China's Changing Map

PRAEGER LIBRARY OF CHINESE AFFAIRS

PRAEGER LIBRARY OF CHINESE AFFAIRS

General Editor: Donald W. Klein, Columbia University

China is one of the world's oldest civilizations and one of the least known or understood. Its rich history has much to contribute to our understanding of man; its experiences in modernization are relevant to other developing nations; its crucial role in Asian and world politics makes imperative a fuller comprehension of the Chinese past and present.

The volumes in this multidisciplinary series will explore central issues of China's political, social, and economic structure, its foreign relations, its philosophy and thought, and its history, civilization, and culture. The contributors to the series represent a wide variety of approaches and attitudes, and all are specialists in their respective fields. Included in the series are the following works:

Ralph C. Croizier, ed., *China's Cultural Legacy and Communism* (1970)

Alexander Eckstein, ed., *China Trade Prospects and U.S. Policy* (1971)

Donald G. Gillin, *History of the Chinese Civil War, 1945–50* (1972)*

James P. Harrison, *A History of the Chinese Communist Party* (1972)*

Li Jui, *Comrade Mao Tse-tung's Early Revolutionary Activities,* trans. by Anthony W. Sariti, with an introduction by Stuart R. Schram (1972)*

John M. H. Lindbeck, *Understanding China: An Assessment of American Scholarly Resources* (1971)

Michel Oksenberg and Frederick C. Teiwes, eds., *The Chinese Communist Bureaucracy at Work* (1972)*

Lucian W. Pye, *Warlord Politics: Conflict and Coalition in the Modernization of Republican China* (1971)

Theodore Shabad, *China's Changing Map: National and Regional Development, 1949–71,* rev. ed. (1972)

William W. Whitson, with Chen-hsia Huang, *The Chinese Communist High Command: A History of Military Politics, 1927–70* (1972)

* *Title and publication date are not yet final.*

China's Changing Map

National and Regional Development, 1949-71

COMPLETELY REVISED EDITION

THEODORE SHABAD

PRAEGER PUBLISHERS
New York • Washington

BOOKS THAT MATTER
Published in the United States of America in 1972
by Praeger Publishers, Inc.
111 Fourth Avenue, New York, N.Y. 10003

This is a revised edition of the book first
published in 1956 by Frederick A. Praeger, Inc.

© 1956, 1972 by Theodore Shabad

Library of Congress Catalog Card Number: 71-178868

Maps by Vaughn Gray

Printed in the United States of America

Contents

List of Maps

List of Tables

The present, second edition of *China's Changing Map,* first published in 1956, was undertaken in the face of a virtually complete blackout on economic information imposed by the Chinese authorities in 1960. The secrecy began after the failure of the Great Leap Forward, an attempted crash program of intensive economic development, and there were no indications at the time of publication of this book that it might be lifted. For the past decade, scarcely any significant information about the national economy and population or about regional and local development has been made public in Communist China. There have been no announcements of such key production items as the magnitude of coal or steel output or the size of harvests. Routine information ordinarily found in annual statistical abstracts is completely unavailable for China on a current basis.

Not even during the most stringent suppression of economic information in the Soviet Union, from 1947 to 1955, was the secrecy as severe as it has been in China since 1960. In the Soviet Union, percentage changes of output of various industries were systematically published and could be applied to known base data. Technical journals could be used effectively for research. In the case of China, the publication of most books, journals, and newspapers has been embargoed, first after 1960 and then to an even more absolute degree after the start of the Cultural Revolution in 1966. It is fair to say that China has gone further than any major nation in modern times to suppress even the most elementary information about the state of its population and economy.

Despite these problems, valiant attempts have been made by foreign scholars, notably economists, to analyze the trickle of material emanating from China, and, by building on the known information for the 1950's, to construct models of possible economic development during the last decade. Most of these studies have been concerned with macroeconomics, sectoral output, national product and income, and other economic aggregates. Few publications have been concerned with the spatial details of China's economic development in the 1960's.

The second edition of *China's Changing Map* is the result of an effort to sift through the same limited body of information that has been used by economists, but to sort and arrange it on a regional basis, with particular reference to China's resource-oriented industries and associated industrial complexes. Like the first edition, the second edition does not purport to be a comprehensive treatment of the geography of China. Both physical geography and historical geography have been covered ably elsewhere. The author has set himself a more limited and specific objective: to trace the changes that have occurred on the map of China, both the political map of territorial-administrative organization and the economic map of resource development.

In its aim, substance, and methodology, the second edition has been conceived in the image of the author's *Geography of the USSR,* published in 1951, and his more recent *Basic Industrial Resources of the USSR,* which appeared in 1969. An attempt has been made to focus on recent resource development projects in China and the associated development of urban centers.

Part I surveys China as a whole. The physical setting of the country is discussed concisely, to the extent that it is essential for an understanding of man's use of the land. The political geography of China is treated with particular reference to the complex territorial-administrative organization of the country and changes in provincial boundaries. In the absence of official data on territorial change and population growth during the 1960's, the 1970 areas and populations of provinces have been estimated roughly by the author on the basis of available information. The discussion of China's ethnic groups and their autonomous territorial units has been thoroughly revised. In the economic section, available production statistics for the 1950's are given for the principal sectors and commodities, together with a range of published Western guesstimates for the 1960's. The distribution of railroads has been updated.

Part II, the regional treatment, is essentially the heart of the book. Here, political administrative and economic changes are discussed in detail, province by province. As in the first edition, emphasis is placed on resource development, industrial construction, urbanization, and the distribution of ethnic groups and their local government areas. The grouping of provinces into major natural regions, such as the North China plain, the loesslands, or the Southeast coastal uplands, has been preserved. To ensure systematic coverage of industrial complexes, a particular effort has been made to touch on all the 170 or so major cities ("shih") of China, as well as former cities, and to suggest economic activities that may have led to their growth or decline.

Vaughn Gray, who designed and drafted the maps for the first edition, has revised them for the new edition. They are intended to serve as general location maps. Places that could not be mapped because of space limitations are generally oriented in the text with reference to a more important center that does appear on the maps.

In the matter of place-name spellings, the author was again confronted with a choice between the simple, though inconsistent Chinese post-office names and the more complex, scientific Wade-Giles transliteration system. Because the general reader is presumed to be more familiar with postal spellings (for example, Peking, Foochow) than with Wade-Giles forms (Pei-ching, Fu-chou), the postal style has been used in text and maps. However, cross-references from Wade-Giles transliterations, as well as from the Chinese Communists' own phonetic Pinyin transcription (in the examples, Beijing and Fuzhou), have been included in the index for all place names. In non-Chinese regions, such as Inner Mongolia, Sinkiang, and Tibet, indigenous forms have been used whenever they were known, but the official Chinese phonetic character transcription of the non-Chinese names is cross-indexed.

In the use of territorial-administrative terms, some Chinese words such as "chou" and "hsien" have been retained to avoid ambiguity, while other generic terms, such as province, are given in the traditional English translation. With regard to the rendering of physical generic terms, such as "kiang," "ho," "shui" (all meaning "river"), and "shan" ("mountain"), the following practice has been adopted: When the specific part of a place name is a single character, the Chinese generic has been used, again to avoid ambiguity; for example, Han Kiang and Han Shui (two different streams), instead of the ambiguous Han River. When the specific part of the name is made up of two or more characters, the English generic has been added, on the ground that the specific name sufficiently identifies the feature; for example, Yungting River instead of Yungting Ho. Similarly, in discussing the administrative units known as "hsien" ("counties"), the term "hsien" has been made part of the name if the specific is a single character and has been dropped from the name when the specific consists of two or more characters. Conventional English forms have been used for a number of well-known features, such as Yellow River instead of Hwang Ho.

The book is limited to the territory under the actual control of the Peking Government. Therefore, Taiwan and the foreign territories of Hong Kong and Macao have been omitted.

New York
September, 1971

Part I

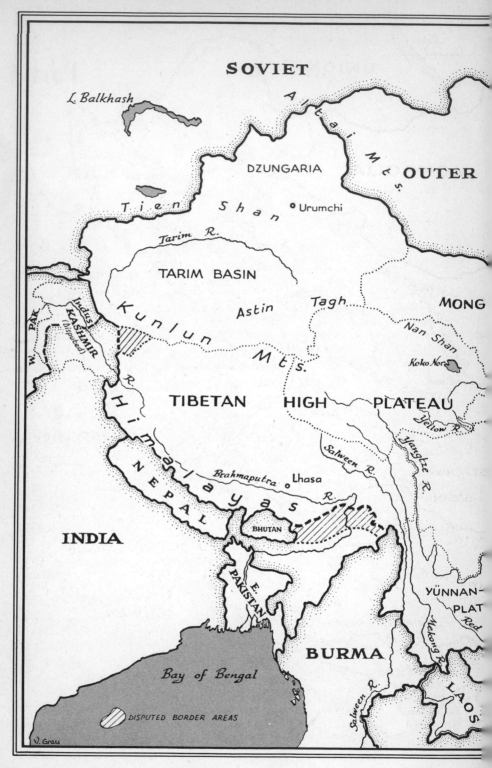

1. Physical Features of China

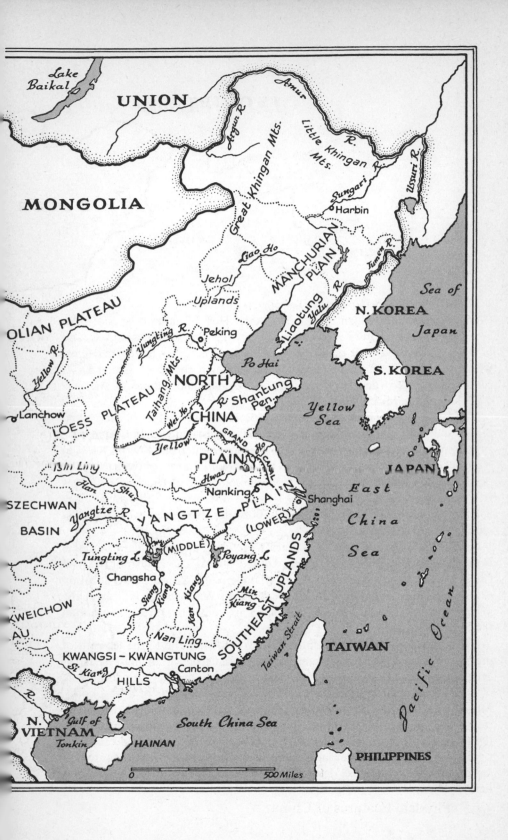

1. The Physical Setting

LOCATION AND BOUNDARIES

China occupies a dominant position in Asia. Her 3.7 million square miles cover a compact territory larger than that of the United States and second in the world only to that of the Soviet Union. Unlike her Soviet neighbor, which occupies the northern fringe of the Eurasian continent, China has a central location, bordering on virtually all the mainland nations of Asia except those of the Middle East.

The latitudinal position of China corresponds closely to that of the United States and both countries have the same east-west spread. If China were superimposed on North America, she would reach from Puerto Rico to Hudson Bay, and from the Atlantic to the Pacific. In terms of the geography of the Soviet Union, China extends from the longitude of Omsk (73 degrees E.) to Khabarovsk (135 degrees E.) over a distance of 3,000 miles. The country's north-south range is about 2,500 miles, from tropical Hainan Island to subarctic Siberia.

In climatic terms, and thus in natural vegetation and soils, eastern China is the rough equivalent of the eastern United States. The industrial heart of China, in the Peking-Mukden-Dairen triangle, corresponds to the location of the urban belt extending from New York to Washington. However, the more important agricultural zones of China are somewhat farther south than the most populous parts of the United States.

The core areas of both the United States and China lie to the leeward of great continents in the battleground of polar and tropical air masses. However, China extends westward and ends in the dry middle-latitude climate of arid central Asia, without the relief of the oceanic effects of a west coast. Moreover, China has much less level land than the United States, especially in the west and south. About one-half of China exceeds one mile in elevation. The inhospitable character of climate and topography is reflected particularly along China's international borders. Through the centuries, towering mountains or parched deserts have impeded China's intercourse with her neighbors.

4

China borders on eleven nations. They are North Korea, the Soviet Union, Outer Mongolia (Mongolian People's Republic), Afghanistan, Pakistan's section of Kashmir, India, Nepal, Bhutan, Burma, Laos, and North Vietnam.

China's frontier with North Korea is neatly defined by the Yalu and Tumen rivers, whose combined courses cut across the base of the Korean peninsula between the Yellow Sea and the Sea of Japan. Traffic over the Yalu-Tumen frontier is among the most active along China's frontiers. The rivers are crossed by a number of rail lines linking the industrial areas of North Korea with adjacent Manchuria. The two main routes are the west-coast railroad, crossing the Yalu at Tantung-Sinuiju and serving Pyongyang, and the east-coast line, which bridges the Tumen River and goes on to the Korean centers of Chongjin, Kim Chak, Hungnam, and Wonsan.

Of the 880-mile border between China and North Korea, dating from Chinese-Japanese treaties of 1895 and 1910, an undemarcated 40-mile stretch in the Changpai Mountains has been the subject of a dispute. Korean maps have tended to show the frontier along headwaters of the Yalu and Tumen rivers rising in the Paitow Shan (Korean: Paektu San), at 8,993 feet the highest peak of the Changpai Mountains. Chinese maps have in the past drawn the border along the southeast slopes of the Paitow Shan, leaving the disputed area of about 100 square miles within China. However, since about 1960, Chinese maps have shown the boundary as passing through the peak itself, suggesting that Peking may have relinquished its claim.

The Soviet Union's frontier with China is interrupted by Outer Mongolia. Most of the eastern section of the Soviet-Chinese border is formed by the mighty Amur River and its tributaries, the Ussuri and the Argun. Little traffic passes this effective river barrier separating Manchuria and Siberia. While population is relatively concentrated along the Trans-Siberian railroad on the Soviet side, the Chinese bank is sparsely settled. Among the few Amur River towns that exchange goods are Blagoveshchensk in the Soviet Union and Aihui (Heiho) in Manchuria. Most of the Soviet-Chinese traffic across the Manchurian frontier moves over the Chinese Eastern railroad, a branch of the Trans-Siberian that originally crossed Manchuria as a short cut to the Soviet Far East. The railroad crosses the frontier at Manchouli, at its western end, and at Suifenho, in the east. Suifenho, together with the Soviet border town of Grodekovo, handles the limited traffic between Manchuria and the Vladivostok area of the Soviet Far East. In the late 1960's, one local passenger train a day crossed the border here each way. The Manchouli station, which handles much of China's overland traffic with the Soviet Union, is situated opposite the Soviet border town of Zabaykalsk. (The Soviet town was originally known as Otpor, meaning "rebuff," and was given its present name, meaning "Transbaykalia," in 1958, when the Soviet Union and China still maintained a public stance of amity.) Manchouli's significance as the principal continental gateway to China declined in 1955 with the opening of the Trans-Mongolian railroad, and again in

1960 with reduction of the volume of traffic as Soviet-Chinese relations cooled.

The Manchurian-Siberian river frontier, about 2,300 miles long, is based to a large extent on the treaties of Aigun and Tientsin, both concluded in 1858, which established the Amur River boundary, and the Treaty of Peking (1860), which defined the Ussuri River border. These accords were among "unequal treaties" challenged by the Chinese in the early 1960's as having been imposed by strong imperialist nations on a weak China in the nineteenth century. Disputes over islands in the Amur and Ussuri rivers erupted in scattered armed clashes in 1968 that brought Soviet-Chinese relations to their lowest point. Tension was somewhat relieved with the beginning of frontier negotiations in 1969.

Near Manchouli begins the 2,700-mile-long border with Outer Mongolia, based on a treaty of December, 1963. The frontier had previously been shown as undetermined on Chinese maps and as fixed on Soviet and Mongolian maps. The 1963 agreement followed roughly the previous Soviet-Mongolian delineation, with minor adjustments. The boundary line crosses the steppe and desert of the Gobi, where nomad herdsmen are normally the only population elements. The only major trade route across this frontier has been the highway from Peking to Ulan-Bator via Kalgan, paralleled since 1955 by the Trans-Mongolian railroad from Peking to Ulan-Bator via Tsining. The rail route, which crosses the boundary at the Chinese town of Erhlien Hot and the Outer Mongolian station of Dzamyn Ude, saves 720 miles from the Moscow-Peking run through Manchuria. It handled a substantial part of Soviet-Chinese overland traffic in the late 1950's but, together with the Manchurian route, declined in the 1960's as trade between the two countries became negligible.

West of Outer Mongolia, the Soviet-Chinese border resumes along a segment of 1,850 miles, which, together with the Manchurian portion, makes a total boundary length of 4,150 miles between the Soviet Union and China. The Central Asian portion, between the Kazakh, Kirghiz, and Tadzhik republics on the Soviet side and Sinkiang on the Chinese side, runs alternately along mountain ranges and across valleys that are the natural gateways for overland traffic in this part of the frontier. Most of the Kazakh and Kirghiz boundaries date from the Treaty of Chuguchak (Tarbagatai) of 1864. The upper valley of the Ili River, including the town of Kuldja, which was seized additionally by the Russians in 1871, was recovered by the Chinese in 1881 under the Treaty of St. Petersburg (where it was signed), referred to by the Chinese as the Treaty of Ili. Part of the Tadzhik boundary along the Sarykol Range of the Pamirs is based on a British-Russian agreement of 1895 and has not been formally accepted by the Chinese, who show this segment on their maps as undelimited.

The main northern highway crossings along the Inner Asian frontier between the Soviet Union and China are in the upper Irtysh valley at Chimunai (China) and between Chuguchak (the present Tahcheng) on the

Chinese side and Bakhty on the Soviet-Kazakh side. Farther south are the Dzungarian Gates, a historic routeway that was to have been used by the projected Sinkiang railroad between the Soviet Union and China. The Soviet segment of this rail line was inaugurated in 1960 to the frontier station of Druzhba ("friendship"), but the Chinese segment between Urumchi and the border has not been completed. In the upper Ili valley, a motor road crosses the boundary between Hocheng on the Chinese side and Khorgos on the Soviet side. In contrast to the northern low-level valley routes, the southern segment of the Inner Asian frontier is crossed by two mountain highways running from Sinkiang into the Kirghiz S.S.R. at Torugart Pass, north of Kashgar, and at Irkeshtam, west of Kashgar.

Between China and Afghanistan, a short 47-mile border along a watershed at the eastern end of the Wakhan panhandle has existed in practice since the British-Russian agreement of 1895. This boundary was affirmed by a Chinese-Afghan treaty in November, 1963.

Pakistan inherited conflicting Chinese and Indian frontier claims in the Karakoram Range as a result of the Pakistani-Indian dispute over Kashmir since 1947. The Kashmir cease-fire line of 1949 gave Pakistan control over the northwestern portion of Kashmir. Pending a final solution of the Kashmir dispute, China agreed in 1963 to a provisional settlement of the Chinese-Pakistani frontier as far east as the Karakoram Pass, the anchor of the Kashmir cease-fire line. The settlement followed natural features, assigning the Shaksgam-Muztagh valley in the upper reaches of the Yarkand River to China, and the valleys of the Indus drainage basin to Pakistan. Overland traffic between Pakistan and China was facilitated with the completion of a motor road in 1971 through Gilgit, Hunza, and Misgar, and Khunjerab Pass into Sinkiang, replacing an ancient caravan route across Mintaka Pass to the west.

The border with India, Nepal, Sikkim, and Bhutan follows the formidable mountain barrier of the Himalayas, long inaccessible to motorized traffic and crossed only by a few caravan routes. The Indian portions include the so-called western sector, in the Ladakh region of Kashmir; the middle sector, between Ladakh and Nepal; China's frontiers with Sikkim and Bhutan, linked with India by treaty relationships; and the eastern sector, between Bhutan and Burma.

In the western sector, the Chinese-Indian frontier dispute involves mainly the Aksai Chin area of Ladakh. Long limited to conflicting cartographic claims, the Aksai Chin issue flared in the 1950's when the Chinese encroached on the area and upgraded a traditional caravan route between Sinkiang and Tibet across the Aksai Chin to a motor road, inaugurated in 1957. The Chinese were shown to be in actual control of Aksai Chin in the late 1950's, and they retained control after the brief Indian-Chinese border war of November, 1962. In the middle sector, the Chinese claim a few small areas that have been under the actual control of India since the 1950's.

The Chinese-Nepali border, extending 670 miles, long based on a traditional line, was affirmed by a 1961 treaty between the two countries. This segment of the frontier is crossed at Nyalam by the Katmandu-Lhasa motor road, built in the 1960's.

The 140-mile boundary between China and Sikkim, one of the two Indian protectorates along the Chinese frontier, was established by a British-Chinese treaty of 1890. This segment is crossed by the main India-Tibet caravan route, through Kalimpong and Yatung across the Natu La pass. The route was upgraded to a motor highway on both the Indian and Tibetan sides in the late 1950's and early 1960's but carries virtually no trade, in view of the poor state of relations between India and China. A traditional border, 300 miles long, also separates Bhutan, the other Indian protectorate, from China.

Eastward from Bhutan extends another disputed 700-mile segment of the Indian-Chinese frontier, involving about 32,000 square miles of territory. The area is under the actual control of India, which administers it as the Northeast Frontier Agency. The disputed area is bounded on the north by the so-called McMahon Line, drawn at a British-Tibetan-Chinese conference at Simla in 1914 but never formally accepted by China. Chinese maps therefore place the international frontier east of Bhutan along the valley of the Brahmaputra River at the foot of the Himalayas, roughly 100 miles south of the McMahon Line. After India had allegedly encroached slightly beyond the McMahon Line near its western (Bhutan) end, China invaded the disputed Northeast Frontier Agency in the border war of November, 1962, but then withdrew again to the McMahon Line under a unilateral cease-fire.

On the Burmese frontier, the Chinese relinquished a claim to the headwaters of the Irrawaddy River in a frontier settlement signed in January, 1960. The Burmese, in return, assigned to China three disputed villages in the Hpimaw area, northeast of Myitkyina, and part of the Wa states east of the Salween River. The Chinese-Burmese boundary, 1,300 miles long, is crossed by the Burma Road, a major supply route in World War II that still retains some significance for foreign trade.

The Chinese frontier continues through mountainous terrain shared with Laos, along a 260-mile segment, and with North Vietnam, for a distance of 800 miles. Transportation links with northern Laos were improved in the late 1960's by the construction of a motor road between southern Yünnan and Laotian areas controlled by the Neo Lao Hak Sat. Traffic between China and North Vietnam relies mainly on two rail routes. One is the old French-built railroad between Kunming, the capital of Yünnan Province, and Hanoi. This line, a natural outlet for Yünnan Province, was partly dismantled during World War II and subsequent civil warfare, but was restored in the late 1950's. The other railroad, between Kwangsi and North Vietnam, was completed in 1952.

Also part of China's international boundary are the two short segments separating Portuguese-controlled Macao and British-controlled Hong Kong from the mainland. A fifteenth-century wall across a narrow isthmus forms the frontier of Macao, granted to Portugal under a perpetual leasehold that was reaffirmed in 1904. Hong Kong, granted to the British by the Treaty of Nanking in 1842, was expanded in 1860 by the addition of Kowloon, and again in 1898 through a 99-year lease on the mainland and island areas known as the New Territories. Hong Kong is separated from the mainland by a delimited boundary 155 miles long, of which 80 miles run along the Shumchun River, a border stream.

Other areas outside the control of mainland China, and therefore not covered in the present account, are the territories held by the Chinese Nationalist Government of Taiwan. In addition to Taiwan proper, they include the Pescadores island group and the so-called offshore islands off the coast of Fukien, notably Quemoy, near the port of Amoy, and Matsu, near Foochow.

GEOLOGIC STRUCTURE

In broad sweeps, the geologic history of China can be discussed in terms of the Chinese platform, a stable, rigid section of the earth's crust, and a series of enclosing unstable zones or geosynclines that have produced the great Himalayan, Kunlun, and Tien Shan uplifts in the west and the oceanic trough and island arc off the eastern coast.

Two areas of somewhat differing geologic history make up the Chinese platform. They are, on the one hand, the Sinian shield, covering almost all of North China and Manchuria and a large part of the Northwest, and the South China massif, which includes the Szechwan basin and China south of the Yangtze River.

The Sinian shield dates from Pre-Cambrian times. It is a part of the Chinese platform that has been a region of emergence through most of its history, and its formations are largely of nonmarine origin. Continental development occurred in the Proterozoic era, the Upper Cambrian, Devonian, and Lower Carboniferous periods and since the Upper Permian. Marine invasions, dated from the end of the Proterozoic, the Lower Cambrian, Ordovician, and Upper Paleozoic, left limestone and shale formations. The sedimentary cover is generally thin and discontinuous. Rocks of the ancient metamorphic basement outcrop over large areas, consisting of Archeozoic gneisses and crystalline schists and of Early Proterozoic micaceous schists, phyllite, and quartzite.

The South China massif, in contrast to its northern counterpart, has generally been a region of subsidence and has been subjected to marine invasions over a longer period of time. Sediments show a fairly complete stratigraphic record, with all marine systems from the Upper Proterozoic to the Triassic represented. The southern massif finally became emergent in the Late Triassic. Basement rocks are of Proterozoic origin, except along the coast where Archeozoic formations outcrop.

The northern and southern parts of the Chinese platform are separated by a narrow folded zone that gave rise to the Tsin Ling mountain system in the Hercynian revolution (Upper Paleozoic) and the Kilien Mountains of the Nan Shan system in the earlier Caledonian revolution (Lower Paleozoic).

In the Cretaceous period occurred the greatest mountain-building time of the Chinese platform. It is known as the Yen Shan revolution, for its type locality at the northern edge of the North China plain. In the course of the Yen Shan upheaval, the platform was broken into a series of separate blocs that continued to maintain their rigidity. These blocs are Shantung-Liaotung, Manchuria, Ordos, Szechwan, and Tarim. The mountains formed in the Yen Shan revolution trend typically northeast-southwest and are especially developed in the South China massif.

After the Yen Shan period, which incidentally corresponds to the Laramide revolution that gave birth to the Rocky Mountains in North America, deposition of the products of continental erosion continued on the rigid blocs. They began to subside, except for the Shantung-Liaotung massif, which continued to retain its mountain characteristics. The subsiding blocs of the Chinese platform were covered with Mesozoic-Cenozoic redbeds of fluvial and lacustrine origin. The largest accumulation occurred in the foothills of the western Kunlun (Yarkand depression), the central Tien Shan (Kucha depression), and the Nan Shan (Kansu depression). The total thickness of sediments reached 25,000 to 30,000 feet.

Among relatively recent formations are the Manchurian and North China plains, which subsided along fairly clearly defined fault lines. However, while the present rolling topography of the Manchurian plain is largely of erosional origin, the North China lowland is entirely the product of the accumulation of sediments of the Yellow River.

Volcanic activity related to the Yen Shan revolution produced rhyolite and andesite lava flows in the Great Khingan, the Peking hills, Shantung, and the southeast coast. Among intrusive rocks, granite predominates, forming large masses near the southeast coast and smaller bodies in the Yin Shan of Inner Mongolia, the Peking hills, and the Lüliang Mountains of Shansi. Tertiary and Pleistocene basalt flows underlie large areas in the Great Khingan and the East Manchurian uplands, the Alashan Mountains, the Luichow peninsula, and northern Hainan.

The Tien Shan–Altai tectonic zone of China includes the central and eastern sections of the Tien Shan, the Dzungarian massif, the Tarbagatai and Saur Mountains, the Zaisan depression, and the Mongolian Altai.

The Tien Shan penetrates into China from the Soviet Union and tapers off gradually in both width and elevation. It consists of a number of parallel ranges of varying geologic ages. A central zone, including the Narat Range, is made up of Pre-Cambrian formations (crystalline schist, slate, phyllite). Adjoining it on the north (Borokhoro Range) and south (Kokshaal-Tau) are thick sandstone, shale, and limestone formations of Cambrian-Ordovician and Lower Devonian age. Finally, the outer zones consist of Upper Paleozoic sandstone and shale.

The Dzungarian massif consists essentially of undisturbed horizontal sedimentary strata ranging from Lower Carboniferous marine formations through Middle and Upper Carboniferous volcanic deposits, Lower Permian sandstone and shale, and coal-bearing sandstone and argillite of the Upper Triassic and Jurassic, to continental deposits of Cretaceous and Tertiary origin.

The Tarbagatai and Saur Mountains on the Soviet border are made up of strongly warped Silurian shale and sandstone overlain unformably by Middle Paleozoic volcanic materials. The Zaisan depression, which is occupied by the upper Irtysh River, is filled with unconsolidated marine sediments of the Middle and Upper Paleozoic era. The Mongolian Altai consists of two geologic zones. The northern high-elevation zone consists of Lower Paleozoic shale and sandstone, while the southern foothill belt is made up in large part by outcrops of the Pre-Cambrian basement.

It would thus appear that the Tien Shan–Altai geosyncline filled with sediments during the Lower Paleozoic era. These sediments were uplifted during the Middle and Upper Paleozoic into the original mountain system. The Dzungarian massif, which had passed through a continental period while the geosyncline was being filled with marine sediments, subsided at the time of the mountain-making. Dzungaria then passed through a marine invasion, followed by lacustrine deposition.

The Kunlun Himalaya zone is made up of the mountain systems of the Kunlun and the Himalaya, separated by the high plateau of Tibet. The Kunlun system, formed in the Lower and Middle Paleozoic era, has the following geologic make-up: Its northern ranges consist of phyllitized shale and sandstone of Proterozoic age. Gneisses and schists of Archeozoic age and granite intrusions characterize the middle section. The southern slopes, facing Tibet, are made up of intensely warped sandstone and shale of the Lower Paleozoic.

The Himalayan branch arose during the Alpine revolution. The axis of the system consists of Pre-Cambrian gneiss and schist. Thin strata of Upper Paleozoic, Triassic, and Jurassic age cover the flanks. Igneous rocks are represented by post-Cretaceous granite intrusions and rhyolite and andesite lava flows of the same period. The geologic history of the Tibetan plateau is only sketchily known. Scattered data indicate a wide development of Upper Paleozoic, Jurassic, Cretaceous, and Tertiary deposits.

TOPOGRAPHIC FORMS

The topography of China reflects the tectonic history of the region. The mountains produced by the Yen Shan revolution of the Cretaceous period trend characteristically northeast-southwest. Other mountain ranges, formed predominantly during the earlier Caledonian and Hercynian revolutions of the Paleozoic era typically strike east-west. These two intersecting patterns have formed a checkerboard-like configuration that can be traced with relative ease through most of China.

The easternmost of the Yen Shan tectonic lines is evident in the Southeast uplands of the coastal provinces of Chekiang and Fukien. This massif, consisting of several parallel ranges, rises to 3,500–5,000 feet in the Wuyi and Tienmu Mountains along the western margins. It is adjoined by a synclinal zone, also following the northeast-southwest trend, occupied by the lowlands of the Hwai Ho and the lower Yangtze River and the valleys of the Kan Kiang in Kiangsi Province and the Tung Kiang and Pei Kiang in Kwangtung Province. This is followed by an anticlinal zone that can be traced from the East Manchurian uplands, through the Liaotung peninsula, Shantung, the mountains on the Hunan-Kiangsi border, and as far as the Luichow peninsula and Hainan. Then comes the most extensive lowland belt of China, ranging from the Manchurian plain through North China, the Tungting Lake and Siang Kiang plain, to the coastal plain on the Gulf of Tonkin.

This broad synclinal zone stops abruptly at the great continental scarp that can be traced through eastern China. The scarp lies along the eastern edge of the Great Khingan Mountains, continues along the Taihang Mountains overlooking the North China plain, and can be traced along the eastern edge of the Szechwan mountain rim and the Kweichow plateau. Virtually all of China below 1,500 feet lies east of this scarp line. To the west, covering 85 per cent of the nation's territory, lie plateaus, highlands, and rugged mountains, with a predominant east-west orientation. Only the Alashan Mountains in Ningsia have retained the typical northeast-southwest trend found east of the scarp.

Four equally spaced east-west structures can be distinguished in China. The northernmost, situated chiefly in Outer Mongolia, penetrates into China in the Ilkhuri and Little Khingan Mountains of northern Manchuria. The next tectonic line is best expressed in the Yin Shan of Inner Mongolia, north of the Yellow River bend. The third, and most important, system is the Tsin Ling. This rugged mountain range, rising to 13,500 feet in southern Shensi, is an extension of the Nan Shan, itself a continuation of the Kunlun system. The Tsin Ling acts as a major climatic barrier to monsoon rainfall from the south and dust-laden desert winds from the north. It is the most important geographic boundary of China, determining the distribution not only of soils and vegetation, but also of cultivated crops, customs, and Mandarin dialects. The southernmost east-west structure is the Nan Ling system, forming the northern boundary of the Si Kiang drainage basin and of Kwangtung Province. The Nan Ling is a geographic boundary, second in importance only to the Tsin Ling divide. It defines the Cantonese language area, the tropical part of China, and the region of two successive rice crops a year. The Nan Ling is the only east-west structure that penetrates prominently east of the great continental scarp.

The elevated part of China west of the scarp is dominated by the Tibetan highlands. These comprise the loftiest and most extensive plateau in the world, at an average elevation of 15,000 feet, enclosed by the towering mountain systems of the Himalaya and the Kunlun. Along their northwestern margin, the Tibetan highlands drop abruptly to the 2,500-foot-high Tarim basin. This desert-filled depression, in turn, is separated by the Tien Shan mountain system from the Dzungarian steppe basin farther north. The two depressions and the intervening mountain barrier constitute the Chinese political unit of Sinkiang. Northeast of the Tibetan highlands extends the vast 3,000-foot-high Mongolian plateau. This desert and steppe peneplain is the dominant topographic feature of the province of Kansu and Inner Mongolia. Between the Mongolian plateau and the Tsin Ling divide is the dissected loess plateau, a region where fine silt blown from the desert in the north forms a veneer over the entire landscape.

East of the Tibetan highlands and south of the Tsin Ling divide, the Cretaceous-Tertiary lake basin of Szechwan drops to an elevation of 900 feet. The Szechwan basin, now filled with buff, red, and purple sandstone and shale, is frequently called the Red basin. It is the only major population and agricultural center west of the continental scarp.

Southeast of the Tibetan highlands and south of the Szechwan basin is the plateau region of Kweichow and Yünnan. The Kweichow plateau at 4,000 feet and the Yünnan plateau at 6,000 feet rise in a sort of steplike formation from the eastern lowlands to the western highlands. The western part of Yünnan is a continuation of the canyon country of eastern Tibet, from where Southeast Asia's great streams and intervening high ranges fan out into the Indochinese peninsula.

COASTS

China's coastline of 7,000 miles touches on three seas of the Pacific Ocean: the Yellow Sea, the East China Sea, and the South China Sea. With the exception of parts of the South China Sea, these bodies of water are on the continental shelf separated from the deeper reaches of the Pacific proper by the East Asian island arc. China's coast extends from Tantung, at the mouth of the Yalu River on the Korean border, in the north, to Tunghing, on the North Vietnamese border, in the south. It is shared by the provinces of Liaoning, Hopei, Shantung, Kiangsu, Chekiang, Fukien, Kwangtung, and Kwangsi.

In the north, the Yellow Sea penetrates westward between the rocky peninsulas of Liaotung and Shantung and forms the large embayment of Po Hai, formerly called Gulf of Chihli. The Po Hai receives major rivers of North China, including the Liao Ho, the Hai Ho, and the Yellow River. The bayshore is generally shallow and smooth and offers few good harbors. The old port of Yingkow at the mouth of the Liao Ho has been silting up. The principal ports along this part of the coast are Chinwangtao, an outlet for the Kailan coal mines, and the new outer port of Tientsin at Tangku. The development of Hulutao, much discussed shortly after World War II, has not materialized. The best natural Yellow Sea harbors are situated on the rocky peninsulas. They are Dairen and the naval base of Port Arthur on the Liaotung peninsula, and the ports of Chefoo, Weihai, and especially Tsingtao on the Shantung peninsula. South of Shantung and as far as the Yangtze River mouth, the coast is again characterized by shallow water and an evenness of shoreline. The only port is Lienyünkang, eastern terminus of the Lung-Hai railroad.

South of the Yangtze River mouth, the coast of China is rocky and indented, with numerous islets and inlets. The East China Sea extends from the Yangtze mouth to the Taiwan Strait. Its chief ports are Shanghai, China's foremost metropolis, Ningpo, Wenchow, and Foochow. South of the strait is the South China Sea, with the ports of Amoy, Swatow, Canton, Britain's Hong Kong, and Tsamkong (Chankiang). Hainan is the largest Chinese island under control of the Peking regime. The government also claims jurisdiction over the islands of the South China Sea extending as far as Lat. 4 degrees N.

CLIMATE

China's climate is dominated by air-mass movements known collectively as the winter and summer monsoons. In winter, heavy out-radiation over the Asian continent chills the air and creates a stationary high-pressure area known as the Siberian High. In January, the center of this high is situated south of Lake Baikal in Outer Mongolia. At that time of the year, a region of low pressure forms over the northern Pacific in the area of the Aleutian Islands. Cold, dry air masses of polar continental origin move successively from the area of the Siberian High toward the Pacific, forming what is known as the winter monsoon. Strong northerly winds accompanying these air flows carry a negligible amount of precipitation but bring dust storms that are common throughout North China during the winter months.

During the summer, the continental interior is overheated and becomes warmer than the ocean. The expanding and rising continental air creates a low-pressure system in the area of the winter high. At the same time, a region of high pressure forms over the relatively cooler Pacific in the area of the Hawaiian Islands. A succession of hot, moist air masses invades China from the southeast. When this air is lifted, by either mountain or cold-front wedges in its path, abundant precipitation results.

China's climate is thus alternately continental and dry in winter and maritime and wet in summer. The seasonal shifts in air circulation take place in April and September. The winter and summer monsoons vary in strength and permanence. In winter, the opposing high- and low-pressure cells are situated relatively close to each other. As a result, the pressure gradient is strong and the cold, dry northerlies blow steadily and with considerable force. During the summer, the pressure cells are much farther apart, the pressure gradients are weaker and winds associated with the summer monsoon are variable both in strength and in direction. The relative strength of the winter and summer monsoons explains why the cold, dry Polar Continental air affects a much greater area of China during a longer period of time than the warm, moist invasions of Tropical Maritime air.

Superimposed on the basic to-and-fro seasonal circulation are lesser air-mass movements, middle-latitude cyclones, and tropical cyclones (typhoons). The middle-latitude cyclones, many of which are believed to be of European origin, follow a number of paths from west to east across China. Most of them pass eastward through the Yangtze valley and across the North China plain. These cyclones, formed by the interaction of opposing warm and cold air masses, produce most of the precipitation throughout China. A considerable amount of precipitation, especially along the southeast coast, is related to the passage of typhoons. These tropical cyclones arise in the area of the Marshall Islands of the Pacific and follow more or less regular paths to the northwest. They either strike the China coast or recurve northeastward toward Japan, bypassing the mainland. Typhoons are most common between June and August. Their passage produces heavy rain squalls, contrasting with the usual gentle drizzles associated with the westerly cyclonic storms.

As might be expected from the monsoonal circulation pattern, seasonal temperatures are sharply differentiated through most of China. The greatest annual temperature range is found in northern Manchuria, where the January average drops to $-13°$ F ($-25°$ C), while in July the mercury climbs to $70°$ F ($20°$ C) as a monthly average. The annual temperature range decreases gradually toward the south. In tropical Hainan it is only 15 degrees compared with the more than 80 degrees in northern Manchuria. As a result of the regular increase of average January temperatures from north to south, the winter isotherms are all aligned from east to west. The January isotherm of $32°$ F follows the Hwai Ho valley, the Tsin Ling divide, and curves around the west rim of the Szechwan basin into southern Tibet. During July, temperatures are more uniform, with an average of $70°$ to $85°$ F ($29°$ C). The highest summer temperatures are found in the lowlands of eastern China and the South China hills, as well as in the Tarim basin of Sinkiang. The lowest average July readings occur in the Tibetan highlands, the Altai Mountains, and the northern Khingan of Manchuria.

Precipitation shows even greater regional contrasts than temperature. It is the chief climatic factor differentiating North China and South China. South of the Tsin Ling divide and the Hwai Ho valley, annual rainfall is from 40 to more than 80 inches. Precipitation decreases rapidly toward the north and west. It is 25 inches in the North China plain and Manchuria and less than 4 inches in the Mongolian desert plateau and the Tarim basin. Most of China's rainfall occurs during the summer monsoon. But while South China receives some rain throughout the year, North China has virtually no precipitation in winter under the influence of the cold dry air of the northerly monsoon.

RIVER PATTERNS AND PROJECTS

The pattern of China's major rivers is determined by the east-west structural trend of the nation's topography. As a result, these streams all flow eastward to the Pacific. Tributaries are in part defined by the northeast-southwest trend of the Yen Shan structures. This is especially true in South China where many tributaries join the eastward-flowing streams at right angles.

The northernmost river system is that of the Sungari, which flows through Manchuria to the Amur River on the Soviet-Chinese border. The Sungari receives the Nun Kiang (Nonni) and is navigable for river steamers during the six-month ice-free season. It serves the cities of Kirin, Harbin, and Kiamusze, in addition to Tsitsihar on the Nun Kiang. The large Fengman hydroelectric station is just above Kirin.

Southern Manchuria is drained by the Liao Ho, which enters the Po Hai at Yingkow. Unlike the mountain-fed Sungari, the Liao Ho rises in the semi-arid Mongolian plateau and is navigable only for flat-bottomed junks in its lower reaches. The Yalu and Tumen rivers on the Korean-Chinese border are used chiefly for timber-floating and are of limited importance for navigation. The Shuifeng (Supung) hydroelectric station on the Yalu is shared by China and North Korea.

Southwest of the Liao Ho system, beyond the small coastal drainage basin of the Lwan Ho, is the complex system of the Hai Ho. The Hai Ho itself is only a short stream flowing 30 miles from Tientsin to the sea. It is the outlet of five major tributaries that drain the North China plain and converge fanlike at Tientsin, causing a flood problem. To reduce this threat, flood-control reservoirs have been built on the tributaries—notably the Kwanting reservoir northwest of Peking in 1954 and the Miyün reservoir northeast of Peking in 1959—and additional seaward outlets have been constructed to bypass the Hai Ho north and south of Tientsin.

The great river of North China is the Yellow River, known in Chinese as the Hwang Ho. The basin of this 2,900-mile-long stream is bounded on the north by the Yin Shan and on the south by the Tsin Ling divide. The Yellow River rises at an elevation of 15,000 feet in the Tibetan highlands. Its rapid upper course cuts gorges through easily eroded loess formations as the stream describes the great bend around the resistant Ordos plateau. After the Yellow River enters the North China plain, its gradient is greatly reduced and the silt-laden stream is no longer able to carry its load at reduced velocity. Extensive deposition follows. Over the years the river aggraded its lower course to such an extent that the channel was built up above the level of the surrounding countryside. The river's natural levees had to be heightened by artificially constructed embankments to prevent flooding.

The Yellow River has repeatedly broken through its containing dikes and changed course, spreading its alluvium over the North China plain. There have been nine major course changes in the history of the Yellow River. Until 1194, the river reached the sea at various points of the Po Hai north of the Shantung peninsula. In that year, one arm entered the sea south of Shantung through the valley of the Hwai Ho. After nearly seven centuries of southeasterly flow, the Yellow River resumed its northeasterly course about 1855, in what is essentially its present channel. Once again, the river was diverted toward the Hwai Ho basin in June, 1938, but this time its dike was broken intentionally to slow the Japanese advance in China. The breach was sealed in March, 1947, and the Yellow River returned to its old course.

The Communists have given renewed attention to the problem of flood control along the Yellow River. The solution of the problem requires a complex system of flood-detention reservoirs in the upper reaches. As a stopgap measure, the Peking regime has strengthened the dikes along the lower course and provided spillways, particularly at Litsing, near the mouth, where ice-jams frequently cause flooding in the spring. The People's Victory Canal, completed in 1953, diverts some of the water of the Yellow River into the Wei Ho at Sinsiang.

In July, 1955, an over-all water-resource development program for the Yellow River was made public. The plan, covering half a century of work, called for the construction of a number of multipurpose dams and reservoirs along the Yellow River, soil conservation, and irrigation projects. Smaller reservoirs on upstream tributaries were to be designed to prevent the silting of the mainstream installations. The first phase of the program, to be completed within fifteen years, envisaged hydroelectric stations of one million kilowatts each at Sanmensia, on the Honan-Shansi border, and in the Liukia gorge, on the Kansu-Tsinghai boundary. Work on these and other projects was accelerated during the Great Leap Forward but was then interrupted in 1960 with the failure of that crash development effort and the departure of Soviet technicians. Except for small, scattered irrigation projects, the Yellow River development program appears to have been dormant in the 1960's.

The principal tributaries of the Yellow River are the Wei Ho in Shensi and the Fen Ho in Shansi. No tributaries enter the elevated channel of the river in its lower course. Because of its lack of navigability and the ever-present flood danger, few large cities have developed along the Yellow River. The stream flows past Lanchow in Kansu and Yinchwan in the Ningsia Hui Autonomous Region, Paotow in Inner Mongolia, Kaifeng in Honan, and Tsinan in Shantung.

The Hwai Ho is the largest river between the Yellow River and the Yangtze and drains the southeastern margin of the North China plain. A relatively short river—675 miles long—the Hwai Ho is subject to severe summer flooding. When the Yellow River usurped the channel of the Hwai Ho before 1855, and again from 1938 to 1947, the invading stream deposited vast amounts of sediment in the Hwai Ho channel, disrupting its natural course to the sea. The Hwai Ho discharged its water into the fluctuating lakes Hungtse and Kaoyu, which enlarged in times of flood over vast areas.

Part of the water from the naturally mouthless Hwai Ho followed the Grand
Canal to the Yangtze; another part made its way through shifting channels
to the sea.

In 1950, the Peking regime embarked upon an ambitious program of
Hwai Ho flood control. The plan called for the construction of detention
reservoirs (some with power-generating capacity) on the upstream tributaries, the dredging of the main channel and strengthening of dikes, flood-
diversion dams and reservoirs in mid-course, and the digging of a new outlet
to the Yellow Sea from Hungtse Lake, in the lower reaches of the Hwai Ho.
The outlet, known as the North Kiangsu Canal, was inaugurated in 1952.
Of twenty-seven planned detention reservoirs, about ten have been completed. To relieve the load on the Hwai Ho during the flood stage, a parallel
outlet channel, the New Pien Canal, was dug in the late 1960's to collect
part of the discharge of left tributaries and divert it into Hungtse Lake. The
canal follows roughly the course of a waterway of the same name that existed under the Sui Dynasty (A.D. 581–618).

The Yangtze River, 3,400 miles long, is the longest river of China and
by far its most important waterway. Rising in the Tibetan highlands, the
Yangtze traverses central China from west to east, linking the interior of
the country with the maritime routes of the Pacific. Navigation starts at
the western edge of the Szechwan basin and proceeds past Chungking, Wuhan, and Nanking to the sea near Shanghai. Wuhan is accessible to ocean-
going vessels, but difficult gorges above Ichang restrict upstream navigation
to 500-ton steamers. The chief tributaries are the Min Kiang and Kialing
River in Szechwan, the Han Shui in Hupei, the Siang Kiang in Hunan, and
the Kan Kiang in Kiangsi. The latter two flow through the Tungting and
Poyang lakes, natural flood-reservoirs for the surplus waters of the Yangtze.
Although the Yangtze carries less sediment than the Yellow River—600 million tons a year compared with 4,000 million tons—and aggrades its channel
to a lesser extent, it nevertheless presents a flood threat in summer. In the
middle 1950's, two flood-detention basins were built in the middle Yangtze
reaches, in Hupei Province, to accommodate excess flood waters. The Kingkiang basin, with a capacity of 5.5 billion cubic meters, was built in 1952–
53 south of Shasi. The second basin, with a storage capacity of 2.2 billion
cubic meters, was completed in 1956 between Mienyang and Hanyang, in
the angle formed by the Yangtze and its left tributary, the Han Shui. The
drainage basin of the Yangtze River, between the Tsin Ling divide and the
Nan Ling in the south, covers about one-fifth of China. It is, moreover, the
most populated and economically the most important fifth of the nation.

South of the mouth of the Yangtze River are a number of coastal stream
basins draining the provinces of Chekiang, Fukien, and easternmost Kwangtung. Each of the principal streams is associated with a rivermouth city.
They are the Tsientang River with Hangchow (which is not a seaport), the
Wu Kiang with Wenchow, the Min Kiang with Foochow, the Lung Kiang
with Amoy, and the Han Kiang with Swatow.

In southern China, south of the Nan Ling divide, three rivers converge on the Canton delta. They are the Tung Kiang, the Pei Kiang, and the Si Kiang. The Si Kiang, the most important of the three from the point of view of navigation, rises in the Yünnan plateau and traverses Kwangsi and western Kwangtung from west to east.

Except for the upper reaches of the great rivers of Southeast Asia, the rest of China is occupied by internal drainage basins. These are the arid parts of the country, including Inner Mongolia, Kansu, Sinkiang, and most of Tsinghai and Tibet. The upper Irtysh River, which leaves China through a back door, ultimately finds its way to the Arctic Ocean.

SOILS AND VEGETATION

A combination of climate and natural vegetation acting on a variety of parent materials has produced an infinite complexity of soils in China. The effect of the vegetation cover plays a secondary role in many parts of the country, particularly in densely settled areas where virtually the entire land has been put under cultivation and little of the original vegetation remains.

Just as China can be divided into North and South in discussions of other aspects of physical geography, the country falls conveniently into northern and southern soil groups. In North China, where rainfall is limited and grassland vegetation prevails in uncultivated areas, soils tend to be rich in lime and soluble plant nutrients. They are called pedocals, or soils with an excess of calcium carbonate (lime). In South China, where rainfall is more abundant and forest vegetation predominates, soils tend to be leached and poor in humus. They are called pedalfers because the excessive leaching leaves behind aluminum and iron hydroxides.

Pedocals occur in the arid, semi-arid, and subhumid climatic regions of China. They range from subhumid chernozems (black earths) through chestnut and brown soils to arid desert soils. Chernozems are among the most fertile in the world, but in China they are restricted to northern Manchuria. Most of them are cultivated in soybeans and wheat and other grains. Their original vegetation cover is tall-grass steppe. Chestnut and brown soils occupy the arid side of the chernozem belt. They contain less humus and are consequently lighter in color, lightness increasing with aridity. These soils make up a large part of central Manchuria and Inner Mongolia, as well as the northeastern margins of the Tibetan highlands and the moister parts of Sinkiang. Short-grass steppe is the typical vegetation. The very light-colored, high-lime soils of the loesslands of Shansi, Shensi, and southeastern Kansu are related to the chestnut soils. Gray desert soils, the most arid phase of the pedocal series, extend through the great inner Asian desert belt from the Taklamakan desert in Sinkiang through northern Kansu into the border area between Inner and Outer Mongolia. Here short grass and brush is the natural vegetation. Agriculture is limited to irrigated oases.

Deciduous and coniferous upland forests are found in North China in the mountains enclosing the Manchurian plain, the Taihang Mountains, the Yen

Shan, and the hills of the Shantung and Liaotung peninsulas. The Manchurian forests, which crown the Great and Little Khingan ranges and the East Manchurian uplands, are developed on podzol soils characterized by an ash-colored horizon below the top soil layer. The upland forests enclosing the North China plain are associated with brown soils that are very much like the podzols, though less intensely leached. These brown forest soils are found in Liaotung, Shantung, the Taihang scarp, as well as in the Tsin Ling divide, which separates the North China and South China soil groups.

Perhaps the most important agricultural soil of North China is the calcareous alluvium developed on the floodplain of the North China lowland. Unlike the foregoing zonal soils, which have been developed through the prolonged action of climate and vegetation zonation, the alluvium is called intrazonal because it has been formed mainly through the depositional action of streams within zones. The texture of the alluvium ranges from coarse sand close to the streams to silt at greater distances from the rivers. The coarse sand, often accumulated in the form of natural levees, is a poor soil, while silt is highly productive. Century-long cultivation of these soils has left virtually no trace of the original vegetation. Wheat and cotton are cultivated in silty soils, while tobacco and peanuts are favored by the sandy soils. A special type of alluvial soil is the so-called shakiang soil. This type is characterized by lime concretions in its lower horizons. The concretions are believed to come from the ground water that has been saturated with calcium carbonate. The shakiang soils are developed in the flat topography of central Honan and northwest Anhwei, as well as in western Shantung.

In South China, intrazonal alluvial soils are found immediately south of the major soil divide. Unlike their northern counterparts, the southern alluvial soils are leached under the increasingly humid conditions and are noncalcareous. They are ideally suited for rice cultivation. Periodic flooding of the rice fields has developed a dense impervious clay horizon, which in turn has become an asset in keeping the fields flooded. These rice paddy soils are best developed in the middle and lower Yangtze valley.

The most important zonal soils in South China are lateritic red and yellow soils. They are characterized by advanced chemical and mechanical decomposition of the parent rock under humid, subtropical conditions, accumulation of hydroxides giving the soils their characteristic color, low humus content and hence low fertility. Both red and yellow soils are associated with subtropical forests. Red soils predominate in the hill country south of the Yangtze, the southeast coastal uplands, the Kwangtung-Kwangsi hills, and Yünnan. Yellow soils are associated chiefly with the Kweichow plateau. A distinctive purple-brown soil found in the Szechwan basin is derived from the highly colored shales and sandstones of Cretaceous and Triassic age.

Most of South China's red and yellow soils are associated with subtropical evergreen broadleaf forest (pine, fir, bamboo). Cultivators have used these soils for tea, tung trees, and, to some extent, for rice. In general the soils are of little agricultural value. The distinctive purplish soils of the

Szechwan basin are largely cultivated. Rice is the dominant crop, but there is also a diversified production of corn, sweet potatoes, and tobacco. Pine, cypress, bamboo, and oak are found on the uncultivated slopes.

The southeastern margins of the Tibetan highlands have relatively high precipitation (about 40 inches a year). Here coniferous forest is developed on predominantly podzolic soils. Farther northwest, on the Tibetan plateau, soils and vegetation vary frequently in accordance with slope insolation. Northward-facing slopes, which receive less sunshine and are consequently cooler and moister, are generally forested or covered with tall grass. Southward-facing slopes, which are more exposed to the sun, are drier and display predominantly short- and tall-grass associations. In the desolate central part of Tibet, soils are poorly developed and vegetation is extremely meager.

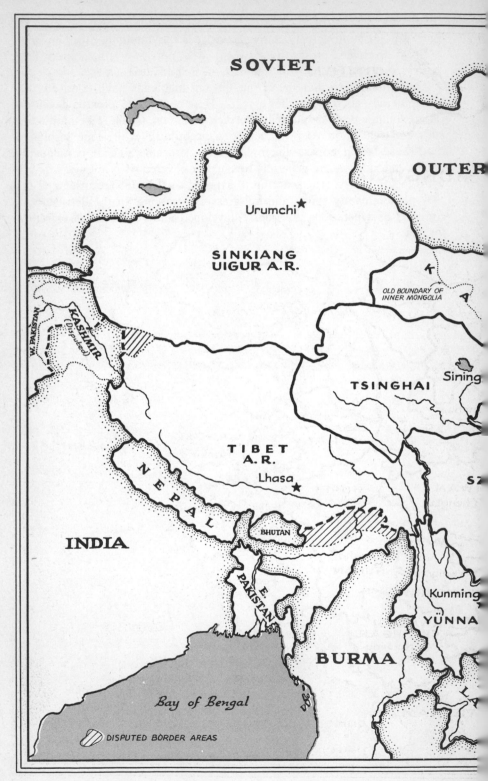

2. Political Divisions of China

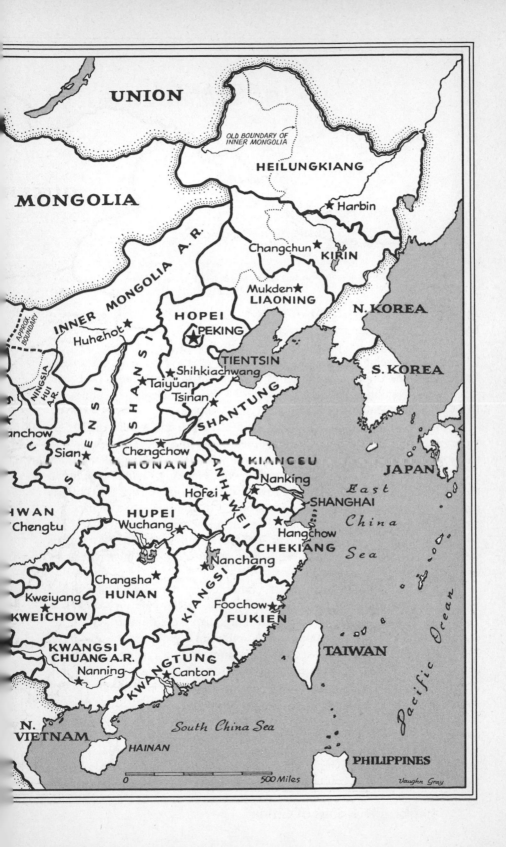

UNION

MONGOLIA

OLD BOUNDARY OF
INNER MONGOLIA

HEILUNGKIANG

★ Harbin

INNER MONGOLIA A.R.

Changchun ★ KIRIN

Mukden ★
LIAONING

N. KOREA

Huhehot ★

HOPEI
★ PEKING

NINGSIA HUI A.R.

APPROX. BOUNDARY

S H A N S I

Shihkiachwang ★
Taiyüan ★
Tsinan ★

TIENTSIN

S. KOREA

SHANTUNG

anchow

Sian ★

Chengchow ★

HONAN

KIANGSU

Nanking ★

JAPAN

HWAN
Chengtu

HUPEI
Wuchang ★

Hofei ★

A N H W E I

SHANGHAI ★

East
China

Hangchow ★
CHEKIANG

Sea

Nanchang ★

Changsha ★
HUNAN

KIANGSI

Foochow ★
FUKIEN

Kweiyang ★

KWEICHOW

KWANGSI
CHUANG A.R.
Nanning ★

★ Canton

KWANGTUNG

TAIWAN

Pacific Ocean

N.
VIETNAM

HAINAN

South China Sea

PHILIPPINES

0   500 Miles

Vaughn Gray

2. The Political Framework

PROVINCIAL CHANGES SINCE 1949

By an act of the Nationalist Government on June 5, 1947, China was divided into thirty-four provinces (not including Taiwan), one territory (Tibet), over which the Chinese then had no effective control, and twelve cities under the direct jurisdiction of the central Government. The twelve cities were Nanking, Shanghai, Peiping, Tsingtao, Tientsin, Chungking, Dairen, Harbin, Hankow, Canton, Sian, and Mukden.

According to the China Handbook, 1950, the provinces were further divided into 2,023 hsien and fifty-five cities under the direct jurisdiction of the provincial governments. As some of the provinces were considered to be too extensive for effective administration, the Nanking regime established the intermediate level of administrative district ("hsing-cheng ch'ü"). The hsien of twenty-three provinces were grouped in administrative districts instead of being directly subordinated to the provincial Government. (According to later Communist sources, the provinces under the Nationalists were divided into 2,016 hsien, fifty-seven provincially administered cities, and 209 administrative districts.)

This was the administrative pattern inherited by the Communists at the time of the proclamation of the Chinese People's Republic on October 1, 1949. The Peking regime proceeded to reorganize the administration in accordance with existing conditions and the program of political consolidation. The nation was divided into six greater administrative regions ("ta hsing-cheng ch'ü"). These major regional divisions, each in turn subdivided into a number of provinces, represented various stages of Communist power consolidation in China. In 1950, when the greater administrative regions were established, the Northeast (Manchurian) region, for example, was completely consolidated, while agrarian reform was in progress in the East and Center-South and counterrevolutionary activity was still a major factor in the Southwest. The division of China into six major regions made it possible for the Peking regime to adopt specific regional measures. The greater administrative regions and their provinces and regionally administered cities were:

(1) North China (Hua-pei), with the provinces of Hopei, Chahar, Pingyüan, Shansi, and Suiyüan, and the cities of Peking and Tientsin. The North China region was at first directly under the Central Government, where a special Ministry for North China was set up for its administration. A regional administrative committee was set up as late as December, 1951.

(2) Northeast (Tung-pei), with the provinces of Liaotung, Liaosi, Kirin, Sungkiang, Heilungkiang, and Jehol, and the cities of Mukden, Fushun, Anshan, Penki and Port Arthur–Dairen. After the end of World War II, the Nationalist Government divided Manchuria into nine provinces (Liaoning, Antung, Liaopei, Kirin, Sungkiang, Hokiang, Heilungkiang, Nunkiang, and Hsingan), plus Jehol. This administrative pattern was never put into effect, because the Nationalists failed to gain full control of Manchuria. The Nationalist setup was superseded by five Communist provinces, plus Jehol, which made up the Northeast region. Because Manchuria was the most advanced region from the point of view of Communist power consolidation, a so-called Northeast People's Government functioned there from August, 1949, to November, 1952. This regional government had greater powers than the bodies set up in the other greater administrative regions.

(3) East China (Hua-tung), with the provinces of Shantung, Kiangsu, Anhwei, Chekiang, Fukien, and the cities of Shanghai and Nanking (in 1952, Nanking was placed under the provincial jurisdiction of Kiangsu). The East China region was supposed to include Taiwan, in case of the island's occupation by the Communists. Kiangsu and Anhwei were each administered after 1949 as two separated provincial units, situated north and south of the Yangtze River, to conform with varying stages of Communist consolidation. North and South Anhwei were recombined in August, 1952, and North and South Kiangsu in the following November.

(4) Center-South (Chung-nan), with the provinces of Honan, Hupei, Hunan, Kiangsi, Kwangtung, Kwangsi, and the cities of Wuhan (Hankow, Hanyang, Wuchang) and Canton.

(5) Southwest (Hsi-nan), with the provinces of Szechwan, Kweichow, Yünnan, Sikang, Tibet, and the city of Chungking. Szechwan was administered in four sections until 1952.

(6) Northwest (Hsi-pei), with the provinces of Shensi, Kansu, Ningsia, Tsinghai, Sinkiang, and the city of Sian.

The Inner Mongolian Autonomous Region (set up in 1947) was independent of the system of greater administrative regions.

In November, 1952, occurred the first major reorganization of the political-administrative system. The six major regional authorities, which until that time had wielded considerable powers, were reduced to mere supervisory bodies. This measure was designed to strengthen Communist consolidation at the provincial level, looking toward ultimate abolition of the supraprovincial structure. The provinces of Chahar and Pingyüan in North China were abolished. Chahar had been greatly reduced in area because of territorial transfers to Inner Mongolia, and the rump was considered to be too small to function as a province. The rest of Chahar was divided between Shansi and Hopei. Pingyüan had been created in 1949 out of the Communist Shansi-Honan-Hopei border region that existed during the civil war. The new province, made up largely of parts of Honan and Shantung, failed to achieve provincial unity. No provincial center arose, with the former Shantung section gravitating toward Tsining and the Honan portion toward Sinsiang. Short-lived Pingyüan was dissolved in 1952, and the previous provincial borders were approximately restored. The temporary divisions of Kiangsu, Anhwei, and Szechwan were terminated at this time, and Nanking was placed under provincial rule.

After November, 1952, mainland China had thirty-one provinces, including Inner Mongolia and Tibet (now independent of the Southwest region), and twelve regionally administered cities. Two more such cities—Changchun and Harbin—were added late in 1953 in Manchuria.

A second major administrative reorganization was announced June 19, 1954. This time, the greater administrative regions were abolished altogether and the provinces placed directly under the central government. Several provinces were eliminated and combined. In Manchuria, Sungkiang was incorporated into Heilungkiang, and Liaotung and Liaosi were combined to form Liaoning. In the Northwest, Ningsia was incorporated into Kansu. The province of Suiyüan was merged with the Inner Mongolian Autonomous Region. Eleven of the fourteen cities that had been regionally administered were placed under provincial jurisdiction. Only Peking, Tientsin, and Shanghai remained under central administration.

The changes of June, 1954, left China with twenty-seven mainland provinces, including Tibet and Inner Mongolia, and three centrally administered cities.

In a further provincial shift, announced in July, 1955, the provinces of Sikang and Jehol were abolished. Sikang proper (east of the upper Yangtze River) was merged with Szechwan, while the Chamdo area (west of the upper Yangtze) was acknowledged as being part of autonomous Tibet. Jehol, like Chahar, had lost substantial northern territory to Inner Mongolia and was evidently judged to be too small to function as a separate province. It was therefore divided among Inner Mongolia, Liaoning, and Hopei. The 1955 shift reduced the number of Chinese mainland provinces to twenty-five, including Tibet and Inner Mongolia, plus the three centrally administered cities of Peking, Tientsin, and Shanghai. In September, 1955, Sinkiang Province was converted into the Sinkiang Uigur Autonomous Region on the basis of the Uigur ethnic minority, which then represented a majority of the Sinkiang population.

In the late 1950's, further adjustments in first-order provincial-level units took place. In 1958, Tientsin was demoted from centrally controlled city to subprovincial level, and placed under the jurisdiction of Hopei Province. (It was to regain its first-order status in 1967.) Also in 1958, Kwangsi Province was transformed into the Kwangsi Chuang Autonomous Region on the basis of the Chuang ethnic minority, which made up a substantial part of the population. Still another first-order ethnic autonomous unit, the Ningsia Hui Autonomous Region, was created in the same year, having been carved out of Kansu Province, which had absorbed the old Ningsia Province in 1954. In contrast to the more extensive old Ningsia, the new autonomous region was limited to a smaller area around the Yellow River's Ningsia plain, where the Hui (Chinese Moslems) represented a significant population element.

The present pattern of first-order autonomous regions was completed in 1965, when the Tibet Autonomous Region was formally established, signifying a consolidation of Communist Chinese control. Tibet had previously been administered by what was technically known as the Preparatory Committee for the Tibet Autonomous Region. Also in 1965, a major territorial shift took place at the provincial level, as the Kwangsi Chuang Autonomous Region gained frontage on the Gulf of Tonkin with the transfer of a coastal area that had been traditionally part of Kwangtung Province (except for a brief period, 1951–55, when it was also part of Kwangsi).

The most recent administrative change affecting China's provincial pattern was the partial dismemberment of the Inner Mongolian Autonomous Region in 1969. Both the east and the west wing of the region were detached and incorporated into adjoining provinces with which these areas had stronger economic and transport links than with the main central portion of Inner Mongolia in what used to be Chahar and Suiyüan. The three eastern leagues (subprovincial civil divisions) were reincorporated into the Manchurian provinces, with Hulunbuir going to Heilungkiang Province, Jerim to Kirin Province, and Jo-uda to Liaoning Province. The western wing of Inner Mongolia in the Alashan Desert, which had passed from Kansu to Inner Mongolia in 1956, was incorporated partly into the Ningsia Hui Autonomous Region and into Kansu Province.

Although not strictly part of the civil administrative pattern, China's military regions gained significance as supraprovincial units during the Cultural Revolution after 1966, when the regional bureaus of the Chinese Communist Party became inoperative through the dismantling of the Party apparatus. The Party's regional bureaus had maintained supraprovincial jurisdiction after the six greater administrative regions (Northeast, North, East, Central-South, Northwest, Southwest) had been abolished in 1954. With the apparent elimination of the Party bureaus and the growing role of the military in civil administrative affairs, the military regions seem to have assumed supraprovincial administrative functions. Of the twelve regions in 1970, four correspond to single province-level units. Eight comprise two or more provinces, in which case, each individual province is constituted as a

TABLE 1
MAJOR ADMINISTRATIVE DIVISIONS OF CHINA (1970)

Former Greater Administrative Regions	Military Region	Province-Level Divisions
Northeast	Mukden (Shenyang)	Heilungkiang Kirin Liaoning
North	Peking	Hopei Peking City Tientsin City Shansi Inner Mongolian Autonomous Region
East	Tsinan Nanking	Shantung Kiangsu Shanghai City Anhwei Chekiang
	Foochow	Fukien Kiangsi*
Central-South	Wuhan	Hupei Honan
	Canton	Kwangtung (with Hainan) Kwangsi Chuang Autonomous Region Hunan
Northwest	Lanchow	Kansu Shensi Ningsia Hui Autonomous Region Tsinghai
	Sinkiang	Sinkiang Uigur Autonomous Region
Southwest	Chengtu Kunming	Szechwan Yünnan Kweichow
	Tibet	Tibet Autonomous Region

* From 1950 to 1954, Kiangsi was subordinate to the Central-South Region.

military district. Hainan Island, which occupies a special position as an administrative district ("hsing-cheng ch'ü") within Kwangtung Province, is the only military district below provincial level. Other subprovincial civil divisions, whose designation was changed in 1971 from special district ("chuan ch'ü") to area ("ti-ch'ü"), correspond to military subdistricts in the parallel military hierarchy.* Table 1 correlates the old greater administrative regions, as represented by the regional party bureaus, and the present military regions with the provincial structure.

THE ADMINISTRATIVE SYSTEM

The framework of Communist China's administrative structure was originally established by Article 53 of the 1954 Constitution. It divided the

* As part of the 1971 reform, Hainan Island was also designated an "area," but its status in the military hierarchy remained unclear.

country into provinces ("sheng"), autonomous regions ("tzu-chih ch'ü"), and certain cities ("shih") that were directly under the jurisdiction of the central government. According to the 1954 Constitution, provinces and autonomous provinces were divided in turn into autonomous chou ("tzu-chih chou"), hsien, autonomous hsien ("tzu-chih hsien"), and cities. Hsien and autonomous hsien were subdivided into hsiang (rural townships), national hsiang, and towns ("chen").

Autonomous regions, autonomous chou, and autonomous hsien are areas of national autonomy in which ethnic minority groups are granted the right to self-administration under local leaders in a way that assures effective political control. These national autonomous areas are discussed in greater detail in the section on ethnic groups.

Although the administrative structure followed essentially the guidelines laid down by the 1954 Constitution, its provisions were interpreted liberally in practice. Some hsien were placed under the jurisdiction of cities, resulting in some very large urban areas, and an intermediate administrative level, the special district ("chuan ch'ü"), was interposed in virtually all provinces and autonomous regions between the province level and the hsien level. In addition, the hsiang, or lowest-level rural civil division, was replaced during the Great Leap Forward of 1958 by the commune ("kung-she"). Both the special district and the commune were formally acknowledged in the draft 1971 Constitution, which otherwise affirmed the administrative pattern established in 1954. However, in 1971, the Peking regime changed the term "special district" to that of "area" ("ti-ch'ü").

As of the end of 1970, China had twenty-one ordinary provinces, five autonomous regions, and three cities (Peking, Tientsin, Shanghai) under central-government control. The provinces and autonomous regions, in turn, were broken down into twenty-nine autonomous chou, 170 special districts (areas), about 2,000 hsien and seventy autonomous hsien, and 170 cities. For greater clarity, the administrative system will be discussed here in terms of the different orders of subordination.

First-Order Divisions. These are the provinces, autonomous regions (for the principal and areally most extensive ethnic minority groups), and the centrally administered cities. A comparison between the postwar Nationalist political map and the present Communist administrative pattern shows a decline in the number of provinces, the appearance of the autonomous regions (some of them converted from ordinary provinces), and a reduction in the number of centrally administered cities. The reduction in the number of provinces took place generally in the outlying parts of China, including Manchuria. The historical provincial pattern of China proper has remained virtually undisturbed (see Map 2). The autonomous regions have been established mainly in areas outside China proper with significant ethnic minorities. Out of the eight largest minority groups, five (Chuang, Uigur, Hui, Tibetan, and Mongol) have been granted the status of autonomous region, equivalent to province. The three others (Yi, Miao, Manchu) have not reached that level of administration because of either a low level of cultural development or excessively scattered areal distribution or, as in the case of the Manchus, virtual assimilation with the ethnic Chinese. The number of centrally administered cities declined from twelve, in the Nationalist postwar pattern, to three (Peking, Tientsin, Shanghai). As noted earlier, only Peking and Shanghai were under central authority, while Tientsin was temporarily demoted to subprovincial level from 1958 to 1967.

Intermediate-Level Divisions. This subprovincial level of the administrative hierarchy, although not explicitly provided in the 1954 Constitution, has existed since the early stages of Communist administration. This level consists of three basic types of units: the special district ("chuan ch'ü"), the autonomous chou, and cities directly under province jurisdiction. The special district, which is essentially the successor of the Nationalists' administrative district ("hsing-cheng ch'ü"), combines groups of hsien into regional patterns within provinces. It is apparently designed to interpose an intermediate level of administration between province and hsien and thus avoid the need for direct provincial administration of the many hsien. Apparently because the term "special district" implied impermanence, it was officially changed in 1971 to that of area ("ti-ch'ü"). Its equivalent in national minority areas is the autonomous chou, which occurs in portions of provinces dominated by ethnic groups with a significant population and level of economic and cultural development. Most of the twenty-nine autonomous chou have been organized in the non-Chinese ethnic territories of the southwestern and northwestern parts of the country. In the urban category, the intermediate level of administration is represented by about eighty cities that have reached a sufficiently large population or advanced economic development to be considered equivalent to the areas (special districts) or autonomous chou. Like these administrative areas, the subprovincial or intermediate-level cities are directly under provincial administration. Three provinces contain unique administrative units at the intermediate level. In Kwangtung Province, the island of Hainan is constituted as an administrative district ("hsing-cheng ch'ü"), Communist China's only unit of this type, equivalent to the regular areas (or special districts) on the Kwangtung mainland. An autonomous chou on Hainan, that of the Li and Miao ethnic groups of the island, is, contrary to the general pattern, subordinate to the Hainan Administrative District rather than directly to Kwangtung Province. In a reverse situation, in the Sinkiang Uigur Autonomous Region, two of the areas (Tahcheng and Altai) are subordinated to an autonomous chou (Ili Kazakh Autonomous Chou). Finally, a special terminology is used in the Inner Mongolian Autonomous Region for the intermediate administrative divisions, which are there known as leagues (Chinese "meng," Mongol "chuulgan" or "aymag"). Thus, instead of regular areas, Inner Mongolia is subdivided at the intermediate level into four leagues: Silingol, Ulanchab, Ikh Jo, and Bayan Nor.

Second-Order Divisions. This level is represented basically by the hsien (county-size units), autonomous hsien, and equivalent cities. Despite frequent administrative changes involving the merger or separation of hsien, the number of these units has remained remarkably stable, around 2,000. The number of hsien per province or autonomous region tends to vary widely, from fewer than twenty in small Ningsia Hui Autonomous Region to 180 in populous Szechwan Province. The average is about eighty per province, and the average population about 300,000. As for the intermediate level, a distinctive terminology for second-order divisions is used in the Inner Mongolian Autonomous Region, where they are known by the traditional administrative term "banner" (Chinese "ch'i," Mongol "hushuun"). In Tibet, official Chinese usage is "hsien," but the Tibetan term is "dzong," sometimes rendered phonetically in Chinese as "tsung." Autonomous hsien are the equivalent of ordinary hsien in national minority areas that are not large enough in area or population or not sufficiently developed culturally and economically to merit the higher status of autonomous chou. Similarly cities at the second-order hsien level are generally less developed industrially and have a smaller population than cities at the intermediate, subprovincial level. Like the other second-order administrative units, hsien-level cities have been subordinated to the areas or autonomous chou. At the end of 1970 there were about ninety such cities in China.

Third-Order Divisions. The second-order divisions, hsien and autonomous hsien, are further broken down into basic rural and urban administrative units. The basic rural units in the early years of Chinese Communist rule were the hsiang and, in small ethnic minority areas, the nationality hsiang. There were about 220,000 hsiang. During the middle 1950's, however, the hsiang became increasingly obsolete as the collectivization drive in agriculture produced large farm units that supplanted the administrative functions of the hsiang. This process culminated in 1958 in the formation of rural communes ("kung-she"). The number of communes, initially about 24,000, was increased in the early 1960's to its present level of about 75,000. Although the commune became the basic rural political unit below the hsien level, it is further broken down into production brigades ("sheng-chan ta-tui"), usually named for a village but sometimes numbered, and then into production teams ("sheng-chan tui"), which are generally numbered. A complete designation of a rural locality would thus range from production team through brigade, commune, hsien, and administrative area to province. The basic urban administrative unit below the hsien level is the town ("chen"). These towns, numbering about 5,000 in the 1953 census, owe their urban status mainly to the presence of a local farm market rather than to modern industry. Industrial development of substantial significance would normally be reflected in the promotion of a town to city ("shih") status. The administrative seat of a hsien is usually a market town. In this connection, a distinctive aspect of Chinese hsien nomenclature needs to be mentioned. The name of any hsien automatically applies to its administrative seat, even though the town serving as the hsien seat may also have its own local name. When the administrative headquarters of a hsien moves, as frequently happens in China, the old seat assumes its local name and the hsien name is applied to the new seat. This explains why a particular hsien name may be applied to different towns on maps published at different dates. Although towns are generally subordinate to hsien, in one unique situation, in Yünnan Province, a town ("chen") is equivalent to a hsien. This is Wanting, a Chinese border station on the Burma Road.

As in the Soviet Union, changes in the administrative structure of China can be interpreted in the context of economic development. The appearance of new hsien in previously unsettled territory suggests agricultural development through irrigation or the plowing up of virgin lands. An example of such a hsien is Yuyi (which means "friendship"), established in 1959 in Heilungkiang Province on newly reclaimed land east of Kiamusze, and named in honor of the Soviet-Chinese amity of that period.

Administrative changes are an even more sensitive indicator of urban industrial development. Here the key is the establishment of a city ("shih"). In the early stages of Communist rule in China, the urban administrative structure did not yet reflect industrial development. Some cities inherited from the Nationalist administrative pattern were large trade centers without modern industry, for example, Kaishow in Anhwei Province, a Hwai Ho junk-navigation head on the Honan border. In the 1950's, as the urban system was modified to reflect industrial growth, some of these old market cities lost their city status. Kaishow, for example, was demoted to town (hsien seat) in 1954. At the same time, the urban pattern was made more responsive to industrial and mining developments. At first, beginning about 1951, a distinctive designation, industrial-mining district ("kung-k'uang ch'ü"), was used for such development projects in their early stages. After such a project had sufficiently developed and reached a certain population level, say, 50,000, it was raised to city status. The coking-coal center of Fengfeng in southern Hopei, for example, was among the first places designated as a mining district, about 1951, and was raised to the status of city in 1954. (Two years later, it was incorporated into the expanding urban complex of Hantan.) Actually, no more than about fifteen such urbanized districts were created, and the practice faded in the late 1950's. The last mining district appears to have been the copper-mining center of Tungchwan in Yünnan Province, created in 1954 and raised to city status in late 1958. Since then, developing mining or industrial centers have been raised directly to the status of city, usually from town level, without the intermediate stage of industrial or mining district.* The three levels of cities may be presumed to reflect relative population size and industrial significance, although these relationships are probably not strictly observed. In general, however, a city under central government authority may be expected to per-

* In the summer of 1971, Chinese broadcasts began to refer to at least one of these mining cities (Tungling in Anhwei Province) as a "t'e-ch'ü" (special area) rather than "shih" (municipality). However, it was not immediately apparent whether a new terminology was being introduced into the administrative hierarchy.

form more important functions than a city at subprovincial level (under provincial authority), and a subprovincial city is probably more significant than a city at hsien level (under the authority of the area). Some of the subprovincial cities have large areas, including many hsien, under their jurisdiction, for example, Tantung in Liaoning Province and Hangchow in Chekiang Province.

POPULATION CHARACTERISTICS

The total population of China has long been a matter of confusion and controversy, except during a brief period in the middle 1950's, when a population census was held as of June 30, 1953 (enumeration in some areas was not completed until 1954), followed by annual official estimates based on population registration until the year-end of 1957. When the Communists came to power in 1949, they used the figure of 475 million for total population. This was presumed to have been based on a count made by the Nationalist government after its establishment in 1928. The enumeration, conducted over a period of two years and published in 1931, yielded the figure of 474,787,386. Nationalist figures in subsequent years generally were between 450 million and 500 million. The last Nationalist enumeration, based in part on estimates by local officials, yielded 463,493,418 for June, 1948. The 475-million figure appeared in Communist publications from 1949 until the publication of the 1953 census results in 1954. During these early years, other figures ranging from 483 million to 575 million were also published by Peking at one time or another.

The 1953 census results gave China's population as 582.6 million. According to the annual year-end estimates, the national population rose at a rate of natural increase of slightly more than 2 per cent annually, reaching 646.5 million by the end of 1957. Thereafter, with the imposition of secrecy on economic and demographic statistics, no more official estimates were issued on a regular basis. In the summer of 1964, a new population registration, unpublicized in official media, is reported to have been conducted, although there appears to be some doubt whether it was successfully carried through on a nationwide scale. In the meantime, the rounded figure of 650 million was used through the early 1960's for the national total, superseded about 1966 by the figure of 700 million. During the Cultural Revolution, as new local governing agencies, the Revolutionary Committees, were established in 1967 and 1968, population figures were made public for provinces and other first-order divisions, yielding 712 million for the national total. Some analysts interpreted these figures as the delayed results of the reported 1964 count. Other observers, finding these figures inconsistent with past rates of natural increase, voiced doubt that they referred to any particular year, such as 1964, and regarded them simply as the latest data available in each area. This view was strengthened in 1969 and 1970 as additional provincial population figures began to be cited in official Chinese media. In some areas, the latest data showed an unlikely stagnancy in population from the late 1950's through the entire decade of the 1960's, for example, a steady population figure of 70 million for Szechwan; in other areas, the provincial populations were shown to have risen substantially, particularly in places known for significant in-migration, for example, Heilungkiang Province, Inner Mongolia, and Sinkiang.

On the basis of the limited amount of information available as of 1970, it would appear, therefore, that the population of China and its provinces, let alone its major cities, cannot be estimated accurately. A wide range of values, generally clustered between 750 million and 800 million, has been suggested for year-end 1970. For the purpose of this book, the author has

TABLE 2

AREA AND POPULATION OF MAJOR ADMINISTRATIVE DIVISIONS

(*area in thousand square miles; population in millions*)

	1957 Area	Population in 1957 Area		1970 Area	1970 Population
		1953 Census	1957 Official Estimate	(*author's estimates*)	
Provinces					
Anhwei	54	30.7	33.6	54	39
Chekiang	39	22.9	25.3	39	31
Fukien	48	13.1	14.7	48	18
Heilungkiang	179	11.9	14.9	280	25
Honan	65	44.2	48.7	65	55
Hopei	75	37.9	41.5	75	46
Hunan	81	33.2	36.2	81	41
Hupei	72	27.8	30.8	72	35
Kansu	142	11.3	12.8	190	16
Kiangsi	64	16.8	18.6	64	25
Kiangsu	40	40.9	45.2	40	51
Kirin	72	11.3	12.6	110	21
Kwangtung	89	36.7	38.0	83	40
Kweichow	67	15.0	16.9	67	20
Liaoning	58	20.6	24.1	90	29
Shansi	61	14.3	16.0	61	20
Shantung	59	48.9	54.0	60	60
Shensi	76	15.9	18.1	76	22
Szechwan	220	65.7	72.2	220	75
Tsinghai	280	1.7	2.1	280	2.5
Yünnan	168	17.5	19.1	168	24
Autonomous Regions					
Inner Mongolia	457	7.3	9.2	225	9
Kwangsi Chuang	85	17.6	19.4	91	25
Ningsia Hui	25	1.6	1.8	40	2.5
Sinkiang Uigur	640	4.9	5.6	640	10
Tibet	470	1.3	1.3	470	1.5
Centrally Administered Cities					
Peking	6.6	2.8	4.0	6.6	7
Shanghai	2.2	6.2	6.9	2.2	10
Tientsin	1.2	2.7	3.2	1.2	4
CHINA	3,700	582.6	646.5	3,700	about 765

attempted to adjust scattered official Chinese population figures for provinces, autonomous regions, and centrally administered cities, and arrives at a total of about 765 million (Table 2).

A rough age-group breakdown in the 1953 census showed that China's was a young population. About 15.6 per cent of the total was under four years old, compared with 8.7 per cent in the United States at the same date, and 41.1 per cent was less than eighteen years old, compared with 32.6 per cent in the United States. Men outnumbered women by 107.5 to 100. The predominance of males has been typical of China's population.

The 1953 census classified about 35 million persons, or 6 per cent of the population, as national minorities. According to the census instructions, the determination of linguistic or other ethnic affiliation was to be left to each household head. He was expected to list the national minority of which he considered himself to be a member. The census summary contained total numbers for the ten minority groups exceeding one million in population. The data for smaller groups were disclosed in other sources. A detailed discussion of ethnic groups and their distribution appears in the following section.

The population classified as urban in the June, 1953, census was 77.2 million, of which 43.5 million resided in cities ("shih") and 33.7 million in other urban places, mostly towns ("chen"). Official data, apparently based in part on the 1953 census and in part on population registration, have been published for China's total population and the urban-rural breakdown for the period 1949–57 (Table 3). The figures show that urban population rose more rapidly than rural population during this period, as might be expected during a period of industrialization and the associated flow of population from rural to urban areas. Urban population rose by an average of 7 per cent a year from 1949 to 1957 compared with a mean annual rural population growth of 1.4 per cent. The population influx into cities apparently continued during the Great Leap Forward of 1958–59 and reached 130 million some time in the early 1960's. Beginning in 1961, an effort was made to limit urban growth, in connection with a slowdown of industrializa-

TABLE 3

URBAN-RURAL POPULATION OF CHINA, 1949–57

(*year-end figures, in millions*)

	Total	Urban	Rural
1949	541.7	57.7	484.0
1950	552.0	61.7	490.3
1951	563.0	66.3	496.7
1952	574.8	71.6	503.2
1953	588.0	77.7	510.3
1954	601.7	81.5	520.2
1955	614.7	82.9	531.8
1956	627.8	89.2	538.6
1957	646.5	99.5	547.0

tion, and to transfer manpower to the countryside. The percentage of urban population probably remained more or less stagnant during the 1960's, at about 15 to 20 per cent of total population, so that a presumed total population of 750 to 800 million at year-end 1970 may have included an urban component of 130 to 150 million.

The 1953 census reported twenty-five cities of more than 500,000 population, seventy-seven cities in the 100,000–500,000 size class, and sixty-two cities of less than 100,000. For most of these places, official estimates were announced as of year-end 1957, and these have been used in the present book in addition to the 1953 census figures. The population data for the

TABLE 4

POPULATION OF CHINA'S LEADING CITIES

(*in thousands*)

	1953 Census	1957 Estimate	1970 Estimate
Shanghai	6,204	6,900	10,000**
Peking	2,768	4,010	7,000**
Tientsin	2,694	3,200	4,000
Mukden (Shenyang)	2,299	2,411	3,000
Wuhan	1,427	2,146	2,700
Chungking	1,773	2,121	4,400**
Canton (Kwangchow)	1,599	1,840	3,000**
Harbin	1,163	1,552	2,000
Port Arthur–Dairen*	1,200	1,508	
Nanking	1,092	1,419	1,700
Sian	787	1,310	
Tsingtao	917	1,121	
Chengtu	857	1,107	1,700
Taiyüan	721	1,020	
Fushun	679	985	
Changchun	855	975	
Kunming	699	880	
Tsinan	680	862	
Tzepo	184	806**	
Anshan	549	805	
Tangshan	693	800	
Hangchow	697	784	800
Chengchow	595	766	1,100
Changsha	651	703	800
Lanchow	397	699	
Süchow	373	676	
Tsitsihar	345	668	
Soochow	474	633	
Foochow	553	616	700
Wusih	582	613	
Shihkiachwang	373	598	
Kirin	435	568	
Nanchang	398	508	
Kweiyang	271	504	

* This urban area is officially known as Lüta, for the Chinese names of the two component cities—*Lü*shun (Port Arthur) and *Ta*lien (Dairen). The population of Dairen alone was 766,000 in 1953 and 800,000 in 1957.

** Includes substantial rural areas under the jurisdiction of the central city.

twenty-five cities of 500,000 or more in the 1953 census appear in Table 4. Cities in the interior are found to have grown at a more rapid rate during the middle 1950's than coastal cities. This was in accordance with the policy of achieving a more uniform distribution of industry, theretofore concentrated in Manchuria and along the coast.

About 75 per cent of China's population lives in 15 per cent of the nation's territory. This is the eastern lowland and hills area situated east of the great continental scarp formed by the Khingan-Taihang-Kweichow plateau line. The only major population concentration west of that line is in Szechwan, which is the country's most populous province.

The greatest density is found in the middle and lower reaches of the Yangtze valley. There a density of 2,000 to 2,500 persons to the square mile is not uncommon, although the overall average in the lowlands is more nearly 1,000 to 1,200. Similar densities occur in the Canton delta and in the coastal plains of Kwangtung and Fukien. More than one-fifth of the nation's population is found in the North China plain, one of the original Chinese settlement areas. There the average density is 650 per square mile.

Outside of the areas of greatest concentration, major densities are found in the Szechwan basin (500 per square mile) and in southern Manchuria (400 per square mile). Beyond that, settlement decreases rapidly toward the western mountains and deserts, which are virtually devoid of settlement.

ETHNIC GROUPS

Like the Soviet Union, China is a multinational state. However, the Chinese majority is by far more predominant in China than the Russian or Slavic group is in the Soviet Union. Russians make up about one-half of the Soviet population; including the Ukrainians and Belorussians, the proportion rises to nearly 75 per cent. In China, the Chinese account for 94 per cent of the total population. This difference in the relative predominance of the basic ethnic groups has determined the basic political structure of the two nations. The Soviet Union is juridically a union of sixteen republics. According to Article 17 of the 1936 Constitution, this union is voluntary and the republics reserve the right of free secession. It is unlikely that any republic will ever raise the issue of secession, but juridically it has that right. China, on the other hand, is a unified multinational state. According to Article 3 of the 1954 Constitution, national autonomous units are inalienable parts of the People's Republic of China.

The primary doctrinal basis of Chinese Communist policy with respect to national minorities was originally set forth in the Common Program of the Chinese People's Political Consultative Conference, promulgated in September, 1949. Articles 50–53 assert the equality of the nationalities and the need for regional autonomy based on the preservation of language, customs, and religious beliefs.

The first autonomous region was set up even before the promulgation of the Common Program. It was Inner Mongolia, declared to be autonomous as early as May, 1947. The next important national unit was the Kantse Tibetan area, founded in November, 1950. Thereafter, national autonomous units were created at a rapidly increasing rate. Most of the areas were established in the course of 1953 and 1954. These autonomous areas varied greatly in size and population. They ranged from the Inner Mongolian region, which initially had an area of 255,000 square miles and a population of 2,500,000, to national units at the hsiang ("village") level. Despite the evident disparity in size and importance, all areas bore the uniform designation of "autonomous region" ("tzu-chih ch'ü").

It was only with the proclamation of the 1954 Constitution that a system of gradation was established. The system, already discussed under the administrative structure, ranges from autonomous region, corresponding to a province, through the autonomous chou, at the subprovincial level of the area, to the autonomous hsien, equivalent to hsien. In the late 1960's, there were five autonomous regions, twenty-nine autonomous chou, and sixty-six autonomous hsien. They are grouped in Table 5 by ethnic minorities. Of the more than fifty ethnic groups for which the Chinese have published total population figures, about thirty-five are represented in autonomous areas. Autonomous units grouping more than one ethnic minority are repeated for each minority in Table 5.

In the following discussion, China's ethnic groups are classified insofar as possible on the basis of language affiliation. Two major language families include virtually all the languages spoken in China. They are the Sino-Tibetan family, also known as the Indo-Chinese, and the Altaic family, comprising the Turkic, Mongolic, and Tungusic subfamilies. Outside of these two great language families are the Koreans, sometimes linked to the Altaic family; the Mon-Khmer languages, considered part of an Austro-asiatic family; and the Tadzhiks of Sinkiang, an Indo-European group.

Sino-Tibetan (Indo-Chinese) Family. The Chinese are, of course, the dominant ethnolinguistic group of China, having numbered 546.3 million in the 1953 census, or 94 per cent of the population. The ethnic Chinese are known in Chinese as Han, for the Han Dynasty (206 B.C.–A.D. 220). The Chinese people, in the sense of the people of China, are known in Chinese as "Chung-hua jen-min" or "Chung-kuo jen-min."

Chinese, a major group of the Sino-Tibetan language family, is a monosyllabic tone language written by means of characters representing words. While the character script is used throughout the Chinese-language area, the spoken language has regional phonetic differences, especially in southern China, where a rugged topography has led to the formation and preservation of regional dialects.

Spoken Chinese can be divided into two major groups, separated roughly by a northeast-southwest line joining the mouth of the Yangtze River and the border of North Vietnam. North of this line are the so-called Mandarin dialects, spoken by 380 million according to the 1953 census. There are three major forms of Mandarin ("kuan-hua," meaning "official language") : the

TABLE 5
ETHNIC MINORITIES OF CHINA

Ethnic Group (1953 census, in thousands)	Province	Autonomous Areas*
Chuang (7,030)	Kwangsi	Kwangsi Chuang Autonomous Region
	Yünnan	Wenshan Chuang-Miao AC
	Kwangtung	Linshan Chuang-Yao AH
Uigur (3,640)	Sinkiang	Sinkiang Uigur Autonomous Region
Hui (Dungan) (Chinese Moslems) (3,556)	Ningsia	Ningsia Hui Autonomous Region
	Kansu	Linsia Hui AC Changkiachwan Hui AH
	Sinkiang	Changki Hui AC Yenki Hui AH
	Tsinghai	Hwalung Hui AH Menyüan Hui AH
	Hopei	Tachang Hui AH Mengtsun Hui AH
	Kweichow	Weining Yi-Hui-Miao AH
	Yünnan	Weishan Yi-Hui AH
Yi (Nosu, Lolo) (3,254)	Szechwan	Liangshan Yi AC Yenyüan Yi AH
	Yünnan	Tsuyung Yi AC Hungho Hani-Yi AC Lunan Yi AH Nankien Yi AH Ninglang Yi AH Oshan Yi AH Kiangcheng Hani-Yi AH Weishan Yi-Hui AH
	Kweichow	Weining Yi-Hui-Miao AH
Tibetan (2,776)	Tibet	Tibet Autonomous Region
	Tsinghai	Haisi Mongol-Tibetan-Kazakh AC Hainan Tibetan AC Haipei Tibetan AC Hwangnan Tibetan AC Ngolog Tibetan AC Yüshu Tibetan AC
	Szechwan	Ahpa Tibetan AC Kantse Tibetan AC Muli Tibetan AH

* AC = Autonomous chou
  AH = Autonomous hsien

TABLE 5 (*continued*)

Ethnic Group (*1953 census, in thousands*)	Province	Autonomous Areas*
Tibetan (*continued*)	Kansu	South Kansu Tibetan AC Tienchu Tibetan AH
	Yünnan	Titsing (Tehtsin) Tibetan AC
Miao (2,511)	Kweichow	Southeast Kweichow Miao-Tung AC South Kweichow Puyi-Miao AC Sungtao Miao AH Tzeyün Miao-Puyi AH Anlung Puyi-Miao AH Chenfeng Puyi-Miao AH Chenning Puyi-Miao AH Wangmo Puyi-Miao AH Weining Yi-Hui-Miao AH
	Hunan	West Hunan Tuchia-Miao AC Chengpu Miao AH
	Yünnan	Wenshan Chuang-Miao AC Pingpien Miao AH
	Kwangsi	Tamiaoshan Miao AH Lunglin Multinational AH Lungsheng Multinational AH
	Kwangtung	Hainan Li-Miao AC
Manchu (2,419)	Liaoning Heilungkiang Kirin	None
Mongol (1,463)	Inner Mongolia	Inner Mongolian Autonomous Region
	Heilungkiang	Hulunbuir League Durbet Mongol AH
	Kirin	Jerim League South Gorlos Mongol AH
	Liaoning	Jo-uda League Fusin Mongol AH Kharachin East Wing AH
	Ningsia	Alashan East Banner
	Kansu	Alashan West Banner Edsin Banner North Kansu Mongol AH
	Tsinghai	Haisi Mongol-Tibetan-Kazakh AC Honan Mongol AH
	Sinkiang	Bayan Gol Mongol AC Borotala Mongol AC Khobuk-Saur Mongol AH

* AC = Autonomous chou
  AH = Autonomous hsien

TABLE 5 (*continued*)

Ethnic Group (*1953 census, in thousands*)	Province	Autonomous Areas*
Puyi (Chungchia) (1,248)	Kweichow	South Kweichow Puyi-Miao AC Tseheng Puyi AH Anlung Puyi-Miao AH Chenfeng Puyi-Miao AH Chenning Puyi-Miao AH Wangmo Puyi-Miao AH Tzeyün Miao-Puyi AH
Korean (1,120)	Kirin	Yenpien Korean AC Changpai Korean AH
Tung (713)	Kweichow	Southeast Kweichow Miao-Tung AC
	Hunan	Sinhwang Tung AH Tungtao Tung AH
	Kwangsi	Sankiang Tung AH
Yao (666)	Hunan	Kianghwa Yao AH
	Kwangtung	Juyüan Yao AH Linnam Yao AH Linshan Chuang-Yao AH
	Kwangsi	Tayaoshan Yao AH Pama Yao AH Tuan Yao AH Lungsheng Multinational AH Tunghing Multinational AH
	Yünnan	Hokow Yao AH
Pai (Minchia) (567)	Yünnan	Tali Pai AC
Tuchia (549)	Hunan	West Hunan Tuchia-Miao AC
Kazakh (509)	Sinkiang	Ili Kazakh AC Barkol Kazakh AH Mulei Kazakh AH
	Kansu	Aksai Kazakh AH
	Tsinghai	Haisi Mongol-Tibetan-Kazakh AC
Hani (Woni, Akha) (481)	Yünnan	Hungho Hani-Yi AC Kiangcheng Hani-Yi AH
Thai (Tai) (479)	Yünnan	Hsishuangpanna Thai AC Tehung Thai-Chingpo AC Kengma Thai-Wa AH Menglien Thai-Lahu-Wa AH
Li (361)	Kwangtung	Hainan Li-Miao AC

* AC = Autonomous chou
AH = Autonomous hsien

TABLE 5   (*continued*)

Ethnic Group (*1953 census, in thousands*)	Province	Autonomous Areas*
Lisu (317)	Yünnan	Nukiang Lisu AC
Wa (Kawa) (286)	Yünnan	Simeng Wa AH Tsangyüan Wa AH Kengma Thai-Wa AH Menglien Thai-Lahu-Wa AH
She (Yü) (219)	Chekiang Fukien	None
Tungsiang (156)	Kansu	Tungsiang AH
Nasi (Nakhi, Moso) (143)	Yünnan	Likiang Nasi AH
Lahu (139)	Yünnan	Lantsang Lahu AH Menglien Thai-Lahu-Wa AH
Shui (134)	Kweichow	Santu Shui AH
Chingpo (Kachin) (102)	Yünnan	Tehung Thai-Chingpo AC
Kirghiz (71)	Sinkiang	Kizil-Su Kirghiz AC
Tu (Mongor) (53)	Tsinghai Kansu	Huchu Tu AH None
Daghor (Daghur, Daur) (44)	Heilungkiang	Mo-li-ta-wa Daghor AH
Mulao (43)	Kwangsi	None
Chiang (36)	Szechwan	Mowwen Chiang AH
Pulang (Palaung) (35)	Yünnan	None
Salar (31)	Tsinghai	Shunhwa Salar AH
Russians (23)	Heilungkiang	None

* AC = Autonomous chou
AH = Autonomous hsien

TABLE 5 (*continued*)

Ethnic Group (*1953 census, in thousands*)	Province	Autonomous Areas*
Kolao (Gelao) (21)	Kweichow	None
Sibo (19)	Sinkiang	Chapchal Sibo AH
Achang (18)	Yünnan	None
Maonan (18)	Kwangsi	None
Pumi (15)	Yünnan	None
Tadzhik (14)	Sinkiang	Tash Kurghan Tadzhik AH
Uzbek (14)	Sinkiang	None
Nu (Lu) (13)	Yünnan	Kungshan Tulung-Nu AH
Tatar (6.9)	Sinkiang	None
Evenki (Solun) (5)	Heilungkiang	Evenki AH
Paoan (5)	Kansu, Tsinghai	None
Vietnamese (4)	Kwangsi	Tunghing Multinational AH
Yüku (Sary-Uigur) (3.9)	Kansu	South Kansu Yüku AH
Menpa (3.8)	Tibet	None
Penglung (2.9)	Yünnan	None
Tulung (2.4)	Yünnan	Kungshan Tulung-Nu AH
Orochon (Oronchon) (2.3)	Heilungkiang	Orochon AH
Gold (Hoche, Nanay) (0.5)	Heilungkiang	None

* AC = Autonomous chou
  AH = Autonomous hsien

Northern, or Peking, dialect, spoken throughout North China, Northwest China, and Manchuria north of a line formed by the Tsin Ling divide and the Hwai Ho; the Upper Yangtze, or Chengtu, dialect in Southwest China; and the Lower Yangtze, or Nanking, dialect in southern Anhwei and northern Kiangsu. Efforts are being made to transform the Northern Mandarin into China's national spoken language. Associated with the Mandarin dialects is Hunanese, in central and southern Hunan, with about 26 million speakers; the Hweichow dialect, in the Tunki region of southernmost Anhwei, with 7 million speakers; and the Kiangsi, or Kan, dialect, spoken by 13 million.

The most important Chinese language south of the linguistic divide is the Shanghai, or Wu, dialect, spoken in southern Kiangsu and in Chekiang by 46 million people in the 1953 census. This is followed southward along the coast by the Foochow, or Min, dialect, spoken by 7 million in the Min Kiang basin of northern Fukien. It is adjoined in the south by the Amoy-Swatow dialect of southern Fukien, about 15 million strong. To the west is the area of the Hakka language, spoken by 20 million in southernmost Kiangsi and northeastern Kwangtung. Another major southern Chinese language, second only to the Shanghai dialect, is Cantonese, spoken by 27 million people. Cantonese is the vernacular of central and western Kwangtung and southern Kwangsi. The Amoy-Swatow, Hakka, and Cantonese dialects are spoken by most overseas Chinese, who emigrated from these southern regions of China.

The Chinese Communists distinguish two national minorities that are also Chinese-speaking. They are the Hui (Chinese Moslems) and the Manchus.

The Hui, known in Russian as Dungan, are distinguished from ethnic Chinese mainly because of their affiliation with the Sunni branch of Islam. There are several theories regarding the origin of these Chinese Moslems. According to one view, they are descendants of Moslems who settled in China in the thirteenth and fourteenth centuries and adopted Chinese language and culture. Another theory suggests that they are derived from Chinese colonists who settled in the Northwest and adopted Islam. The 3.6 million Hui reported in the 1953 census are unusually widely distributed, with at least a few thousand represented in virtually every province of China. However, their traditional areas of settlement are Ningsia, Kansu, Tsinghai, and Sinkiang. The concentration of 577,000 Hui in the Ningsia plain led to the formation in 1958 of the Ningsia Hui Autonomous Region, one of the five province-level autonomous areas of China. In Kansu, with a Hui population of 535,000 in the 1953 census, the Linsia Hui Autonomous Chou and the Changkiachwan Hui Autonomous Hsien have been established. In Tsinghai, with a Hui population of 252,000, two autonomous hsien—Hwalung and Menyüan—have been set up. And in the Sinkiang Uigur Autonomous Region, 134,000 Hui are constituted as the Changki Autonomous Chou and Yenki Autonomous Hsien. Outside this core region in Northwest China, we find large Hui populations in Honan (387,000),

Hopei (376,000, with two autonomous hsien), Shantung (246,000), and Anhwei (136,000). Hui concentrations have also given rise to autonomous areas in Southwest China: Yünnan, with 217,000 Hui in 1953, contains Weishan Yi-Hui Autonomous Hsien, and Kweichow (41,000) has a Wei-ning Yi-Hui-Miao Autonomous Hsien. In general, however, the Hui are too disseminated to justify the creation of autonomous areas. Many live in cities; for example, there were 84,000 in Peking and 30,000 in Shanghai in the 1953 census.

The criteria used by the Chinese Communists in distinguishing a Manchu ethnic group are not entirely clear. Of the 2.4 million people reported as Manchu in the 1953 census, only a negligible number, if any, can be considered as having preserved any cultural traits of the original Manchu people of Manchuria who conquered China in the seventeenth century and founded the Manchu (Ch'ing) Dynasty (1644–1912). Though originally related to the Tungus in the Tungusic branch of the Altaic language family, the Manchus adopted Chinese language and culture and are virtually indistinguishable from ethnic Chinese, except insofar as they consider themselves descendants from the original Manchus. Still settled mainly in Manchuria, the Manchus have not been organized in distinctive autonomous areas. Their main areas of distribution in the 1953 census were as follows: Liaoning—1.1 million, Heilungkiang—630,000, Kirin—333,000, and Hopei—206,000 (plus 81,000 in Peking).

In addition to the Chinese-language group, the Sino-Tibetan family includes the Thai, Miao-Yao, and Tibeto-Burman groups, all of which are represented in China.

The Thai group, in turn, breaks down into three branches: the Thai-Chuang branch, about 9 million strong in China; the Tung-Shui branch, with 850,000 speakers; and the separate Li language of Hainan.

By far the most numerous ethnic group of the Thai-Chuang branch, in fact the largest ethnic minority of China, is the Chuang people, settled in a compact area in western Kwangsi, where they account for about 70 per cent of the population. Though originally established only as an autonomous chou in western Kwangsi, the Chuang rose in status in 1958, when the entire province was converted into the Kwangsi Chuang Autonomous Region. It contains 6.5 million of China's 7 million Chuang. Most of the others, sometimes distinguished as a separate Nung group (198,000 in the 1953 census) and the related ethnic minority of the Sha (112,000), are settled in adjoining southeastern Yünnan, together with Miao groups, and are constituted as the Wenshan Chuang-Miao Autonomous Chou. A small eastern enclave of Chuang in the Hunan-Kwangsi-Kwangtung border area is included in the Linshan Chuang-Yao Autonomous Hsien of Kwangtung Province.

Two small ethnic groups closely related to the Chuang are distinguished within the basic Chuang settlement area. They are the Mulao, numbering 43,000 in 1953, and the Maonan (18,000), both settled northwest of Liuchow without separate autonomous territorial status.

North of the Chuang settlement area is the large Puyi ethnic group of southwest Kweichow. The Puyi, formerly known as the Chungchia, number 1.2 million and are settled chiefly in the valley of the Peipan Kiang (northern branch of the Pan Kiang). Since the Puyi settlement area is intermixed with Miao population, the two groups share most of the autonomous areas established in this region: the South Kweichow Puyi-Miao Autonomous Chou and the joint autonomous hsien of Anlung, Chenfeng, Chenning, Tzeyün, and Wangmo. A separate Puyi hsien is at Tseheng.

The Thai ethnic group proper is represented by 479,000 people in Yünnan Province in two major settlement areas. One, inhabited by about 150,000 Thais speaking the Lü dialect on the Burma-Laos border, is constituted as the Hsishuangpanna Autonomous Chou. The other, in western Yünnan, is settled by about 175,000 Thais who are more closely related to the Shans of Burma and live in proximity with the Chingpo (Kachin) ethnic group. They form the Tehung Thai-Chingpo Autonomous Chou. Between these two main areas, Lü-speaking Thai elements are associated with the Lahu and Wa in the triple-nationality Menglien hsien, and with the Wa in Kengma hsien.

The two components of the Tung-Shui branch are settled in the Kweichow-Hunan-Kwangsi border region. The more numerous Tung (713,000 in 1953) are settled mainly in southeast Kweichow, where they form a joint autonomous chou with the Miao. Branches in Kwangsi (150,000 Tung in 1953) are constituted as the Sankiang Tung Autonomous Hsien, and in Hunan (125,000) as Tungtao and Sinhwang hsien. The 134,000 Shui are settled entirely in southeast Kweichow, where they form the Santu Shui Autonomous Hsien.

Somewhat separated geographically and culturally from the other members of the Thai ethnolinguistic group is the Li people of Hainan Island. Numbering 361,000 in the 1953 census, the Li are constituted, together with 16,000 Miao, as the Hainan Li-Miao Autonomous Chou. In contrast to the other, rice-growing members of the Thai group, the Li economy is traditionally based on the raising of water buffaloes.

The Miao-Yao group, formerly associated with the Mon-Khmer family, is now considered to be related to the Sino-Tibetan family. Its two principal components are the Miao people, totaling just over 2.5 million in the 1953 census, and the Yao, with 666,000. Both differ from some of the more compact ethnic minorities of southern China in having a widely dispersed distribution. The Miao have their basic settlement areas in Kweichow, with a Miao population of 1.4 million, and Hunan, with 380,000. In Kweichow, the ethnic group is associated with the Tung in the Southeast Kweichow Miao-Tung Autonomous Chou, and with the Puyi in the South Kweichow Puyi-Miao Autonomous Chou, as well as in five joint Puyi-Miao autonomous hsien. In western Kweichow, a small Miao area is associated with Yi and Hui elements in Weining hsien. In northeast Kweichow, the Sungtao Miao Autonomous Hsien is part of a compact Miao area that extends into western Hunan, where it is part of the West Hunan Tuchia-Miao Autonomous Chou. Chengpu hsien in southwest Hunan represents another small Miao area. Though also numerous in Kwangsi (204,000) and in Yünnan (360,000), the Miao are settled in these provinces in scattered groupings, represented only in a few cases in the autonomous territorial structure. In Kwangsi, the Miao have autonomous status in Tamiaoshan hsien, in a hill area of that name as well as in the two multinational hsien of Lungsheng and Lunglin; and in Yünnan in Wenshan Chuang-Miao Autonomous Chou and in Pingpien Miao Autonomous Hsien. More than 80,000 Miao in southwest Szechwan have no autonomous status, but the 16,000 on Hainan Island share an autonomous chou with the Li people.

A small group, the Kolao (Gelao), numbering 21,000 in 1953, lives in an isolated section of western Kweichow, and is believed to be related linguistically to the Miao.

The Yao have their main settlement area in the Kwangsi-Hunan-Kwangtung border region. In Kwangsi, with a Yao population of 469,000, or 70 per cent of all Yao in China, the group forms a compact settlement area in the Ta Yao Shan hills, where a Yao autonomous hsien has been established. Two other Yao hsien are farther west, at Pama and Tuan. In Hunan, with 70,000, the Yao form Kianghwa Autonomous Hsien. And, across the border in Kwangtung (with 41,000 Yao) are the Yao hsien of Juyüan and Linnam and the joint Chuang-Yao hsien of Linshan. In Yünnan, which has a Yao population of 72,000, the Hokow Yao Autonomous Hsien is situated on the border of North Vietnam.

A poorly defined component of the Miao-Yao group is the She (or Yü) people of isolated mountain areas of Chekiang and Fukien, believed to be related to the Yao. The She are not represented in the autonomous structure. Of a total number of 219,000 in 1953, one-third was reported in Chekiang and two-thirds in Fukien.

The Tibeto-Burman group includes three major branches: the Tibetan proper, the Yi, and the Kachin (Chingpo). The group is associated areally with the Tibetan highlands and the canyon country adjoining in the southeast, and totals 8.4 million people within China.

The Tibetan branch is areally, though not numerically, the most widespread of the ethnic minorities in China. The 2.8 million Tibetans, found throughout the Tibetan highlands, have one of the oldest cultures among the ethnic groups, with a distinctive alphabet dating from the seventh century. They are Lamaist by religion, agriculturists in the valley bottoms of southern Tibet, and nomadic herders over the vast reaches of the highlands. Tibetans are distributed as follows by provinces: 1.27 million in Tibet proper, including the Chamdo district; 713,000 in Szechwan; 516,000 in Tsinghai; 205,000 in Kansu; and 67,000 in Yünnan. Tibet was formally established in 1965 as the Tibet Autonomous Region after many years of provisional status under a so-called Preparatory Committee, established in 1955. Formal creation of the autonomous region was evidently delayed by

a Tibetan revolt of 1959 that led to the flight of the Dalai Lama. The Tibetans of Szechwan are organized in two autonomous chou—Kantse in the
western part of the province, and Ahpa in the northwest. The Muli Tibetan
Autonomous Hsien covers a smaller settlement area in southwestern Szechwan. Sparsely settled Tsinghai is covered almost entirely with Tibetan ethnic territorial units at the autonomous chou level. They are the Hainan,
Haipei, Hwangnan, Ngolog, and Yüshu areas, as well as the Haisi area,
which the Tibetans share with Mongols and Kazakhs. The Tibetans of
Kansu are constituted as the South Kansu Tibetan Autonomous Chou and
the Tienchu Tibetan Autonomous Hsien. Finally, in Yünnan, the Titsing
(Tehtsin) Tibetan Autonomous Chou has been established at the border of
Tibet and Szechwan.

Several minor ethnic groups are closely related to the Tibetans proper
and are found on the margins of the Tibetan settlement area. The largest of
these minorities is the Chiang (36,000 in the 1953 census), who form the
Mowwen Chiang Autonomous Hsien within the Ahpa Tibetan Autonomous
Chou of Szechwan. Two smaller ethnic communities, the Nu (13,000) and
the Tulung (2,400), share the Kungshan Autonomous Hsien of northwestern Yünnan, in the upper valley of the Salween River. Since 1962, the Chinese Communists have distinguished yet another small community, the
Menpa of southern Tibet, numbering 3,800.

The Yi branch, including the Yi proper (the former Nosu or Lolo) and
associated ethnic groups (Hani, Lisu, Nasi, Lahu, Achang), is numerically
the most important of the Tibeto-Burman ethnolinguistic groups, with a
settlement area extending from Szechwan through Yünnan and into western
Kweichow. The Yi proper have their homeland in the Liangshan Yi Autonomous Chou of southwestern Szechwan, with a smaller outlier in Yenyüan
Yi Autonomous Hsien to the southwest of the Liangshan area. Szechwan
contains 1.1 million Yi out of a total of 3.25 million Yi in southwest China,
or about one-third. The Kweichow outlier of the Yi settlement area, with
about 275,000 Yi, is constituted in part as the triple-nationality Weining
hsien, shared with Hui and Miao elements. The largest number of Yi live in
Yünnan Province (1.85 million in 1953), but, in contrast to the compact
settlement of the Liangshan Yi of Szechwan, the Yünnan Yi are widely dispersed, constituting one autonomous chou—Tsuyung—and four autonomous
hsien—Lunan, Nankien, Ninglang, and Oshan. A fifth hsien, Weishan, is
shared with a Hui community. The Yi also share an autonomous chou,
Hungho, and the adjoining Kiangcheng hsien with the Hani, one of the
ethnic groups closely associated with the Yi proper.

The Hani, numbering 481,000, are settled on the right bank of the Red
River, on the Yünnan border with North Vietnam, and, together with Yi
and Chinese on the economically developed left bank, form the Hungho
Hani-Yi Autonomous Chou. The Kiangcheng hsien adjoining in the southwest, also borders on Laos and North Vietnam.

The Lisu, another major minority associated with the Yi, are settled in the Salween River canyon of western Yünnan, where they form the Nukiang Lisu Autonomous Chou, Nu Kiang being the Chinese name for the Salween. They numbered 317,000 in the 1953 census, and have some affinity with the nearby Kachins.

The Nasi, or Nakhi (143,000 in 1953), have their settlement area in northwest Yünnan, in the bend formed by the Kinsha River, the upper course of the Yangtze. There they form the Likiang Nasi Autonomous Hsien. The Nasi, formerly known as Moso, have some common traits with the neighboring Tibetans.

The Lahu, who numbered 139,000 in 1953, have some common cultural features with the Wa people of the Mon-Khmer family, with whom the Lahu are associated in southwest Yünnan, in the canyons between the Mekong and Salween rivers. The Lahu form an autonomous hsien in the basic settlement area around Lantsang, and share the adjoining Menglien hsien with Thai and Wa elements.

The smallest of the tribes associated with the Yi are the Achang (18,000 in 1953), forming an enclave without autonomous status within the Tehung Thai-Chingpo Autonomous Chou, in proximity with the dominant Thai and Chingpo (Kachin) groups.

The Chingpo (Kachin) branch is represented primarily in northern Burma. China's 102,000 members of this ethnic group are associated with the Shan-like Thai in the Tehung Thai-Chingpo Autonomous Chou of western Yünnan. (Chingpo is the Chinese phonetic rendering of the Kachins' self-designation, which is also spelled Chingpaw. Kachin is the Burmese name of the group.)

The Pai ethnic group (formerly called Minchia) is also related to the Yi branch, but was not officially recognized in the autonomous territorial structure of Yünnan until 1956 because of heavy assimilation with the Chinese. They were found to number 567,000 in the 1953 census, and are settled compactly in what is now the Tali Pai Autonomous Chou, in the area of the lake Erh Hai. In contrast to most of the other Yünnan ethnic minorities, who are largely mountain dwellers, the Pai are valley people, engaged in agriculture and trade.

Yet another minority, the Tuchia of Hunan, was recognized relatively late as a distinctive ethnic group, related to the Yi. The Tuchia, numbering 549,000 as of 1953, were identified mainly in the northern part of the West Hunan Miao Autonomous Chou, which was accordingly renamed the West Hunan Tuchia-Miao Autonomous Chou in 1957.

Also part of the great Sino-Tibetan language family is a small Vietnamese community of about 4,000, identified in Tunghing Multinational Autonomous Hsien of Kwangsi, on the Gulf of Tonkin and adjoining North Vietnam. The Vietnamese plains dwellers are associated in the hsien with Yao elements in the adjoining hills and with Kwangsi's dominant Chuang people.

The Altaic Family. Shifting from the intricate ethnic patterns of subtropical Southwest China, to the vast arid Northwest, we find China's other great language family, the Altaic, with its Turkic and Mongolic subfamilies.

The most numerous are the Turkic groups, virtually all Moslems, totaling 4.3 million people. By far the most important is the Uigur people, who now live chiefly in the oases around the Tarim basin of Sinkiang and numbered 3.64 million in the 1953 census. They are descendants of Uigurs who once had a state in what is now Mongolia, but were driven westward in the ninth century by ancestors of the modern Kirghiz. A distinctive ancient Uigur alphabet was adopted in the thirteenth century by the Mongols and later by the Manchus, while the Uigurs shifted to the Arabic script with Islamic culture. Since 1955, the Uigurs are the titular ethnic group of the Sinkiang Uigur Autonomous Region, although an influx of Chinese in the late 1950's and through the 1960's into this strategic area adjoining the Soviet Union appears to have deprived the Uigurs of their former numerical majority.

Related historically to the Uigurs is the small Yüku (Sary-Uigur or Yellow Uigur) community of 3,900 people of Kansu, in the foothills of the Nan Shan. This group of stockherders, which appears to have split off from the ancient Uigurs in their westward migration, has adopted Lamaism and other cultural features of the Mongols. It forms the South Kansu (Sunan) Yüku Autonomous Hsien. (Yüku is the Chinese phonetic rendering of Uigur or Yugur, another form.)

Also culturally and linguistically close to the Uigurs of Sinkiang is the small Chinese Uzbek minority of 14,000, settled predominantly in the larger towns of Sinkiang. The main Uzbek settlement area is in Soviet Central Asia. The 1953 census also reported 6,900 Tatars in Sinkiang towns. Two other Turkic peoples identified predominantly with Soviet Central Asia are represented in Sinkiang and adjoining provinces. They are the Kazakhs, who numbered 509,000 in the Chinese census of 1953, and the Kirghiz, with 71,000. Both are predominantly stockherders.

The Chinese Kazakhs are found predominantly in the northern, Dzungarian portion of Sinkiang, where they form the Ili Kazakh Autonomous Chou. This autonomous area includes the Kazakhs of the upper Irtysh valley, the so-called Kara Irtysh or Black Irtysh, and the Kazakhs of the mountain valleys of the Kunges, Tekes, and Kash rivers (headstreams of the Ili). Farther east in Sinkiang, Kazakh communities are constituted as the Mulei and Barkol autonomous hsien. A Kazakh hsien, Aksai, has been established in northwestern Kansu, and to the south, in Tsinghai, the Kazakhs share the Haisi autonomous chou with Mongols and Tibetans. The Tsinghai Kazakhs, settled around Golmo, south of the Tsaidam Basin, were moved there after a revolt of Sinkiang Kazakhs was suppressed in 1936.

The Kirghiz ethnic group of China is settled in the foothills of the Tien Shan and the Pamirs, ranging in an arc behind the oases of the western Tarim basin of Sinkiang. Much of the Kirghiz settlement area is included in the Kizil-Su Kirghiz Autonomous Chou. Like the Kazakhs, the Kirghiz are predominantly nomad stockherders.

The easternmost Turkic community in China is the distinctive Salar ethnic group (31,000 in 1953), settled on the right bank of the Yellow River in northeast Tsinghai. The Salar, believed to be descendants of the ancient Oghuz people, are constituted as an autonomous hsien around Shunhwa. They have been influenced by neighboring Tibetan and Mongol as well as Chinese communities.

The Mongols proper, the principal element of the Mongolic branch of the Altaic language family, numbered 1.46 million in the Chinese census of 1953. They were among the first Chinese ethnic minorities that received autonomous territorial status, when the Inner Mongolian Autonomous Region was established in 1947, two years before the Communists assumed power in Peking. At its greatest extent, from 1958 to 1969, Inner Mongolia contained 997,000 Mongols, or roughly two-thirds of China's total Mongol population. However, the cession of Inner Mongolian areas to Manchuria in late 1969 probably reduced the number of Mongols in the autonomous region to 500,000 or 600,000, out of a total regional population of about 9 million. The territorial transfers raised the Mongol population of Manchuria from 320,000 to more than 700,000. Heilungkiang, which had 38,000 Mongols, some of whom formed an autonomous hsien, acquired the entire Hulunbuir League, with a Mongol population of about 100,000, mostly Barga Mongols. Kirin, with 47,000 Mongols, centered in the South Gorlos hsien, obtained the Jerim League, with an estimated Mongol population of 200,000. And Liaoning, which already had 235,000 Mongols, constituted in two autonomous hsien, added the Jo-uda League, with perhaps 100,000 more. By contrast, the large westernmost section of Inner Mongolia, the Alashan Desert, divided in 1969 between the Ningsia Hui Autonomous Region and Kansu Province, had only a sparse population of a few thousand Mongols. The cession of the Alashan East Banner to Ningsia may have involved perhaps 5,000 Mongols, and transfer of the Alashan West Banner and the Edsin Banner to Kansu about 10,000. In addition, Kansu also had the North Kansu (Supei) Mongol Autonomous Hsien, with 3,000 Mongols.

Two other Chinese provinces with significant Mongol minorities are Sinkiang, with 58,000 in the 1953 census, and Tsinghai, with 26,000. The Mongols of Sinkiang are constituted into two autonomous chou—Borotala and Bayan Gol—and the autonomous hsien of Khobuk-Saur. In Tsinghai, the Mongols are associated with Tibetans and Kazakhs in the Haisi autonomous chou, and also have the Honan Mongol Autonomous Hsien.

Although the Mongols of Outer Mongolia abandoned the ancient Mongol alphabet in favor of the Cyrillic after World War II, the traditional vertical script continued to be used by the Mongols of China. Tentative plans to convert to the Cyrillic were made in Inner Mongolia in 1955, but were later abandoned as the political split between China and the Soviet Union developed.

Four small ethnic groups are related to the Mongols within the Mongolic ethnolinguistic branch: the Tu (Mongor), Tungsiang, Paoan, and Daghors.

In contrast to the nomadic herding economy of the Mongols proper, these smaller communities have adopted a settled mode of life and engaged in agriculture.

The Tu group of northeast Tsinghai, numbering 53,000 in 1953, is believed to derive from Mongols who settled in the Koko Nor area in the twelfth century. Because of long separation from the main Mongol linguistic area, the Tu language has preserved archaic features still reflected in the Mongol written language. The Tu minority is constituted as the Huchu Tu Autonomous Hsien. (The alternate term Mongor apparently reflects the Chinese pronunciation of "Mongol," changing *l* to *r*.)

The Tungsiang (156,000 in 1953), unlike other Mongolic groups, have adopted Islam, presumably because they live near Hui (Chinese Moslems) in southern Kansu. The name of this group means "eastern village" in Chinese, an allusion to their location east of the city of Linsia, where they are constituted in an autonomous hsien.

Another Mongolic ethnic group of Moslem religion is the Paoan, 5,000 strong in 1953. The Paoan, who lack separate autonomous status, live in Kansu, west of Linsia, near the Tsinghai border.

Far removed from this cluster of three related communities in the Tsinghai-Kansu area is a Mongolic group, the Daghors (Daghurs, Daurs) of Heilungkiang Province in Manchuria. Numbering 44,000 in the 1953 census, the Daghors are believed to be Mongolized Manchus. They form the Moli-ta-wa Autonomous Hsien in Heilungkiang.

If we discount the assimilated Manchu people discussed earlier, the Tungusic branch of Altaic includes four small ethnic groups in China: the Evenki, the Orochon and Gold of Manchuria, and the Sibo of Sinkiang.

The Evenki, who numbered 5,000 in 1953, are seminomadic herders in the Great Khingan Mountains of Manchuria. An Evenki community, also known as Solons, which formed militarized elements of the Manchu armed forces, is constituted as an autonomous hsien on the southern outskirts of the city of Hailar.

The Orochon, similar to the Evenki herders in mode of life, are also settled in the Greater Khingan, where their autonomous hsien is situated. They number about 2,300.

The Gold, only 500 strong, are a primitive fishing people in the swampy area between the lower Sungari River and the Amur. They are known as Hoche in Chinese and as Nanay in the Soviet Union; an alternate name in the Western literature is Fishskin Tatars.

The Sibo are a geographical oddity in the sense that they are descendants of a militarized Manchu group, resettled in the eighteenth century far from the main Manchu settlement area to guard the western borders of China. Numbering 19,000 in the 1953 census, the Sibo form the Chapchal Autonomous Hsien in the Ili valley of western Sinkiang, on the frontier of the Soviet Union.

The Koreans. The Koreans, sometimes regarded as part of the Altaic family, number 1.12 million in China and are settled in Manchuria along the North Korean boundary. Their main area of settlement is in the Yenpien Korean Autonomous Chou of Kirin Province, with an additional autonomous hsien at Changpai to the southwest. Kirin has a Korean population of 765,000, compared with 239,000 in Heilungkiang and 116,000 in Liaoning. Korean villages, which engage in irrigated rice-growing, lumbering, and craft industries, are situated in river valleys and along railroads used by Koreans in their northward migration into China after the 1870's.

The Mon-Khmer Family. The Mon-Khmer linguistic family of Southeast Asia is represented in Yünnan Province by the Wa (formerly Kawa), the Pulang (Palaung), and the Penglung.

The Wa group, by far the most numerous, with 286,000 in 1953, lives along the mountainous frontier between Yünnan and Burma in the Salween-Mekong watershed. It is constituted in two autonomous hsien—Simeng and Tsangyüan—and shares two others with Thai and Lahu elements. The Pulang (Palaung), numbering 35,000 in 1953, also reside on the Yünnan-Burma border, but east of the Mekong River. Finally, the smallest of the Mon-Khmer groups, the Penglung (2,900 in 1953), forms an enclave adjoining the Achang settlement area in Tehung Thai-Chingpo Autonomous Chou of western Yünnan.

The Tadzhiks. An Indo-European ethnic group is the Tadzhik community on the eastern slopes of the Pamirs in southwest Sinkiang. These Tadzhiks, numbering 14,000 in 1953, are constituted as the Tash Kurghan Autonomous Hsien. The Sinkiang Tadzhiks are related to the Wakhan, Shugnan, and Rushan Tadzhiks in the Soviet portions of the Pamirs.

A large Russian ethnic minority in Manchuria, which rose to be as high as 250,000 in the early twentieth century, has been largely repatriated to the Soviet Union. It included both urban residents, notably in Harbin and smaller towns along the Russian-built Chinese Eastern railroad, and farmers in the so-called Three Rivers area on the right bank of the Argun River. The 1953 census of China reported 23,000 Russians; their number declined further to 9,800 by 1957.

In summary, China's ethnic minorities belong to two major language families: the Sino-Tibetan in the southwestern quadrant of the country and the Altaic in the northwestern quadrant. Economically, most of these ethnic minorities are farmers like the basic Chinese population. The total nomadic herding population is about 3.5 million, including chiefly Tibetans, Mongols, and Kazakhs. Certain small tribes, such as the Orochon of Manchuria, make hunting their chief source of livelihood. In religion, 8 million minority people are Moslems. They include the Uigurs and the Hui, each with about 3.6 million persons, Kazakhs, Tungsiang, Kirghiz, Salar, and others. Tibetans and Mongols, the Tu and Yüku, are Lamaists, and the Thai peoples of Southwest China are predominantly Theravada Buddhists. Other groups engage in various shamanistic practices.

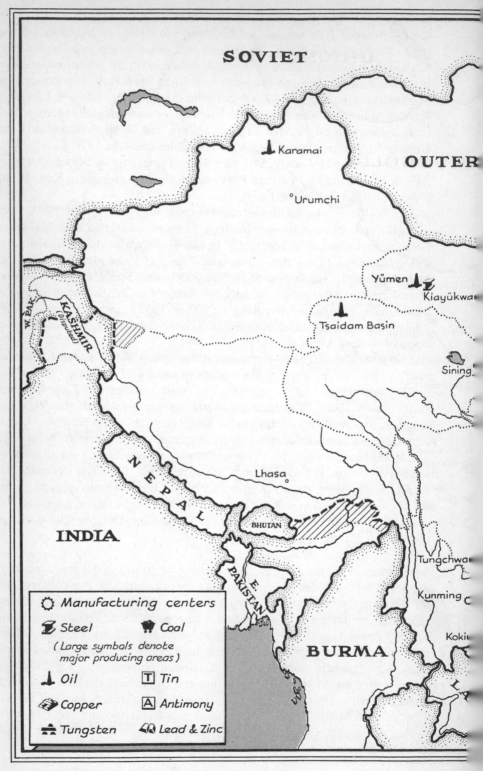

3. Economic Centers of China

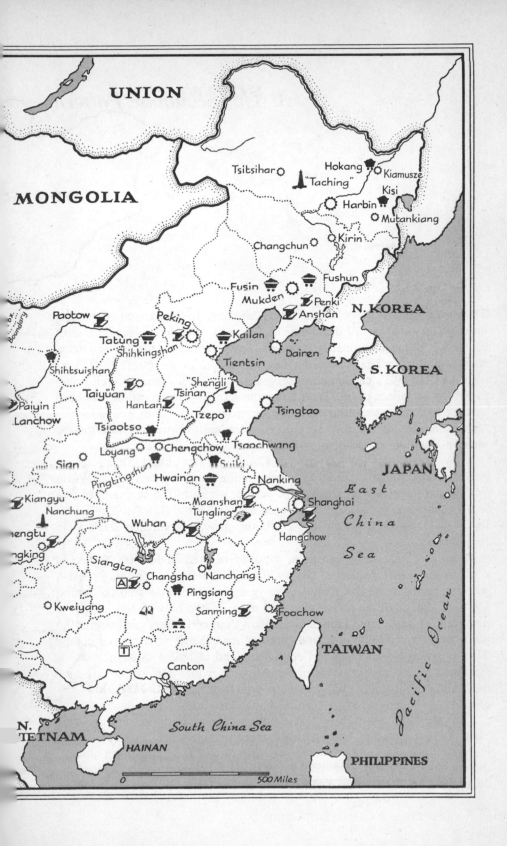

UNION

MONGOLIA

Tsitsihar
Hokang
"Taching"
Kiamusze
Kisi
Harbin
Mutankiang
Changchun
Kirin
Fushun
Fusin
Mukden
Penki
Anshan
N. KOREA
Paotow
Peking
Kailan
S. KOREA
Tatung
Shihkingshan
Tientsin
Dairen
Shihtsuishan
Paiyin
Taiyüan
"Shengli"
Tsinan
Lanchow
Hantan
Tsingtao
Tsiaotso
Tzepo
Loyang
Chengchow
Tsaochwang
Sian
Pingtingshun
Suiki
Hwainan
Nanking
JAPAN
Kiangyu
Maanshan
Tungling
Shanghai
East
Nanchung
hengtu
Wuhan
Hangchow
China
ngking
Siangtan
Sea
Changsha
Nanchang
Kweiyang
Pingsiang
Sanming
Foochow
TAIWAN
Canton
Pacific Ocean
N.
TETNAM
South China Sea
HAINAN
PHILIPPINES

0   500 Miles

3. The Economic Pattern

The economic history of Communist China can be broken down roughly into two major phases of development. The first, well-documented phase of the 1950's began with orderly economic development on the Soviet model, with emphasis on heavy industry, but culminated in the Great Leap Forward of 1958–59, a chaotic crash program. The second phase, which began in 1960 with failure of the Great Leap and a three-year recession, has been marked by a more balanced economic-development program, veiled by virtually complete statistical secrecy on even the most elementary information about population and economic performance.

From the Communist take-over of China in 1949 until 1952, the economy passed through a period of rehabilitation from the ravages of World War II and the civil war. During this period, whose mixed economy of private industry and state-controlled sectors resembled the New Economic Policy of the early 1920's in the Soviet Union, prewar production levels were roughly restored.

In 1953, China embarked upon a policy of industrialization by forced draft in the Soviet pattern of the 1930's. The guidelines for this program were contained in the first Chinese five-year plan, which covered the period 1953–57, although the actual plan was made public only in July, 1955. It provided for more rapid growth of industry than agriculture, and within the industrial sector it favored capital goods at the expense of consumer goods. The supply of Soviet industrial equipment and technical assistance was a significant aspect of this phase of development, which also stressed the industrialization of China's underdeveloped interior regions. By the end of the first five-year plan, private enterprise had been virtually eliminated.

The year 1958 was to have marked the beginning of the second five-year plan (1958–62), which had been announced in September, 1956. However, in apparent dissatisfaction with the existing rate of economic development, the Chinese leadership embarked in 1958 on a program of accelerated industrialization that became known as the Great Leap Forward. In addition to continued heavy investment in capital-goods industries, this crash program also called for a vast number of small rural industrial projects, typified by the backyard-iron-furnace movement. At the same time, agricultural cooperatives established in the preceding plan period were combined into larger, more regimented production units known as communes. As a result of the Great Leap Forward, production goals set originally for 1962 in the second five-year plan had already been reached or exceeded in 1959, according to official figures that now appear to have been inflated. According to the 1960 economic plan, made public in March, 1960, the pace set by the Great Leap was to have continued. However, the leadership evidently attempted to accomplish too much too fast. As a statistical blackout descended on China in 1960, the crash program collapsed, and the Soviet Union, which had frowned on the Great Leap experiment, withdrew its economic aid. The Chinese economic advance was disrupted.

In the economic crisis of 1960–62, economic-development policies were reviewed. Forced-draft industrialization, with emphasis on heavy industry, was abandoned in favor of more balanced, moderate economic growth, in which agriculture and related industries were given priority. Uneconomical small-production establishments built during the Great Leap were closed, investment was greatly reduced, and production increases after the 1960 collapse were achieved mainly through use of underemployed existing output capacity. Through the first half of the 1960's, the Chinese economy slowly recovered, and it may have again reached the 1959 peak level of the Great Leap by 1966, as the Cultural Revolution started.

However, the upheavals associated with the Cultural Revolution, a wide-reaching purge, in which the existing Communist Party machinery was dismantled, evidently set back economic production for at least two years. As order was restored in the wake of establishment in 1967–68 of the Revolutionary Committees, the new agencies of local administration, the economic picture brightened again, and previous peak production levels were apparently restored in 1969. In an effort to speed development, the leadership again encouraged the widespread growth of small-scale rural industrial projects, but on a more balanced level than during the hectic Great Leap. In the meantime, it was disclosed that a third five-year plan had been in operation from 1966 to 1970, and that a fourth plan (1971–75) was about to begin. But in the continuing embargo on national statistical indicators, no information about either plan was revealed.

In the following discussion of individual sectors of the Chinese economy, an attempt is made to trace statistical trends, at least for the 1950's, structural changes, and shifts in geographical distribution insofar as the limited information permits.

INDUSTRY

Statistical Questions. As long as statistical information was published, the Chinese reported aggregate growth of economic production in terms of an official index of the gross value of industrial and agricultural output. This index represented the total value of the output of farms and industrial establishments in constant prices. During the five-year plan of 1953–57, gross value was reported in 1952 prices. The gross-value index exaggerates the level of production because the value of goods processed successively by two or more establishments figures in the gross-value product of each establishment. This double counting is more serious in industry, where products pass through more processing stages, than in agriculture. Western economists have made independent estimates of a more accurate measure of economic growth, the net product, or value added, which excludes the cost of materials. Choh-ming Li has computed that, during the first five-year plan, the net product was about 75 per cent of the gross product in agriculture, 50 per cent in heavy industry, 30 per cent in handicrafts, and 20 per cent in light industry. However, since the ratio of net to gross product has been relatively constant, the gross-value figures are presented here as a rough measure of the rate of growth (Table 6).

TABLE 6

GROSS VALUE OF INDUSTRIAL AND AGRICULTURAL PRODUCTION

(*1949 to 1958, in billion 1952 yüan*)

	1949	1952	1953	1954	1955	1956	1957	1958 Plan
Industry and handicrafts	14.0	34.3	44.7	52.0	54.9	70.4	78.4	
Industry proper	10.8	27.0	35.6	41.5	44.8	58.7	65.0	72.0
Modern industry	7.9	22.0	28.8	34.0	37.1	50.4		
Factory handicrafts	2.9	5.0	6.8	7.5	7.7	8.3		
Domestic handicrafts	3.2	7.3	9.1	10.5	10.1	11.7	13.4	
Agriculture and rural subsidiary output	32.6	48.4	49.9	51.6	55.5	58.3	60.3	64.3
TOTAL	46.6	82.7	94.6	103.6	110.4	128.7	138.7	

(*1957 to 1960, in billion 1957 yüan*)

	1957	1958 Plan	1958 Actual Orig.	1958 Actual Rev.	1959 Plan Orig.	1959 Plan Rev.	1959 Actual	1960 Plan
Industry and handicrafts	70.4		117	117	165	147	163	210
(Industry proper)		(64.4)						
Commune industries				6.4			12	19
Rural				6.0			10	15
Urban				0.4			2	4
Agriculture proper	53.7		88	67	122	74	78	88
(plus subsidiary work)	(64.9)	(68.8)						
TOTAL	124.1		205	184	287	221	241	298

NOTE: The two sets of figures for actual 1958 performance and the 1959 plan result from an official revision of original 1958 data that were acknowledged to have been inflated, particularly in agriculture, and a corresponding adjustment of the 1959 plan.

During the first five-year plan, as noted earlier, the Chinese computed the gross product for comparative purposes in constant prices of 1952. However, in the course of the plan period, several price adjustments were not reflected in the gross product figures. There was a general tendency toward increases in prices of some farm products and toward reduction for most industrial products. Moreover, many products first turned out after 1952 lacked 1952 prices. It was therefore decided that, starting from 1958, a new statistical series would express the gross product in constant 1957 prices. The differences between the 1952 and 1957 prices are evident from Table 6. For 1957, industrial output in 1957 prices was about 8 billion yüan lower than in 1952 prices, reflecting the price cuts on industrial products during the 1952–57 period. In agriculture, on the contrary, gross output in 1957 prices was about 4.5 billion yüan higher, indicating the price increases for farm products.

In addition to the change in price level, some structural changes were made in the classification of gross product, particularly with respect to handicrafts. Domestic handicrafts, operated primarily on a private basis in the early 1950's, were almost totally converted into cooperatives by 1956 and thus were not significantly different from so-called factory handicrafts already included under the industry heading. Beginning in 1958, therefore, handicrafts were no longer separated statistically from industry. However, during the Great Leap, before statistical secrecy was imposed in 1960, the Chinese authorities issued data on the output value of industry operated by rural and urban communes, as distinguished from industry run by central, provincial, and local (hsien) government. These commune industry figures have been included in Table 6.

Changes of Emphasis. Table 6 also illustrates the extent to which industry and handicrafts developed more rapidly than agriculture during the first five-year plan and the Great Leap. In the 1952–57 period, the output of industry proper rose 240 per cent, from 27 billion to 65 billion yüan (1952 prices), and handicraft production increased by 83 per cent. The 1957 gross output of agriculture, by contrast, was only 25 per cent above 1952 output. The gross value of agricultural output rose slowly, despite the fact that this category included not only strictly agricultural activity, such as crop-raising and animal husbandry, but also the value of output of subsidiary rural occupations. In the statistical change of base from 1952 to 1957 prices, the value of output of subsidiary rural activities was eliminated from the gross agricultural product, which was thereafter limited to the value of crops and animal products. This change in statistical definition reduced the agricultural product (in 1957 prices) from 64.9 to 53.7 billion yüan as of 1957. Part of the value of the subsidiary work was transferred to the light-industry sector, but some household activities, such as tailoring and shoemaking for the household's own use, were probably omitted altogether from the gross product.

As a result of these statistical revisions, the lag of agricultural output was further enhanced after 1957. During the Great Leap, the output of the new statistical category of industry and handicrafts rose by 230 per cent, from 70.4 billion yüan in 1957 to 163 billion in 1969, compared with a 46 per cent increase in agriculture. This lag in the farming sector accounted in part for the collapse of the Great Leap and the ensuing reorientation of industrial priorities, giving greater weight to chemical fertilizers, farm implements, and other industries supporting agriculture.

The blackout on economic information imposed in 1960 makes it difficult to assess the rates of growth during the past decade. It is believed, however, that after the recession of 1960–62 the economy gradually recovered and may have reached the Great Leap levels again by 1970, or a gross value of output of close to 300 billion yüan (in 1957 prices). In view of the continued rapid rates of growth of industrial production, with more weight given to agricultural-support industries, industry in 1970 may have accounted for three-fourths of the total value of output, or about 220 billion yüan, and agriculture for one-fourth, or about 75 billion yüan.

The priority the Chinese accorded to heavy industry during the first five-year plan and the Great Leap emerges clearly from Table 7. This table

TABLE 7

OUTPUT OF HEAVY AND LIGHT INDUSTRY

| | 1952 Yüan | | | | | | | 1957 Yüan | | | |
	1949	1952	1953	1954	1955	1956	1957	1957	1958	1959	1960 Plan
Industry proper	10.8	27.0	35.6	41.5	44.8	58.7	65.0				
Industry and handicrafts								70.4	117	163	210
Heavy industry	3.1	10.7	14.7	17.6	20.6	29.2	34.3	32.9	67	96	127
Machinery	0.2	1.4	2.2	2.6	3.0	5.8	6.2	10	19		
Light industry	7.7	16.3	20.9	23.9	24.2	29.5	30.7	37.5	50	67	83

distinguishes the output of heavy industry—mainly capital goods (with a subcategory for machinery)—from light industry, primarily consumer goods. As part of the 1957 statistical revision, the breakdown into the heavy- and light-industry sectors is based on industry proper in 1952 yüan for the period up to 1957 and on the aggregate category of industry and handicrafts in 1957 yüan after 1957. During the 1952–57 period, production of heavy industry rose by 320 per cent, from 10.7 billion to 34.3 billion yüan (1952 prices), compared with an 89 per cent growth of light industry, from 16.3 billion to 30.7 billion yüan. The share of heavy industry within all industry rose from 39.7 per cent in 1952 to 52.8 per cent in 1957, when, for the first time, it exceeded the value of light industry. As a result of the combination of handicraft statistics (mainly the consumer goods of light industry) with those of industry proper, the share of light industry again exceeded that of heavy industry. But with the continued priority given to heavy industry during the Great Leap, the output of that sector almost tripled in 1958–59 compared with a 79 per cent rise in light industry. Although the use of the gross value statistics somewhat distorts the relationship between the heavy- and light-industry sectors (because of different degrees of double-counting), it seems clear that producer-goods industries grew about twice as fast as consumer-goods industries in the 1950's. With the reappraisal of priorities in 1960, it may be assumed that the discrepancy in growth rates between the two industrial sectors was adjusted in favor of light industry. However, the extent of that adjustment has been obscured by statistical secrecy.

Structural Changes. In addition to changes in emphasis on particular sectors of the economy, there have also been significant changes in the institutional structure of China's industry. These changes involved primarily the gradual transfer during the first five-year plan of the private sector of industry to government control. The Peking regime inherited a sizable government-industry sector from the Nationalists. This was gradually enlarged through expropriation, the establishment of joint state-private establishments, and the fostering of cooperatives (in the handicraft sector). The trend is illustrated by Table 8. The table shows that, by 1956, private in-

TABLE 8

INSTITUTIONAL CHANGES IN INDUSTRY AND HANDICRAFTS
(*value of output, in billion 1952 yüan*)

	1949	1952	1953	1954	1955	1956	1957
State industry	3.7	14.3	19.2	24.5	28.1	38.4	
Cooperatives	0.07	1.1	1.7	2.4	3.4	12.0	
State-private	0.2	1.4	2.0	5.1	7.2	19.1	
Private industry	6.8	10.5	13.1	10.3	7.3	0.03	
Individual craftsmen	3.2	7.1	8.6	9.6	8.8	0.8	
TOTAL	14.0	34.3	44.7	52.0	54.9	70.4	78.4

NOTE: Some totals do not add up because of rounding.

dustry had been virtually eliminated, having passed largely to the joint state-private sector, where the government exercised effective control. In addition, almost all private craftsmen had been joined into cooperatives. As a result of these structural changes, the share of national income derived from the state sector of the economy (mainly modern industry and transportation as well as state farms) rose between 1952 and 1957 from 19 to 33 per cent; the share of the cooperative sector (agriculture, handicrafts, simple local transportation, and trade) from 1.5 to 56 per cent, and the share of the joint state-private sector (in modern industry and transportation) from 0.7 to 8 per cent. At the same time, the share of small-scale private (individual) enterprise (in agriculture, handicrafts, trade) dropped from 72 per cent to 3 per cent, and the share of large-scale (capitalist) enterprise (in modern industry and transportation) from 7 per cent to less than 0.1 per cent.

Fuel and Power Industries. Coal is by far the most important fossil fuel in the Chinese economy, accounting for more than 90 per cent of all energy resources. It provides the basic fuel for the electric-power industry, for iron and steel and other metal smelting, and for the nation's railroads. A distinctive aspect of China's coal economy is the large household consumption of coal for heating and cooking. In 1957, the last normal statistical year, households consumed about 50 per cent of the total coal supply, industry 35 per cent (including metallurgy and power plants, each 10 per cent), and railroads almost 10 per cent. Most of China's coal output consists of bituminous types (about 80 per cent in 1957), which include coking coals for the iron and steel industry. Anthracite, used mainly for domestic heating, accounted for 17 per cent, and lignite only about 3 per cent.

Coal production before the Communist take-over ranged from 30 to 40 million tons annually during the late 1930's to a peak of 65.8 million tons in 1942, when output was spurred by the Japanese war economy in Manchuria and other occupied parts of China. Under Communist rule, the coal industry gradually rose from a low of 32.4 million metric tons in 1949 to 66.5 million tons in 1952. During the first five-year plan, it benefited from large-scale investment, which brought output to 131 million tons by 1957. The coal industry was then caught up in the Great Leap, which resulted in a boom in the handicraft sector, as the authorities encouraged the digging of shallow, primitive mines all over the country. The last official data placed the production goal for 1960 at 425 million tons, of which probably 20 to 25 per cent was to be produced in the ephemeral handicraft mines (Table 9). The goal was said to have been achieved, but coal-mining, together with the rest of the economy, declined in the early 1960's after the collapse of the Great Leap. Estimates for the following years vary, but production is believed to have recovered gradually to more than 200 million tons by the middle of the decade before being set back again briefly during the early convulsions of the Cultural Revolution. Output in 1970 may have been again around 300 million tons as a new small-mines drive got under way.

Two-thirds of China's coal production is concentrated in the northeast quadrant of the country, where it serves the industrial base of Manchuria and North China. In 1957, the last year for which geographical distribution is available, Manchuria and North China each produced 43 million tons, or, together, two-thirds of the national output. In Manchuria, steam coals for electric-power generation are provided mostly by the large strip mines of Fushun and Fusin, each yielding on the order of 10 to 20 million tons a year. Coking coal for the iron and steel industry at Anshan in southern Manchuria is provided mainly by the underground mines of Hokang, Shwangyashan, and Kisi in northern Manchuria. In North China, the principal producer of steam coals is the Kailan basin around Tangshan, which supplies power plants in the Peking-Tientsin industrial district and sends its surplus southward through the coal-shipping port of Chinwangtao. A significant supplier of coking coal is the Fengfeng basin near Hantan. The

TABLE 9
COAL PRODUCTION
(in million metric tons)

	Modern Industry	Handicrafts	Total
1942	62.0	3.8	65.8
1949	31.0	1.4	32.4
1952	63.5	3.0	66.5
1953	66.6	3.1	69.7
1954	79.9	3.7	83.6
1955	93.6	4.7	98.3
1956	105.9	4.4	110.3
1957	123.2	7.5	130.7
1958	219	51	270
1959	ca. 280	ca. 70	348
1960 (plan)	ca. 300	ca. 100	425 (plan)

NOTE: The breakdown for 1959 and for the 1960 plan is estimated.

Tatung mines of northern Shansi also have a wide marketing area within North China. Yet another major coal-mining producer is the Hwainan basin of Anhwei, which accounted for half of East China's 1957 output of 16 million tons.

Since the first five-year plan (1953–57), new coal-mining centers have been developed on the southern and western margins of the old northeastern industrial quadrant, partly in conjunction with the construction of new iron-and-steel plants at Wuhan on the Yangtze River and at Paotow on the upper Yellow River. The principal new coking coal supplier for Wuhan is Pingtingshan, a new mining city of central Honan, which now supplements shipments from the older mines at Pingsiang in western Kiangsi. Another recent development is the so-called Hwaipei ("north of the Hwai Ho") coal district of northern Anhwei, with its urban center in the new city of Suiki. On the western margins of China's basic industrial region, a major coal district has arisen in support of the Paotow iron-and-steel plant on the border between Inner Mongolia and the Ningsia Hui Autonomous Region. The district consists of a cluster of three new cities—Shuitsuishan in Ningsia and Wuta and Haipowan in adjoining Inner Mongolia.

Petroleum was long a negligible element in the Chinese fuel economy and was supplemented by shale oil as well as by synthetic oil produced by hydrogenation of bituminous coal. In fact, during the 1950's, crude-oil figures included production from all these sources (Table 10).

The earliest major producing field was Yümen, in Kansu, where operations began in 1939, and about 1 million tons were produced in 1958. In that year, another major western field, at Karamai in Sinkiang, was put into production and soon matched Yümen's output. Production also began during the Great Leap in a smaller oil field discovered near Nanchung in Szechwan. A fourth development during this period, in the Tsaidam Basin of Tsinghai Province, was largely discontinued after the collapse of the Great

TABLE 10
CRUDE-OIL PRODUCTION
(*in million metric tons*)

	Natural Petroleum	Synthetic and Shale Oil	Total
1942	0.07	0.77	0.84
1949	0.07	0.05	0.12
1952	—	—	0.44
1953	—	—	0.62
1954	—	—	0.79
1955	0.48	0.49	0.97
1956	0.56	0.60	1.16
1957	0.85	0.61	1.46
1958	1.47	0.79	2.26
1959	*ca.* 2.7	*ca.* 1.0	3.7
1960 (plan)	*ca.* 3.4	*ca.* 1.8	5.2

NOTE: No breakdown is available for 1952, 1953 or 1954. The breakdown for 1959 and 1960 Plan is estimated.

Leap. (After stagnating through the 1960's, the development of Tsaidam was resumed in 1969.) China's oil production, which may have reached 3 million tons by 1960 from these western fields, rose dramatically in the following years as a result of the discovery of an oil field in northern Manchuria that soon became the leading producer, contributing at least half of the total output. Because the new development was announced after the imposition of secrecy in 1960, it has been consistently identified in official Chinese publications only by the code name Taching, meaning "great celebration," and has not been located geographically. However, on the basis of Western analysis of scattered information, it has been identified as being in the Anta area, on the Chinese Eastern railroad west of Harbin. Yet another code-named oil discovery was reported in the middle 1960's, this one called Shengli ("victory") and tentatively located on the lower Yellow River in northern Shantung. Little information about this development has become available.

As a result of the development of Taching, the Chinese were able to phase out imports of refined products from the Soviet Union, which were as high as 2.9 million tons in 1961. By the middle 1960's, when the Chinese announced that they had achieved self-sufficiency in crude-oil production, total domestic output may have been 8 million tons. As the Taching field and the western producing areas were further expanded, China's petroleum output may have approached 20 million tons by 1970.

China's petroleum-refining capacity is concentrated in three old coastal refining centers, Shanghai, Dairen and Chinsi, and in the newer inland center of Lanchow, opened in 1958. Before the start of operations at Lanchow, crude oil from the western fields moved to both Shanghai and Dairen, which also refined imported crude. The construction of the Lanchow refinery and the development of the Taching field in Manchuria reoriented flow patterns.

Lanchow henceforth became responsible for refining the crude oil supplied by the Yümen and Karamai fields, while the coastal refineries shifted increasingly in the early 1960's to Manchurian crude. A new small refinery at Nanking and the Shanghai complex may also be handling crude oil shipped from Szechwan on the Yangtze River. In addition to the big refineries in consuming areas, there are smaller installations in the producing fields.

Shale-oil production was long limited to the coal-mining center of Fushun, where oil shale is recovered from the rock overlying the coal in strip mines. Two shale refineries at Fushun produce a total of more than 1 million tons of oil. A second shale-oil project was undertaken in the late 1950's at Mowming in western Kwangtung and began operation in 1961. Total shale-oil production in China may be about 2 million tons.

A liquid-fuel industry based on hydrogenation of coal was developed in Manchuria under the Japanese, who operated synthetic-oil plants at Fushun and Chinchow. Smaller plants based on the coal-hydrogenation principle were built during the Great Leap in many parts of China. Total national production of synthetic fuel may be on the order of several hundred thousand tons.

China's limited resources of natural gas appear to be concentrated entirely in the Szechwan basin, where gas has been used for centuries to evaporate salt brine in the salt-producing center of Tzekung (the former Tzeliutsing). A newer gas field, discovered in the middle 1950's south of Chungking, appears to have been producing since the early 1960's. Total gas production in Szechwan may be about 10 billion cubic meters a year and is used for carbon-black manufacture and fuel. No information is available on the use of gas associated with oil production.

The electric-power industry, as might be expected, is concentrated in the northeast industrial quadrant of the country. Industry is by far the most important power consumer, absorbing 90 per cent of the total electricity output, with negligible portions going to rural electrification and transportation. Thermal-power plants, mostly coal-fired, account for four-fifths of total generation of electrical energy, and hydroelectric plants for one-fifth. During the first five-year plan, thermal-power capacity rose from 1.8 million kilowatts in 1952 to 3.5 million in 1957, while hydroelectric capacity increased from 0.2 million to 1 million kilowatts (Table 11). Almost half of the generating capacity added during the five-year period—1.2 million kilowatts out of a total of 2.5 million—was installed in Manchuria, which in 1957 generated 47 per cent of China's total electricity output (Table 12). During the Great Leap, ambitious plans were announced for the construction of hydroelectric plants in many parts of China, but as Soviet aid in supplying power-generating equipment was withdrawn in 1960, only some of these projects were completed. The largest are: the Sinan plant of western Chekiang, with a designed capacity of 650,000 kilowatts, of which the first unit was installed in 1960; the Cheki station of northwest Hunan, with a de-

TABLE 11

ELECTRIC-POWER PRODUCTION

	Output (billion kilowatt-hours)			Year-end Capacity (million kilowatts)		
	Total	Thermal	Hydro	Total	Thermal	Hydro
1941	6.0			2.5		
(pre-1949 peak)						
1949	4.3	3.6	0.7	1.8	1.6	0.2
1952	7.3	6.0	1.3	2.0	1.8	0.2
1953	9.2			2.4		
1954	11.0			2.6		
1955	12.3			3.0		
1956	16.6	13.1	3.5	3.6	2.8	0.8
1957	19.3	14.6	4.7	4.5	3.5	1.0
1958	27.5	22.0	5.5	6.3	5.1	1.2
1959	41.5	33.7	7.8	9.5	7.9	1.6
1960 (plan)	55.5–58			13.7		

NOTE: No breakdown is available for 1953, 1954 or 1955, and the 1960 Plan.

TABLE 12

REGIONAL ELECTRIC-POWER PRODUCTION*

	1952		1957	
	Output	Capacity	Output	Capacity
Manchuria	2.6	0.7	8.2	1.9
North China	1.3	0.4	3.1	0.7
East China	2.3	0.6	4.0	0.9
Central-South	0.7	0.2	2.2	0.5
Southwest	0.3	0.09	1.0	0.2
Northwest	0.08	0.02	0.8	0.2
Total	7.3	2.0	19.3	4.5

* Output in billion kilowatt-hours; capacity at year-end in million kilowatts; some columns do not add up because of rounding.

signed capacity of 435,000 kilowatts, inaugurated in 1962, and the Sunfung (Sinfeng) station of Kwangtung, with a designed capacity of 210,000 kilowatts, which began operation in 1960. Among the more spectacular projects, some in the 1-million-kilowatt class, that were not completed in the 1960's are the great hydroelectric stations of the Yellow River, the Sanmen plant in western Honan, and the Liukia and Yenkuo projects upstream from Lanchow in Kansu. The Chinese do not appear to have developed nuclear power for civilian electricity generation on a significant scale.

The last official power production figure announced by the Chinese at the end of the Great Leap was the 1960 plan calling for 55.5 to 58 billion kilowatt-hours. However, as the economic recession began in the second half of 1960, the actual output is believed to have been short of the 50 billion mark. After having dropped in the early 1960's to perhaps as low as 30 billion kilowatt-hours, electric-power generation slowly recovered through the decade and, after a temporary setback during the early part of the Cultural Revolution, may have reached 50 billion kilowatt-hours or more by 1970. By that time, the Chinese were reported to be capable of manufacturing generating units of more than 100,000 kilowatts and installing 220-kilovolt transmission lines.

On a regional basis, three major power systems may be distinguished, coinciding with some of the most highly industrialized sections of the country. By far the largest is the Manchurian system, with a total installed capacity of 3 million kilowatts interconnected by 220-kilovolt lines. The principal components of the Manchurian system are the old 560,000-kilowatt Fengman hydroelectric station on the upper Sungari River above Kirin and large thermal plants at Harbin, Mukden, and the coal centers of Fushun and Fusin. The 700,000-kilowatt Supung hydroelectric station, which China shares with North Korea, also feeds some of its output into the Manchurian system. Adjoining the system on the southwest is the Peking-Tientsin power grid, with thermal stations in these two industrial centers and at Tangshan, the heart of the Kailan coal basin. The Peking-Tientsin system has a capacity of more than 1 million kilowatts. A transmission line connecting it with the Manchurian grid was reported under construction in the late 1960's. The third major power system, with a total capacity of about 2 million kilowatts, is the Shanghai-Hangchow grid. Its basic producers are the Sinan hydroelectric station and thermal-power plants in Shanghai, Wangting (near Wusih), and Nanking, linked by 220-kilovolt transmission lines.

Lesser power grids are associated with industrial clusters elsewhere through the nation. In North China, they include the Taiyüan-Yangchüan industrial district of central Shansi and the Chengchow-Loyang district of Honan; in East China, the power grid based on the Hwainan coal basin and serving Anhwei Province was interconnected in the 1960's with the Nanking-Shanghai system; in Central China are the Wuhan industrial cluster and the central Hunan power grid connecting the Changsha-Chuchow industrial district with the Cheki hydroelectric plant. In the south, thermal-power capacity at Canton is interconnected with the Sunfung (Sinfeng) hydroelectric station. In Southwest China are the industrial clusters of Chungking and Kunming, and, in the Northwest, the Paotow and Lanchow power and industry combinations.

The Iron and Steel Industry. Before the Communist take-over, the only large integrated iron and steel plant was the Anshan complex of Manchuria, founded in World War I and expanded by the Japanese in the late 1930's. Smaller capacities, mainly for pig-iron smelting, existed at Peking (in the Shihkingshan plant), Taiyüan, and Chungking. Soviet dismantling of the Anshan installations after World War II had brought Anshan to a virtual standstill, and China's production of iron and steel was minimal in 1949. Output gradually rose through the 1950's, as a result of reconstruction and more intensive utilization of Anshan capacity and the expansion of iron and steel plants elsewhere in China. By the end of the first five-year plan, the

TABLE 13

IRON ORE, PIG-IRON, AND INGOT-STEEL PRODUCTION

(*in million metric tons*)

	Iron Ore	Pig Iron			Ingot Steel		
		Total	Modern	Crafts	Total	Modern	Crafts
1943		1.8			0.9		
(pre-1949 peak)							
1949		0.25			0.16		
1952	4.3	1.93	1.9	0.03	1.35		
1953	5.8	2.23	2.17	0.06	1.77		
1954	7.2	3.11	2.96	0.15	2.23		
1955	9.6	3.87	3.63	0.24	2.85		
1956	15.5	4.83	4.78	0.05	4.47		
1957	19.4	5.94	5.86	0.08	5.35		
1958	40	13.7	9.5	4.2	11.1	8.0	3.1
1959	60	20.5	*ca.* 10	*ca.* 10	13.4	*ca.* 10	*ca.* 3.4
1960 (plan)		27.5	*ca.* 14	*ca.* 14	18.4	*ca.* 13	*ca.* 5.4

country produced 5.9 million tons of pig iron and 5.4 million tons of ingot steel.

During the Great Leap, a crash program of iron and steel expansion involved four kinds of development: (1) the inauguration of two additional large integrated iron and steel plants at Wuhan in central China and at Paotow in Inner Mongolia; (2) the integration of other plants that formerly produced mainly pig iron (for example, Peking) or only steel (Shanghai); (3) the construction of several new medium-size and small integrated plants (Hantan in Hopei, Sanming in Fukien, Kiangyu in Szechwan), although many other projects in this category were abandoned after the collapse of the Great Leap; (4) the ephemeral backyard-furnace drive, which was abandoned because of its high cost and the poor quality of its products. The all-out effort during the Great Leap raised pig-iron output to more than 20 million tons in 1960, about evenly divided between conventional plants and primitive handicraft furnaces, and ingot-steel production to more than 13 million tons, including three-fourths in conventional open-hearth furnaces and converters. During the undocumented period of the 1960's, steel output is believed to have dropped initially to about 8 million tons during the recession after the Great Leap, rising to perhaps 12 million tons by the middle of the decade. After a brief setback to about 10 million tons during the early phase of the Cultural Revolution, steel production probably resumed its climb and may have reached 18 million tons by 1970 as many small iron and steel projects planned or begun during the Great Leap were completed. The corresponding pig-iron figure for 1970 is assumed to be close to 25 million tons as a result of a renewed local ironworks drive.

The following iron and steel districts can be distinguished. The Manchurian district, accounting for nearly half of the national output, consists of the large integrated Anshan complex, the smaller Penki plant, specializing in low-phosphorus pig iron and high-grade alloy steels, and a few steel plants supporting metal-fabricating industries in the larger manufacturing centers. The Shanghai-Maanshan district combines the iron-mining and pig-iron capacity of Maanshan (Anhwei Province) with the steel-ingot and finishing mills of Shanghai. An attempt was made during the Great Leap to integrate the Maanshan plant by adding some steel capacity, and the Shanghai complex by adding blast furnaces, but the complementary character of the two centers has been preserved. The Wuhan iron and steel plant, which derives its ore from the nearby Tayeh mines, is the larger of the two new integrated complexes inaugurated during the Great Leap. It has three blast furnaces, two opened in 1958–59 and the third in 1969, for a combined capacity of 2.5 million tons of pig iron a year. Steel capacity is believed to be less, so that surplus pig iron may be moving down the Yangtze River to the Shanghai steel complex.

The Lungyen-Peking-Taiyüan iron and steel district consists of the Lungyen mine near Süanhwa and the two integrated plants of Peking and Taiyüan. The Shihkingshan plant at Peking has a pig-iron capacity of about 1 million tons and added steel-making capacity during the Great Leap. Taiyüan was China's second largest iron and steel plant during the middle 1950's, before the expansion program during the Great Leap altered the regional pattern. It may also be near the 1-million-ton class.

Paotow, the second new iron and steel center, has apparently lagged behind the original plans. The first blast furnace, with a capacity of close to 1 million tons of pig iron, was inaugurated in 1959, followed by the first steel converter the next year. However, the project then stagnated through the 1960's, and the second blast furnace and converter opened in 1970. The ore for the Paotow complex is provided by the Paiyünopo (Bayan Obo) mine to the north. In Southwest China is another integrated iron and steel plant at Chungking, also in the 1-million-ton category. Partly dependent on longhaul pig iron in the middle 1950's, some from as far away as Anshan, the Chungking complex was fully integrated during the Great Leap through construction of additional blast-furnace capacity. Yet another integrated iron and steel complex has long been planned in the Kiuchüan district of Kansu Province, based on iron-ore deposits at Kingtiehshan nearby. There were no reports of development during the Great Leap and through the early 1960's. However, the formal establishment of the urban district of Kiayükwan on the proposed site in 1965 suggested renewed interest in the project, and a major iron-smelting plant was, in fact, reported to have been inaugurated in Kansu in 1970.

Finally, there is an important iron-ore mining operation on Hainan Island. It was developed during World War II by the Japanese as a raw-material source for Japanese iron and steel plants. Since the completion of a railroad to the mainland port of Tsamkong in 1955, much of Hainan's ore has been moving through the Tsamkong terminal to various mainland iron and steel plants.

Among ferroalloys, China is short of nickel, chromium, and cobalt, which must be imported or for which substitutes need to be used in the manufacture of alloy steels. The country has an adequate supply of manganese and molybdenum, and is a leading producer of tungsten. Manganese is supplied mainly by mines near Siangtan in Hunan Province, west of Wuchow in Kwangsi, and at Wafangtze in Manchuria's Liaoning Province. Molybdenum was long supplied by the Yangkiachangtze mine near Chinsi in Liaoning, but additional supplies may have become available as coproducts of copper and tungsten developments. The principal tungsten-producing area is around Tayü in southern Kiangsi, with additional output from adjacent parts of southern Hunan and northern Kwangtung.

The production of base metals appears to be adequate, although some shortages have been reported from time to time. Several small deposits have long been worked in southern Manchuria, with a lead smelter and a copper refinery at Mukden. Outside Manchuria, lead-zinc mining seems to be concentrated in central Hunan and northern Kwangtung. The old lead-zinc mine of Shuikowshan supplies refining facilities in the Chuchow-Changsha industrial district. Additional smelting capacity has been reported at Shiukwan in Kwangtung. A lead smelter is also in operation at the tin-mining center of Kokiu. Several copper developments have been reported during the 1960's, although the precise status of each is unclear. They are Tungling in Anhwei Province, Paiyin near Lanchow in Kansu Province, and Tungchwan in Yünnan Province. In all three cases, mining developments have been significant enough to give rise to urban districts in the administrative hierarchy. Other copper developments, not reflected in the administrative pattern, have been reported from Showwangfen, southwest of Chengteh in Hopei Province, and from the Hwangshih area in Hupei.

Export metals, aside from tungsten, include tin, antimony, and mercury. The leading tin center of Kokiu in Yünnan Province, with additional output by the Hohsien district of eastern Kwangsi and in association with the tungsten of southern Kiangsi. The greater part of antimony production comes from the old mining center of Sikwangshan in central Hunan. The principal mercury-mining district is on the Kweichow-Hunan border, in the Fenghwang-Tungjen area.

In light metals, aluminum production is concentrated mainly in an old Japanese-built reduction facility, reopened in early 1955 at Fushun in southern Manchuria, apparently using aluminous shale from nearby deposits. It produced about 20,000 tons of aluminum in 1957. An aluminum reduction plant was inaugurated in November, 1959, at Lanchow in Kansu Province, but its future development is unclear in view of failure to complete the planned low-cost sources of hydroelectric power on the Yellow River. Aluminum facilities have been reported at Paotow, Wuhan, Hofei (in Anhwei), and Lanchi (in Chekiang), but there is little information on the distribution of aluminum-bearing raw materials or alumina plants. According to a 1970 report, two alumina plants are in operation in China. One, originally designed for 35,000 tons, was completed within two years (evidently during the Great Leap) and was subsequently expanded to a capacity of 300,000 tons of alumina by the late 1960's. This plant may be associated with the Fushun reduction facility and the alumina capacity suggests an aluminum output of 150,000 tons by 1970. The second alumina plant, at an unspecified location, was originally planned for a capacity of 1 million tons but was completed by the late 1960's with only 200,000 tons. The combined alumina output of 500,000 tons would correspond to 250,000 tons of aluminum. Large magnesite deposits in the Tashihkiao-Yingkow district of southern Manchuria are used mainly for the production of refractories. Some magnesium metal is believed to be produced by an old Japanese-built reduction plant at Yingkow. Uranium is believed to be mined in Sinkiang and southern China for use in nuclear-weapons production and limited civilian applications.

Among nonmetallic industrial minerals, the most important is salt, which is obtained from coastal salines, from brine wells, and from desert salt lakes. The principal coastal fields are in Kiangsu, Shantung, Hopei, and Liaoning on the Yellow Sea and its embayments. Brine wells are significant in Szechwan (at Tzekung), and desert lakes are worked for salt and associated minerals (borax, bromine, iodine) in Tsinghai and Inner Mongolia. Most of China's output is used for food purposes, with only a relatively small part serving as a raw material for alkali-chlorine plants. Since most of China's salt production is dependent on natural evaporation in coastal salt fields, production has tended to fluctuate (Table 14). However, it is believed to have been expanded significantly since the imposition of statistical secrecy in 1960, with some estimates placing output as high as 15 million tons by 1970.

Asbestos production is believed to have been increasing in China, with most of the output coming from the Shihmien deposit in Szechwan. Fluorspar, mined mainly at Wuyi in Chekiang, has been exported, mostly to Japan. Cement production has been steadily growing in conjunction with in-

TABLE 14
SALT PRODUCTION
(*in million metric tons*)

1949	2.99
1950	2.46
1951	4.35
1952	4.95
1953	3.57
1954	4.89
1955	7.54
1956	4.94
1957	8.28
1958	10.4
1959	11
1960	14
(plan)	

TABLE 15
CEMENT PRODUCTION
(*in million metric tons*)

1949	0.66
1950	1.41
1951	2.49
1952	2.86
1953	3.88
1954	4.60
1955	4.50
1956	6.39
1957	6.86
1958	9.30
1959	12.27
1960	16
(plan)	

dustrial construction, particularly during the 1950's, when it apparently topped 10 million tons during the Great Leap (Table 15). It dropped during the retrenchment of the early 1960's, but is believed to have approached the 15-million-ton level by 1970. Cement plants have been expanded or newly built outside the northeast industrial quadrant, with major facilities at Tatung (Shansi Province), Yaohsien (Shensi), Yungteng (Kansu), Kiangyu (Szechwan), Kweiyang (Kweichow), Liuchow (Kwangsi), Canton, Siangsiang (Hunan), Nanping (Fukien), and Kiangshan (Chekiang).

Machinery industries have been given high priority in Chinese industrial development, particularly since 1960, when the heavy flow of Soviet equipment ceased. The leading manufacturing centers are Mukden in Manchuria, which, because of its proximity to the Anshan steel complex, has traditionally specialized in heavy machinery, and Shanghai, whose skilled labor force has focused on precision goods. The production of heavy machinery has also expanded in Harbin in northern Manchuria, and in the new iron and steel center of Wuhan in central China. Shanghai, Harbin, and Mukden are also the principal centers for the manufacture of power-generating equipment and other electrical-engineering goods.

The automotive industry had its beginnings at the large motor-vehicle plant inaugurated in 1956 at Changchun in Manchuria but was supplemented during the 1960's by smaller manufacturing facilities at Peking, Shanghai, Tientsin, and Nanking. Similarly, the tractor industry began with a major plant at Loyang in 1958, but was subsequently enlarged with smaller installations at Tientsin, Shanghai, and Mukden. Dairen, Tientsin, and Shanghai are the principal shipbuilding and repair ports, while aircraft are assembled at Mukden and Nanchang. Railroad equipment plants are concentrated mainly in Manchuria, at Dairen, Changchun, and Tsitsihar, with additional facilities at Tsingtao, Wuhan, Chuchow and elsewhere.

The Chemical Industry. China's chemical industry developed slowly during the documented 1950's but was reported to have received greater priority in the 1960's, particularly in chemical fertilizers and petrochemicals.

TABLE 16
CHEMICAL PRODUCTION
(in thousand metric tons)

| | Chemical Fertilizer | | | Sulfuric | Soda | Caustic |
	Total	Nitrogen	Phosphate	Acid	Ash	Soda
1941	227	227	—			
(pre-1949 peak)						
1949	27	27	—	40	88	15
1950	70	70	—	49	160	23
1951	134	134	—	149	185	48
1952	194	188	6	190	192	79
1953	249	249	—	260	223	88
1954	321	321	—	344	309	115
1955	345	324	21	375	405	137
1956	663	563	100	517	476	156
1957	803	683	120	632	506	198
1958	1,244	900	344	740	640	270
1959	1,765	1,390	375	1,060		
1960 (plan)	2,800			1,500		

NOTE: Blank spaces above indicate no data; — indicates no significant production.

The old chemical centers were associated with the coke-byproducts plants of the Manchurian iron and steel industry and with alkali-chlorine plants based on salt electrolysis. Early coke-products plants at Anshan and Penki in Manchuria yielded ammonium sulfate, which was long the main chemical fertilizer produced by Chinese industry. A Japanese-built chemical center at Kirin, also in Manchuria, yielded acetylene and its derivatives by the calcium carbide route. Sea salt was the raw material used for an alkali industry at Dairen and Chinsi in southern Manchuria and at Tientsin and Shanghai. Salt brines served as the basis for a chemical industry at Tzekung in Szechwan. During the first five-year plan, chemical production was also expanded at Nanking and Taiyüan. Production statistics for that period appear in Table 16.

By 1957, total chemical-fertilizer production in China was about 800,000 tons, including about 680,000 tons of nitrogenous fertilizer (mostly ammonium sulfate) and 120,000 tons of phosphatic fertilizer. During the Great Leap, and particularly in the 1960's, emphasis was given to the further development of the chemical-fertilizer industry, mainly through the construction of a network of small and middle-size plants. These plants produced simple fertilizers, such as ammonium bicarbonate and ammonium chloride, with a low nitrogen content, and simple ground phosphate from newly developed deposits. By 1965, these small facilities accounted for 12 per cent of China's total fertilizer output, estimated at 5 million tons. After the brief disruption of the Cultural Revolution, the small-plants campaign accelerated during the late 1960's, and by 1970 these local establishments accounted for as much as 40 per cent of total production. An official statement that the new fertilizer capacity installed in 1970 exceeded by 30 per cent the total capacity added from 1958 to 1969 suggests the intensity of the campaign at the turn of the decade. In view of this all-out local effort and the continued construction of modern nitrogenous and phosphatic fertilizer plants, total fertilizer output in 1970 may be estimated at 14 million tons. The emphasis on fertilizer production may be expected to continue into the 1970's as one approach to a guaranteed food supply.

A more modern phase of the chemical industry was associated with petrochemicals, based on oil refineries at Dairen, Shanghai, and, after 1958, at Lanchow. The refinery at Lanchow is presumed to provide the feedstocks for a synthetic-rubber plant that was inaugurated there in 1959. The range of petrochemicals produced at these refining centers was further diversified during the 1960's, yielding resins, plastics, and other derivatives. Rubbertire production during the first five-year plan, then still based on imported natural rubber, rose from 417,000 in 1952 to 880,000 in 1957, with a major manufacturing center at Mutankiang in Manchuria.

Forest Products. China's forest resources, yielding building timber, firewood, pulp, and paper, are concentrated in Manchuria, the principal producing area, as well as in Central-South China, and in the Southwest. The principal lumbering districts in Manchuria are the Great Khingan Mountains, with centers in the Ituliho area, and the Little Khingan Mountains around Ichun. Timber in Manchuria, mainly Dahurian larch, Japanese birch, and Korean pine, is shipped by railroad to sawmills and pulp and paper plants for processing. The principal centers are Kiamusze and Mutankiang in Heilungkiang Province, and in Kirin and Tumen in Kirin Province.

The principal species in central and south China, between the Tsin Ling and Nan Ling ranges, are the cunninghamia and the cypress. Specialty trees in the subtropical and tropical regions of China are the camphor tree, which yields an important essential oil; the sumac, whose nutgall is a source of tannin; Chinese ash, on which scales deposit Chinese insect wax; the lacquer tree, a sumac whose berries yield a fat known as Japan wax; the eucommia, which yields gutta-percha, a natural rubber; and an evergreen oak, whose bark yields cork. In contrast to Manchuria, where forest products move mainly by rail, in Central-South China, logging streams play a more important role. Among the leading wood-products centers are Canton and Nanping (Fukien Province). In southwestern China, the principal timber region is the Ahpa Tibetan Autonomous Chou of Szechwan, which yields valuable spruce and fir species. The production trend in timber and paper during the 1950's appears in Table 17. Paper production is broken down into modern paper-mill production and handicraft establishments, which produce fine Chinese paper by traditional methods. After having topped 40 million cubic meters during the Great Leap, timber output is believed to have declined to less than 30 million cubic meters during the early 1960's as part of the general economic retrenchment. Rising again through the decade, except for a brief setback during the Cultural Revolution, it may again have reached 40 million cubic meters by 1970. Similarly, paper pro-

TABLE 17
TIMBER AND PAPER PRODUCTION

	Timber (in million cubic meters)	Paper (in thousand metric tons)		
		Total	Modern	Handicraft
1943			165	
(pre-1949 peak)				
1949	5.67	228	108	120
1950	6.64	380		
1951	7.64	492		
1952	11.20	539	372	167
1953	17.53	667	427	240
1954	22.21	842	556	286
1955	20.93	839	589	250
1956	30.84	998	746	252
1957	27.87	1,221		
1958	35.0	1,630		
1959	41.2	2,100	1,700	400
1960 (plan)	47	2,800		

duction, having reached 1.7 million tons in modern paper mills during the Great Leap (and more than 2 million if handicraft paper is included), is believed to have recovered these levels by 1970.

Consumer Goods. Consumer-goods production, as noted earlier (see Table 7), increased less rapidly than heavy industry during the first five-year plan (1953–57) and the Great Leap, so that its share in total industrial output declined from 60 per cent in 1952 to 47 per cent in 1957 (in comparable 1952 prices). The trend continued during the Great Leap after the statistical conversion to a 1957 price level. It is assumed that greater priority was given to consumer-goods production during the 1960's, but statistical documentation is lacking for that period.

A leading branch of consumer-goods industries is the manufacture of cotton yarn and cloth as well as silk and wool fabrics. China's cotton crop is grown mainly in the North China plain and in the Wei Ho valley of southern Shensi. The great cotton-milling centers have been traditionally along the eastern seaboard at Tientsin, Tsingtao, and Shanghai, which alone had almost 50 per cent of the nation's cotton spindles. As a result, three-fourths of the cotton crop or more had to be shipped to the coastal mills for conversion into textiles. In an effort to bring industry closer to sources of raw material, the Chinese fostered the construction of cotton mills in the cotton-growing area, notably at Shihkiachwang, Peking and Hantan in Hopei Province, Chengchow in Honan, and Sian and Sienyang in southern Shensi. China's spindle inventory in 1952 was about 5.5 million, and the addition of 2.6 million spindles during the first five-year plan, mostly in new mills in the cotton belt, raised the total to 8.1 million spindles in 1957. The loom inventory during that year was 132,000. The increase in cotton-milling capacity is reflected in the growth of production during the 1950's (Table 18).

TABLE 18
COTTON TEXTILE PRODUCTION

	Cotton Yarn (in million bales)*	Cotton Cloth (in million meters)
1949	1.8	1,890
1950	2.41	2,520
1951	2.68	3,060
1952	3.62	3,830
1953	4.1	4,690
1954	4.6	5,230
1955	3.97	4,360
1956	5.25	5,770
1957	4.65	5,050
1958	6.1	5,700
1959	8.25	7,500
1960 (plan)	9.0	7,600

* One bale = 400 pounds.

Year-to-year fluctuations correspond to variation in the cotton crop, with one year's lag; for example, a drop in the cotton harvest 1954 and 1956 was reflected in a decline of cotton textile output in 1955 and 1957. After having approached 8 billion meters during the Great Leap, cotton cloth production is believed to have declined sharply (by one-half or more) during the early 1960's. Recovery is assumed to have been slow, but may have reached or exceeded the Great Leap levels by 1970.

Despite the development of mills in the cotton belt, most of the textile output remains concentrated along the coast, particularly in the Shanghai-Nanking-Hangchow triangle. This area also accounts for most of the silk and woolen goods. In the silk industry, natural silk, produced either by mulberry-fed worms or by oak-fed worms (as in Shantung and Liaoning), has been supplemented in the 1960's by increasing amounts of man-made fibers, particularly viscose rayon and acetate yarn, for which a raw-material base is available in the form of cotton linters. Advances have also been made in producing noncellulosic fibers, such as polyamides (nylon), acrylics (orlon), and polyesters (dacron) on the basis of byproducts of petroleum-refining.

An important indicator among processed foods is sugar, which is derived mainly from sugar cane in Fukien, Kwangtung, Kwangsi, and Szechwan. Sugar-beet production has been fostered in northern Manchuria and, on irrigated land, in Inner Mongolia, and Sinkiang. Among the major sugar refineries in the cane belt are those of Canton in Kwangtung and Neikiang in Szechwan. Beet-sugar processing centers include Harbin, Kiamusze, and Tsitsihar in Manchuria; Paotow and Huhehot in Inner Mongolia, and Shihhotze in Sinkiang. Sugar is being refined both in modern mills and in handicraft establishments, especially in the cane-sugar regions. By the end of the first five-year plan in 1957, modern mills produced 575,000 tons and craft mills 289,000 tons out of a total production of 864,000 tons (Table 19).

TABLE 19
REFINED SUGAR PRODUCTION
(*in thousand metric tons*)

	Total	Modern	Handicraft
1949	199		
1950	242		
1951	300		
1952	451	249	202
1953	638	298	340
1954	693	347	346
1955	717	410	307
1956	807	518	289
1957	864	575	289
1958	900		
1959	1,100		
1960 (plan)	1,300		

After having topped 1 million tons during the Great Leap, total sugar output declined but is believed to have recovered rapidly during the 1960's and may have been as high as 2 million tons by 1970. Since the sugar-refining season after harvest generally spans two calendar years, the statistics for calendar years usually include about two-thirds of the previous year's crop and one-third of the current year's crop processed in the autumn.

Other consumer products, such as wheat flour, edible oils, fish, and meat, are produced mainly in areas of population concentration, including southern Manchuria, the North China plain, and the Shanghai district. In assessing the production of consumer goods in China, it must be borne in mind that processed foods are intended essentially for the urban segment of the population.

Before ending the discussion of industry, a few words need to be said about the geographical distribution of industrial establishments. Historically, industry has developed along the coast, with relatively few major establishments inland. Before 1949, more than 70 per cent of industry was located in coastal centers. At the start of the first five-year plan, seven coastal provinces and the three centrally administered cities accounted for 73 per cent of the total gross value of industrial output, with Shanghai and Tientsin alone representing 30 per cent of the total. In an effort to achieve a more uniform distribution of industry, bringing processing plants closer to resource bases in the interior and thus promoting the industrialization of underdeveloped inland provinces, the first five-year plan placed emphasis on industrial development of the interior. Of 694 major development projects, 472 were located in inland provinces. Notable examples were the two new iron and steel complexes of Paotow and Wuhan, the petrochemical industry of Lanchow, and manufacturing at Chengtu. The redistribution policy seems to have undergone some change, however, following the collapse of the Great Leap and the withdrawal of Soviet technical aid. Some major inland projects, such as the great hydroelectric complexes on the Yellow

River, do not appear to have been completed, hampering industrial development of the western regions. Although centrally located Wuhan seems to have been developed more or less according to plan, the iron and steel project at more remote Paotow has lagged. The loosening of Soviet-Chinese ties and Peking's reorientation of trade may also have been a factor in focusing attention increasingly on the developed coastal regions during the 1960's.

AGRICULTURE

Lest a detailed industrial description give the reader a misleading impression, it must be emphasized at this point that China is still essentially an agricultural country. About 85 per cent of the population is rural, and of these 600 million people more than 500 million are engaged in the growing of food crops. Agricultural produce, moreover, provides the raw material for at least half of China's industrial production. And it is the export of farm products that has supplied much of the foreign exchange needed for the import of industrial equipment.

To be sure, industry was the more dynamic factor of the Chinese economy during the 1950's. It was noted earlier that during the first five-year plan the output of industry proper (not counting handicrafts) rose 240 per cent from 1952 to 1957, compared with a 25 per cent rise in the value of agricultural production. This trend continued to grow during the Great Leap, and the lag of the agricultural sector is generally regarded as a factor in the collapse of that crash program. Although a reallocation of priorities in favor of agriculture is known to have occurred during the 1960's, the full extent of that reorientation has remained veiled in statistical secrecy.

Agriculture in China has been characterized by intensive cultivation with high yields per unit area and low output per man. Out of the nation's total area of 950 million hectares, about 110 million hectares (270 million acres) are under cultivation, or 0.14 hectare per person, compared with five times as much cultivated land per person in the United States. Another way of expressing this unfavorable balance between land and population is to say that, with only 7.8 per cent of the world's cultivated area, China must support almost 25 per cent of the world's population. This imbalance is generally viewed as a major deterrent to the country's economic progress.

The Chinese Communists have attempted to improve the agricultural situation by changing the institutional framework. These changes can be discussed in terms of three periods: an initial land reform after the Communist take-over (1949–52), a period of progressive collectivization (1953–57), and the period since the establishment of communes during the Great Leap Forward in 1958.

For purposes of the initial agrarian reform, the Communists classified peasants into four major categories: landlords, who owned more than 50 mou (3.3 hectares) per household and did not work their own land; rich peasants, who owned 30 to 50 mou (2 to 3.3 hectares) and depended only in part on their own labor; middle peasants, 10 to 30 mou (0.7 to 2 hectares), owner-operators; and poor peasants, less than 10 mou, largely tenant farmers. The land reform had been carried out piecemeal as the Communists gained control of China. By June, 1950, when the reform law was officially promulgated, one-third of the country with a population of 145 million people had already been affected. It was basically completed in 1951 and 1952. The net effect was to confiscate excess land from large holdings and to redistribute it to peasants with little or no land. A total of 47 million hectares was appropriated and distributed among 350 million peasants. Landlords and rich peasants were virtually eliminated as a class; middle peasants represented about two-thirds of the total households and poor peasants about one-fourth as a result of the redistribution.

The land reform had scarcely been completed when the Communists proceeded to implement a program of collectivization to ensure political control over the countryside. In the initial stage, mutual-aid teams, a simple form of agricultural cooperation, began to function in the early 1950's, even while the redistribution of land was still going on. There were nearly 10 million such cooperative groups at their peak in 1954. Mutual-aid teams joined together in work projects, while land, animals, and tools remained the property of peasant households. In an overlapping development, mutual-aid teams began to be consolidated into agricultural producer cooperatives, in which land, though privately owned, was pooled for cultivation, and members were compensated on the basis of labor and land contributed. By the end of 1956, about 680,000 such cooperatives had been formed, comprising 120 million families, or 96 per cent of all peasant families. In yet another overlapping phase, the original cooperatives were converted into actual collective farms, in which virtually all land was turned over to common ownership (except for small private plots) and remuneration was based on labor alone. By the end of 1957, China's agriculture was thus organized into more than 700,000 collective farms, comprising more than 90 per cent of the rural households.

The commune movement, beginning in mid-1958, was an effort to organize rural labor to an even greater degree in mass projects designed to advance the economy during the Great Leap Forward. In the second half of 1958, 700,000 collective farms were merged into about 25,000 communes, which became the basic units of rural administration replacing the old unit of rural government known as the "hsiang." The commune, as initially conceived, regimented peasants in all aspects of life through virtual elimination of private ownership, the use of communal kitchens, nurseries, old people's homes, and other communal institutions. The excessive centralization of control soon proved to be ineffective, and, in 1959, a subdivision of the commune, the production brigade, became the basic accounting unit directing the activities of rural production. After the failure of the Great Leap, the commune system was further revised, and the production team, a subdivision of the brigade, was designated as the basic unit of rural production in 1962. While this reorganization of functions was implemented in the early 1960's, the original 25,000 communes were increased to 74,000, containing 700,000 brigades and 5 million production teams, each team being made up of an average of 20 households.

In addition to these forms of collective farming, the Communist institutional structure also contains state farms, which are operated as government establishments hiring labor and paying wages. Originally established as experimental and seed-selection stations, the state farms have been used increasingly in remote, sparsely populated areas where new land has been put under cultivation after reclamation. There were about 2,000 state farms in the 1950's, and the number is reported to have increased in the 1960's.

An expansion of the area under cultivation is one of the measures advocated in a national agricultural development program of 1956–67, which was adopted in draft form in 1956 and approved in 1960. Although the time period originally envisaged has passed, the program still serves as a general guideline for the long-range development of agriculture. Reclamation of new land in areas of marginal agricultural production is documented only for the first five-year plan, when 3.9 million hectares were said to have been reclaimed, raising the total cultivated area from 107.9 million hectares in 1952 to 111.8 million in 1957 (Table 20). Much of the new land was put under cultivation in northern Manchuria, Inner Mongolia, and Sinkiang. During the 1960's, no further statistics were released, but it is assumed that

TABLE 20

CULTIVATED LAND AND CROPPED AREA

(*in million hectares*)

| | Cultivated Land | | | | | Cropped Area | |
| | | | Irrigated Land | | | | |
	Total	Dry Land	Total	Irrigated Dry Land	Paddy	Total	Food Grains Alone
1949	97.9	71.8	26.0	3.2	22.8		101.6
1950	100.4						104.8
1951	103.7						107.0
1952	107.9	77.2	30.8	4.9	25.9	141.3	112.3
1953	108.5	77.6	31.0	5.0	26.0	144.0	114.3
1954	109.4	77.8	31.6	5.3	26.3	147.9	116.3
1955	110.2	78.1	32.1	5.5	26.5	151.1	118.4
1956	111.8	74.2	37.6	10.2	27.4	159.2	124.3
1957	111.8					157.2	120.9
1958	108.7					158	121.3

NOTES: The cropped area refers to the area of crops sown or harvested. Because some land produces more than one crop a year, the cropped area tends to be larger than the cultivated land.

The total irrigated portion of cultivated land is made up of paddy, or land where rice is grown in water, and irrigated dry land, where irrigation water is applied to land that would normally be dependent on natural precipitation.

Some rows do not add up because of rounding.

the new emphasis on agriculture, involving further reclamation of outlying marginal land and a host of local labor-intensive projects in the main population areas, may have further increased the cultivated area by, say, 10 per cent to about 120 million hectares.

In addition, a major effort was concentrated on improving existing farmland through the development of irrigation and flood-control projects, higher fertilizer application, improved mechanization, better seed selection, expansion of multiple cropping, insect and disease control, and other techniques of intensive agriculture. The yields per unit area established as the goal of the 1956–67 program still serve as the objectives to be attained. For grains, the plan called for an ultimate target of 400 chin per mou (3 tons per hectare) in the area of lowest yields, north of the Yellow River; 500 chin per mou (3.75 tons per hectare) in an intermediate area between the Yellow River and the Hwai Ho; and 800 chin per mou (6 tons per hectare) in the highest-yield areas, south of the Hwai Ho and the Yangtze River. Individual production teams in the North that achieve not only the long-range productivity planned for their area, but even the higher goals set for southern China are set to have "crossed the Yangtze River."

Food Grains. The long-range yield goals reflect the primary division of China into two basic grain areas: The North is a dry, dust-blown land of wheat and lesser grains, such as millet and kaoliang, with generally lower yields; the South is green and humid and devoted almost entirely to high-yield rice as the predominant food crop. Chinese Communist food-grain statistics include not only rice, wheat, and lesser grains but also the grain equivalent of potatoes (sweet and white) converted at the rate of four tons of potatoes to one ton of grain (Table 21).

It is generally accepted that by the start of the first five-year plan in 1953, production had recovered from the levels that followed World War II and the Chinese civil war and roughly regained prewar output. Then followed a few years of rapid expansion, ending in 1956. The last year of the first five-year plan, 1957, already suggested signs of stagnation, particularly in wheat and potatoes, even though the total food-grain crop was said to have increased slightly over 1956, to 185 million tons. The first year of the Great Leap Forward, commencing in 1958, was evidently a good year, although the original claim of 375 million tons was acknowledged officially to have been in error and was revised to 250 million tons. Most Western specialists on the agriculture of China consider even the revised figure exaggerated, and their estimates have ranged around 200 to 210 million tons. The official Chinese figure for 1959 was even higher—270.05 million tons —whereas foreign observers reported, on the basis of weather conditions and other direct indications, that the 1959 crop was actually 20 to 30 million tons below the record 1958 level. Although an official goal of a 10 per cent increase was set for the 1960 food crop, a further decline to about 160 million tons is believed to have occurred. At any rate, the poor agricultural performance is assumed to have been a factor in the collapse of the Great

TABLE 21

FOOD-GRAIN PRODUCTION

(area in million hectares; output in million metric tons)

	All Food Grains		Rice		Wheat		Lesser Grains		Potatoes	
	Area	Output	Area	Output	Area	Output	Area	Output	Area	Output
1949	101.6	108.2	25.7	48.7	21.5	13.8	47.4	35.8	7.0	9.9
1950	104.8	124.7	26.1	55.1	22.8	14.5	48.2	42.7	7.7	12.4
1951	107.0	135.1	26.9	60.6	23.1	17.3	48.7	43.2	8.3	14.0
1952	112.3	154.4	28.4	68.4	24.8	18.1	50.4	51.5	8.7	16.4
1953	114.3	156.9	28.3	71.2	25.6	18.3	51.3	50.7	9.0	16.7
1954	116.3	160.5	28.7	70.9	26.9	23.5	50.9	49.2	9.8	17.0
1955	118.4	174.9	29.2	78.0	26.7	23.0	52.5	55.0	10.0	18.9
1956	124.3	182.6	33.3	82.5	27.3	24.8	52.7	53.4	11.0	21.9
1957	120.9	185.0	32.3	86.8	27.5	23.7	50.6	52.6	10.5	21.9
1958	121.3	250.0	32.7	113.7	26.6	29.0	45.7	62.0	16.3	45.4
		(215.2)								
1959		270.1								
		(192.7)								
1960		(161.3)								
1961		(189.2)								
1962		(203.8)								
1963		(218.9)								
1964		(237.8)								
1965		(258.0)								
(preliminary)										

NOTES: Food-grain output figures in parentheses, beginning in 1958, are purportedly official data given by Chinese officials in Peking privately to a visiting Pakistani agricultural delegation in 1965 (S. Swamy and S. J. Burki, "Foodgrains Output
in the People's Republic of China, 1958–1965," *The China Quarterly,* No. 41 [Jan-
uary-March 1970], 58–63).

This official series meshes with the official Chinese data of the first five-year plan
period (1952–57), then appears to correct the apparently inflated figures originally
announced for 1958 and 1959. It agrees roughly with unofficial Western estimates for
1960 (at about 160 million metric tons), but then shows far more rapid improvement
during the first half of the 1960's, so that, by 1965, the spread between this series and
unofficial Western estimates was 50 to 70 million tons.

Some area and output figures do not add up to the totals because of rounding.

Potato output data are given in grain equivalents, equal to one-fourth of the actual
weight of the potato crop.

Leap, and no official results for 1960 were announced, as statistical secrecy
was imposed.

During the 1960's, foreign observers attempted to estimate agricultural
production on the basis of scattered official reports of percentage change,
weather conditions, policy pronouncements, and the flow and balance of
foreign trade. There appears to be a consensus that the increasing priority
given to agriculture during the decade has produced a more or less steady
growth of food-grain production. But the unofficial estimates range widely.
From a low point of about 160 million metric tons in 1960, the crop is believed to have reached a level of 180 to 200 million tons by 1965. These

estimates are substantially below purportedly official data given by Chinese officials in Peking to a visiting Pakistani delegation in 1965. According to these estimates, the food crop rebounded from the 160-million level of 1960 to a preliminary figure of more than 250 million tons in 1965. In view of Chinese official statements that bumper crops were harvested annually from 1963 through 1970, it may be assumed that the high levels achieved in the middle 1960's continued through the rest of the decade. As in the case of China's population, we thus have a significant range of possible food-crop figures for 1970, from a low of perhaps 200 to a high of possibly as much as 240 million metric tons.

One of the basic factors in increasing yields has been irrigation. The statistics on irrigated land are conflicting, even for the normally well-documented period of the first five-year plan (1953–57). What appears to be the most reliable source (the 1956 statistical abstract published in 1957, cited in the bibliographic note) begins with 26 million hectares irrigated in 1949 and rises through 30.8 million hectares in 1952 to 37.6 million hectares by 1956 (Table 20). This source breaks the irrigated area down into a paddy sector (land where rice is grown in water), which remained relatively steady at roughly 26 to 27 million hectares, and an ordinary irrigation sector (irrigated dry land), which showed significant increase. The official report on fulfillment of the first five-year plan, issued in 1959, said the total irrigated area rose from 21.1 million to 35.6 million hectares in 1957. At any rate, the total irrigated area at the end of the first five-year plan appears to have been around 35 million hectares. During 1958, the first year of the Great Leap, a virtual doubling of the irrigated area was claimed, raising the total to about 66 million hectares. Such an increase has been widely discounted by Western specialists, and official Chinese statements later conceded that only about half of that area could be adequately irrigated, with the rest requiring additional work. It is presumed that during the 1960's, when greater priority was given to agricultural development, much of the area claimed to be under irrigation during the Great Leap was further improved, accounting in part for the reported gains in agricultural output.

The principal beneficiary of improved irrigation is rice, which is China's most important food crop. It accounts for about 45 per cent of all food grains. Rice is cultivated almost entirely south of the Tsin Ling divide and the Hwai Ho, where it is favored by the warm, humid climate and the impervious clay-pan soils that retain irrigation water. The major rice-surplus regions are the Red Basin of Szechwan and the "rice bowls" of the middle and lower Yangtze valley. In Szechwan, roughly 40 per cent of the cropped area is in paddy land, yielding 60 per cent of the provincial food crop. In the Yangtze valley, rice, a summer crop, is generally alternated with winter wheat. In the double-cropping region of southernmost China, two complete crops of rice can be grown. The total cropped rice area in the late 1950's was about 33 million hectares (Table 21), with an average yield of 2.5 to 3 tons of rice per hectare. These yields are believed to have risen during the 1960's, accounting in large part for the reported increases in output.

In terms of harvesting season, three types of rice crop are distinguished: the early crop, the late crop, both obtained from double-crop land in the extreme south, and the main semi-late crop, which is grown in the single-cropped area of Szechwan and the Yangtze valley. Judging from the crop data for 1957 and 1958, the most significant increases in output are being achieved in the southern double-cropped area, where the early and late crops combined exceed the single semi-late crop of central China.

Wheat is the characteristic food grain of North China, where it is cultivated mainly in the winter-wheat and kaoliang region of Hopei, Honan, and Shantung, favored by calcareous alluvial soils and moderate precipitation. The total wheat area has remained fairly stable at about 26 million hectares with average yields fluctuating around 1 ton per hectare. The higher-yielding varieties of winter wheat account for 85 to 90 per cent of total production. The rest represents spring wheat, which is grown in Manchuria and north of the Great Wall, where colder winters and a shorter growing season do not favor winter wheat.

The lesser grains grown in China account for about 30 per cent of the total food crop. They include kaoliang, millet, corn, and barley. Since wheat and rice alone are inadequate to feed the Chinese population, these lesser grains are a significant element in the nation's food production. In mountain areas and in some parts of North China, they represent the basic diet. They are also used in part as raw materials for the food-processing industry and as forage for livestock. Kaoliang, a sorghum, is associated as a summer crop with winter wheat in the North China plain and with soybeans in Manchuria. The term "kaoliang," which means "tall millet," is used by the Chinese in North China and Manchuria. In Szechwan, where it is believed to have originated, it is known as "shu-shu," meaning millet from Shu, an ancient name of Szechwan. The annual kaoliang crop is about 12 million tons. Millet, which yields a similar amount, is more drought-resistant than kaoliang and is grown farther west. It is associated with winter wheat in the loesslands of Shansi, Shensi, and southeastern Kansu. Corn is found widely in a belt extending from Yünnan through Szechwan to North China and southern Manchuria. To the northwest of this zone, the climate is too dry and the growing season too short. To the southeast, corn is generally replaced by rice and sweet potatoes. The normal corn crop is of the order of 15 to 20 million tons. Barley, like wheat, is a winter crop and is cultivated mainly in the Yangtze valley. In hilly areas where rice is not grown, barley represents the main food crop. It occupies a special position in the Tibetan highlands, where it is the staple food in a roasted and ground form known as tsamba. The annual crop in China is about 8 million tons.

The tuber component of the food crop, consisting largely of sweet potatoes, is produced mainly in southern China. Sweet potatoes can be grown in hilly areas on sandy and stony soils unsuitable for more demanding crops. White potatoes, relatively new in China, are found mainly in the vicinity of urban, industrial areas of North China and Manchuria. The production of all tubers, including both sweet and white potatoes, was fairly steady during the first five-year plan, ranging from 17 to 22 million tons in grain-equivalent, one-fourth of the actual weight. In the crash program of 1958, the production of tubers was reported to have doubled as the cultivated area was rapidly expanded into marginal land. The high level is not believed to have been maintained during the 1960's.

Oil-Bearing Crops. By far the most important of these is soybeans, which used to be classed with the food grains in official Chinese statistics until 1955. Soybeans are a distinctive crop of Manchuria but are also grown in North China. They used to be a major export crop, but as domestic needs increased, the soybean exports declined, particularly after 1960. The area in soybeans has remained fairly steady, and there has been little fluctuation in output of this crop, which is a major source of edible oil and of feed cakes for livestock (Table 22). Other significant oilseeds in China are peanuts and rapeseed. Peanuts are grown mainly in Shantung, which normally yields a third of the crop, and in the neighboring provinces of Hopei, Honan, and Kiangsu. The total cropped area has been about 2.5 million hectares and the output about 3 million tons. Lesser oilseeds are rape, which is cultivated in Szechwan, Hunan, and Kiangsi, and sesame, grown in Honan and Hupei. Perilla, linseed, and hempseed are Manchurian crops. A major source of industrial oil, used for high-grade varnishes and enamels, is tung oil, produced by the tung tree. The nation's leading tung-oil producers are the provinces of Szechwan, Hunan, Kwangsi, and Hupei.

TABLE 22

OIL-BEARING CROPS

(area in million hectares; output in million metric tons)

	Soybeans		Peanuts		Rapeseed	
	Area	Output	Area	Output	Area	Output
1949	8.3	5.1	1.3	1.3	1.5	0.73
1952	11.7	9.5	1.8	2.3	1.9	0.93
1953	12.4	9.9	1.8	2.1	1.7	0.88
1954	12.7	9.1	2.1	2.8	1.7	0.88
1955	11.4	9.1	2.3	2.9	2.3	0.97
1956	12.0	10.2	2.6	3.3	2.2	0.92
1957	12.7	10.0	2.6	2.6	2.4	0.91
1958		10.4	2.4	2.8	2.35	1.1
1959		11.5				

Fiber Crops. The most important is cotton, with about half the nation's output coming from the North China plain and the loesslands, and the other half from the Yangtze valley. Most of the cotton crop consists of native Chinese cotton, with a short stable up to one inch in length. Higher-yielding, long-staple varieties are grown on irrigated land in the Wei Ho valley of southern Shensi and elsewhere. The cotton crop is closely reflected in the

TABLE 23
GINNED COTTON CROP

	Area (in million hectares)	Output (in million metric tons)
1949	2.77	0.44
1952	5.58	1.30
1953	5.18	1.18
1954	5.46	1.07
1955	5.77	1.52
1956	6.26	1.45
1957	6.33	1.64
1958		2.10
1959		2.41

volume of textile production, with a poor cotton year generally resulting one year later in a drop in cotton-cloth output. The fluctuations in the cotton crop during the documented period of the 1950's appear in Table 23. During the 1960's, the cotton crop is assumed to have reverted to its pre–Great Leap levels of about 1.5 million tons of cotton lint a year.

Among China's lesser vegetable fibers are jute and the related kenaf (ambari) as well as ramie, hemp, and flax. Jute, which requires the warm, humid climate of southern China, and kenaf, more adaptable to northern conditions, both yield a coarse fiber for sacking. Jute flourishes in Chekiang, Anhwei, and Kiangsi, while kenaf is also grown in Manchuria and North China. Total fiber production from jute and kenaf was 305,000 tons in 1952; it dropped to 137,000 tons in 1953–54, because of acreage cuts, and recovered to 308,000 in 1957. About 2.2 kilograms are needed for the manufacture of a sack, so that the crop would appear sufficient for 135 million burlap bags. China is the third largest producer of jute and kenaf, after Pakistan and India. Another bast fiber, more distinctive of China, is ramie, used in the making of finer industrial fabrics. The main producing areas are Kiangsi, Hupei, Hunan, and Szechwan, which yield about 70 per cent of the total crop of about 40,000 to 50,000 tons a year. Hemp and flax are grown for their oilseed and their fiber in the cooler climates of Manchuria and North China.

Natural silk production, a traditional activity in China, flourished in the early decades of the twentieth century, when Chinese silk was a major export commodity. It declined during World War II because of the destruction of mulberry trees, on whose leaves the domestic silkworm feeds. By 1949, the domestic silk cocoon crop was 30,900 tons, one-fifth of prewar levels. During the first five-year plan, production was about twice the 1949 output. About 80 per cent of the domestic cocoon crop is harvested in the Yangtze delta provinces of Kiangsu and Chekiang, as well as in Kwangtung and Szechwan. In addition to the domestic mulberry-fed silkworm, silk is also produced from wild silkworms that feed on oak leaves. Wild silk, which yields shantung and pongee fabrics, is collected in Shantung and Liaoning.

TABLE 24

SILK COCOON PRODUCTION

(*in thousand metric tons*)

	Total	Domestic Silk	Wild Silk
1949	42.8	30.9	11.9
1952	123.3	62.2	61.1
1953	71.6	59.3	12.3
1954	90.8	65.1	25.7
1955	130.8	67.0	63.8
1956	134.2	72.4	61.8
1957	111.5	67.5	44.0

Production trends in wild silk have tended to be erratic compared with the more stable levels in domestic raw silk (Table 24).

Sugar Crops. China obtains her sugar supply from both sugar cane, the more important source, and sugar beets. Sugar cane is grown mostly in Fukien, Kwangtung, and Kwangsi, as well as in Szechwan. During the first five-year plan, the cropped area rose from 182,000 hectares in 1952 to 270,000 in 1957, and the cane crop from 7.1 million tons to 10.4 million tons, a growth in both area and production of about one-third. Sugar beet area expanded more rapidly in northern Manchuria and in irrigated lands of Inner Mongolia, from 35,000 to 165,000 hectares, or fourfold, and this was reflected in an increase in the beet crop from 479,000 tons in 1952 to 1.5 million tons in 1957. In the late 1950's, China derived about 85 per cent of its sugar from cane and 15 per cent from beets. Area and production trends during the 1950's are shown in Table 25.

TABLE 25

SUGAR CANE AND BEET PRODUCTION

(*area in thousand hectares; output in million metric tons*)

	Sugar Cane		Sugar Beets	
	Area	Output	Area	Output
1949	108	2.64	16	0.19
1952	182	7.12	35	0.48
1953	192	7.21	49	0.51
1954	219	8.59	73	0.99
1955	204	8.11	115	1.60
1956	221	8.66	149	1.65
1957	270	10.4	165	1.5
1958		13.5		2.9

Tea and Tobacco. A distinctive Chinese commodity, tea, like natural silk, has been lagging far behind former output levels. In its heyday, in the 1880's, the Chinese tea crop was about 240,000 metric tons, and the country was the world's tea-supplier. It has since then been replaced by India and Ceylon. China produces three types of tea, depending on the method of manufacture: black tea, which is allowed to ferment before the firing or drying process; oolong tea, which is partly fermented; and unfermented

TABLE 26
TEA PRODUCTION
(in thousand metric tons)

1949	41.1
1952	82.4
1953	84.7
1954	92.1
1955	108.0
1956	120.4
1957	111.5
1958	141

green tea. The most important districts for green tea are Pingshui and Lungtsing in northern Chekiang, and Liuan and Tunki in Anhwei. Black tea is made in Kimen (Keemun) in southern Anhwei, and in Wenchow in southern Chekiang, while oolong tea stems mainly from Fukien. Other tea-producing provinces are Hupei and Hunan. National production during the 1950's appears in Table 26. Output increases were achieved largely by doubling the tea-cultivation area, which reached 382,000 hectares in 1957, but yields per unit area were far below the levels achieved in India and Ceylon.

Tobacco acreage was expanded during the 1950's, but production was unsteady (Table 27) as annual yields remained generally low. Tobacco is cultivated almost everywhere in China, from Manchuria in the northeast to Yünnan in the southwest, but the principal producing areas are Honan and Shantung.

TABLE 27
TOBACCO PRODUCTION

	Area *(in thousand hectares)*	Output *(in thousand metric tons)*
1949	61	43
1952	186	222
1953	191	213
1954	218	232
1955	252	298
1956	385	399
1957		256
1958		380

Animal Products. In a country as densely populated as China, little land can be spared for pasture except in the outlying arid range lands. More food can be obtained through direct consumption of crops than by feeding them to livestock. Because of this, per capita consumption of meat is one of the smallest in the world, although total production is relatively large. The most numerous domestic animals are hogs, which can live on farm refuse, and pork accounts for the bulk of meat production. The hog population ranged from 90 million in 1952 to 146 million in 1957 and was reported to have

TABLE 28
LIVESTOCK POPULATION
(*in millions*)

| | Hogs | Sheep and Goats | Draft Animals | | | |
			Cattle	Horses	Donkeys	Mules
1949	58	42	44	4.9	9.5	1.5
1952	90	62	57	6.1	11.8	1.6
1953	96	72	60	6.5	12.2	1.6
1954	102	81	64	6.9	12.7	1.7
1955	88	84	66	7.3	12.4	1.7
1956	84	92	67	7.3	11.7	1.7
1957	146	99	64	7.5	10.9	1.8
1958	160	109	65	7.5	10.6	1.6
1959	180	112	65	7.6		

increased further to 160 million in 1958 and 180 million in 1959 during the Great Leap, although these high figures may be inflated. It is believed that many animals were slaughtered during the period of collectivization. After the recession of the early 1960's, hogs are again assumed to have regained or exceeded the pre–Great Leap levels (Table 28). Hogs are raised throughout China proper and are particularly numerous in provinces with the largest rural populations, such as Szechwan. In addition to providing most of the meat consumed, they also supply hog bristles, a traditional Chinese export item.

There are virtually no hogs in the loesslands and the Northwest inhabited by Moslems, and these areas have a large sheep and goat population, which in the first five-year plan ranged from 62 million in 1952 to 99 million in 1957. Further advances were reported during the Great Leap, to 109 million in 1958 and 112 million in 1959. These gains were less spectacular than for hogs, and therefore appear more credible. Moreover, goals for sheep- and goat-holdings were not achieved. The sinking of new wells and the development of irrigation facilities in grazing lands of the Northwest are believed to have favored further increases in sheep and goat herds during the 1960's. Holdings have been stagnant for large draft animals (cattle, including water buffaloes, horses, donkeys, and mules), which compete more than other livestock for feed with the farm population. Moreover, peasants slaughtered animals rather than give them to collectives and communes.

Fish are an important dietary supplement near the seashore and near inland ponds and canals. Major marine fisheries extend along the coastal provinces of southern China, notably Chekiang, Fukien, Kwangtung, and Kwangsi, and more than one-half of the total catch comes from the sea. A distinctive aspect of Chinese fisheries is the extensive practice of fish culture, both in shallow coastal waters and in inland ponds and lakes, supplementing the natural yield. In the late 1950's, as much as one-third of the total catch was derived from fish culture. The main marine species caught by China's fishing fleet include mackerel, sardine, yellow croaker, cod, and

TABLE 29
CATCH OF FISH AND OTHER AQUATIC PRODUCTS
(in million metric tons)

pre-1949 peak	1.6
1949	0.45
1950	0.91
1951	1.33
1952	1.67
1953	1.90
1954	2.29
1955	2.52
1956	2.65
1957	3.12
1958	4.06
1959	5.02
1960 (plan)	5.8

skate. Inland, the main species are believed to be carp and related fish, as well as some shrimp. The catch during the 1950's appears to have steadily increased, although the reported Great Leap levels may have been inflated (Table 29) and the total volume was probably set back to about 3 million tons in the early 1960's, to be followed by renewed gains.

TRANSPORTATION

One of the problems faced by the Chinese Communists has been the construction of a transportation network to meet the demands of expanded economic development. Like the Soviet Union, China is essentially a railroad nation, with waterways and motor roads playing a secondary role. Before the Great Leap, with its emphasis on local water and road traffic, China's railroads accounted for two-thirds of the tonnage of freight loadings and three-fourths of the freight traffic (in ton-kilometers). It was therefore natural for the Chinese to undertake an ambitious railroad-construction program during the first five-year plan, particularly in the western inland regions. However, after the collapse of the Great Leap, further construction was virtually halted and did not resume until the late 1960's.

The Chinese Communists inherited a total length of 25,900 kilometers (16,200 miles)* of main-line railroads, of which about one-half covered Manchuria. A large part of the rail net had been put out of operation or even dismantled during World War II and the Civil War ending in 1949. But in a postwar rehabilitation effort, the Communists succeeded in having 22,000 kilometers, or 85 per cent, open to traffic by the end of 1949 (Table 30). During the 1950's, the restoration of the remainder of the rail net was associated with an ambitious program of construction of new main lines. These new trunk lines served a variety of purposes. Some, like the Lanchow-Sinkiang railroad, built over an eleven-year period, from 1953 to 1963, were designed to open up the western parts of the country to development.

* A kilometer equals five-eighths of a mile.

TABLE 30
LENGTH OF RAILROAD ROUTES OPEN TO TRAFFIC
(*in thousand kilometers*)

1949	22.0
1950	22.5
1951	23.4
1952	24.5
1953	25.1
1954	25.9
1955	27.2
1956	29.2
1957	29.9
1958	31.2
1959	32
1960	32.6
1963	34.2

Others, like the access routes to Amoy and Foochow on the Taiwan Strait, had military significance. Still others, running mainly north-south, represented attempts to improve interregional links by connecting east-west lines. Some of these new interregional lines, like the Paoki-Chengtu railroad, opened in July, 1956, and the Paotow-Lanchow line, completed in August, 1958, also played a significant role in spurring economic development along the way. Still other railroads provided China with additional international connections. Through the 1950's, more than 10,000 kilometers were added to the main-line network, including 8,000 kilometers of new line and 2,000 kilometers of rehabilitated old lines. (These figures do not include double-tracking or more than 5,000 kilometers of industrial spurs and another 5,000 kilometers of narrow-gauge forest railway built during the 1950's.)

One of the earliest construction projects completed by the Chinese Communists was the 420-kilometer Laipin-Pingsiang railroad in Kwangsi, connecting the Chinese railroad system at its previous railhead of Laipin with the town of Pingsiang on the frontier of North Vietnam. After the Indochina armistice of 1954, North Vietnamese, aided by Chinese railroad workers, restored the line between Hanoi and the Chinese border, and the following year, through traffic was inaugurated between Peking and Hanoi. This railroad was to play an important role in supplying arms and other matériel to North Vietnam. Another joint Chinese–North Vietnamese project was the reconstruction of the old French railroad, built between Kunming and Hanoi in 1910 to provide an outlet for Yünnan's tin. The railroad was fully restored in 1957.

Related to the Kwangsi rail system is the construction of the Litang-Tsamkong (Chankiang) railroad, opened to traffic in July, 1955. This 318-kilometer line linked the Kwangsi railroad with the Kwangtung port of Tsamkong, fostering subsequent development of the port by opening up an extensive hinterland. A spur was completed in 1959 from Limkong, on the Litang-Tsamkong main line, to the new oil-shale mining center of Mow-

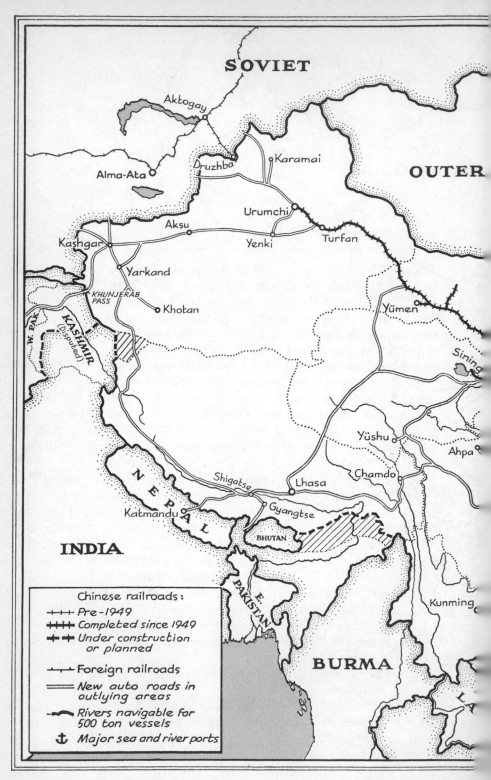

4.   Transportation Lines of China

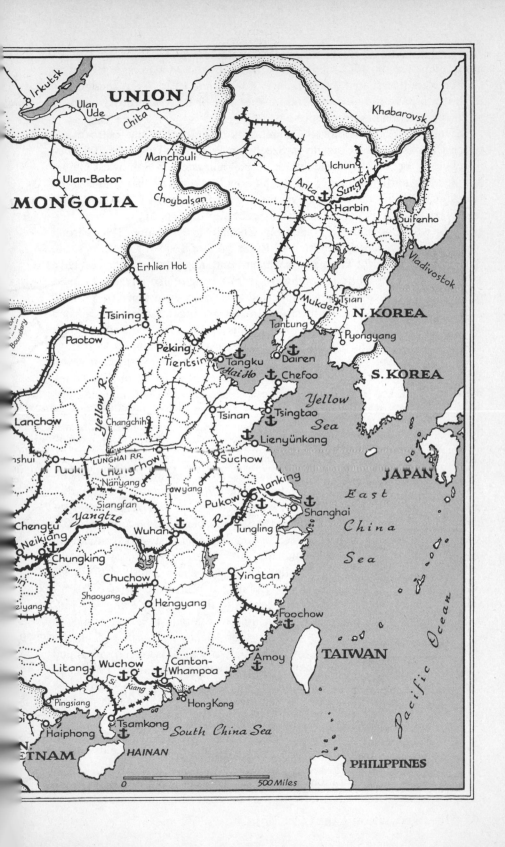

ming. Plans for the construction of a railroad from Mowming eastward to Canton were interrupted by the failure of the Great Leap. Construction was reported to have resumed in 1966, at the start of the Cultural Revolution, but no completion has been reported.

In July, 1952, the Chinese Communists completed a key railroad between Chungking and Chengtu in Szechwan Province. This line, 505 kilometers long, became the basic link of a new rail system in Southwest China. Planned and partly completed by the Nationalists, the railroad connects the two principal cities of Szechwan via the sugar cane center of Neikiang. Two lines were to be built southward from Szechwan to Yünnan, one from Neikiang to Kunming and the other from Chengtu to Kunming. The railroad from Neikiang reached the Yangtze River port of Ipin in October, 1958, thus completing a 72-kilometer segment, and no further advances have been reported. The railroad southward from Chengtu also advanced only a relatively short distance and was reported to have reached Omei in 1965.

However, a third line southward from the Chungking-Chengtu railroad did reach Kunming in the mid-1960's, thus establishing the first rail link between Szechwan and Yünnan. That line runs from Chungking, south to Kweiyang, the capital of Kweichow Province, and then west through Kweichow to Yünnan. Construction on the line southward from Chungking began in 1958, and a bridge across the Yangtze River near Chungking was inaugurated in November, 1959. After an apparent interruption of work in the early 1960's, after the collapse of the Great Leap, construction was resumed in 1964, and the Kweiyang-Chungking railroad was completed in 1966. Meanwhile work had also resumed on the next leg, between Kweiyang and Chanyi, the railhead of an old line from Kunming. This segment, too, was apparently completed in the middle 1960's. Kweiyang had earlier been reached by a railroad from Kwangsi, when the last remaining 145-kilometer gap between Tuyün and Kweiyang was closed in December, 1958. Still another rail link in Kweichow, this one running eastward from Tuyün toward Hunan, has not been completed.

While rail projects gradually filled in empty spaces south of the basic Chungking-Chengtu line, it was also connected northward by a 680-kilometer railroad running north from Chengtu to the east-west Lung-Hai railroad at Paoki. The Lung-Hai railroad, one of the oldest east-west lines in China, was originally opened in 1916 between Süchow, in northern Kiangsu, and Tungkwan, on the Honan-Shensi border. It was subsequently extended westward, reaching Sian in 1935, Paoki in 1937, Tienshui in 1945, and Lanchow in 1952. The construction of the Chengtu-Paoki line across the Tsin Ling divide posed major engineering problems, requiring 41 tunnels in one stretch of 26 miles. When it was finally completed in July, 1956, it provided the first rail link between Szechwan's rich regional economy and the rest of China and reduced Szechwan's dependence on the rapids-strewn Yangtze River as an outlet.

Some of the more ambitious railroad projects have been undertaken by the Communists in China's Northwest. After Lanchow was reached in 1952 by the extension of the Lung-Hai railroad from Tienshui, work continued almost immediately on the great Lanchow-Sinkiang line, which was envisaged as a link with the Soviet Union through the center of Asia. Under the plan, the Chinese were to build the portion from Lanchow through the Kansu corridor and through Sinkiang to the Soviet border, a distance of 2,350 kilometers, and the Russians were to construct the 312-kilometer Soviet portion from the border to Aktogay, on the Turksib railroad. Railroad construction crews started from Lanchow in late 1952 and advanced rapidly through the Kansu corridor during the period of the five-year plan and the Great Leap, to reach Hami in 1960. The rate of advance slowed during the post–Great Leap recession, and Urumchi, the capital of Sinkiang, was reached only in 1963. This completed a 1,900-kilometer segment from Lanchow. By that time, Soviet-Chinese relations had deteriorated to the point that the rest of the Chinese portion of the project, a 450-kilometer line beween Urumchi and the Sinkiang border, was abandoned. The Russians, in the meanwhile, had completed in 1960 their section from Aktogay to the new border station, ironically called Druzhba ("friendship"). Even incomplete, the Lanchow-Sinkiang railroad represented a significant achievement by fostering the development of the western oil fields of Yümen and Karamai and providing a modern transport outlet for the cotton and animal products of Kansu and Sinkiang.

At the eastern end of the Sinkiang railroad, further construction integrated this line firmly into the Chinese rail system and transformed Lanchow, rail-less until 1952, into a major transport hub. The key project was the 990-kilometer railroad between Paotow and Lanchow, paralleling the upper course of the Yellow River. The railroad, inaugurated in August, 1958, not only provided a direct link between the new Sinkiang railroad and the old Peking-Paotow line, thus establishing a connection between the Northwest and North China, bypassing the Lung-Hai railroad. It also linked two new industrial centers of the country—Paotow, with its iron and steel plant, and Lanchow with its petrochemical industry—and helped to open up resources on the upper Yellow River, notably the coking coal of the Shihtsuishan district. Another project in the Lanchow area, completed in 1959, was a shorter railroad running westward to the Sining area, the most highly developed portion of Tsinghai Province. This line was envisaged as extending ultimately to the resource-rich Tsaidam Basin. But because of abandonment of the development of Tsaidam during the recession after the Great Leap, the railroad was not extended beyond lake Koko Nor, where it serves Haiyen, a reputed nuclear-weapons development center.

While work was proceeding on the Sinkiang line through the Kansu corridor, the Soviet Union, Outer Mongolia, and China combined their efforts to complete a shorter link between China and the Soviet Union. This route connects Tsining (on the Peking-Paotow railroad) with Ulan-Bator, Outer Mongolia's capital, and the Trans-Siberian railroad at Ulan-Ude. The Ulan-

Ude–Ulan-Bator segment had been completed in 1947, and the new Tsining–Ulan-Bator railroad was inaugurated at the end of 1955. The new Trans-Mongolian link between China and the Soviet Union sliced about 650 miles from the previous route between Peking and Moscow through Manchuria and soon became the principal overland connection between the two countries. In 1959, the last full year of heavy Soviet economic aid to China, the Trans-Mongolian railroad handled three times more freight than the Manchurian link.

The construction of the Trans-Mongolian route, and later the building of the Paotow-Lanchow railroad, placed an unprecedented traffic burden on the old Peking-Paotow line, built between 1909 and 1923. As part of a general improvement and modernization of the old line to Paotow, the alignment near Peking was straightened by construction in 1955 of a 100-kilometer bypass between Fengtai, on the southwest outskirts of Peking, and Hwailai (Shacheng). This cutoff eliminated excessive grades and the light rail construction of the original Nankow Pass section of the Peking-Paotow line.

In the well-developed Manchurian rail network, new construction during the 1950's and 1960's was limited largely to timber railroads in the Great Khingan and Little Khingan mountains, China's principal lumbering regions. These special-purpose forest railroads were driven northward from Yakoshih, on the Chinese Eastern Railroad, in the Great Khingan, and northward from Ichun in the Little Khingan. Another major rail project, completed in the early 1960's, was a direct outlet from the newly developed Taching oil field at Anta, bypassing the heavily traveled Harbin-Mukden railroad. An old Japanese-built rail link between Chengteh and Peking, dismantled in the late 1940's, was restored over an altered alignment between Chengteh and Hwaiju and was opened to traffic in 1960.

Elsewhere in China proper, rail construction was limited largely to short lines giving access to coal mines and other newly developed resource sites. Two projects were of significance for broader regional development. One was the Fukien railroad, constructed in two stages, which linked Foochow and Amoy, two important ports, to the Chinese rail system at Yingtan. The Yingtan-Nanping-Amoy line was inaugurated in April, 1957, followed in December, 1958, by the Nanping-Foochow segment. The Fukien rail project improved the position of the two ports, then subject to harassment from Nationalist offshore islands in the Taiwan Strait, by providing direct connections with their hinterland. Another major rail-construction project in China proper was the 420-kilometer line completed late in 1965 between Wuhan and Tankiangkow, on the upper Han Shui. This railroad was originally envisaged as an access route to a hydroelectric project site at Tankiangkow, which has been stagnant since the Great Leap. But the line also represents the first segment of a major cross-country rail project that would connect Wuhan with both Sian and Chungking.

Most of China's railroad net is single-tracked, but the main trunk lines carrying the heaviest traffic are being gradually double-tracked. During the early reconstruction period, 1950–52, almost 1,000 kilometers of old double-track line was restored, raising double trackage to 1,457 kilometers by the end of 1952. During the period of the first five-year plan, 423 additional kilometers of double-track line was restored and 894 kilometers was newly double-tracked. By the end of the 1950's, double-trackage included the basic north-south Manchurian trunk line, from Harbin through Changchun and Mukden to Dairen; the Mukden-Tientsin-Peking line, and the northern (Peking-Chengchow) segment of the main Peking-Wuhan-Canton railroad. In the 1960's, work has slowly continued on double-tracking the Chengchow-Wuhan-Changsha section of the north-south trunk line, on portions of the Tientsin-Nanking-Shanghai line, and on the Chengchow-Loyang-Sian segment of the Lunghai railroad. Rail transportation was greatly aided by the construction of bridges across the Yangtze River, providing direct links between the rail systems of southern and northern China and eliminating the need for ferry service. In addition to the bridge at Chungking, opened in 1959, Yangtze River crossings were also inaugurated in 1957 at Wuhan and, in 1969, at Nanking.

The double-tracked main lines carry five times or more the average traffic density of the Chinese rail net, which is one of the most heavily used in the world. While the total length of rail lines open to traffic rose by 22 per cent during the five-year period 1953–57, freight traffic in ton-kilometers more than doubled. The strain on the rail system further rose during the Great

TABLE 31

FREIGHT TRAFFIC VOLUME
(*t = freight loadings in million metric tons;*
t/km = freight traffic in billion metric ton-kilometers)

	Railroads		Waterways		Trucking		Total	
	t	t/km	t	t/km	t	t/km	t	t/km
pre-1949 peak	137	40	13	13	8	0.5	158	54
1949	56	18	5	4	6	0.3	67	23
1950	100	39	7	3	9	0.4	116	43
1951	111	52	10	7	14	0.6	135	59
1952	132	60	14	11	22	0.8	169	72
1953	161	78	20	14	31	1.3	212	93
1954	193	93	29	19	43	1.9	265	114
1955	194	98	36	24	49	2.5	278	125
1956	246	120	47	28	79	3.5	372	152
1957	274	135	54	34	84	3.9	412	173
1958	381	186	76	44	176	7.0	634	236
1959	542	263	123	55	340		1,005	
1960 (plan)	720		170		540		1,430	

NOTES: During the Great Leap, the freight traffic shown in the table was supplemented by so-called local or native means of transport, which were reported to have carried 691 million metric tons in 1958 (for a total of 1,324 million) and 1,207 million in 1959 (for a total of 2,212 million).
Some rows do not add up because of rounding.

Leap Forward and may have been a factor in the collapse of that crash program. The share of rail traffic in the total movement of goods appears in Table 31. After the spurt associated with the Great Leap, rail traffic is assumed to have dropped back to the level of the late 1950's, or about 300 million tons of freight originated, and 150 billion ton-kilometers of traffic performance. After a gradual rise of rail-transport work in the early 1960's, another temporary decline seems to have occurred during the disorders associated with the Cultural Revolution in 1966–67, but the transport situation was again reported to be improving by 1970.

Water-borne transportation breaks down into inland shipping, which handles about three-fourths of the tons originated on waterways, and coastal shipping, which handles one-fourth. However, because of the generally greater length of haul in coastal shipping, its share in ton-kilometer performance is about 40 per cent compared with 60 per cent on inland waterways. Actually only three major rivers are suitable for the large-scale movement of goods on inland waterways. They are the Yangtze, the Si Kiang (West River) and the Sungari River in Manchuria. Other streams and canals are accessible to shallow-bottom barges and junks. The Yangtze is by far China's most important waterway, penetrating deeply into the hinterland as far as Szechwan. It alone handled 70 per cent of all the waterway tonnage in the late 1950's. Major ports are Chungking, Wuhan, Nanking, and Shanghai. The Si Kiang, in southern China, handles part of the trade of eastern Kwangsi and western Kwangtung between the ports of Wuchow and Canton. The Sungari, which serves northern Manchuria, has most of its traffic between Harbin and Kiamusze. Its international significance as a tributary of the Amur River has declined during the period of cool relations between the Soviet Union and China.

The principal coastal port is Shanghai, which serves as the basic transshipment center between Yangtze River traffic and coastal shipping. It also handles as much as half of China's foreign trade. To the north are the ports of Lienyünkang, eastern terminus of the Lunghai railroad; Tsingtao, on the Shantung peninsula; and Tientsin, China's second largest port since its old harbor facilities were expanded by addition of the deep-water port of Sinkang ("new harbor"). Dairen is the port of Manchuria. In southern China, the operations of the ports of Foochow and Amoy have been somewhat impeded by the hostilities between Communist China and Taiwan's Nationalist government. The principal ports are Canton, with the outer harbor of Whampoa, and the growing port of Tsamkong (Chankiang), which has steadily expanded since it was reached by a railroad in 1955.

Trucking plays a major role in the outlying western regions still without railroads, particularly on the Tibetan highlands. The most important highways are the Szechwan-Tibet and Tsinghai-Tibet motor roads, both opened in 1954, and the Sinkiang-Tibet road, inaugurated in 1957. Motor roads played a key role in the effort to develop the mineral resources of the Tsaidam basin, before that program was shelved after the collapse of the Great

Leap. Some Chinese industrial centers, notably the oil field of Karamai in Sinkiang, are still heavily dependent on motor traffic.

Airlines link Peking with most of the large cities of China. International services, long oriented mainly toward the Soviet Union, North Korea, and North Vietnam, now link China also with Burma, Pakistan, and Western Europe. Further extensions may be expected as China continues to establish diplomatic relations with other countries. Domestic routes cover about 35,000 kilometers, with major traffic centers at Peking, Shanghai, Canton, Wuhan, Chungking, Sian, Lanchow, and Urumchi. Before the disruptive spurt of activity during the Great Leap, China's airlines reported a freight turnover of about 8 million metric ton-kilometers and passenger traffic of 80 million passenger-kilometers.

FOREIGN TRADE

China's foreign trade has undergone important changes in both its direction and its structure, reflecting the different economic policies pursued since 1949. In the 1950's, when domestic priorities were on the development of heavy industry with Soviet assistance, trade was primarily with the Soviet Union and other Soviet-bloc nations and involved an exchange of traditional Chinese agricultural and mineral exports and textiles for Soviet machinery and some raw materials (mainly petroleum and refined products) designed to contribute to the growth of the industrial base. The policy of heavy reliance on the Soviet bloc was reinforced by a Western embargo on trade with Communist China after its intervention in the Korean War (1950–53). This phase in the history of Chinese foreign trade reached a peak in 1959, when total exchanges with the Soviet bloc amounted to $3 billion, or 70 per cent of China's total trade of $4.4 billion (Table 32). Machinery and industrial equipment amounted to about 40 per cent of total imports.

The collapse of the Great Leap in 1960, followed by the withdrawal of Soviet economic and technical aid and a restructuring of Chinese domestic priorities, resulted in a fundamental reorientation of China's trade. Geographically, it shifted increasingly during the 1960's from reliance on the Soviet bloc to Japan and Western Europe (notably West Germany, Britain, France, and Italy). By 1970, when trade had virtually recovered the Great Leap levels after the recession of the early 1960's, the former relationship between Communist and non-Communist trade had been almost exactly reversed. Western trade accounted for 75 per cent of the total, and Communist trade for 25 per cent. Among the Communist countries, the Soviet Union's trade with China had fallen behind trade volumes by Cuba, Albania, and Rumania. The new Chinese economic policy of balanced development, with greater attention to agricultural improvement, was reflected in growing imports of chemical fertilizers to spur farm output and of some agricultural products (wheat, cotton, sugar, and jute) to supplement domestic production. Industrial machinery and complete plants, instead of being furnished by the Soviet Union, were now being sought in Japan and

TABLE 32
CHINA'S FOREIGN TRADE
(total turnover in billion dollars)

		Communist Nations		Non-Communist Nations		
	Total	Total	USSR	Total	Western Europe	Japan
1950	1.62	0.60	0.58	1.02	0.16	0.06
1951	2.05	1.03	0.81	1.02	0.23	0.03
1952	1.94	1.32	0.97	0.62	0.11	0.02
1953	2.28	1.56	1.17	0.72	0.23	0.03
1954	2.54	1.88	1.34	0.66	0.19	0.06
1955	2.80	1.99	1.39	0.81	0.25	0.11
1956	3.20	2.13	1.50	1.07	0.36	0.15
1957	3.16	1.95	1.28	1.21	0.39	0.14
1958	3.94	2.41	1.52	1.53	0.65	0.11
1959	4.35	2.98	2.05	1.37	0.65	0.02
1960	4.05	2.62	1.67	1.43	0.64	0.02
1961	3.00	1.69	0.92	1.31	0.39	0.05
1962	2.72	1.42	0.74	1.30	0.33	0.09
1963	2.85	1.26	0.60	1.59	0.37	0.14
1964	3.30	1.11	0.45	2.19	0.45	0.31
1965	3.91	1.15	0.42	2.76	0.69	0.47
1966	4.26	1.05	0.32	3.21	0.90	0.62
1967	3.93	0.86	0.11	3.07	1.01	0.58
1968	3.89	0.98	0.10	2.91	0.88	0.57
1969	3.9	1	0.06	2.9		0.63
1970	4.3	1		3.3		0.83

Western Europe. The development of China's domestic oil-resources, particularly in the Taching field of Manchuria, virtually eliminated the importation of petroleum products. China's exports continued to be high-value food products (rice, vegetables, processed foods), supplemented by an increasing volume of textiles and manufactured goods, but shipments of minerals, once a major item, lagged behind the export levels of the 1950's.

Part II

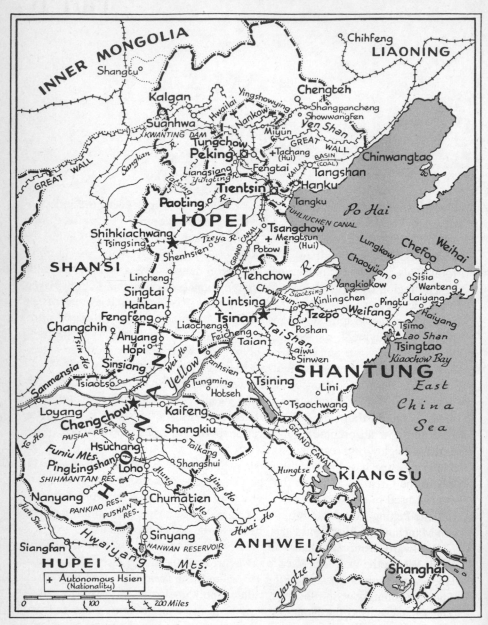

5. North China Plain

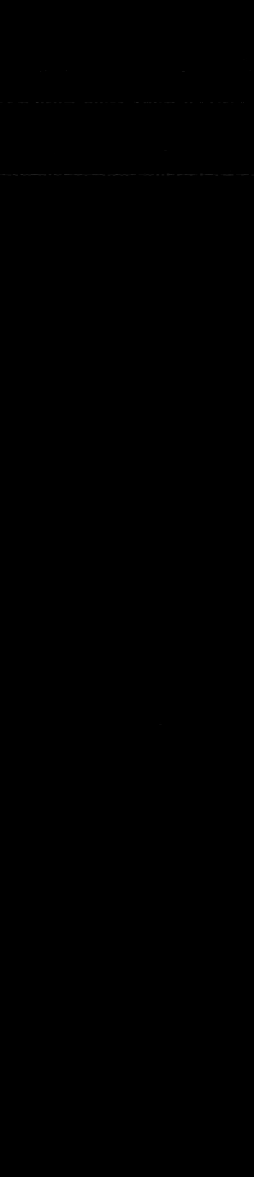

4. The North China Plain

The North China plain includes the provinces of Hopei (with the independent cities of Peking and Tientsin), Honan, and Shantung. The region covers an area of 200,000 square miles, or 5 per cent of the area of China. Its 1970 population was about 170,000,000, or 22 per cent of the nation's total. This represents an average population density of 850 per square mile.

The region owes its unity to the depositional work of the Yellow River, for which it is sometimes named the Yellow River plain. It is one of the best-defined geographical regions of China, bounded by the Yellow Sea and its great embayment, the Po Hai, in the east, by abrupt mountain scarps in the north and west, and by lower hills in the southwest. Only in the southeast does the region pass gradually into the Lower Yangtze plain.

The northern mountain border, where the Yen Shan is the most prominent range of hills, is crowned by the Great Wall. Several important pass-gates in the northern border have served as historic invasion routes in the past and now accommodate major transportation routes between the plain and the neighboring regions.

Perhaps the best-known routeway is Shanhaikwan (mountain-sea-pass), where the Great Wall meets the sea. This is the principal gateway to Manchuria, used in the seventeenth century by the invading Manchu tribes. Today the Peking-Mukden double-tracked main line passes here, joining southern Manchuria, China's industrial heart, to the rest of the nation.

Westward from Shanhaikwan, the northern border follows the Great Wall. Where the wall is pierced by two streams, the Lwan Ho and the Chao Ho, are two minor passes linking Hopei with the former province of Jehol. They are Sifengkow, in the Lwan valley, and Kupehkow, in the Chao valley. The Japanese used the Kupehkow route in the construction of the railroad from Peking to Chengteh in 1939. Reconstruction of the line was completed in 1960 by a different pass-route.

Northwest of Peking, the wall-crowned Yen Shan is crossed by Chüyung-kwan pass near Nankow, a town for which the pass is often named in the

Western literature. This gateway is to Mongolia what Shanhaikwan is to Manchuria. It is crossed by the old Peking-Kalgan railroad, a former key transportation link between North China and Inner Mongolia. The main traffic now uses the Fengtai-Shacheng cut-off through the Yungting valley.

The Taihang Mountains, which border the North China plain on the west, are an escarpment of the loess upland province of Shansi. These mountains, rising suddenly from the plain to more than 3,000 feet, present a solid front inhibiting transportation. Only one of several passes constitutes a major routeway. That is the Niangtzekwan, used by the railroad from Shihkia-chwang to Taiyüan.

In western Honan, where the North China plain is encroached upon by the Funiu Mountains and its outliers, the Lung-Hai railroad is restricted to a number of passes between the mountains and the Yellow River. These passes are, from east to west, the Hulaokwan, the Hankukwan, and, in the extreme west on the Shensi border, the major gateway of Tungkwan at the right angle bend of the Yellow River.

Finally, along the southern margins of the plain, the Hwaiyang Mountains are crossed by a low pass known as the Wushengkwan. This gateway also has been put to good use by China's railroad-builders in laying the track for the Peking-Hankow trunk line.

Thus surrounded by mountains, the North China plain is in itself a region of very low relief. The product of alluvial deposition of the Yellow River and other streams descending from the loessial uplands in the west, the plain stands in sharp contrast to the bordering mountains that rise to more than 3,000 feet above the nearly level lowland.

The Yellow River enters the plain along the Honan-Shansi border and then proceeds on its aggraded, dike-enclosed course 450 miles east and northeast to its mouth on the Po Hai. This course has been used by the river since 1855, except for the relatively brief diversion from 1938 to 1947, when the stream flowed southeast into the Hwai Ho system. The North China plain can be compared to a gigantic alluvial fan over which the course of the Yellow River has swept back and forth like the tail of a gigantic dog. Because the Yellow River flows at an elevation of ten to twenty feet above the surrounding countryside, it receives no tributaries throughout its entire lower course in the North China plain. Only two streams join it immediately after its exit from the mountains; they are the Tsin Ho, which descends from the Shansi plateau, and the Lo Ho, which flows to the Yellow River from the Funiu Mountains.

North of the Yellow River, in Hopei, the North China plain is drained by the complex river system of the Hai Ho. The Hai Ho itself is only a short stream flowing thirty miles from Tientsin to the sea. But it is the outlet of five major streams converging fanlike at Tientsin. These are the Northern Canal, a section of the Grand Canal formed at Tungchow east of Peking; the Yungting River, rising in northern Shansi as the Sangkan River; the Tatsing River, formed in central Hopei; the Tzeya River, formed in south central Hopei by the junction of the Huto and Fuyang rivers; and the Southern Canal, a section of the Grand Canal that receives the Wei Ho from northern Honan. A flood-prevention program in the Hai Ho basin in the 1950's and 1960's has included the construction of reservoirs in the upper reaches and the widening of channels in the lower sections of streams.

South of the Yellow River, the North China plain is drained by the Hwai Ho, whose principal tributaries rise in southern Honan. The longest affluents, including the Ying Ho and the Hung Ho, rise in the Funiu Mountains.

East of the Grand Canal, which connects the Hwai Ho and Hai Ho river systems, are the Shantung uplands, a region of ancient metamorphic and igneous rocks that have resisted weathering. These uplands once were an island, later transformed into a peninsula as the shifting Yellow River gradually filled in the sea on the northern and southern sides of the uplands. The highest part of the uplands, the Tai Shan (5,000 feet), is a mass of basic extrusive rocks standing out sharply in fault scarps above the surrounding plain. On its eastern side, the Tai Shan is separated by the Kiaolai corridor from the hills that form the actual Shantung promontory, rising to 3,700 feet in the Lao Shan northeast of Tsingtao. The Kiaolai corridor is a broad water-level valley extending across the Shantung peninsula from Laichow Bay in the north to Kiaochow Bay in the south. Under the Ming dynasty (1368-1644), a canal was built through this corridor, connecting the Po Hai and the Yellow Sea. The waterway has fallen into disuse.

In accordance with the relief, the North China plain presents two contrasting types of coastlines. The shore north of the Yellow River mouth is low-lying and simple, with virtually no natural harbors. Although the shore line is one of submergence, the absence of relief in the initial topography has resulted in a simple coast. The only natural port along this coast is Chinwangtao.

The coast of Shantung, by contrast, is rocky and much indented. It abounds in natural harbors, of which the most important are Lungkow, Chefoo, Weihai, and the port of Tsingtao on Kiaochow Bay.

The climate of the North China plain is the monsoon-controlled variety of the humid middle-latitude continental climate. It is distinguished by hot, rainy summers when the region is dominated by Tropical Maritime air masses and by cold, dry winters under the influence of Polar Continental air. The typical annual temperature range is from 25° F (—4° C) in January to 80° F (27° C) in July. The annual range is greater inland, while somewhat warmer winters and cooler summers prevail along the Shantung coast.

Rainfall reaches a maximum in July, with virtually all the precipitation occurring from May through September. The average annual total is 25 inches, with generally higher amounts along the coast and toward the south. Strong winds associated with the northwest monsoon blow loess from the western uplands, spreading it throughout the level plain.

The windblown loess and the river-laid alluvium provide the parent material for the calcareous and saline young alluvial soils typical of the flood plains of North China. In poorly drained areas with a high water table, both in inland lake depressions and near the coast, salinity increases and tends to depress fertility. In the mountain margins of the North China plain and the Shantung uplands, brown podzolic soils support a mixed deciduous and coniferous forest where natural vegetation remains. The peculiar shakiang soil, characterized by poor drainage and a horizon of lime concretions, occurs in central Honan and in Shantung at the west foot of the Tai Shan. Noncalcareous recent alluvial soils are found in southern Honan.

The predominantly calcareous alluvium of the North China plain and the summer rainfall have made the region one of the most important agricultural areas of China. This is the so-called winter wheat–kaoliang region. Irrigation is uncommon. Wheat and barley are the two winter grains, while kaoliang, millet, and corn are planted in the summer. The North China plain produces about one-half of China's total output of each of these grains. Rice cultivation is quite insignificant and is pursued in southernmost Honan. Soybeans are widely grown throughout the region, which produces about one-third of China's total output.

The Shantung peninsula is China's leading peanut-growing area, and the North China plain as a whole produces about 75 per cent of China's peanuts. The alluvial soils also favor the growing of cotton, of which the entire region produces about two-thirds of China's total. Like peanuts, tobacco is favored by the sandy soils of Shantung and Honan, while fruit is also associated with the podzolic brown upland soils.

Fisheries are widely developed off the North China coast, particularly around the rocky Shantung peninsula. There the indented coastline and the abundance of offshore islands favor the growth of plankton and other fish food.

Livestock-raising is an auxiliary activity of the farm population. Oxen, donkeys, and mules are particularly common, as they serve as important draft animals. Hogs are fed on the byproducts of agriculture and sheep are raised chiefly for meat.

Industrially, the North China plain is important as a coal-producer, with the main mines found along the foot of the northern and western mountain margins and in the Shantung uplands. Iron ore is found chiefly in the Lungyen deposit outside the North China plain itself, but also in small amounts in Shantung. Important salterns are exploited along the coast. Manufacturing industry is concentrated in the Peking-Tientsin belt, along the Tsinan-Tsingtao railroad and in northern Honan.

Railroads are the main form of transportation in the North China plain, which has the densest rail net south of the Great Wall. Waterways play a minor role because of their shallowness and irregular flow. Roads are only of local importance.

The relatively dense railroad development results from a combination of factors. Railroads focused from the very start on Peking, the nation's capital; the predominant lowland relief facilitated railroad construction; the importance of railroads was greatly enhanced through the virtual absence of good navigable waterways; and, finally, construction of lines was sponsored in part by foreign interests active in North China. The Peking-Hankow and Tientsin-Pukow railroads are the main north-south trunk lines, while the Lunghai, Tsingtao-Tsinan-Tehchow-Shihkiachwang, and Tientsin-Peking connections provide east-west links.

Except for the Hai Ho below Tientsin, which is accessible to small coastwise vessels of less than 3,000 tons, North China's waterways are suitable only for junk traffic. The main junk arteries are the combined Wei Ho and Southern Canal route and the Siaotsing River, a delta arm of the Yellow River. Ocean-going trade proceeds through the ports of Chinwangtao, Tientsin-Tangku, Chefoo, Weihai, and Tsingtao.

The densely-settled North China plain has a homogeneous Chinese population speaking the northern Mandarin dialect. While population density is about 850 or more per square mile in the plain proper, it ranges from 150 to 400 in the hilly parts of Shantung, where arable land is more limited. The only ethnic minorities are a few scattered communities of Chinese Moslems (Hui), two of which, in Hopei Province, have been constituted as autonomous hsien.

HOPEI PROVINCE

Capital: Shihkiachwang; area: 75,000 sq. mi.; population: 46 million

PEKING

Area: 6,600 sq. mi.; population: 7 million

TIENTSIN

Area: 1,200 sq. mi.; population: 4 million

Before 1949, Hopei, including the present independent-city areas of Peking and Tientsin, had an area of 54,000 square miles and an estimated population of 29 million. In 1949, Hopei ceded about 4,000 square miles of territory along its south and southeast borders to the newly formed province of Pingyüan and to Shantung. From 1949 to 1952, the provincial area was 50,000 square miles, and the population was estimated at 31 million. In November, 1952, Hopei regained virtually all the territory ceded in 1949 and, furthermore, acquired about 15,000 square miles of the abolished province of Chahar. Within these expanded boundaries, the 1953 census recorded a population of 41.5 million, including 2.8 million for Peking and 2.7 million for Tientsin. In early 1956, Hopei annexed the southern part of the abolished Jehol Province with a 1953 population of 1.9 million. This brought the Hopei total within the expanded territory to 43.4 million as of the 1953 census and to 48.7 million as of the 1957 year-end estimate, including 4 million for the then independent city of Peking and 3.2 million for the then subprovincial city of Tientsin. In a subsequent minor boundary adjustment, Hopei ceded the hsien of Shangtu, northwest of Kalgan, to Inner Mongolia early in 1962.

The independent municipal area of Peking was expanded several times after 1949, reaching its present limits in October, 1958. Tientsin was also established as an independent city directly under the central government after 1949, but lost that status in April, 1958, when it became a city under the jurisdiction of Hopei Province. Independent-city status was restored to Tientsin in 1967.

Until the annexation of parts of Chahar and Jehol, Hopei had been entirely within the North China plain. The northern territorial gains projected part of Hopei onto the Inner Mongolian plateau and the Jehol uplands, where natural conditions differ considerably from those of the North China plain. Both January and July average temperatures are about 5°F (2.5°C) lower than those prevailing in the North China plain, but, more important, average annual precipitation drops to 15 inches from the average of 25 inches in the plain. These climatic differences can be explained by the location of the former Chahar and Jehol areas with respect to the climatic source regions. These areas are more exposed to the cold, dry Polar Continental air dominating the region during the winter, which accounts for the lower January temperature. On the other hand, they are situated in the lee of the Yen Shan, which offers a considerable obstacle to the hot and rainy Tropical Maritime air originating in the seas off China. The climatic barrier of the Yen Shan operates to depress the July temperature and the annual precipitation.

The chernozems and the dark chestnut soils developed in the former Chahar area are among the most fertile soils of China, but limited rainfall greatly restricts their usefulness. In contrast to the North China plain, all crops are summer-grown, with spring wheat, millet, and potatoes the chief products. On the drier margins, extensive livestock-raising is the principal activity.

In the greater part of Hopei, conditions typical of the North China plain prevail. The province is one of China's leading winter wheat and cotton areas. Wheat is grown throughout the plain and soybeans chiefly in the seaward area. Cotton is concentrated in the river basins of the Wei Ho, Tatsing River, Tzeya River, and the Northern Canal.

Hopei Province accounts for more than 5 per cent of China's food crop from a sown area of 8 million hectares. About 40 per cent of the total grain area is in wheat. The province grows also about 20 per cent of the nation's cotton from an average sown area of 1 million hectares. Oil crops take up about 470,000 hectares, with about 65 per cent of this area planted in peanuts. Conditions in the province are favorable for fruit-growing, especially along the foot of the bordering mountain ranges. Tientsin is known for its pear orchards; Liangsiang, a southwest suburb of Peking, for its chestnut trees; and Shenhsien for its peaches.

As part of the flood-prevention program in the basin of the Hai Ho, several projects have been completed in Hopei Province: The Kwanting reservoir on the Yungting River northwest of Peking, the Miyün reservoir on the Pai Ho, northeast of Peking, and a variety of channel widening and straightening operations to avoid the converging of flood waters in the Tientsin area.

The Kwanting reservoir was built between October, 1951, and May, 1954. Situated 45 miles northwest of Peking, just beyond the Great Wall, the reservoir was formed by construction of an earth dam, 150 feet high and 1,000 feet long, across a gorge of the Yungting River. When filled to capacity, the reservoir covers an area of 85 square miles. A multipurpose project, it serves for flood control, irrigation, and power generation, through three 10,000-kilowatt turbines installed in 1955.

The Miyün reservoir, completed in 1959 about 50 miles northeast of Peking, is also reported to have a generating capacity of 30,000 kilowatts, installed in 1960. A smaller reservoir, the Ming Tombs reservoir, northwest of the Chinese capital, was built in 1958. It is the source of a water-supply aqueduct to Peking.

Old channels have been widened, and new channels and seaward outlets have been constructed in the 1950's and 1960's for most of the tributaries of the Hai Ho converging on Tientsin. Some of the most extensive work has been carried on along the Tatsing and Tzeya rivers. Construction of an alternate outlet, the Tuhliuchen Canal, was completed in 1953. The outlet, named for a village near the Tatsing-Tzeya confluence, was further improved in 1969–70. At the same time, the channels of some of the northern tributaries of the Hai Ho, east of Peking, were strengthened in mass projects at the end of the 1960's.

Among mineral resources, coal is by far Hopei's principal asset, with deposits found chiefly along the south foot of the Yen Shan and the east foot of the Taihang Mountains.

The best-known and one of China's most important coal fields is the Kailan basin, named for the towns of Kaiping and Lwanhsien (sometimes Lanhsien). Exploited since 1879, the Kailan basin owed its development primarily to a favorable seaboard location that assured it a bunker market at its ice-free port of Chinwangtao. It produces good steam-raising coal and has in the past yielded coal suitable for coking. It has long been a leading producer. The principal mines of the Kailan basin are Sükochwang near Tangshan, Makiakow near Kaiping, Chaokochwang, Tangkiachwang, and Linsi near Kuyeh, all along the Peking-Mukden railroad. The Kailan coal basin is believed to be producing 10 to 15 million tons a year.

The Kailan field is situated 60 miles west of its shipping port of Chinwangtao. Just north of the port, in the foothills of the Yen Shan, are the smaller coal mines of Shihmenchai near Liukiang.

West and southwest of Peking, within the capital's municipal limits, are a number of small coal mines in a tectonically much disturbed zone. These mines are Mentowkow, Changkowyü, Chaitang, and Chowkowtien. They are situated on spurs of the Peking-Hankow railroad. The Mentowkow anthracite mine, the largest of this group, is linked directly by rail with

Peking. The Peking mines are known collectively as the Kingsi ("west of the capital") coal district, which is believed to have a combined mining capacity of more than 5 million tons, mostly anthracite.

Farther south, along the east foot of the Taihang Mountains, are the coal mines of Tsingsing, west of Shihkiachwang near the Shansi line, and Lincheng and Fengfeng, both on spur lines of the Peking-Hankow railroad. Fengfeng, situated in southernmost Hopei near the Honan border, has developed as a major coking coal supplier for North China's steel plants. It was set up as a special mining district in 1950 and existed briefly as a city (1955–56) before being incorporated into the growing industrial municipality of Hantan. The Fengfeng coal mines produce more than 5 million tons a year and help supply the coking coal needs of iron and steel plants at Hantan, Shihkingshan (west of Peking), and Taiyüan. A coal-dressing plant with a capacity of 2 million tons opened in 1959 at Matow, a rail junction south of Hantan where the 12-mile spur from the Fengfeng mines joins the main line.

Small coal mines are at Yingshowying, southwest of Chengteh on the railroad to Peking, and at Siahwayüan, southeast of Süanhwa.

One of China's main iron-ore sources was acquired by Hopei with the annexation of part of Chahar in 1952. That is the iron-ore district known variously as Lungyen (for the Lungkwan and the Yentungshan deposits) or Süanlung (for the towns of Süanhwa and Lungkwan). The ore is sedimentary hematite, of relatively high grade (50 per cent iron), and siliceous. Its phosphorous content is too high for Bessemer treatment, but it is suitable for basic open-hearth furnaces. The reserves have been put at 400 million tons. Mining began in 1919 at the Yentungshan deposit, just northeast of Süanhwa, from where the ore was shipped by rail to the Hanyang works. But operations ceased soon thereafter and were not renewed in earnest until the Japanese occupation during World War II. The Japanese built a 30-mile rail spur to the Pangkiapu deposit, east of Süanhwa, and built several small blast furnaces to smelt the ore on the spot. By 1942, annual output reached 900,000 tons of ore. After having been shut down for nine years, three blast furnaces were rebuilt in 1953 at Süanhwa and were reported in 1958 to be producing 260,000 tons of foundry iron suitable for making castings. A powder metallurgy plant opened there in 1969. Most of the Lungyen iron-ore output, which was 1.4 million tons in 1958, is shipped to the integrated iron and steel plant of Shihkingshan, and partly to Taiyüan and Anshan.

Small iron mines at Tzeshan, just southwest of Wuan, in southernmost Hopei, also yield a high-grade hematite, with an iron content of 50 to 60 per cent, for use in the integrated iron and steel plant of nearby Hantan.

Aside from the basic minerals of coal and iron, Hopei also has deposits of copper, tungsten, manganese, and gold on the northern and southern slopes of the Yen Shan. Economically the most important is the copper deposit of Showwangfen, 30 miles south of Chengteh, which has been developed since the Great Leap. Gold is mined in the Yen Shan, notably in the Malanyü lode mine near Tsunhwa, which has been in operation since 1932.

A significant mineral is salt, produced in the Changlu salines of Tientsin. The salines extend along the coast of the Po Hai north and south of Tientsin's outer port of Tangku and account for about one-fourth of China's salt production. Most of the output is used for seasoning food, but about 25 per cent or more provides raw material for the caustic soda and chlorine-based chemical industries of the Tientsin area.

Hopei's coal, mainly Kailan steam coal, is the principal fuel used in the province's electric-power industry. The principal generating plants are associated with the industrial centers of Peking, Tientsin, and Tangshan, which are connected by a power-transmission grid of 220-kilovolt lines (converted from 110 kilovolts in 1971). The capacity at Tangshan in the Kailan field is believed to be in excess of 300,000 kilowatts, and that at the Tientsin heat and power station is estimated at about 150,000 kilowatts. The Peking power complex includes two major installations, the Shihkingshan station, next to the iron and steel plant, west of Peking, and a thermal-power plant in the eastern industrial suburbs of Peking. The Shihkingshan station, with an original capacity of 40,000 kilowatts in the 1950's, was expanded during the Great Leap to more than 100,000 kilowatts. A 100,000-kilowatt unit was added in 1968. The East Peking station was inaugurated in 1958 with a 50,000-kilowatt unit and was planned to reach a capacity of 250,000 kilowatts. The northern Hopei power grid has been extended northwest from Peking via the 30,000-kilowatt Kwanting hydroelectric station to a power plant at the Siahwayüan coal mine, which serves the Kalgan-Süanhwa industrial complex. South of Peking, along the main railroad to Chengchow, smaller thermal-power stations, on the order of 50,000 kilowatts, operate in the industrial areas of Paoting, Shihkiachwang, and Hantan. The Shihkiachwang power plant burns coal from the nearby Tsingsing mine, and the Hantan plant from the nearby Fengfeng mine.

Hopei's industries are concentrated in a T-shaped belt extending along the Kalgan-Peking-Tientsin railroad to the Kailan coal basin, and from Peking southward through Paoting and Shihkiachwang to Hantan.

The iron and steel industry is represented by several establishments, including the integrated plants of Shihkingshan and Hantan, the pig-iron plant of Süanhwa, and the steel plants of Tientsin and Tangshan. The Shihkingshan plant in the Peking municipal district is by far the most important of these enterprises. It is situated on the Yungting River, 12 miles from Peking's western gates and on the rail spur to the anthracite mine of Mentowkow. Shihkingshan was founded shortly after World War I and was expanded in World War II under Japanese occupation. By 1957, the plant's blast-furnace department produced 430,000 tons of pig iron from a medium-size furnace originally built in 1924 and from three smaller furnaces. During the Great Leap, a 1,000-cubic-meter blast furnace was inaugurated in 1959, equal in capacity to the four older installations taken together and raising the plant's pig-iron capacity to the 1-million-ton level. At the same time, steel-making capacity began to be added during the Great Leap; however, the Shihkingshan plant was not fully integrated until 1969, when a blooming mill was placed into operation. Until that time, Shihkingshan ingot steel had to be sent elsewhere for conversion into blooms, billets, and other semifinished products. The plant uses iron ore from the Lungyen district and coking coal mainly from Fengfeng. Shihkingshan pig iron, in addition to being locally converted into steel, is also shipped to the steel plants at Tangshan, Tientsin, and Shihkiachwang for use in combination with scrap metal.

The medium-size integrated iron and steel plant of Hantan, in southern Hopei, dates from the Great Leap. The first blast furnace, with a working volume of 255 cubic meters and an annual pig-iron capacity of 125,000 tons, was inaugurated in 1959. The Hantan plant also has steel-making capacity and finishing mills and produces some ferroalloys. Its total iron and steel capacity is probably less than 500,000 tons a year.

The iron and steel plants provide metal for fabricating industries concentrated in the manufacturing centers of Peking, Tientsin, Tangshan, Kalgan, and Shihkiachwang, with rolling-stock, machine-tool, and a variety of machinery plants. Cement for industrial and housing construction is provided by mills at Tangshan, Liuliho (southwest of Peking), and Hantan (inaugurated in 1969). The coal port of Chinwangtao has a large glass factory.

As China's major cotton-growing area, Hopei has also played an important role in the cotton textile industry. In the past, most of the spinning capacity was concentrated in Tientsin, which accounted for as much as 90 per cent of the spindles before 1949, and a large share of the provincial cotton crop was shipped to Shanghai mills. In an effort to assure more uniform distribution of the cotton textile industry, new mills were built in the 1950's in Peking, Shihkiachwang, and Hantan, along the Peking-Chengchow railroad in the heart of the Hopei cotton belt. As a result of this spatial redistribution, the share of the Tientsin mills in the provincial industry dropped to about 50 per cent, while that of the new milling centers in the cotton belt rose from 5 per cent in 1949 to almost 50 per cent in 1957.

Hopei's urban pattern has undergone extensive changes since 1949 as a result of industrialization and frequent administrative shifts (see Table 33). In addition to the two independent municipal districts of Peking and Tientsin, Hopei Province has one city, Shihkiachwang, the capital, at subprovincial level, and eight cities at hsien level: Tangshan, Chinwangtao, Chengteh, Kalgan, Paoting, Singtai, Hantan, and Tsangchow.

Peking, China's ancient capital, has once again reverted to its political pre-eminence. As Yenking, it was the capital of the Liao dynasty set up in the tenth century by the Kitan Tatars who had invaded North China from the north. The city's name changed frequently under subsequent dynasties. It was Chungtu under the Chin dynasty set up in the twelfth century by the Golden Horde. The city's greatest period came in the late thirteenth century, when Kublai Khan moved his capital here from Karakorum. During this period, the city was called Tatu by the Chinese and Khanbalyk by the Mongols. The latter name was rendered Cambaluc by Marco Polo, who visited here about 1275. The city continued as capital under the Mongols' Yüan dynasty until 1368. Under the early Mings, it was briefly replaced by Nan-

TABLE 33
CITIES OF HOPEI

City	City Level	Function	Population (*in thousands*)		
			1953	1957	1970 est.
Peking	province	manuf.	2,768	4,010	7,000
Tientsin	province	manuf., port	2,694	3,200	4,000
Shihkiachwang	subprovince	manuf.	373	598	
Tangshan	hsien	manuf., coal	693	800	
Kalgan	hsien	manuf.	229	480	
Hantan	hsien	coal-steel	50–100	380	
Paoting	hsien	manuf.	197		
Chinwangtao	hsien	port	187		
Chengteh	hsien	manuf.	93		
Singtai (1953–58, 1961–)	hsien	manuf.	50–100		
Tsangchow (formed 1961)	hsien	trade			

Former Cities	Period	Function	Disposition
Fengfeng	1955–56	coal	merged with Hantan
Hanku	1953–58, 1960–62	chemicals	merged with Tientsin
Potow	1953–58	trade	subhsien town
Süanhwa	1953–55, 1960–62	iron	hsien seat
Tungchow	1953–58	trade	merged with Peking

king but resumed its political leadership in 1421 under the name of Peking ("northern capital"). It retained the name and the leadership through the Manchu dynasty (1644–1911) and into the early years of the Republic. In 1928, the Nationalists transferred the seat of government to Nanking, and Peking was renamed Peiping ("northern peace"), a name it had briefly held under the early Mings. In 1949, the city once again became China's capital under its historic name.

The present city pattern dates from the days of Kublai Khan. Peking proper consists of two contiguous walled cities: the Inner City (a rectangle measuring 4 miles by 3 miles) adjoined on the south by the Outer City (5 miles by 1.5 miles). The innermost part of the Inner City is the old imperial palace of the Mings and Manchus, historically known as the Forbidden City and now converted into a museum. It is surrounded by the former Imperial City, whose walls were razed after 1949. This central part of the Inner City is the most beautiful of the capital, set among lakes and parks. It is the seat of the government, which has its offices around the elongated lake called Chungnanhai. Southeast of the Imperial City is the Legation Quarter, where foreign powers were permitted to establish offices after the Boxer Rebellion of 1900. Along the south edge of the Imperial City, Chang An Chieh, one of the capital's main thoroughfares, leads past Tien An Men ("gate of heavenly peace"), Peking's Red Square and scene of political meetings and demonstrations.

The Outer City, which contains the famous Temple of Heaven and the Temple of Agriculture, is the commercial quarter and has only about one-fourth the population of the Inner City. At the wall separating the two cities is Chien Men, Peking's main railroad station.

The capital's higher educational institutions are situated largely in the western suburbs along the road leading to the old summer palace and the Western Hills, a resort area. City planning has provided for further residential and educational development west and northwest of the city proper, with industries concentrated east of the city.

Industrial development of Peking before 1949 involved the Mentowkow anthracite mines and the Shihkingshan iron and steel plant west of the city, and the Changsintien locomotive and rolling-stock shops and the Fengtai bridge girder plant to the southwest. Industrial expansion accelerated during the Great Leap, with metal-fabricating plants (machine tools, ball bearings, motor vehicles and engines), electronics (computers), and chemicals (nitrogen fertilizers, synthetic fibers, vinyl resins). Many of the new industries were located east of Peking proper along the railroad to Tungchow. The vinyl chloride plant, opened in 1965, is situated at Shunyi, 15 miles northeast of Peking.

Increasing industrialization and Peking's new political role as the nation's capital led to repeated expansions of its municipal area under central government jurisdiction. Shortly after 1949, the area increased from 270 to 500 square miles, and, in 1953, further annexation of territory placed Peking's western municipal limits along the Great Wall, giving the district an area of 1,750 square miles. The census of June, 1953, recorded a population of 2.8 million within the municipal area, including 1,050,000 in the twin-walled central city—830,000 in the Inner City and 220,000 in the Outer City. In 1958, the municipal district was further enlarged in two separate annexations. The first, in March, 1958, included a suburban ring, with the eastern suburb of Tungchow, and expanded the municipal area to 3,400 square miles and the population from 3.6 million to 5.3 million. The second 1958 annexation, in October, was mainly northward to include relatively more sparsely populated mountain areas, such as the Miyün district, where a flood-control reservoir was under construction. The second annexation expanded the Peking municipal area to its present size of 6,600 square miles, with a 1958 population of about 6 million.

Historically, Peking has occupied a strategic position in the North China plain near the gateways to Mongolia and Manchuria and was usually the first Chinese city to fall to the invaders. In the past, Peking, or rather its river port of Tungchow, ten miles east, was the northern terminus of the Grand Canal, which linked the northern capital with the southern parts of the country. In the railroad age, Peking has maintained its importance as a transportation focus. Lines radiate from here to Wuhan and Canton, Kalgan and Paotow, Tientsin and Mukden, Tungchow and Chengteh. The railroad through Tientsin to Mukden is one of the busiest in China, carrying coal from the Kailan mining district, salt from the Tientsin salines, and pig iron and steel and manufactured goods from Peking and Tientsin. The westward rail outlet from Peking toward Paotow was improved with the construction in 1955 of a new 65-mile segment between Fengtai (southwest Peking suburb) and Hwailai (Shachcng) along thc vallcy of thc Yungting River, avoiding the steep grades and tight curves of the older segment between Nankow and Hwailai. The importance of this western outlet was further enhanced with the completion of the Trans-Mongolian Railroad to the Soviet Union in 1956 and the extension of the Paotow line toward Lanchow in 1958.

Just 70 miles southeast of the capital stands Tientsin, China's third largest city. Like Peking an independent municipal district directly under the central government, Tientsin has a quite different personality. While Peking still retains the charm of classical Chinese culture and the dignity of an ancient imperial capital, Tientsin is the product of the machine age, a bustling industrial center of the Western type. Of little significance until the mid-nineteenth century, Tientsin was occupied by the British and French in 1858 and 1860 and thereafter opened to foreign trade. Concessions were granted to Britain, France, Japan, Germany, Italy, Austria-Hungary, Belgium, and Russia, and, after the city's destruction in the Boxer Rebellion (1900), the city walls were razed and reconstruction proceeded along Western lines.

Tientsin has developed as a natural outlet for the products of North China and Inner Mongolia. It is situated on the Hai Ho, 25 miles from the sea, at the point where five major streams converge to form the short outlet to the Po Hai. The large amounts of sediments brought from the entire Hai Ho system choke the river and form offshore sand bars. Only continuous dredging has been able to keep the waterway open for small vessels. At high tide and under the best conditions, ships of 3,000 tons and a 15-foot draft were able to make their way to Tientsin along the tortuous course of the Hai Ho. Medium-size ocean vessels were forced to anchor 25 to 30 miles out at sea off the Taku Bar. With the aim of improving accessibility, the Japanese initiated port-improvement work during World War II. Construction of an artificial outer harbor near Tangku, opposite Taku on the north bank of the Hai Ho estuary, was continued after the war. Sinkang (the "new port") was formally opened in October, 1952. A deep-water area of about 7 square miles is now protected by two moles against further deposition of riverborne sediments. The new harbor can accommodate four 10,000-ton and five 3,000-ton ships. A lock gives access to the Hai Ho itself and permits smaller ships to go up the river to Tientsin. The port freezes for about two months in winter but is usually kept open by icebreakers. In severe winters, Tientsin's traffic can be detoured through the port of Chinwangtao.

Tientsin's importance for maritime trade is matched by its landward communications. Aside from being situated on the Peking-Mukden railroad, with its high traffic-density, Tientsin is the northern terminus of the Tientsin-Pukow railroad, which terminated at Pukow, opposite Nanking, before the Yangtze River bridge was completed in 1969. Through Peking, Tientsin has rail access to Inner Mongolia. Small junks can make use of the waterways converging at Tientsin, particularly the Grand Canal–Wei Ho route leading to Sinsiang in northern Honan.

As one of China's leading ports, Tientsin has also developed into a key industrial center, noted particularly for its cotton and woolen mills and food-processing industries. Since 1949, greater attention has been devoted to the city's metallurgical and metal-fabricating industries, which include a steel plant (using long-haul pig iron and scrap) and the manufacture of textile, chemical, and oil equipment, motor vehicles, tractors, bicycles, and diesel engines. An important chemical industry, based on the Changlu salines in the Tientsin area, has been in existence since 1914. Its plants, at Taku on the south bank of the Hai Ho, Tangku on the north bank, and Hanku farther north, produce soda ash, caustic soda, and chlorine derivatives from the electrolysis of salt.

Like Peking, Tientsin expanded its municipal area after 1949. At first, the Tangku-Taku port area was incorporated into Tientsin, increasing the urban district from 21 to 100 square miles. The next step was to join the two sections into an enlarged municipal district of 900 square miles, which had a population of 2.7 million in the 1953 census. In 1962, the Tientsin urban area annexed the chemical center of Hanku, expanding to its present territory of about 1,200 square miles. Tientsin ceased to be a municipal district under central government jurisdiction in April, 1958, when it was made a city within Hopei Province. At the same time, the provincial government was moved from Paoting to Tientsin. Independent city status was restored to Tientsin in 1967, and this time the provincial capital was moved from Tientsin to Shihkiachwang.

Hopei's third largest city is Tangshan, the industrial metropolis of the Kailan coal basin. With a 1957 population of about 800,000, it includes a considerable part of the Kailan basin within its municipal boundaries. It has steel and cement industries and a large power plant based on the local coal resources. Tangshan is on the Peking-Mukden railroad, about halfway between Tientsin and Chinwangtao, its two ports. Chinwangtao is Hopei's only ice-free port and handles chiefly the shipments of Kailan coal. Southwest of Chinwangtao is Pehtaiho, one of China's most popular beach resorts.

Other key centers of the North China plain section of Hopei Province are situated along the Peking-Chengchow railroad. Paoting, the provincial capital before 1958, is an agricultural center with processing industries and distribution functions. It acquired a viscose rayon plant in 1960, using local cotton linters as raw material. Shihkiachwang is a rail hub and cotton-milling center at the junction of the Peking-Hankow and Tehchow-Taiyüan lines. Shihkiachwang was only a small village 50 years ago. It developed rapidly as a railroad center, especially after the narrow-gauge line to Taiyüan was converted to standard gauge and the connecting railroad from Tehchow was built by the Japanese. The city had a population of 598,000 in 1957. Farther south, beyond Singtai, another local agricultural center, is the growing urban complex of Hantan. Originally a minor agricultural-trade town, Hantan at first acquired a cotton textile industry in the early 1950's. The development of the coking-coal mines at Fengfeng (included in the Hantan municipal limits in 1956) and the presence of iron ore at nearby Tzeshan led to the development of an iron and steel industry at Hantan during the Great Leap. It was followed in the early 1960's by the construction of an unidentified mining and metallurgical complex, probably involving nonferrous and rare metals, with its mine at Kwangshantsun ("ore-mining settlement"), on a 20-mile rail spur northwest of Hantan. A large cement plant was added to the growing industrial center in 1968.

In the southeastern part of Hopei, along the Tientsin-Pukow railroad and Grand Canal, Tsangchow has been the regional center since it was raised to city status in 1961. It replaced the market town of Potow, to the southwest, which was temporarily established as a city from 1953 to 1958.

In former Chahar, the plateau section of Hopei, Kalgan and Süanhwa are the principal urban centers. Kalgan, whose Chinese name is Changkiakow, is a historic transportation and commercial center on the southern margin of Inner Mongolia. Here converge rail lines from Peking and Paotow and highways from Ulan Bator and the Chahar and Silingol leagues of Inner Mongolia. Although Kalgan is situated outside the political frontiers of the Inner Mongolian Autonomous Region, the city continues to play a major role in the life of the adjoining Inner Mongolian leagues. Kalgan is situated on a branch of the Yang Ho, a headstream of the Yungting River. It consists of a Chinese section on the western (right) bank and a Mongol section and railroad settlement on the eastern bank. It receives hides and wool from the northern steppe and ships tea, cotton goods, sugar, and tobacco to the herders. Developed as a trade center under the Manchu Dynasty, Kalgan long handled the tea traffic on the overland route from China to Russia. The city expanded after it was reached by the railroad from Peking in 1909. Further expansion followed the construction of the railroad across Mongolia toward the Soviet Union. Kalgan has cotton and woolen mills, manufactures coal-mining and drilling equipment, and acquired a viscose rayon mill in 1968.

Süanhwa, the iron-mining and smelting center 15 miles southeast of Kalgan, forms a single conurbation with Kalgan. At various times, Süanhwa existed as a separate city (1953–55 and 1960–62); at other times, it was incorporated into the Kalgan urban district, together with the coal-mining town of Siahwayüan, 15 miles southeast of Süanhwa.

Chengteh, the former capital of Jehol Province, passed to Hopei in 1956. Situated on a tributary of the Lwan Ho, the city is the economic center of the southern Jehol uplands. Chengteh was long oriented toward the Manchurian province of Liaoning, with which it had good rail communication. The Japanese built a railroad in 1938 linking Chengteh with Peking via the Kupehkow Pass in the Great Wall, but this line was destroyed during World War II. When it came to rebuilding a rail link between Chengteh and Peking in the 1950's, the line was relocated farther south to provide access to the coal mine of Yingshowying and the copper center of Showwangfen, south-west of Chengteh. The new Chengteh-Peking railroad was inaugurated in 1960.

Hopei Province has two autonomous hsien based on the Chinese Moslem nationality: Tachang, east of Peking, and Mengtsun, southeast of Tsang-chow. These hsien were first established in 1955 and, after having been tem-porarily abolished in 1958, were restored in 1962.

HONAN PROVINCE

Capital: Chengchow; area: 65,000 sq. mi.; population: 55 million

Honan temporarily ceded its section north of the Yellow River to the short-lived province of Pingyüan from 1949 to 1952 but was then restored to its pre-1949 area and had a population of 44.2 million in the census of June, 1953. In minor boundary adjustments with Shantung during the 1960's, Honan gave up Tungming on the south bank of the Yellow River late in 1962, and acquired Fanhsien on the north bank late in 1964.

The eastern half of Honan, both north and south of the Yellow River, is an integral part of the North China plain, with the typical winter wheat and kaoliang crop association. In both sown area and output, Honan is China's leading producer of wheat, which occupies 35 per cent of the total cultivated acreage in the province. Soybeans are also a significant crop, in the eastern part of the province. Among the principal industrial crops are cotton, which is cultivated throughout the province, and tobacco, which is concentrated around Hsüchang in central Honan. Among the oilseeds, sesame does well in the Hwai Ho basin in the southeast, and peanuts favor the sandy soils near the Yellow River in the northeast.

In the western part of Honan, the easternmost mountains of the Tsin Ling system reach elevations up to 6,000 feet in the Funiu Mountains. This hilly region, where the sown area is greatly reduced and settlement is sparse, stands in sharp contrast to the intensively cultivated plains of the province. However, the mountains perform a useful function in sheltering part of Honan from the cold northwesterly winter monsoon. This sheltered area, centered on Nanyang in the southwestern part of Honan, has an agriculture similar to the rice-wheat association of the Middle Yangtze plain. In this southward-oriented area, rice, wild silk, and the cultivation of sesame play an increasing role in the rural economy. Although Nanyang is linked by railroads with the rest of Honan, its natural outlet is the Han Shui, major tributary of the Yangtze in the south.

River-reclamation work in Honan has been concerned with regulation of the Yellow River and the Hwai Ho system. Work along the Yellow River has included the strengthening of dikes that contain the stream at a level above the surrounding countryside and the construction of the People's Vic-tory Canal. This 30-mile-long canal links the Yellow River north of Cheng-chow with the Wei Ho at Sinsiang. The canal, which runs parallel to the Peking-Hankow railroad, was completed in 1953. A combined navigation and irrigation project, the new waterway diverts Yellow River water to the shallow Wei Ho and supplies a system of irrigation ditches between Sinsiang and the Yellow River. The raised water-level has made the Wei Ho navigable for 100-ton junks from Sinsiang to Tientsin.

The ambitious flood-control program for the Yellow River announced in the middle 1950's provided for construction of the Sanmensia ("three-gate-gorge") hydroelectric dam on the Honan-Shansi border, at a point where two islands split the flow of the Yellow River into three channels. The dam, to be built between 1957 and 1961, was expected to have a capacity of 1 million kilowatts and to reduce the maximum flood stage from 37,000 cubic meters to 8,000 cubic meters a second. Construction began during the winter 1956–57, and the new town of Sanmensia at the dam site was inaugurated in March, 1957. The flow of the Yellow River was diverted temporarily from the site in 1958, and concrete pouring began in the spring of 1959. However, the failure of the Great Leap and the departure of Soviet advisers prevented completion of the project. The first of eight planned 137,500-kilowatt generating units, which was delivered in 1960, before the cessation of Soviet aid, was reported to have been installed by 1963, but no power production is believed to have been started. Another major Yellow River project, the Taohwayü diversion dam near Chengchow, also remains to be realized. It was designed to increase the irrigated area north and south of the river and to open the lower course to navigation by 500-ton junks.

In the Hwai Ho system, work has continued for several years on the construction of detention reservoirs in the headwaters of the Hwai Ho and its tributaries. These reservoirs have been built roughly along a north-south line west of the Peking-Hankow railroad. Five projects have been completed thus far in this zone. They are, from north to south, the reservoirs of Paisha (1952), Shihmantan (1951), Pankiao (1952), Pushan (1954), and Nanwan (1955).

Coal is the province's principal mineral resource, with deposits continuing south from Hopei along the east foot of the Taihang Mountains. Like their northern neighbors, the Honan deposits are linked by spurs to the main Peking-Hankow railroad. Until the late 1950's, the principal producer was the anthracite-mining complex of Tsiaotso, on a railroad spur west of Sinsiang. The Tsiaotso mines, dating from the beginning of the twentieth century, have been expanded and are believed to yield more than 5 million tons of anthracite a year. Established at first as a special industrial-mining district, Tsiaotso was raised to the status of city in 1956, reflecting its increased economic significance.

Two other major coal-mining centers, each producing coking-grade bituminous coal, have been developed in Honan since the late 1950's. Hopi, in northernmost Honan, arose in 1957 on the site of a small, primitive operation in a deposit of lean coal, low in volatile content. A city was established in that year, and the mining complex was linked by a 12-mile rail spur with Tangyin, on the main Peking-Hankow line. Five mines with a combined capacity of about 3 million tons are believed to be in operation at Hopi. Pingtingshan, the other new coal-mining city, was developed from scratch on a deposit of fat coal, high in volatile matter, in the eastern outliers of the Funiu Mountains in central Honan. Here, too, a city was founded in 1957, and the growing mining complex was linked by a 38-mile railroad with the junction of Mengmiao, on the main line just north of the regional center of Loho. The coal seams in the Pingtingshan area are at depths of less than 1,500 feet, reach 50 feet in thickness, and extend over a distance of about 50 miles. Beginning in the late 1950's and continuing through the 1960's, a series of mines was constructed at Pingtingshan, making it Honan's leading coal producer and a significant supplier of coking coal for the Wuhan iron and steel industry. Annual production is believed to be less than 10 million tons a year. Two lesser coal mines are the Sinmi mine at Mihsien, on a rail spur from Sincheng, and the Yilo mine at Yiyang, on a 14-mile rail spur southwest of the industrial city of Loyang. At both the Sinmi and the Yilo complexes, new mining capacity was added in the early 1960's.

Honan's coal production, pending completion of the dormant Sanmensia hydroelectric project, is the principal source of industrial power for the province's growing manufacturing cities. A 110- and 220-kilovolt grid links thermal-power stations at Chengchow, Loyang, Kaifeng, and Sinsiang. These and other urban centers are situated along the two main rail lines intersecting at Chengchow: the east-west Lung-Hai railroad and the Peking-Hankow line.

The dominant urban center (Table 34) is Chengchow, capital of the

TABLE 34
CITIES OF HONAN

City	City Level	Function	Population (in thousands)		
			1953	1957	1970 est.
Chengchow	subprovince	manuf.	595	766	1,100
Loyang	subprovince	manuf.	171	500	
Kaifeng	subprovince	manuf.	299	320	
Shangkiu	hsien	trade	134		
Sanmensia	hsien	hydro project (dormant)			
Anyang	hsien	manuf.	125		
Hopi	hsien	coal			
Sinsiang	hsien	manuf.	171		
Tsiaotso	hsien	coal			
Hsüchang	hsien	trade	58		
Loho	hsien	trade			
Pingtingshan	hsien	coal			
Sinyang	hsien	trade			
Nanyang	hsien	trade			

Former Cities	Period	Disposition
Chowkow	1953–58	now Shangshui hsien seat
Chumatien	1953–58	now town in Kioshan hsien

province since it succeeded Kaifeng in 1954. Chengchow owed its growth originally to location at the intersection of two of China's main trunk railroads. It developed as a marketing city for the agricultural output (cotton, wheat) of central Honan. Because of its situation in the heart of China's cotton belt, the availability of manpower, and transport routes, Chengchow was one of the inland cities earmarked in the early 1950's for industrial development with emphasis on textiles and processed foods. The city has four cotton mills, with a combined capacity of more than 400,000 spindles and 15,000 looms, and two textile-machine plants, completed in 1950 and 1958. The food-processing industry includes a large flour mill and an oil-and-fats factory. New industrial construction, mainly in the western and northern outskirts, led to a rapid population increase from 595,000 in 1953, to 766,000 in 1957, and to 1.1 million in the late 1960's. Reconstruction of the Yellow River bridge, north of the city, in 1960 further strengthened the Chengchow transport position.

Other urban centers along the Lung-Hai railroad are Kaifeng, Loyang, and Shangkiu. Kaifeng, Honan's former capital, is one of China's oldest cities. It was China's capital for more than 200 years under the so-called Five Dynasties (907–960) and the Northern Sung Dynasty (960–1127). It owed its political importance to its central position in the North China plain and to good water communications with the southeast. The city gradually lost its economic importance as the waterways silted up and the Yellow River presented an increasing flood threat. With the rise of Chengchow in the twentieth century, economic activities slowly shifted to the new rail hub, and this movement culminated with the transfer of the provincial capital in 1954. In the census of 1953, Kaifeng had a population of 299,000 compared with Chengchow's 595,000. Since then, Kaifeng has undergone a rebirth, with the construction of an agricultural machinery plant and the opening of a nitrogen fertilizer plant, which went into operation in 1964. Hydrogen for ammonia synthesis is obtained presumably from Honan's coal resources by the water-gas reaction, in which air and then steam are blown over red-hot coke or coal. Kaifeng is also reported to have a zinc-smelter using the distillation process in which coal or coke is employed as a reducing agent.

At the western end of this central Honan industrial district, another of China's ancient capitals, Loyang, has passed through a renaissance. The center of a small agricultural area irrigated by the Lo Ho, a right tributary of the Yellow River, Loyang was China's capital even before Kaifeng, under the Chou Dynasty (770–255 B.C.) and the Eastern Han Dynasty (A.D. 25–221). Loyang was eclipsed as a political center after the tenth century by Kaifeng. For centuries, it remained a sleepy agricultural town, frequented occasionally by tourists who came to see nearby tombs and ruins that bore witness to the city's former greatness. In 1955, Loyang was rudely awakened when it was chosen as another of China's inland manufacturing centers. In contrast to the textile and food-processing orientation of Chengchow,

Loyang was to become a machine-manufacturing city, relying on the power potential of the Sanmensia hydroelectric project. In rapid succession, several major plants were inaugurated in the late 1950's, manufacturing ball bearings (1957), mining equipment and other heavy machinery (1958), and tractors (1959). Loyang also produces cement and refractory materials. Instead of the cheap power from the Sanmensia project, the city's industries were forced to rely on local thermal-power stations that burn coal from the Yilo mine at Yiyang, southwest of Loyang. The industrial development program raised the city's population from 171,000 in 1953 to more than 500,-000 by the end of the decade.

Shangkiu, in eastern Honan, is another urban center on the Lung-Hai railroad, with predominantly trade and distribution functions. With a population of 134,000 in the 1953 census, Shangkiu serves not only the immediate vicinity within Honan itself, but also adjoining portions of western Shantung, to the north, and of northwestern Anhwei, to the south and east.

Elsewhere in Honan, major urban centers are aligned along the Peking-Hankow railroad. North of the Yellow River are the cities of Anyang and Sinsiang, each associated with a nearby coal-mining complex. Anyang is a local agricultural trade center, long known for excavations of artifacts dating from the Shang (Yin) Dynasty (1766–1122 B.C.). Nearby is the coal city of Hopi. In the Great Leap, Anyang acquired a small iron and steel complex, with a capacity of 100,000 to 200,000 tons, based on Hopi coking coal and local iron reserves. Sinsiang, farther south, is a transportation hub at the crossing of the Peking-Hankow line and the navigable Wei Ho. From here, a railroad leads west to the coal-mining center of Tsiaotso and, since 1961, beyond to Changchih, center of the Luan coal basin in southeast Shansi. Before World War II, another spur extended northeast from Sinsiang to Taokow, then head of navigation on the Wei Ho. The railroad was destroyed during the war and, because of improved shipping conditions on the Wei Ho, was not rebuilt. Sinsiang's industrial base, limited in the past to textiles and food products, was expanded in the early 1960's with construction of a cement plant of 70,000-ton capacity (opened in 1964). A viscose rayon plant, using cotton linters as raw material, was inaugurated in the same year in Sinsiang's northern suburb of Luwangfen. The city was the capital of the short-lived province of Pingyüan (1949–52) and had a population of 171,000 in the 1953 census.

South of the Yellow River, along the railroad leading from Chengchow toward Hankow, are four regional centers that serve the surrounding farming areas. They are, from north to south, Hsüchang, Loho, Chumatien, and Sinyang. Hsüchang, with a population of 58,000 in 1953, is the center of Honan's most important tobacco-growing district. Its regional significance was enhanced in 1968 with the reported completion of a 60-mile rail spur eastward to Taikang on the Kwo Ho, a left tributary of the Hwai Ho. Hsüchang also serves as an outlet for southwestern Honan and its regional center of Nanyang, with which Hsüchang is connected by a highway. But this function is likely to be taken over increasingly by Loho, from which a railroad to Nanyang was reported to have been completed in 1969. Loho, a railroad town with a light-bulb factory, has superseded in its regional trade the older hsien town of Yencheng, just northwest, across the Sha Ho, a headstream of the Ying Ho. The railroad junction of Mengmiao, from which a rail spur leads west to the important coking coal mines of Pingtingshan, is just north of Loho. Chumatien, the next regional center, was a city from 1953 to 1958 but lost its municipal status apparently because of a lag in industrial development. Finally, Sinyang is the economic center of southern-most Honan, where the growing significance of rice reflects the proximity of the Middle Yangtze valley.

Two Honan regional centers are situated at some distance from the main rail lines. They are Nanyang and Shangshui. Nanyang is the main city of the southwestern part of Honan, with wheat, coarse grain, and sesame cultivation. Until 1969, when the city's transport situation was improved by completion of a railroad to Loho, it was dependent on a highway from Hsüchang and on waterways leading to Siangfan in northwest Hupei. Nanyang became a city in 1953, when it had a population of more than 50,000. Shangshui, east of Loho, was long the head of navigation for junks on the Ying Ho, major tributary of the Hwai Ho. The construction of flood-control reservoirs in the upper reaches improved shipping conditions in the 1950's, shifting the navigation head to Loho and resulting in a decline of the trade of Shangshui. This town was known as Chowkiakow before 1950, when it was re-named Chowkow. It had the status of city from 1953 until 1958, when it was demoted and became the hsien seat of Shangshui.

SHANTUNG PROVINCE
Capital: Tsinan; area: 60,000 sq. mi.; population: 60 million

Shantung, like Honan, temporarily gave up part of its territory in 1949 to form the short-lived province of Pingyüan, which lasted until 1952. Shantung was then restored to its pre-1949 area, within which the 1953 census recorded a population of 48.9 million. In minor boundary adjustments with Honan in the 1960's, Shantung gained the hsien of Tungming, on the south bank of the Yellow River, in late 1962, and two years later gave up Fan-hsien, on the north bank.

Shantung Province is about evenly divided between mountains and plains. Lowlands are found along the western border, which is an integral part of the North China plain, and along the Kiaolai corridor, which bisects the peninsula between the two upland masses. The higher western upland, dominated by the Tai Shan, is well inland, while the lower eastern upland forms the Shantung promontory proper.

Shantung has the winter wheat—kaoliang crop association typical of the North China plain. Winter wheat and soybeans are the principal food crops, with wheat accounting for more than 30 per cent of the acreage in food crops, and soybeans 15 to 20 per cent. Both crops are found throughout the province, with soybeans planted in the early summer after the wheat harvest. The principal spring grains are kaoliang, which is generally grown in moister areas, and foxtail millet in drier sections. Cotton and peanuts share the area in industrial crops, with cotton doing best in the calcareous alluvial soils of the Yellow River plain in the northwest, and peanuts favoring light, sandy soils in the uplands. Shantung accounts for about one-half of China's peanut production.

The Shantung peninsula is known for the cultivation of the wild silkworm, which feeds on oak leaves. The wild silk is spun and woven into a thin, soft fabric of yellow-brown silk known as pongee. The best-known wild silk centers are Laiyang, Sisia, Wenteng, and Haiyang, all in the eastern uplands of the Shantung promontory. Chefoo has long been noted as the shipping port for wild silk. Tobacco also favors sandy soils, such as are found near Weifang, and Shantung produces about 20 per cent of China's tobacco. Finally, fruits are a Shantung specialty. Best known are the peaches of Feicheng, pears of Laiyang, persimmons of Taian, and grapes of Tsimo. Fruits are generally exported via Chefoo and Tsingtao.

While richly endowed with agricultural production, Shantung is also a major mineral province. It has been one of China's most important coal producers, with deposits situated along the northern and southwestern margins of the Tai Shan uplands. The northern fields are served by the Tsinan-Tsingtao railroad, and the southwestern fields by spurs of the Tientsin-Pukow railroad. Two major coal basins have given rise to cities at the subprovincial level—Tzepo and Tsaochwang. Two other coal-producing centers, Weifang and Sinwen, are of lesser significance.

The development of the Tzepo coal basin dates from the period of German control of Shantung before World War I. The rank of the Tzepo coals varies from semibituminous in the south, where part of the coal is of coking grade, to semi-anthracite in the north. The coals are relatively low in ash and sulfur and are used mainly as steam-raisers. The Tzepo basin is named for two mining cities, Tzechwan and Poshan, situated on a spur extending south from the junction of Changtien on the Tsingtao-Tsinan railroad. From 1950 to 1954, the Tzepo district included two cities: on the rail spur, the coal-mining center of Tzepo (1953 population: 184,000), with its administrative seat at Poshan; and, on the main line, the trade and light-industry city of Changchow, with its seat at Changtien junction and including the town of Chowtsun, just to the west. In 1954, the two cities were combined in an enlarged Tzepo municipal district, with a 1957 population of 806,000, and its administrative seat was moved from Poshan to Changtien in 1961. In addition to its coal production, estimated at up to 10 million tons a year, Tzepo has a developed refractory material industry, diversified manufacturing, and, at Changtien, a major thermal-power station burning local coal. Just west of the Tzepo basin is the smaller Changkiu coal deposit, now largely depleted.

The other major coal-mining city of Shantung is Tsaochwang, in the southern section of the province, adjoining Kiangsu. The mines are reached by a 20-mile rail spur running east from the junction of Siehcheng (formerly called Lincheng). The Tsaochwang mining complex also dates from before World War I, having arisen in conjunction with the construction of the Tientsin-Pukow railroad. The mines were destroyed during the civil war after World War II and were inoperative until the middle 1950's, when redevelopment began. In early 1960, Tsaochwang was raised to the status of city, suggesting the growing significance of its output. In contrast to the Tzepo deposit, Tsaochwang coal is of coking quality, and annual production is estimated as high as 10 million tons.

The lesser coal-mining center of Sinwen, north of Tsaochwang, is on another spur of the Tientsin-Pukow railroad, running east from Tzeyao junction. The development of the Sinwen mine began in World War II when the rail spur was constructed. Because of the coking quality of Sinwen coal, the operation began to be expanded in the late 1950's and the mining town was given the status of city in 1960. Development apparently did not meet expectations, for municipal status was abolished in early 1965, and Sinwen was demoted to a hsien seat. Coal is also produced in small amounts at Fangtze, a mining suburb south of the regional center of Weifang on the Tsinan-Tsingtao railroad. Fangtze coal, high in ash and noncoking, is used mainly as a local power-station fuel.

Other than coal, Shantung has deposits of iron ore, gold, alunite, kaolin. The iron mine is situated at Tiehshan ("iron mountain") on a short northern spur leaving the Tsinan-Tsingtao railroad at Kinlingchen. This deposit is a contact metamorphic ore body of magnetite-hematite. It has been mined intermittently since 1919. The iron content is 55 per cent, and the ore is nonphosphoric and self-fluxing. The deposit was one of China's ancient iron-smelting centers. Gold is found in small scattered deposits in the eastern uplands, notably at Chaoyüan and Pingtu. Finally, alunite and kaolin are associated with the coal measures of the Tzepo field. They are used in the manufacture of ceramic and refractory products at Tzepo. Since the late 1950's, the higher-grade alumina-bearing materials have apparently also been used as a source of alumina for aluminum reduction.

In the early 1960's, petroleum was reported to have been struck in the so-called Shengli ("victory") field in the Yellow River delta area of northern Shantung, where oil-bearing formations are believed to extend into the offshore shelf. The field is said to be producing perhaps 500,000 tons a year. A petrochemical plant was reported to be operating at Tzepo in 1970.

Except for the ports along the Shantung peninsula, the province's main urban centers (Table 35) have gravitated to the two main rail lines: the Tientsin-Pukow line, crossing the western part of Shantung from north to south, and the Tsinan-Tsingtao line, which links the two largest cities.

Inland rail communications are supplemented by coastwise shipping around the peninsula, but inland waterways, as in the rest of the North China plain, are quite inadequate. The only waterways accessible for junks

TABLE 35

CITIES OF SHANTUNG

City	City Level	Function	Population (*in thousands*)		
			1953	1957	1970 est.
Tsingtao	subprovincial	port, manuf.	917	1,121	
Tsinan	subprovincial	manuf.	680	862	
Tzepo	subprovincial	coal	184	806*	
Tsaochwang	subprovincial	coal			
Weifang	hsien	trade	149		
Chefoo (Yentai)	hsien	port	116		
Weihai	hsien	port			
Tehchow	hsien	trade			
Tsining	hsien	trade	86		

Former Cities	*Period*
Lintsing	1954–63
Taian	1958–63
Lini	1958–63
Liaocheng	1958–63
Hotseh	1960–63
Sinwen	1960–65

* Within expanded boundaries.

are a segment of the Yellow River, from Lokow, the river port of Tsinan, downstream to Litsing, and the Siaotsing River, an arm of the Yellow River delta, which is navigable from Tsinan to the small coastal trade port of Yangkiokow on Laichow Bay of the Po Hai. The Yellow River delta is not navigable below Lintsing because of shallows and silting. The Grand Canal, which crosses the western part of the province from north to south, appears to have been silted up and is used only north of Lintsing, where it joins the Wei Ho, and south of Tsining, where the water level of the canal is maintained by a series of lakes called Nanyang, Tushan, Chaoyang, and Weishan.

Tsingtao, the province's largest city, is the product of Western colonization in China. Ceded to Germany in 1898 as part of the Kiaochow lease, it developed first under German rule and, after 1914, under the Japanese, before it was surrendered to China in 1924. It is one of China's best ports, with a sheltered deep-water harbor at the entrance of Kiaochow Bay. The larger of two ship basins is enclosed by a 2.5-mile-long circular mole and accommodates ships of 30-foot draft. The smaller basin is suitable for coastwise junks. Tsingtao's industries include textiles, automobile tires, flour, vegetable oils, and paper. Heavy industry is concentrated in the northern industrial suburbs of Szefang (locomotive works) and Tsangkow (cement). The population of Tsingtao was 917,000 in 1953 and 1.1 million in 1957. The municipal area goes far beyond the city proper and includes the entire peninsula east of Kiaochow Bay, an area of 300 square miles. In the municipal area rises Lao Shan, highest point of the eastern Shantung uplands, known both as a beach and a hill resort. Having good rail connections with the Shantung hinterland, Tsingtao is the principal maritime outlet for the province's peanuts and soybeans, or their byproducts, as well as coal.

At the other end of Shantung's east-west railroad lies Tsinan, the second largest provincial city. Unlike Tsingtao, Tsinan is an ancient Chinese city that flourished for centuries but one whose importance was greatly enhanced by railroad development. The provincial capital, it is situated on the lower Yellow River, an economic factor of dubious importance, and at the intersection of the Tientsin-Pukow and Tsinan-Tsingtao railroads. Tsinan is the agricultural processing center for western Shantung. Its economy is similar to that of Tsingtao—textiles, flour, vegetable oils. The city consists of the old walled town with scenic Taming Lake and the eastern commercial city. Lokow, the city's river port, is upstream head of navigation on the lower Yellow River and on its arm, the Siaotsing River, which is fed by Taming Lake. Tsinan's population was 680,000 in 1953 and 862,000 in 1957. Additional industrial development since the Great Leap included a small integrated iron and steel complex, machinery (agricultural equipment, machine tools, motor vehicles), and a large thermal-power station in the eastern suburb of Hwangtai.

Between the two termini of the Tsinan-Tsingtao railroad are the mining and industrial city of Tzepo (discussed earlier) and the regional center of Weifang, which serves a large agricultural region at the neck of the east Shantung peninsula. The city of Weifang, with a 1953 population of 149,-000, was formed by merger of Weihsien and the southern coal-mining suburb of Fangtze. It has processing industries for the wheat, tobacco, and peanuts grown in the surrounding area.

Shantung's ports, in addition to Tsingtao, are Chefoo, Weihai, and Lungkow. Chefoo, whose modern Chinese name is Yentai, was opened to foreign trade in 1858 but was never more than a port of local importance for lack of good hinterland communications. It had a population of 116,000 in 1953. Late in 1955, Chefoo was linked by a 114-mile rail branch with the Tsingtao main line. A small iron and steel plant was opened at Chefoo in 1967, with a capacity of about 10,000 tons. Weihai, formerly called Weihaiwei, stands on the site of a Ming Dynasty fort that gave the city its name (Weihaiwei means "awe-inspiring sea fort"). It was leased to Britain in 1898 and served as a British naval base until its return to China in 1930. Lungkow is of minor importance.

Other regional centers in western Shantung are Tehchow, a transportation hub on the Grand Canal–Wei Ho waterway and junction of the Tientsin-Pukow and Tehchow-Shihkiachwang railroads, and Tsining, navigation head for the southern section of the Grand Canal. Tsining, which had a population of 86,000 in 1953, is linked by a 20-mile spur with the Tientsin-Pukow railroad at Yenchow.

A number of regional centers were temporarily raised to the status of cities in the late 1950's and early 1960's but were again demoted to hsien in the absence of industrial growth. They are the Grand Canal towns of Lintsing and Liaocheng; the railroad town of Taian, south of Tsinan; Lini, regional center of southeast Shantung; and Hotseh, in the southwest near the Honan border.

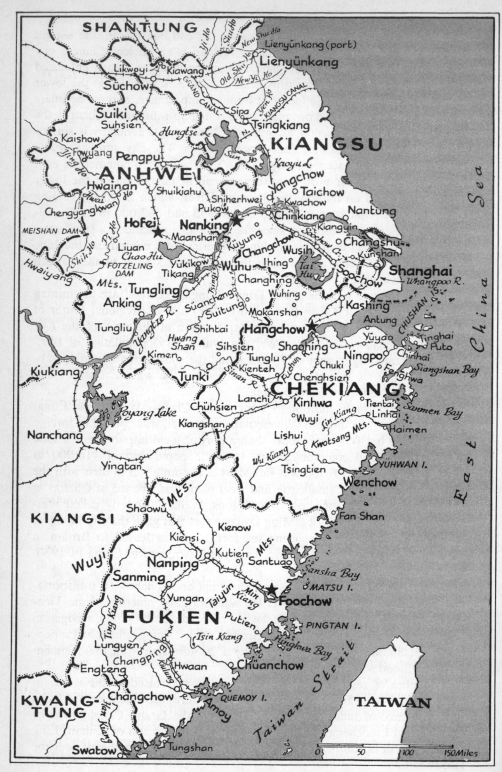

6. Lower Yangtze Plain and Southeast Coastal Uplands

5. The Lower Yangtze Plain

The Lower Yangtze plain includes the provinces of Anhwei and Kiangsu (with the independent city of Shanghai). The combined area of these two provinces is about 95,000 square miles, or 2.5 per cent of all China. Their total population in 1970 was about 100 million, or 13 per cent of the entire nation. The average density of 1,000 persons per square mile exceeds even that of the North China plain.

The region lies on the shore of the Yellow Sea, on both sides of the lower Yangtze River and the Hwai Ho. Unlike the North China plain, it is not sharply delimited by natural features; in fact, it may in part be regarded as a southeastern extension of the northern lowland. Only in the southwest do hill ranges separate the Lower Yangtze plain from the Middle Yangtze plain. Except for occasional hilly sections, the Lower Yangtze plain is an alluvial lowland laid down by the rivers over long ages. It can be divided roughly into three subregions: the Kiangnan plain, the Yangtze–Hwai Ho lowland, and the Wuhu plain.

Kiangnan means "south of the [Yangtze] river" and refers to the triangular delta plain south of the river's estuary. The river once emptied into the ocean above Chinkiang, but the steady accumulation of sediments, of which the Yangtze carries 600 million tons a year, has pushed the delta plain steadily eastward at the rate of one mile every sixty to seventy years. The plain is now crisscrossed by a maze of canals and dotted by a large number of shallow lakes and ponds, of which Tai Hu is the largest. This is one of China's most densely settled industrial and agricultural areas, with the metropolitan centers of Shanghai, Soochow, Wusih, and Chinkiang.

The Yangtze–Hwai Ho lowland north of the Yangtze estuary is the product of deposition of the Yangtze River and the Hwai Ho. The Hwai Ho once had its own outlet to the sea, but in 1194, during one of the periodic course shifts of the Yellow River, this stream usurped the lower course of the Hwai Ho and gradually filled its outlet with sediment. In backing up, the Hwai Ho formed Hungtse Lake, a natural flow-equalizing reservoir, from which it sought outlets via the San Ho and the Grand Canal to the Yangtze and, via constantly shifting channels, directly to the sea. In times of flood, these waterways were unable to contain the rising volume of water, burst their dikes and flooded the surrounding countryside. This is the area where work has been under way since World War II to regulate the Hwai Ho system. The most significant projects thus far have been the North Kiangsu Irrigation Trunk Canal, a new outlet for the Hwai Ho, extending from Hungtse Lake at Kaoliangkien 105 miles northeast to the sea at Pientankang, and the San Ho dam, which regulates the San Ho outlet of Hungtse Lake. The new outlet was completed in 1952, and the San Ho dam in 1953.

In the northernmost part of the Hwai Ho lowland, on the Kiangsu-Shantung border, flood prevention has also been the object of the Yi-Shu project. The Yi Ho and the Shu Ho descend in virtually parallel courses from the Shantung uplands and have often caused floods in northernmost Kiangsu for lack of direct outlets to the sea. Starting soon after 1949, new outlets were built for both rivers directly to the Yellow Sea. The basic work was completed in 1952.

The construction of the North Kiangsu Canal outlet for the Hwai Ho did not entirely resolve the problem of draining flood waters and supplying water to areas in need of irrigation. This led to the concept of building a second new outlet for the Hwai Ho, running from Lake Hungtse northward through a new 120-mile-long channel to the Yellow Sea in the area of Lienyünkang. Such an outlet would ease the drainage load on the North Kiangsu Canal and, at the same time, improve the irrigation of the northernmost section of the province. Construction on the Hwai Ho outlet toward Lienyünkang does not appear to have been started.

The Wuhu plain is formed by Yangtze sediments in a hill-enclosed basin between the Hwang Shan on the south bank of the Yangtze and the Hwai-yang Mountains on the north bank. The northern hills are the easternmost outliers of the central mountain belt and rarely exceed 500 feet in elevation. In the south, the hills are higher, rising to 5,600 feet in the Hwang Shan. Along the Anhwei-Chekiang border, the Tienmu Mountains are the result of volcanic activity and consist largely of black basalt. Nanking, Wuhu, and Anking are the chief cities of the Wuhu plain.

The Lower Yangtze plain is traversed from west to east by the Yangtze River. The river enters the region at Tungliu from its middle plain, flows in a wide, meandering course northeast to Nanking, and turns east a short distance to Chinkiang where the true delta begins. The Yangtze receives no major tributaries throughout the lower plain but is connected by a dense network of minor waterways with both the Hwai Ho system in the north and the Tai Hu system in the south. The Hwai Ho traverses the northern part of the region, generally in an east-northeasterly direction, and receives a number of tributaries, chiefly on the left. The lake Tai Hu is the center of a complex system of lakes and small canals serving the Kiangnan lowland. The chief waterways here are the Kiangnan Canal, the southernmost section of the Grand Canal, Soochow Creek, and the Whangpoo River.

Like the North China plain, the Lower Yangtze plain is dominated climatically by the interplay of Tropical Maritime air masses, which dominate in the summer, and Polar Continental air in the winter. However, because of the more southeasterly position of the Yangtze plain, its climate is more distinctly influenced by summer monsoon conditions than by the cold, dry winter monsoon. The average July temperatures are approximately the same as in the North China plain—about 80° F (27° C)—because of the north-south alignment of the summer isotherms. But the more southerly situation of the region accounts for higher January temperatures of about 35° F (2° C). As in the case of the northern plain, continentality increases inland, with hotter summers and somewhat cooler winters.

A variety of factors combine to produce more or less uniform rainfall distribution throughout the year, certainly the most uniform distribution anywhere in eastern China. The average annual precipitation is 45 inches, almost twice as much as in the northern plain. Moreover, although there is a definite summer maximum, only about 40 per cent of the rainfall comes in the three summer months June through August. The relatively regular annual rainfall distribution results from the combination of the monsoon rains in the spring, cyclonic storms in the summer and winter, and typhoons in the fall.

Three major soil types may be distinguished in the Lower Yangtze plain. The northernmost parts of Anhwei and Kiangsu, which are actually an extension of the North China plain, have calcareous alluvial soils. The middle Hwai Ho valley in Anhwei and the Yangtze valley proper also have alluvial soils, but these are noncalcareous, partly because of the nonloessial character of the rivers' source regions, partly because of greater leaching of the soil. Finally, the hills north and south of the Yangtze River are characterized by leached forest soils, either podzolic types, as in north central Anhwei, or red lateritic soils, as in the southern Anhwei uplands.

The Lower Yangtze plain is one of China's leading agricultural regions, with about 50 per cent of the total area under cultivation. Nowhere is farmland more intensively utilized. Virtually all the land is in crops, with the exceptions of the uplands in southern and central Anhwei and the large area occupied by lakes. Because of the high rural population density, many hands are available to till the land, and farming reaches a high intensity even by Chinese standards.

The region is part of three conventional agricultural divisions. The northernmost section, like the North China plain, belongs to the winter wheat–kaoliang area; the central section is taken up by the Yangtze rice-wheat area, while sheltered southernmost Anhwei is part of the rice-tea area. Rice and cotton are the common summer crops; wheat, barley, and oilseeds are grown in the winter; and tea and silk are distinctive specialty crops.

Summer rice and winter wheat are generally double-cropped throughout the Yangtze valley, with the chief production areas in the Wuhu plain of Anhwei and in the Tai Hu basin of southern Kiangsu around Wusih. Lesser food crops, used in part also as animal feed, are barley, soybeans, corn, and sweet potatoes.

The high rural population density and the abundance of manpower, as well as favorable climatic and soil conditions, have made the Kiangnan lowland of southern Kiangsu one of China's leading silk-producing areas. About 90 per cent of all farm households engage in the cultivation of mulberry trees and the breeding of silkworms. Two silk-production areas are of outstanding importance: the Tai Hu basin, with mills in Soochow and Wusih, and the Wuhu plain, with mills in Nanking, Chinkiang, and Süancheng.

Cotton is grown largely near the coast, where the calcareous alluvium is unsuitable for rice. The coastal alluvium is, moreover, sandy in texture, whereas rice prefers clay-pan soils that permit the fields to be kept flooded. Such sandy, calcareous alluvium is found in northern Kiangsu but also in a strip of the Kiangnan lowland west of Shanghai. There, in the Taitsang-Kunshan area, about 60 to 70 per cent of all land is under cotton. Shanghai is, of course, China's leading cotton-milling center. Nantung, on the north bank of the Yangtze, is known for a long-staple fiber of high quality.

Other crops are oilseeds, grown largely along the Shanghai-Soochow railroad between Kunshan and Soochow west of the cotton belt, and peanuts near the Shantung line in northern Kiangsu. Tea is associated specifically with the Tunki area in southern Anhwei.

The Lower Yangtze plain has long been known as a land of rice and fish. Fisheries abound in the multitude of shallow lakes and waterways, particularly in the lakes Tai Hu and Chao Hu and in the Yangtze estuary. Deepsea fishing activities are centered on the port of Lienyünkang in northern Kiangsu.

Minerals are of moderate importance in the regional economy, with coal, iron ore, pyrites (a sulfur source), and copper the principal products. Coal is mined chiefly at Hwainan and, since the Great Leap, at Suiki, southwest of Süchow. Other mines are at Kiawang, northeast of Süchow. The coal is bituminous and partly of coking quality. Iron ore, mined mainly at Maanshan, provides the basis for an integrated iron and steel industry. Maanshan produces principally pig iron for other steel mills (notably Shanghai) but has also turned out some steel since the Great Leap. Shanghai, which is China's second-ranking steel center (after Anshan), also acquired some pig-iron capacity in the late 1950's. The copper center at Tungling, on the south bank of the Yangtze River in Anhwei, produces blister copper for further electrolytic refining at Shanghai. The coastal salines of Kiangsu have long been important salt-producers, accounting for about 15 per cent of China's total output. The main producing area is the so-called Hwaipei district (north of the Hwai) centered on the port of Lienyünkang. The salt has traditionally gone primarily into food uses, but, with the growth of the chemical industry, a growing share (as much as one-fifth) has been employed as a raw material for the manufacture of sodium, chlorine, and their compounds.

The Lower Yangtze basin, particularly the Kiangnan triangle, has traditionally been China's leading area of light industry, notably cotton and silk textiles, processed foods, paper, and chemicals. These industries developed largely through the stimulus of foreign capital investments in association with a favorable seaboard location, a raw-material base and abundant manpower.

With growing emphasis on the development of heavy industry after 1949, the manufacture of industrial machinery and equipment has forged ahead of light industry, with the principal manufacturing centers at Shanghai, Wusih, and Changchow in Kiangsu, and at Hofei and Pengpu in Anhwei. The chemical industry also expanded, with a petrochemical specialization at Shanghai and a nitrogen and phosphate fertilizer industry at Nanking. The latter has also been promoted as a center of electronics.

The region's economic development was also favored by the establishment of a dense rail net. The most important lines connect Shanghai, Nanking, and Wuhu on the south bank of the Yangtze River. On the north bank are the Tientsin-Pukow railroad, with its Hwainan branch, and the easternmost section of the Lung-Hai line. The transportation net was greatly improved in 1969 with completion of a bridge across the Yangtze River at Nanking, providing for the first time a direct rail connection between the Tientsin-Pukow and Nanking-Shanghai railroads.

Water transportation centers on the great Yangtze artery, which is accessible to ocean-going vessels of 5,000 to 10,000 tons. Smaller vessels, up to a few hundred tons, can navigate the reconstructed Grand Canal and the lower Hwai Ho. A dense network of lesser waterways branching off from these basic transport routes is accessible to smaller junks. Shanghai, the focus of the entire Yangtze basin, is China's greatest seaport, handling a large share of the nation's coastal and foreign trade. A lesser port is Lien-yünkang, the seaside terminal of the Lung-Hai railroad.

The population of the Lower Yangtze plain is homogeneously Chinese but speaking several varieties of Mandarin as well as the Shanghai (Wu) dialect. The northern Mandarin is spoken in the northern section of the region that merges into the North China plain. The Lower Yangtze, or Nanking, form of Mandarin predominates in the central parts of Anhwei and Kiangsu. Closely associated with Mandarin is the Hweichow dialect, spoken by about 7 million people in the Tunki region of southernmost Anhwei. The Shanghai dialect, which is generally considered separate from the various forms of Mandarin, is the principal spoken language of the densely populated Kiangnan lowland of Kiangsu, south of the Yangtze River. Population density in this area rises to more than 1,000 per square mile. Other densely settled areas are in southwestern Kiangsu around Nanking and Chinkiang, and in the Yangtze valley of central Anhwei. The lowest population density —about 150 per square mile—is found in the southern uplands of Anhwei.

KIANGSU PROVINCE

Capital: Nanking; area: 40,000 sq. mi.; population: 51 million

SHANGHAI

Area: 2,200 sq. mi.; population: 10 million

After the Communist take-over in 1949, Kiangsu was administered as two separate units, North Kiangsu and South Kiangsu, separated by the Yangtze River. The province was reunited in November, 1952, at which time it reacquired territory briefly ceded to Shantung and Anhwei. The temporary partition of the province was an outgrowth of the civil war, during which the Communists had held the north bank of the Yangtze for a considerable time before the continued southward advance. The establishment of Communist institutions was therefore further advanced on the north bank than in the south. In view of the difference in existing conditions, the Peking regime found it expedient to administer the two parts of Kiangsu separately until conditions had been equalized. The area of Kiangsu was reduced by about 1,000 square miles in 1955 with the cession of two of the province's northwesternmost hsien—Siaohsien and Tangshan, both just west of Süchow —to Anhwei. The population involved in the transfer was 320,000, according to the 1953 census.

Kiangsu is almost entirely a lowland, except for low hills near the Anhwei border. It is in effect a southeasterly continuation of the North China plain, with similar topography, climate, and soils. Typical Yangtze valley conditions become dominant only in the southern part of the province. Less than one-third of Kiangsu is situated on the south bank of the Yangtze River, and the entire province is crisscrossed by waterways and dotted with lakes. Some of China's largest lakes are here: Hungtse and Kaoyu lakes, which are part of the Hwai Ho reclamation projects, and Tai Hu, on the Chekiang border in the south. The coast is low-lying and straight. Sandbanks offshore hinder navigation, and only in the Yangtze estuary and in the north at Lienyünkang can the coast be approached.

North of the Hwai Ho, winter wheat and summer kaoliang and millet are the chief grains, with cotton (in the Süchow area), corn, soybeans, sweet potatoes also grown in the summer. South of the Hwai Ho, winter wheat and barley and summer rice are the grains, and cotton, soybeans, and silk other key products. During the summer, rice is cultivated on clay pans formed from Yangtze River alluvium, while cotton favors the sandy, noncalcareous, and saline soils found near the coast. Winter wheat is sown on an average of 2.2 million hectares, with the average yield about 1.2 tons per hectare. Kiangsu thus accounts for more than 10 per cent of China's wheat output. In the summer, cotton covers 600,000 or more hectares, yielding about 20 per cent of China's cotton, while rice is sown in about 800,000 hectares, producing about 10 per cent of China's rice. Kiangsu contributes about one-tenth of China's total food-grain production.

Being largely alluvial in origin, Kiangsu is poor in hard-rock minerals. Coal is found at Kiawang (formerly called Kiakiawang) on a 10-mile rail spur north of Süchow on the Shantung border. This coal deposit is an extension of the Tsaochwang deposit farther north in Shantung and yields bituminous coking coal. In the late 1960's, coal deposits were said to have been discovered south of the Yangtze River, and development was reported in the so-called Sunan (southern Kiangsu) mining district, situated probably in the Ihing area. Iron ore is interstratified with coal measures in the north and has been mined in the past at Likwoyi, just northwest of Kiawang on the Tientsin-Pukow railroad. Salt is obtained along the coast, predominantly north of the Hwai Ho, in the special Hwaipei salt district near Lienyünkang. The salt has traditionally been shipped south along the Yen Ho to Sipa (near Tsingkiang) for marketing. In southern Kiangsu, nonmetallics are found near Küyung and Ihing. Küyung limestone is used for the production of cement at Lungtan, on the Yangtze halfway between Nanking and Chinkiang. Ihing clay, mined on the west shore of the lake Tai Hu, has furnished the basis for a ceramic handicraft industry at Ihing itself. One of China's largest phosphate rock deposits, Mienping, in hills near Lienyünkang, was expanded during the Great Leap, yielding both ground rock for direct application and concentrate for the production of superphosphate at Nanking.

Industrial centers (Table 36) are concentrated almost entirely south of the Yangtze River in the Kiangnan lowland. Cotton and silk mills, as well as food-processing plants, are typical of this area. The Kiangnan section is well served by railroads, in contrast to northern Kiangsu, where rail lines are entirely absent except for the Lung-Hai line in the extreme north.

Because of the absence of railroads, waterways play an important role in the transportation of northern Kiangsu. The chief north-south route is the Grand Canal, which was widened and deepened during a major reconstruction project that began during the Great Leap in 1958 and was completed in the early 1960's. Formerly navigable for vessels of about 50 tons deadweight, it can now handle barges of up to 600 tons in the 250-mile section between the Süchow area and the Yangtze River at Kwachow, opposite Chinkiang. The Yen Ho, between Lienyünkang and Tsingkiang, and the North Kiangsu Canal, between Lake Hungtse and the sea, are navigable for smaller junks.

South of the Yangtze, the chief waterways are the Whangpoo River, Soochow Creek, and the Kiangnan Canal section of the Grand Canal. The Kiangnan Canal was built about A.D. 600 from Chinkiang on the Yangtze to Hangchow in Chekiang. It was 200 miles long and about 150 feet wide. It is still navigable all year for small vessels. Silting has been a major problem in the northern part, and vessels, especially during the winter months, use the Wusih-Kiangyin cut-off canal to reach the Yangtze.

Kiangsu contains Shanghai, China's largest city, which is, however, politically independent of the province and comes directly under the jurisdiction of the central government. It is the largest city on the continent of

Asia and one of the largest in the world. In June, 1953, its population was 6.2 million within what was essentially an urbanized area of 350 square miles. But in 1958, in two successive annexations (in February and November), the entire eastern tip of the Kiangnan lowland and Chungming Island in the Yangtze estuary were incorporated in the Shanghai municipal area, adding 1,900 square miles and more than 3 million rural residents to its population. The total population of Shanghai municipality as of 1970 may thus be estimated at about 10 million, of which probably 7 million reside within the central urbanized area.

Shanghai was an unimportant coastal trading center until the mid-nineteenth century, when the Treaty of Nanking (1842) opened the port to foreign trade and abruptly projected it on the world stage. Its growth under the ensuing Western influence has been phenomenal. Its prosperity is also the result of its favorable geographical position near the Yangtze River estuary, the most important navigation artery along the entire China coast. Shanghai's hinterland covers more than 400,000 square miles and has a population of more than 300 million. This tremendous landward empire, combined with the large coastwise trade funneled into the port, has made Shanghai the natural seaward trade focus of central China.

The heart of the city is situated on a tidal flat on the left bank of the Whangpoo River at the mouth of Soochow Creek. Shanghai's commercial core is in the former International Settlement at the river confluence, where broad streets and handsome boulevards are lined by imposing buildings. Here are the thoroughfares historically known as The Bund (along the waterfront) and Nanking Road. The business section is bounded east by the Whangpoo, south by the old Chinese inner city, west by the former hippodrome, now a public park, and north by Soochow Creek. Across Soochow Creek is the industrial section of Hongkew; across the Whangpoo is the right-bank industrial suburb of Pootung. Residential sections surrounding the business center on the southwest and north include the former French Concession and the workers' suburb of Chapei. With growing industrialization, particularly during the 1950's and 1960's, the urbanized area has spread on both sides of the Whangpoo toward its mouth at Woosung on the Yangtze River, as well as toward the northwest, west, and southwest along the rail lines to Soochow and Hangchow.

The city proper is situated about 15 miles from the Yangtze River. Shipping along the Whangpoo has been maintained in the past only through laborious dredging, and a channel of about 30 feet in depth has been provided. Another major obstacle to navigation is presented by enormous sand bars in the Yangtze itself—the Shen Tan (Fairy Flats), situated about 20 miles southeast of Woosung in the Yangtze estuary. A low-water depth of only 18 feet has forced large ships to wait for high tide at that point.

Except for local cotton and silk resources, Shanghai does not owe its economic dominance to a local raw material basis. In fact, its industry has been dependent largely on imported materials. Nearly half of China's imports and exports passed through Shanghai normally before 1949. The chief exports were raw silk, tea, tung oil, eggs, hog bristles, and ores. Imports consisted largely of manufactured goods, food, cotton and woolen goods, petroleum, steel, and chemicals. After 1949, the import of food and consumer goods was greatly curtailed in accordance with the economic policy of the Communists.

In the past, Shanghai has concentrated about one-third of China's industries, fixed industrial capital, and industrial labor force. This proportion declined during the 1950's as new interior areas were being industrialized and China's trade and general economic development were reoriented toward the Soviet Union. However, with increasing coolness between the two countries in the following decade, Shanghai's position was again enhanced as economic development in the old industrialized coastal areas and overseas trade resumed significance for China.

In many ways, Shanghai's position after 1949 can be compared to Leningrad's role after the Bolshevik Revolution in the Soviet Union. Long supplied by foreign raw materials, Shanghai has increasingly looked landward for resources. A large part of its pig iron, for example, is shipped from Maanshan in Anhwei. Like Leningrad, Shanghai has retained its industrial leadership through the presence of a large skilled labor force. To this day, both Leningrad and Shanghai are the only producers of certain specialty products required by the Soviet and Chinese economies.

Shanghai's industrial structure underwent significant change in the 1950's and 1960's as the former importance of the city's textile industry declined, and priority was given to the development of heavy industry, including iron and steel, chemicals, and machine-building. The share of textile industries in the total industrial output declined from 62 per cent in 1949 to 33 per cent in 1958, while heavy industry rose from 17 per cent to 46 per cent. Other light industry, including apparel and food-processing, accounted for about 20 per cent. Although cotton and other textile industries no longer dominate the Shanghai economy as they did before 1949, they still preserve the city's position as China's largest textile producer. In addition to cotton, wool, and natural silk, the Shanghai mills also use synthetic fibers produced by the city's growing chemical industry.

The most significant development in heavy industry after 1949 was the rise of a large iron and steel industry that made Shanghai the second largest steel producer of China, after Anshan and ahead of the new iron and steel centers of Wuhan and Paotow in the interior. At first, Shanghai produced only steel, using both scrap and long-haul pig iron shipped from Anshan and from Maanshan in nearby Anhwei. By 1957, the city was producing 500,000 tons of steel a year. During the Great Leap, a major expansion program added both new steel-making capacity and Shanghai's first blast furnaces to convert the city into an integrated iron and steel complex. Of four planned medium-size blast furnaces, with a combined capacity of 500,000 tons of pig iron a year, two were completed in 1959. However, with steel production estimated at about 2 million tons a year after the expansion, Shanghai still remains dependent on outside pig iron. Most of the new iron and steel industry is situated at Woosung, west of the mouth of the Whangpoo on the Yangtze. In addition to iron and steel, Shanghai also produces ferroalloys, electrolytic copper, and rare metals.

Shanghai's diversified chemical industry, built up mainly in the 1960's, added a wide range of petrochemicals to the earlier specialization in dyes (for the textile industry) and pharmaceuticals. The petrochemical complex, opened in 1965 at Kaokiao, east of the mouth of the Whangpoo River on the Yangtze, uses byproduct gases of the Shanghai oil refinery. The refinery has processed a variety of crude oils from China's far-flung fields but, since the early 1960's, mainly from the Taching field of Manchuria. The petrochemical industry produces raw materials and intermediates for fibers, plastics, and other synthetic end-products. In addition to industrial chemicals, including acids and alkalies, Shanghai also contributes nitrogen fertilizers from an ammonia-based chemical plant that went into operation in 1963.

Most important in the machinery field is the manufacture of electrical equipment (steam turbines, electric motors), heavy machinery, machine tools, and motor vehicles. The Kiangnan shipyard is one of China's leading shipbuilding and repair establishments. Some of the machinery industries are situated at Minhang, a new southern suburb, linked by a 26-mile rail spur with Shanghai. Cement and glass works support the construction program both in the Shanghai area and elsewhere.

In keeping with its level of industrial production, Shanghai is one of China's leading electric-power producers, with three major thermal stations. They are the Yangshupu plant, dating from before 1949 and expanded to more than 200,000 kilowatts; the Chapei station, also an old installation that was renovated and expanded to more than 100,000 kilowatts; and the Wuching heat and power plant, associated with the nitrogen-fertilizer complex. The Wuching plant was inaugurated in 1959 and is also in the 100,000-kilowatt class. The Shanghai power complex is also a key element in a power grid that links the city with Chekiang, Kiangsu, and Anhwei provinces. A 220-kilovolt transmission line feeds power from the Sinan River hydroelectric station to Shanghai. Another line links Shanghai via two intermediate thermal-power stations, at Wangting and Chishuyen, with Nanking and Wuhu, where it connects with a 220-kilovolt transmission line from the power plant at Hwainan.

Virtually all the leading cities (Table 36) of southern Kiangsu are situated along the Shanghai-Nanking railroad. First along this trunk line is Soochow, a silk-milling center with a population of 474,000 in 1953, and 633,000 in 1957. Soochow is situated east of the lake Tai Hu, on the Grand Canal, and near Soochow Creek. It was the capital of the Wu kingdom in the fifth century B.C. After Soochow was declared an open port in 1896, active trade developed in the southern part of the walled town, adjoining the waterways. But the construction of the railroad, which passes north of

TABLE 36
CITIES OF KIANGSU

City	City Level	Function	Population (in thousands)		
			1953	1957	1970 est.
Cities of the Kiangnan lowland					
Shanghai	province	manuf., port	6,204	6,900	10,000
Nanking	subprovince	manuf.	1,092	1,419	1,700
Wusih	subprovince	manuf.	582	613	
Soochow	subprovince	manuf.	474	633	
Changchow	subprovince	manuf.	297		
Chinkiang	hsien	port	201		
Cities of Yangtze–Hwai Ho Interfluve					
Nantung	subprovince	manuf.	260		
Yangchow	hsien	trade	180		
Taichow	hsien	trade	160		
Tsingkiang	hsien	trade	77		
Cities of Lung-Hai Railroad					
Süchow	subprovince	rail hub	373		
Lienyünkang	subprovince	port	208		
Former City					
Changshu (1953–58)		agric.	101		

the town, caused the business section to be shifted to the industrial railroad settlement that developed northwest of the walled town. The proximity of the large economic centers of Shanghai and Wusih overshadowed Soochow as an industrial city. It is known chiefly as an old, unmodified, typically South Chinese city situated in a scenic hill and lake district. It ships raw silk and silk cloth, rice, and vegetables and is noted for its silk mills, embroidery and craft industries. There are some small chemical and ceramics plants, and a new paperboard mill uses rice straw as a raw material.

Twenty-five miles northwest is the industrial city of Wusih. The third largest city of Kiangsu, with a population of 582,000 in 1953, and 613,000 in 1957, Wusih has supplanted Soochow as the economic center of the Tai Hu basin. A small walled town until the late nineteenth century, it then industrialized and made use of modern machine methods, while Soochow retained its ancient handicraft character. Wusih is next only to Shanghai as a textile and food-processing center. Its excellent transportation facilities—railroads, waterways and highways—have made it a natural collecting center of the rich rice, wheat, and silk area of the Tai Hu basin. Since 1949, the traditional silk mills and rice, flour, and oilseed mills have been supplemented by expansion of the manufacture of machinery, notably machine tools and diesel engines. The additional industrial activity has been further enhanced by the construction of a large thermal-power station at Wangting, southeast of Wusih, halfway along the railroad to Soochow. The power plant, with a designed capacity of about 200,000 kilowatts, was inaugurated in 1958 and is a major element in the Chekiang-Kiangsu system. An agricultural center, Changshu, situated east of Wusih and north of Soochow, was demoted from city status in 1958, presumably in the absence of industrial development. It had a population of 101,000 in 1953.

Proceeding along the railroad we come to Changchow, another agricultural and textile center in which machine-building has been assuming growing significance. The city, known as Wutsin before 1949, had a population of 297,000 in 1953. Its machinery industries produce electric motors and diesel engines, agricultural and textile machines. The southeastern suburb of Chishuyen has large locomotive and rolling-stock shops with an associated heat and power station of more than 100,000 kilowatts.

At the point where the Shanghai-Nanking railroad reaches the Yangtze River and the Grand Canal intersects the river stands Chinkiang. The city consists of the old town and a western port and commercial section on the Yangtze River. The port settlement, once a British concession, was returned to China in 1927. Chinkiang had a population of 201,000 in 1953. Before the railroad era, Chinkiang was a flourishing transportation center on the Grand Canal, then the chief link between North and South China. As late as the 1870's, it was held that Chinkiang, not Shanghai, would monopolize the trade of the lower Yangtze River. However, Shanghai did prevail and the rise of that competitor together with the gradual shift of trade from waterways to railroads brought about Chinkiang's relative decline. Today the city is important for its food trade; it ships northern wheat and soybeans southwest along the Yangtze and forwards rice to the northern plain.

Nanking, the second largest city of Kiangsu and the provincial capital, is situated on the lower Yangtze River, about 150 miles from the sea. The city dates from the Han dynasty (second century B.C.) and was variously known as Kinling, Kiangyeh, and Kiangning. The name Nanking dates from the Ming Dynasty and means "southern capital." Nanking was China's capital under several early Chinese dynasties but notably after 1928 under the Nationalists. In 1949, the Communists moved the capital to Peking, but in 1952 Nanking became the provincial capital of Kiangsu, succeeding Chinkiang. Nanking is surrounded by the remains of a circuitous 22-mile-long wall that encloses not only the city proper (3 miles from the Yangtze) but adjacent rural areas. The wall extends to Nanking's waterfront section of Siakwan, which is the city's shipping and commercial suburb. The city's main thoroughfare, Chungshanlu, traverses the walled area from Siakwan to the Chungshan hills, east of Nanking. It passes the Kulou district, an area of parks and residences, and Hsinchiehkow, the central business district. Noteworthy in the eastern hills are tombs of the early Ming emperors and the Sun Yat-sen memorial.

Long China's political center, Nanking was of relatively little importance as an industrial city. Since the early 1950's, its decline in political significance has been matched by industrial expansion, and its population rose from 1.1 million in 1953 to 1.4 million in 1957 and 1.7 million by 1970.

Traditional textile and porcelain industries have given the city's name to nankeen fabric, a hand-loomed cloth of local cotton, and to nankeen porcelain, painted blue on white.

The principal branches of heavy industry before 1949 were chemical fertilizers in the left-bank suburb of Pukow and cement in the eastern suburb of Lungtan, on the railroad to Chinkiang. These activities were expanded after 1949, and others were added. The old ammonium sulfate plant in Pukow was supplemented with the production of sulfuric acid, using pyrites from Maanshan, just across the Anhwei border to the southwest, and superphosphate (since 1958), based on phosphate rock from Lienyünkang. In the late 1960's, Pukow was reported to be manufacturing complex fertilizers containing nitrogen, phosphorus, and potassium. Synthetic fibers (viscose rayon and others) are also being produced. An old radio plant at Nanking provided the basis for an expanded electronics industry. The city's machinery industry, supplied in part by a small local iron and steel plant (opened in 1959), produces power, textile, and agricultural equipment, machine tools, and motor vehicles (heavy-duty trucks). Nanking also has an oil refinery. Connections between the Siakwan section of the city and the left-bank industrial suburb of Pukow were dependent on ferry services until the inauguration of a rail and road bridge in early 1969. The double-decker bridge, more than 3 miles long, connects the Tientsin-Pukow railroad with the rail system on the south bank of the Yangtze River, speeding transportation between North China and Shanghai.

North of the Yangtze River, three urban centers are situated in the immediate vicinity of the river. They are Yangchow, Taichow, and Nantung. Yangchow, called Kiangtu prior to 1949, is situated near the north bank of the Yangtze River opposite Chinkiang. The Grand Canal passes through the city's eastern section. Like Chinkiang, Yangchow had its heyday in the period of the Grand Canal's peak navigation. It flourished particularly under the Sui and Tang dynasties (A.D. 589–907). Yangchow, with a 1953 population of 180,000, is primarily a rice- and salt-marketing center. Rice is traded in the northeastern suburb of Siennümiao, called Kiangtu since 1950. Salt trade is concentrated in Shiherhwei, to the southwest.

Like Yangchow, the city of Taichow, 30 miles to the east, is also primarily a transport and distribution center at the junction of waterways and roads in a region devoid of railroads. Although the construction of a lock system in 1952 provided access to the canal leading south to the Yangtze, the absence of modern industry limited Taichow's status to that of a hsien-level city. In fact, it was temporarily reduced to a hsien town from 1958 to early 1962. Taichow had a population of 160,000 in 1953.

The largest and most industrialized of these north-bank cities is Nantung, nearer the mouth of the Yangtze River. It arose as a cotton-textile town in the late nineteenth century, and also processes grains and oilseeds from the surrounding agricultural area. A superphosphate plant, using ore from Lienyünkang, began operations in 1962. The industries are concentrated in the northwest suburb of Tangkiacha. Nantung had a population of 260,000 in 1953.

Tsingkiang is the urban center of north central Kiangsu. Called Hwaiyin prior to 1949, the city reverted to that name temporarily from 1958 to 1964 and has since been known again as Tsingkiang. It probably has a population of about 100,000. Situated at the intersection of the Grand Canal and the old course of the Hwai Ho, Tsingkiang was a more important trade center before the railroad era. Its regional commerce has been partly absorbed by Pengpu, at the junction of the Hwai Ho and the Tientsin-Pukow railroad. However Tsingkiang still fulfills a useful function as the agricultural center of north central Kiangsu, at the focus of the Grand Canal and the Yen Ho. Grain and salt (marketed at adjacent Sipa) are the main trade goods.

In northernmost Kiangsu, two major cities are situated along the Lung-Hai railroad. They are Süchow and Lienyünkang. Süchow is one of China's major rail cities, situated at the junction of two of the country's most important rail lines, the north-south Tientsin-Pukow railroad and the east-west Lung-Hai railroad. With a population of 373,000 in 1953, it dominates not only the northwestern panhandle of Kiangsu, but also adjacent parts of Shantung, Honan, and Anhwei. The significance of Süchow as a transport center was further enhanced in the early 1960's with the reconstruction of the Grand Canal, which now handles larger volumes of goods trans-shipped from the railroad at Süchow for distribution to central Kiangsu. Among these commodities is coal from the Kiawang mine, northeast of Süchow, and elsewhere around Süchow. Industries include mining equipment, machine tools, and cotton textiles. Süchow was known as Tungshan from 1912 to 1945. A major battle in the Chinese civil war was fought here in November, 1948.

Lienyünkang, the seaside terminal of the Lung-Hai railroad and the only port between Tsingtao and Shanghai, arose through the amalgamation of the three towns of *Sin*pu, Tung*hai* and *Lien*yünkang, the actual rail terminal and port. Until 1961, the combined city was known as Sinhailien. Tunghai, the oldest section of this conurbation, was formerly called Haichow and served as the eastern terminus of the Lung-Hai line. It is an old junk harbor at the head of the combined estuary of the Yen Ho and the old Shu Ho. Made unusable by silting, Tunghai was replaced by the downriver landing and market town of Sinpu. In the 1930's, a deep-water harbor was built south of the estuary on a site sheltered by hills and offshore islands. The new harbor, first called Laoyao, later Lienyün or Lienyünkang ("kang" means harbor), succeeded Tunghai as the terminus of the Lung-Hai line. The port is accessible to small ocean-going vessels of up to 3,000 tons and serves as the base of a fishing fleet. The center of the conurbation of Lienyünkang, which had a population of 208,000 in 1953, is at Sinpu. Included within the Lienyünkang municipal area is the phosphate mining complex of Mienping. A small mine that operated here before 1949 was expanded in 1958 to a capacity of 1.2 million tons of crude rock and 300,000 tons of concentrate. It supplies ore to superphosphate plants at Nanking and at Nantung in southern Kiangsu.

ANHWEI PROVINCE

Capital: Hofei; area: 54,000 sq. mi.; population: 39 million

Like Kiangsu, Anhwei was administered in two sections in the aftermath of the civil war, but Anhwei was reunited in August, 1952, three months before Kiangsu. In November, Anhwei recovered small areas temporarily ceded to Kiangsu, and the province was restored to its pre-1949 boundaries. However, early in 1955, two of the northwesternmost hsien of Kiangsu—Siaohsien and Tangshan, both just west of Süchow—were ceded to Anhwei. The transfer of the two hsien added an area of about 1,000 square miles and a population of 320,000 (1953 census) to Anhwei.

Anhwei may be said to include two distinct natural divisions: the North China plain in the north and the Yangtze valley proper in the south. The northern section, coinciding with the Hwai Ho river system, is typical of the North China plain with its cold, dry winters and hot, rainy summers, calcareous alluvial soils and shakiang soils, and the winter wheat–kaoliang crop association. The southern section, sheltered by low-lying hills, is more typical of Yangtze valley conditions, with more uniform annual precipitation and less severe winters, noncalcareous valley alluvium ringed by podzolic and lateritic upland soils, and the wheat-rice crop association.

Anhwei's grain production is about 6 per cent of China's total. Wheat is the chief winter grain both in the north and in the south, while rice is grown in the summer in the Wuhu plain of the south, particularly in the Chao Hu lake basin north of the Yangtze River. Lesser grains are summer kaoliang in the north and winter barley in the south. Soybeans and sweet potatoes are also grown in the North China plain section.

Cotton is cultivated chiefly in the northern half of Anhwei, but the province as a whole produces only about 5 per cent of the nation's cotton crop. Silk is produced only in the southeast zone bordering on Kiangsu. Anhwei is, however, one of China's leading tea-producing provinces. The chief producing area in the extreme south is centered on Tunki, which produces a green tea, and Kimen, which grows the black keemun tea. A lesser area in the central uplands is Liuan, known for the sunglo leaf.

Anhwei has two of East China's major coal-mining districts: Hwainan ("south of the Hwai"), which is centered on the coal-mining city of Hwainan, on the south bank of the Hwai Ho, and Hwaipei ("north of the Hwai"), which is situated around the city of Suiki, southwest of Süchow.

The Hwainan basin of bituminous coal, partly suitable for coking, went into production in 1929, and the coal was shipped both from the riverside coal harbor of Tienkiaan, downstream along the Hwai Ho, and, after the opening of the Hwainan railroad in 1936, to the Yangtze coal harbor of Yükikow, opposite Wuhu, for trans-shipment to river-going coal vessels.

Early operations were centered just south of Tienkiaan, at Shunkengshan and Kiulungkang. After World War II, geological exploration uncovered additional coal beds west of Tienkiaan, and a rail spur was built 10 miles to the new mining area of Pakungshan. Coal production expanded considerably after 1949 as the entire district was incorporated into a new city of Hwainan, with its center at the old coal harbor of Tienkiaan. The population of Hwainan, 287,000 in 1953, may have risen to 350,000 by 1970. Most of the annual output, estimated at more than 10 million tons, is shipped to Yükikow for distribution mainly upstream along the Yangtze River. Part of the coal, processed in a local coke plant, yields byproduct gases used in the manufacture of nitrogen fertilizer, particularly ammonium sulfate. Hwainan coal is also burned in a major local steam-electric station that is interconnected with small hydroelectric plants on tributaries of the Hwai Ho. A 220-kilovolt grid feeds electricity to the manufacturing cities of Pengpu to the northeast and, across the Yangtze, to Wuhu in the southeast.

The Hwaipei basin developed largely in the 1960's. In the past, bituminous coal was mined here on a small scale in the deposit at Liehshan ("fiery mountain") and shipped down the river Sui Ho to Fulitsi, a station on the Tientsin-Pukow railroad. Large-scale development of the coal basin began in 1958 during the Great Leap, and the first mine opened the following year. A rail spur from Fulitsi replaced the former water route, and, in 1961, the entire Hwaipei coal district was incorporated as the city of Suiki, on the site of the old mining settlement of Suikikow. The basin developed rapidly because of its favorable location near the Lung-Hai and Tientsin-Pukow railroads. Its annual output is estimated at more than 5 million tons.

There are lesser coal mines elsewhere in Anhwei, notably in the Suitung area of southeastern Anhwei, 20 miles southeast of Süancheng. Here, coal measures found on the flanks of the southern Anhwei uplands dip under the alluvium of the Yangtze delta in Kiangsu. The coal is of anthracite rank in the more compressed western part of the Suitung field but is predominantly bituminous in the east.

Small oil deposits of little commercial interest have been observed in the same area of southeastern Anhwei, between Süancheng and Kwangteh. In the middle 1960's, in conjunction with reports of the Shengli ("victory") oil-field development in the lower reaches of the Yellow River in northern Shantung, oil was also reported to have been struck in the Chao Hu basin, southeast of Hofei.

In addition to its two major coal-producers, Anhwei is also well supplied with iron ore, some of it associated with copper. The main iron-mining complex is at Maanshan, on the Kiangsu border north of Tangtu. Large-scale mining operations were initiated here by the Japanese during World War II. They laid a short rail spur from the deposit to the riverside smelting center of Maanshan, where ten small blast furnaces, each with a capacity of 20 tons of pig iron a day, were constructed. After an eight-year suspension, six of the blast furnaces went into operation in 1953, having been re-constructed with a capacity of 100 tons a day. Maanshan developed into a major supplier of pig iron to the Shanghai steel industry, thus reducing the need for long hauls of pig iron from North China and Manchuria. The grow-ing importance of the Maanshan complex led to the incorporation of the mines and smelters as the city of Maanshan in 1956. During the Great Leap, an expansion program added half a dozen more blast furnaces, some of them with a working volume of 250 cubic meters. Finally, the construction of both open-hearth furnaces and oxygen converters resulted in an inte-grated iron and steel operation at Maanshan by 1964. The complex con-tinues to ship most of its pig-iron output to Shanghai but converts some of it locally into crude steel. Total pig-iron production is estimated at 1 million tons or more, with perhaps one-third processed into steel. The Maanshan area is also a producer of pyrites, a source of sulfur for the production of sulfuric acid.

The other mineral complex in Anhwei is the copper center of Tungling ("copper hill"), where mining of copper ore began in the T'ang Dynasty. Modern development began after 1949 with construction of an open pit, a large shaft mine, and a concentrator and smelter producing 95 per cent blister copper. Among the byproduct metals produced with the copper is iron concentrate. The mineral complex was incorporated as a city in 1956 and was first known as Tungkwanshan, for the hill in which the copper operations are located. The city was renamed Tungling in 1958. Mineral products were shipped via the Yangtze River until 1969, when Tungling was reached by a railroad from Wuhu.

A smaller, old iron mine in the Fanchang area, between Tungling and Wuhu, declined in importance with the growth of the Maanshan complex. In the Fanchang operation, dating from 1918, a short narrow-gauge rail-road carried ore from the mine at Taochung to the Yangtze River terminal of Tikang. Maximum production was 200,000 tons a year. But the Tao-chung mine gained new importance with the inauguration in 1970 of a con-centrator for low-grade ore with a capacity of several hundred thousand tons of ore.

Anhwei's principal urban centers are situated along the Yangtze River and on railroads linking Yangtze River ports with the North China plain. The main rail line is the Tientsin-Pukow railroad, which serves the north-eastern part of the province, including the manufacturing center of Pengpu. It is linked by the Pengpu-Shuikiahu line with the Hwainan Railroad, which serves Hofei, the province capital, and the Yangtze coal harbor of Yükikow, opposite Wuhu. A branch from the Tientsin-Pukow railroad to Fowyang was added in 1970. Along the south bank of the Yangtze, a railroad from Nan-king leads via Maanshan to Wuhu and, since 1969, to Tungling. A long-planned southward connection from Wuhu via Kingtehchen to the rail hub of Yingtan has not been completed.

Aside from the Yangtze River, the province's chief navigable artery, water transportation is dependent on three minor streams usable by small vessels that branch off the Yangtze, and on the Hwai Ho in the north. The most important of the Yangtze tributaries is the canalized Yüntsao River (also known as the Yüki), which joins the lake Chao Hu to the Yangtze at Yükikow and permits junks to ascend as far as Hofei. A lock system inaugurated at Yükikow in 1969 opened up this waterway to 1,000-ton vessels. Of less significance are the two other tributaries of the Yangtze, on the right bank. They are the Shuiyang River, navigable from its mouth at Wuhu as far as Süancheng, and the Tsingi River, also from the Wuhu area, as far as Shihtai. A hydroelectric station with a capacity of up to 300,000 kilowatts is planned on the upper reaches of the Tsingi at Chentsun, near Kinghsien.

In the Hwai Ho basin of northern Anhwei, shipping conditions for junks have been improved in connection with the Hwai Ho reclamation project. In the past, large junks were able to ascend the Hwai Ho as far as Chengyangkwan, a river hub at the mouths of the Pi Ho, a right tributary, and the Ying Ho, a left tributary. Among flood-prevention reservoirs thus far completed in northern Anhwei are the Fotzeling reservoir (completed 1954) and the Motzetan reservoir (early 1960's) on the upper Pi Ho, the Meishan reservoir on the upper Shih Ho (completed 1956), and the Sianghungtien reservoir, also on the upper Pi Ho (completed in 1958), all in the Tapieh Mountains. A 40,000-kilowatt hydroelectric station was inaugurated at the Meishan flood-control dam in 1958, and stations with similar capacities were planned at the other two dams, to be linked by 110-kilovolt transmission lines with the thermal-power station of Hwainan. On the left bank of the Hwai Ho, a flood-diversion channel known as the New Pien Ho was inaugurated in 1969, diverting part of the flow of the Sui Ho and the To Ho, left tributaries of the Hwai Ho, directly to Lake Hungtse. Construction on the 80-mile project began in 1966. The New Pien Ho follows the route of the Pien Ho, an ancient canal of the Sui Dynasty (A.D. 581–618).

Hofei and Pengpu, the two principal manufacturing cities of Anhwei north of the Yangtze River, have been developing more rapidly than two other regional centers, Wuhu and Anking, on the Yangtze (Table 37).

Hofei, the provincial capital, was formerly called Luchow. It is situated near the lake Chao Hu, center of a major rice-producing area. In addition to being situated on the Hwainan Railroad, its transport situation was significantly improved with the dredging and canalization of the Yüntsao (Yüki) River leading to the Yangtze. Industrial development began in the 1950's with the relocation of some textile, leather, and other light manufacturing plants from Shanghai. In the Great Leap, Hofei gained a small steel plant to supply a growing machinery industry with metal. The city produces machine tools and equipment for the mining, electrical, and chemical industries. A small aluminum reduction plant was reported completed in the early 1960's. The city's population rose from 183,600 in 1953 to 360,000 in 1957, partly through northward expansion of the municipal area, and was probably close to 500,000 by 1970. Much of the industrial construction at

TABLE 37

CITIES OF ANHWEI

City	City Level	Function	Population (*in thousands*)		
			1953	1957	1970 est.
Resource-oriented Cities					
Hwainan	subprovince	coal power	287	300	350
Maanshan (since 1956)	subprovince	iron			
Tungling (since 1956)	subprovince	copper			
Suiki (Hwaipei) (since 1961)	subprovince	coal			
Regional Centers					
Hofei	subprovince	manuf.	184	360	500
Pengpu	subprovince	manuf.	253	330	400
Wuhu	hsien	manuf.	242	240	300
Anking	hsien	manuf.	105	100	100
Former Cities					
Kaishow (until 1954)		trade			
Sucheng (now Suhsien) (until 1953)		trade			
Tunki (until 1962)		trade			

Hofei and other cities in the province derives its cement from a mill at Chaohsien, southeast of Hofei.

Pengpu, the other manufacturing center of northern Anhwei, owes its development largely to a favorable transport situation, at the junction of the Hwai Ho and the Tientsin-Pukow railroad, and a rail branch connecting with the Hwainan railroad. It is a wheat marketing and processing hub for the agricultural area of the Hwai Ho basin. Its industries, many developed since the 1950's, include machine-building (machine tools, irrigation equipment, farm implements), food-processing (flour, tobacco, meat products), cotton fabrics, glass, paper, and matches. Pengpu's industrial development was associated with population growth, from 253,000 in 1953 to 330,000 in 1957 and 400,000 in the late 1960's.

The two principal regional centers along the Yangtze are Wuhu and Anking. Wuhu, on the river's south bank at the mouth of the Tsingi River, has been the traditional rice-collecting metropolis of southern Anhwei. The construction of the railroad from Nanking and of the Hwainan railroad to Yükikow, the coal terminal opposite Wuhu, further strengthened the city's position as a trade and transport center. Wuhu has some industry, notably a large paperboard mill using rice straw as raw material, but has lagged behind Hofei and Pengpu in manufacturing. This is reflected both in Wuhu's inferior administrative status as a hsien-level city and smaller population (242,000 in 1953, and perhaps 300,000 in the late 1960's).

Anking, on the left bank of the Yangtze, was formerly called Hwaining. A former capital of Anhwei, it lost its political position largely because of poor connections with the rest of the province. It still lacks a rail connection, and its trade is much less significant than that of Wuhu, downriver, or Kiukiang, upriver in Kiangsi Province. Anking's role is limited to that of a subregional center in southwestern Anhwei, and its population has probably changed little since 1953, when it was 105,000.

Somewhat apart from the rest of Anhwei is the isolated, hill-rimmed Tunki area in the extreme south. Here natural conditions are typical of the more southerly tea-rice region. In fact, the area's natural outlet is southeastward along one of the headstreams of the Tsientang River. This is the leading tea area of Anhwei. Noteworthy places in addition to Tunki, largest urban center and administrative seat of the region, are Kimen, the tea-producing town, and Sihsien, formerly called Hweichow. It was once the regional center but has been replaced by Tunki. So isolated is the area that a separate Mandarin dialect, the so-called Hweichow speech, has maintained itself. Relative economic stagnation led to the loss of city status for Tunki in 1962, although it remained the administrative center of the area. Economic development of the isolated region is unlikely until the planned Wuhu-Kingtehchen-Yingtan railroad provides a transport outlet.

6. The Middle Yangtze Plain

The Middle Yangtze plain includes the provinces of Hupei, Hunan, and Kiangsi. The combined area of these three provinces is about 220,000 square miles, or 6 per cent of the nation's total territory. The total population of the region in 1970 was about 100 million, or 13 per cent of China's population. The average density of 450 per square mile is thus considerably below that of the North China plain or the Lower Yangtze region.

Traversed from west to east by the Yangtze River, the region consists essentially of the drainage basins of the three major tributaries of the middle Yangtze: the Han Shui basin in Hupei, the Siang Kiang basin in Hunan, and the Kan Kiang basin in Kiangsi.

Mountains of medium elevation surround the region as a whole and divide the component basins from one another. Separating the region from the North China plain are the Hwaiyang Mountains. In the west, the Middle Yangtze basins border on the Szechwan mountains and the Kweichow plateau. In the south, the basins are separated from Kwangsi and Kwangtung by the Nan Ling divide, one of China's major natural barriers. Finally, in the east are the uplands of Fukien and Chekiang.

The Middle Yangtze plain can be described in terms of three major subdivisions: the Hwaiyang divide in the north, the Middle Yangtze valley proper, and the South Yangtze hills. The Hwaiyang Mountains extend along the Honan-Hupei border from the Nanyang area to the province of Anhwei. In the west they include the low, strongly eroded Tahung and Tungpai hills. These uplands are of ancient origin and have gently rounded contours. A large part of their area is taken up by broad valleys. In the east rise the Tapieh Mountains, with elevations exceeding 3,000 feet. They are characterized by abrupt, deeply dissected scarps on the north side and gentle slopes in the south. The Hwo Shan of the central Anhwei uplands is the eastern most outlier of the Hwaiyang system.

The Middle Yangtze valley proper extends from the Ichang gorges in the west to the Anhwei border. The level, alluvial land of the valley reaches up

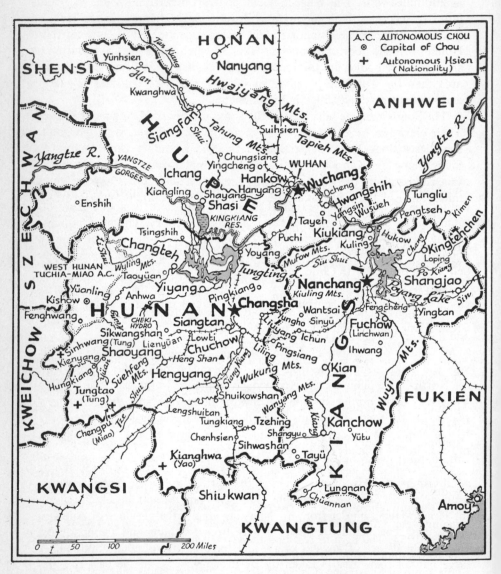

7. Middle Yangtze Plain

into the surrounding mountains. In two localities, between Wusüeh and Tienkiachen on the Kiangsi-Hupei line and between Pengtseh and Tungliu on the Kiangsi-Anhwei line, the hills approach the river on both banks. Elsewhere, the mountains retreat from the river, and the valley is as much as 200 miles wide. The Wusüeh-Tienkiachen constriction divides the valley into two sections: the Tungting and Poyang plains, named for the lakes of the same names. The Tungting plain includes central Hupei and northern Hunan. It is the floor of an ancient lake, of which Tungting Lake and many smaller water bodies are the remains. The Poyang plain occupies a smaller area than the Tungting plain. Lake Poyang was once considerably larger and has been gradually filled in by sediments.

The South Yangtze hills include the southern parts of Hunan and Kiangsi. Their elevation varies from 500 to more than 3,000 feet, with the greater elevations along the provincial borders. The mountain rims enclose the Siang Kiang and Kan Kiang basins like two amphitheaters. The most important ranges along the western margin are the Wuling and Süehfeng mountains. The isolated Heng Shan rises to 4,000 feet in central Hunan overlooking the Siang Kiang valley. The divide between the two river basins is made up by a series of ranges trending northeast-southwest, including the Mufow, Kiuling, Wukung, and Wanyang mountains. Valleys separating these ranges serve as routeways between Hunan and Kiangsi. The isolated Lu Shan, a continuation of the Mufow Mountains, rises to 5,000 feet on the west shore of Lake Poyang. The eastern margins of the South Yangtze hill region are made up largely of the Wuyi Mountains, which form the divide between the Kan Kiang and the southeastern coastal drainage basins.

The Yangtze River is, of course, the region's principal river. It debouches onto the plain at Ichang and traverses it in a meandering course, trending first southeast to Lake Tungting, then northeast to Wuhan, again southeast to Lake Poyang, and turning once more northeast as it enters Anhwei Province. The volume of water varies greatly, being lowest during the winter and highest after the summer rains. Fortunately, the sudden surge of the summer high water seldom produces floods, as the surplus is discharged into the natural reservoirs of the Tungting and Poyang lakes. Dikes encase the middle Yangtze course, whose numerous meanders and irregular channel width offer a relatively low carrying capacity. Occasionally, neither the natural detention basins nor the riverside embankments are able to contain the raging waters. In recent times, two disastrous floods have occurred, in 1931 and in 1954. The fight to regulate the river is a continuing one. Among the measures undertaken since 1949 is the construction of the Kingkiang reservoir south of Shasi, one of several flood-detention basins planned along the middle Yangtze River.

Owing to the moderate barrier effect of the Hwaiyang divide, the Middle Yangtze plain is even less exposed to the northern air masses than the lower reaches of the river. As a result of its sheltered position with respect to the cold, dry Polar Continental air, the January temperatures average 40° F

(5° C) compared with 35° F in the lower plain. The inland location of the middle plain, far from the moderating effect of the sea, also results in higher July averages of 85° F (29° C) compared with 80° F in the lower reaches. Precipitation is abundant and distributed relatively evenly through the year. Of an annual average of 45 inches, about 43 per cent falls in the three summer months June, July, August, 25 per cent in the spring, 21 per cent in the fall, and 11 per cent in the winter.

The Middle Yangtze plain depends for its precipitation largely on turbulence associated with the polar front. Because of the varying intensity of the interaction of the southeastern Maritime Tropical air and the northern Continental air, both flood years and drought years have been produced in the past. Strong southeastern monsoons usually advance as far as the North China plain, which then receives abundant precipitation, while the Middle Yangtze plain to the south suffers drought conditions. Weak summer monsoons, on the other hand, meet Continental air masses over the Yangtze valley, which then has a rainy year, while the Yellow River plain remains dry. This irregular shifting of the polar-front zone produces alternate floods and droughts in the two great Chinese lowlands.

The Yangtze valley proper, including the Tungting and Poyang lake basins, has recent noncalcareous alluvium. Podzols are well developed in the Hwaiyang divide, while lateritic soils predominate in the South Yangtze hills. Red lateritic soils cover most of Kiangsi and Hunan, while yellow soils are restricted to western Hunan adjoining the Kweichow plateau. Agriculturally, the clay pans developed on the valley alluvium are associated with rice, the principal summer crop grown on irrigated land. More than half of the arable land is irrigated, and terracing is common on the hillsides in the south. In terms of the conventional agricultural divisions, Hupei belongs largely to the Yangtze rice-wheat area, in common with the Lower Yangtze plain, while Hunan and Kiangsi are almost entirely in the rice-tea area.

Rice cultivation is favored throughout the region by high summer temperatures and abundant precipitation. It even yields two crops in southernmost Kiangsi, where conditions resemble subtropical Kwangtung. Early-ripening types are grown chiefly north of the Yangtze, while late-ripening varieties and rice used for distilling are cultivated south of the river. The highest yields are obtained in the Yangtze valley proper, where the Tungting and Poyang basins have become known as the "rice bowl" of China. Kiukiang and Changsha are the two great rice markets.

Winter wheat is important only north of the Yangtze. Other winter crops, grown chiefly in the terraced hillsides, include beans, corn, and sweet potatoes.

Tea, also a hillside crop, has three major production centers within the Middle Yangtze area. They are the Siu Shui area of northwest Kiangsi, the Puchi area of southeast Hupei, and the Anhwa area of central Hunan. The leaves in these areas are commonly cured to produce black tea. Hankow and Kiukiang are the regional tea-marketing and -processing centers.

Other important products are cotton, grown in parts of the Poyang and Tungting basins, and ramie and other bast fibers, cultivated chiefly in the South Yangtze hills. Rapeseed and sesame are grown for their oil.

Although much of the region has been cleared of trees, both to make available land and to provide fuel, the original subtropical evergreen broad-leaf forest cover remains in remote and thinly settled upland areas. The stands yield fir, pine, and cypress, as well as bamboo. Although the tung tree is not as important here as in China's Southwest and in the Szechwan basin, the wood oil is produced both in western Hunan and in Kiangsi.

The region is rich in minerals, yielding not only coking coal and iron ore but nonferrous metals. Coking coal from Pingsiang (Kiangsi) and Tzehing (Hunan) must be cleaned in a washing plant at Chuchow to reduce the high ash content. These coal deposits, together with the iron-ore reserves of Tayeh, provide part of the raw material base for the new iron and steel plant at Wuhan. Hunan is China's principal producer of antimony, with the largest mine at Sikwangshan, and a major contributor of manganese (near Siangtan) and zinc-lead-silver ores (Shuikowshan). Kiangsi is the nation's main tungsten-supplier, with mines concentrated in the southern part of the province, notably at Sihwashan near Tayü. The distinctive resources of kaolin and feldspar in northeastern Kiangsi provided the mineral base for the porcelain and ceramics industry of Kingtehchen.

The region's industrial centers are situated along the Yangtze River and the railroad lines. These run in general perpendicular to the river and include the Peking-Hankow-Canton line, the Kiukiang-Nanchang line, and the latitudinal Chekiang-Kiangsi railroad.

The middle Yangtze is accessible to vessels of 5,000 tons in the summer and 2,000 tons in the winter as far as Wuhan. Above Wuhan, 2,000-ton and 1,000-tons ships can reach Ichang in the two seasons, respectively. From the Yangtze, large motorized junks can ascend the Han Shui. The tributary rivers of the Tungting and Poyang basins are also navigable in the lower reaches.

The big industrial centers are the three-city conurbation of Wuhan in Hupei, the increasingly coalescing three-city agglomeration of Changsha, Chuchow, and Siangtan in Hunan, and Nanchang in Kiangsi. Traditional cotton and ramie textile industries, porcelain-manufacturing (Kingtehchen), and flour, oilseed, and tea factories have been supplemented by machinery and other modern manufacturing industries.

The population is particularly dense in the Yangtze valley proper, where it reaches 800 per square mile. Lower densities are found along the Siang Kiang and Kan Kiang valleys—about 350 to 450 per square mile. The most sparsely settled areas are the peripheral South Yangtze hills. Relief is a major determinant of population distribution.

The ethnic make-up of the population is almost entirely Chinese, speaking Mandarin dialects. In Kiangsi, it is the Lower Yangtze variety of Mandarin that predominates, while in Hupei and Hunan, the Upper Yangtze variety is spoken. In southernmost Kiangsi are Hakka-speaking Chinese, and the specific Kan dialect is associated with the Kan Kiang valley. In Hunan, the Hunanese dialect is associated with the Siang Kiang valley. The only non-Chinese minorities are in Hunan. They are the Tuchia of Tibeto-Burman stock, the Tung of Thai stock, and the Miao-Yao group.

HUPEI PROVINCE

Capital: Wuchang; area: 72,000 sq. mi; population: 35 million

Hupei Province occupies a central position in China proper. It is crossed both by the Yangtze River, the nation's chief waterway and east-west transportation artery, and by the Peking-Hankow-Canton trunk railroad. The two national routes meet in the Wuhan conurbation.

The province is about two-thirds lowland (in the east) and one-third upland. The low-lying, lake-studded alluvial plain is bounded by the Hwai-yang divide along the Honan border and by the Mufow Mountains along the Kiangsi line. It continues at water level in the Tungting basin of northern Hunan. In the west, the lowland makes way for the rugged red sandstone outliers of the Szechwan mountain rim.

Through these western uplands the Yangtze River makes its way in precipitous gorges before debouching onto the plain at Ichang. The meandering river proceeds generally eastward through the Hupei lowland past Wuhan, where it receives on the left the Han Shui.

Most of the province is characterized by the rice-wheat crop association. Rice is the main summer crop. Wheat, the winter grain, is sown chiefly in the northern part of the province and milled at Wuhan. Other winter crops are barley, rapeseed, and broad beans. Among the summer crops are cotton, soybeans, and corn. Cotton is grown in the central part of the province and milled into textiles at Wuchang. A distinctive hillside crop is tea. It is cultivated in the uplands west of Ichang and especially on the slopes of the Mufow Mountains near Puchi.

Iron ore in the Tayeh area within the municipal district of Hwangshih is Hupei's principal mineral resource, providing raw material for an old, small iron and steel plant at Hwangshih and the newer, larger, integrated complex built during the Great Leap at Wuhan. Operations in the Tayeh iron deposit date from the 1890's, when a 20-mile railroad was built from the Yangtze riverside terminal of Shihhweiyao to the mine at Tiehshan and Siangpishan. The high-grade magnetite deposit yielded up to 700,000 tons a year in the 1930's and early 1940's, chiefly for export down the Yangtze River to Japan. During the Great Leap, in conjunction with construction of the iron and steel complex at Wuhan, production in the Tayeh area was expanded through excavation of a large open-pit mine, and a 60-mile electrified railroad was completed in 1958 to the Wuhan plant.

Some anthracite is mined in the Hwangshih urban district for local heating uses. For its coking coal, the Hupei iron and steel industry is dependent

TABLE 38

CITIES OF HUPEI

City	City Level	Functions	Population (in thousands)		
			1953	1957	1970 est.
Wuhan	subprovincial	iron-steel, manuf.	1,427	2,146	2,700
Hwangshih	subprovincial	iron ore	111	160	
Shasi	hsien	trade	86	120	
Ichang	hsien	trade	50	110	
Siangfan	hsien	trade	73	100	
Former Cities		Period			
Ocheng		1960–61			
Shayang		1960–61			

on the Pingtingshan mines of Honan, to the north, and the Pingsiang mines of Kiangsi, to the south. During the Great Leap, plans for the development of the so-called Onan (southern Hupei) coal field around Puchi were reported in 1959, with an ultimate production goal of 17 million tons a year. However, development was apparently abandoned with the failure of the Great Leap.

Copper deposits are found south of Hwangshih, between Tayeh and Yangsin, and a small copper-smelter is believed to be operating at Hwangshih. Among nonmetallics, Hupei occupies a key position as China's chief gypsum producer. About 90 per cent of the nation's output originates at Yingcheng, northwest of Wuhan. Limestone deposits near Hwangshih are processsed into cement and lime. Phosphate deposits were discovered in the 1950's in the Chungsiang area, northwest of Wuhan, and a phosphate mine with a capacity of 400,000 tons a year went into operation in 1965.

Nearly all provincial centers (Table 38) are situated along the Yangtze River. They are the Wuhan tri-cities, the iron and steel city of Hwangshih, and the river ports and commercial centers of Shasi and Ichang. A fifth regional center is Siangfan on the middle Han Shui.

Wuhan is the foremost metropolis of central China, dominating the Middle Yangtze plain. This tri-city conurbation consists of Hankow, the largest component, Hanyang, and Wuchang. Hankow, which accounts for about two-thirds of the total population, is a major manufacturing and commercial center. Its development, which paralleled that of Shanghai, began in 1858 when it was one of the first Chinese inland cities to be opened to foreign trade. The city is situated on the left bank of the Han Shui where it joins the Yangtze. The old Chinese part of town extends along the Han, while former foreign concessions line the Yangtze. These concessions, once held by Germany, Russia, Britain, Japan, and France, now constitute the manufacturing and business center of the city. The chief industries are machinery, chemicals, cement, and textiles. The city owes much of its development to the Peking-Hankow-Canton railroad, which crossed the Yangtze by ferry here until the completion of a Yangtze River rail and road bridge in 1957 between Hanyang and Wuchang. A bridge from Hankow to Hanyang across the mouth of the Han Shui had been constructed earlier, in 1954.

Hanyang, situated on the right bank of the Han Shui, has been known in the past as an iron and steel center and arsenal city. Built at the turn of the twentieth century, the metallurgical plant was long the chief iron and steel producer in China proper. After early activity, the plant's production lagged in the 1930's and the installation was finally dismantled and shipped to Chungking in the face of the Japanese advance in 1937. The site of the former steel plant was occupied by a cotton mill in the 1950's, but a steel-making operation was restored in following years. There are also a railroad-tie plant and a paper mill.

Wuchang, the third member of the Wuhan cities, is situated on the right bank of the Yangtze opposite Hanyang and Hankow. It is primarily the administrative and cultural center of the municipality. Here is the seat of the Hupei provincial government, a government mint, and universities. Residential and business sections are situated within the old city wall. Industrial plants and the waterfront are outside the walls. The industries here include cotton, silk, and paper mills; railroad repair shops, and a shipyard. The oldest of the Wuhan cities, Wuchang has preserved much more of the traditional Chinese character than either Hankow or Hanyang. The Hwangholow, a tower on the bank of the Yangtze, is one of the city's sights. Wuhan University is situated in the suburb of Lokiashan, east of the city.

It was northeast of Wuchang, on the right bank of the Yangtze River, that the site for the new Wuhan iron and steel plant was selected during the mid-1950's. The complex arose near the suburb of Tsingshan, 10 miles northeast of the old walled section of Wuchang. Construction began in 1956, and, two years later, the electrified railroad from the Tayeh iron mines, the plant's ore source, was completed. The first blast furnace, with a working volume of 1,386 cubic meters, was inaugurated in September, 1958, and the second, of 1,436 cubic meters, in July, 1959. Construction of the third blast furnace, with a working volume of 1,513 cubic meters, began in 1960 but was interrupted by the failure of the Great Leap, and the furnace was inaugurated only in April, 1969. It gave Wuhan a pig-iron capacity of about 2.5 million tons a year. Crude-steel production began in September, 1959, with completion of a 250-ton open-hearth furnace, followed by several 500-ton furnaces. After a long interval, another open-hearth furnace was inaugurated in December, 1969. Finishing facilities long lagged behind the production of pig iron and crude steel, but, in 1964, a heavy rolling mill was completed for the production of rails, girders, and I-beams. The Wuhan iron and steel plants has provided a metal supply for the city's fabricating industries, which produce heavy machine tools, boilers, diesel engines and electric motors, farm equipment, motor vehicles, and ball bearings. In July, 1971, an aluminum plant was reported inaugurated after nine months' construction.

The construction of the iron and steel complex and associated industrial expansion in the late 1950's and in the 1960's raised the population of Wuhan from 1.4 million in 1953 to 2.1 million in 1957. The estimate for 1970 was 2.7 million.

Hwangshih, on the right bank of the Yangtze, about fifty miles southeast of Wuhan, is a new industrial center. The product of China's industrialization drive, the city was formed in 1950 out of the two riverside towns of Shihhweiyao, former iron-ore loading port, and Hwangshihkang, cement center. (Hwangshih means "yellow stone," the cement rock.) The Tayeh iron mines, west of the river terminals, were included within the Hwangshih municipal district. In addition to shipping ore to the Wuhan complex, the Tayeh mines also supply a small integrated iron and steel plant at Hwangshih. The plant, based on old facilities dating from World War I, was reconstructed and expanded during the Great Leap. In addition to its iron and steel industry, Hwangshih also has a large cement mill, based on nearby limestone deposits, and a small copper-smelter, processing ore mined within the area. The population of the Hwangshih municipal district was 111,000 at the time of the 1953 census and 160,000 in 1957, making it the second largest urban center of Hupei. Hwangshih was envisaged in the early 1950's as the site of the proposed main iron and steel complex of central China, but subsequent study evidently showed the Wuhan site to be more favorable for the development of a large iron and steel industry. Along the 60-mile railroad from the Tayeh iron mines to the Wuhan plant, another small integrated iron and steel complex, with a capacity of 100,000 to 200,000 tons, began to arise in 1958 at Ocheng. This hsien was actually raised to the status of municipality in 1960, but the level of development evidently did not justify such a high administrative level, and Ocheng was returned to hsien status in late 1961.

West of Wuhan are the Yangtze River ports of Shasi and Ichang. Shasi is a water transportation center on the north bank of the Yangtze. It is linked with Hankow, in addition to the river itself, by a junk route utilizing a maze of waterways and lakes north of the Yangtze River. South of Shasi, the Taiping and Owchih canals link the Yangtze with the Tungting basin of northern Hunan. These excellent water routes have made Shasi a natural agricultural market for the surrounding water-logged region. A city of 86,000 in 1953 and 120,000 in 1957, it markets chiefly cotton and grain. Shasi has superseded the older Kiangling, situated five miles west, as the local commercial center. South of Shasi, between the Taiping and Owchih canals, is the Kingkiang flood-detention basin, built in 1952–53. Covering an area of 350 square miles, this dike-enclosed reservoir is controlled at its northern end by the flood inlet gate of Taipingkow, on the Yangtze west of Shasi. The Kingkiang basin is named for the King Kiang, a local name for the Yangtze River in the section north of Lake Tungting. The local market town and water-transport center of Shayang, on the Han Shui, northeast of Shasi, was also briefly raised to city status in 1960, presumably on the basis of development plans. However, these did not materialize, and Shayang was restored to its previous level of market town in Kingmen hsien.

Ichang is noteworthy as the head of navigation on the middle Yangtze River. It is situated at the eastern end of the Yangtze gorges leading to Szechwan, where navigation is restricted to 500-ton vessels. Ichang was primarily a trade center in the past, shipping tung oil, sesame, and grain. Small industries added in the 1950's include a chemical plant that manufactures sulfuric acid from nearby sulfur deposits. The city's population rose from 50,000 in the early 1950's to 110,000 in 1957.

Siangfan, the agricultural and commercial center of the Han Shui valley in northwest Hupei, is a twin city with a combined population of 73,000 in 1953 and about 100,000 in 1957. It was formed in 1950 by a merger of the left-bank town of Fancheng and the right-bank town of Siangyang. As the head of navigation for motorized vessels, Siangfan is the collecting and supply center for the entire northwest section of the province. Its transport situation was greatly improved with completion of a railroad from Wuhan. Construction of the line began in 1958, reached Suihsien by 1961, and was completed to Siangfan at the end of 1965. The railroad may serve as the initial segment of a future trunk line to Sian or Chungking.

Farther upstream along the Han Shui, 40 miles northwest of Siangfan, is the hsien town of Kwanghwa, which under the name of Laohokow was the regional trade center in the 1930's before being superseded by Siangfan. Kwanghwa continued to retain some trade functions as the natural southern outlet for the Nanyang region of southwest Honan until 1969, when the inauguration of the Loho-Nanyang railroad redirected Nanyang's transport connections northward. Just beyond Kwanghwa, in the Han Shui gorges below the mouth of the Tan Kiang, a left tributary, is the site of a proposed 900,000-kilowatt hydroelectric station known as Tankiangkow ("Tan Kiang mouth"). Work on this project began in 1958, a power line from Siangfan was inaugurated the following year, and a rail spur from Siangfan was opened in 1960. But work on the project has apparently stagnated since then.

HUNAN PROVINCE
Capital: Changsha; area: 81,000 sq. mi.; population: 41 million

The province of Hunan coincides approximately with the drainage basin of Lake Tungting. The lake, situated in the northern part of Hunan, fluctuates in volume between the high-water stage in the summer and the low-water stage during the winter. Moreover, silting has somewhat reduced the lake's area in recent years. At comparable seasons of the year, the lake had an area of 1,800 square miles in 1937 and an area of 1,450 square miles in 1946. The lake is linked with the Yangtze River in the northeast at the town of Yoyang. In addition, the western part of the lake is joined to the Yangtze by a number of channels, including the Taiping and Owchih canals.

The lake receives the four main rivers of Hunan. They are the Siang

Kiang, the Tze Shui, the Yüan Kiang, and the Li Shui. Each of these rivers is navigable for junks, the Siang taking the largest vessels, and each river is associated in its lower reaches with a major trade center. These lower river cities are Changsha, the provincial capital, on the Siang, Yiyang on the Tze, Changteh on the Yüan, and Tsingshih on the Li.

Topographically, the province consists of the alluvial basin of Lake Tungting and the valleys of its tributary rivers. These lowlands are enclosed on the west, south, and east by hills of reddish sandstone, rising rarely to more than 3,000 feet. Level land is restricted to the alluvial lowlands. Terracing is widespread on the hillsides.

Hunan is almost entirely in the rice-tea agricultural area of China. Rice is the universal summer crop wherever the land can be irrigated. The Tungting basin and the lower Siang valley are one of China's "rice bowls," with the trade center at Changsha. Hunan produces 15 per cent of China's total rice crop.

Tea is the principal upland crop, accounting for 17 per cent of the nation's total. The tea is grown in the hill ranges separating the major stream valleys. The best-known variety is the Anhwa, which is produced in the Tze Shui valley and shipped via Hankow.

Cotton is cultivated chiefly west of Lake Tungting, near Changteh and Tsingshih. Cotton production is 5 per cent of the national total. Rice acreage in the lowlands is usually planted in wheat, barley, or rapeseed during the winter. Hillside crops, in addition to tea, are corn, soybeans, and sweet potatoes. As part of its effort to increase food production, the Peking regime is encouraging the expansion of sweet potatoes, a high-yield crop, on higher ground.

Distinctive provincial crops, other than tea, are ramie and tung oil. Ramie is grown chiefly in the vicinity of Liuyang and Liling on the east side of the Siang valley. Tung oil is produced chiefly in the western hills of the province. One of the best-known grades of tung oil originates in the area of Hungkiang in the valley of the Yüan Kiang. The so-called Hung oil is shipped down the Yüan to Changteh and from there to Hankow for further distribution.

Fir, pine, and bamboo stands in the uplands of Hunan yield lumber that is floated down the Yüan Kiang to Changteh and the Siang Kiang to Changsha. From these two cities, the lumber is rafted to Wuhan for milling.

Hunan is a conspicuously rich mineral province, particularly in nonferrous metals. The province leads China in the production of antimony and mercury. Its manganese output now probably exceeds Liaoning's. Lead and zinc, tungsten and tin, gold and silver are also produced.

The largest antimony-mining center of China is Sikwangshan, northeast of Sinhwa on the Tze Shui. Lesser antimony mines are found at Panki, southwest of Yiyang, and elsewhere in the Tze Shui basin as well as near Yüanling in the Yüan Kiang basin to the west. Sikwangshan, which accounts for 70 per cent or more of China's total antimony production, has been in operation for hundreds of years, with the modern period of exploitation beginning in the 1890's. Until recently, the crude antimony from Sikwangshan (the name actually means "tin-ore mountain") was trucked to the river landing of Lengshuikiang on the Tze Shui for shipment downriver. Access to the Sikwangshan district was substantially improved in 1960 with construction of the eastern segment of the projected Hunan-Kweichow railroad. The present railhead on this line is Kinchushan, a coal-mining town about 15 miles south of Sikwangshan. In the 1960's, the output of the antimony mines presumably moved increasingly over the railroad for further refining in the Changsha-Chuchow complex.

Hunan's mercury deposits are a continuation of the Kweichow field. The mercury mine is on the Kweichow border at Howtzeping, northwest of Fenghwang, in the southern section of the West Hunan Tuchia-Miao Autonomous Chou. This district accounts for about two-thirds of China's mercury output.

Manganese has been mined since World War I at Shaoshanchung, 20 miles west of Siangtan. After the virtual depletion of high-grade manganese oxides, the mine began to extract low-grade carbonates, which yield nodules of 35 to 47 per cent manganese after calcining. These nodules are of metallurgical grade and are used chiefly in the form of ferromanganese by the steel industry.

China's chief lead-zinc mine outside of Manchuria is Shuikowshan, 30 miles south of Hengyang. This center, insignificant by world standards, also produces silver as part of the mixed ores. The mine and concentrating mill are linked by a short railroad with Sungpai, where a zinc smelter is situated. Lead concentrates are shipped down the Siang Kiang to a smelter at Changsha.

Hunan's tungsten production, often associated with tin, molybdenum, and bismuth, is second only to the tungsten output of Kiangsi Province in China. Hunan accounts for about 10 per cent of the nation's tungsten. The mines are small and widely distributed, with the principal operations in western Hunan near Yüanling, in eastern Hunan near Chaling, and in the southern part of the province at Yaokangsien, 20 miles south of Tzehing, and at Sianghwaling, north of Linwu.

In addition to the silver associated with lead-zinc output, the province is also an important gold producer, with mining centers found both in the western uplands near Taoyüan and Yüanling and in the eastern uplands near Pingkiang.

Hunan also is one of China's phosphate-producing regions, with a mine of 600,000 tons capacity situated at Yungho, northeast of Liuyang near the Kiangsi border. Commercial production appears to have begun on a large scale in 1966, when a 65-mile railroad was completed from Liling through Liuyang to the Yungho mine. The ore is converted into superphosphate at nearby Chuchow.

The province is not a significant coal-producer, but a number of mines help meet local needs. The largest is in the Tzehing area, where a spur from the Sükiatung junction on the Hankow-Canton railroad extends to the mine at Santu. The Tzehing district yields bituminous coal, but much of it is high in ash content and must be cleaned in a large coal-washing plant inaugurated in 1959 at Chuchow. Tzehing is believed to produce about 2 million tons of coal a year. Another, newer source of coal is the Kinchushan deposit, which was reached in 1960 by the eastern segment of the planned Hunan-Kweichow railroad.

The coking-coal deposit of Kinchushan and nearby hematite iron-ore deposits serve as the basis for the small Lienyüan iron and steel plant with a presumed annual capacity of several hundred thousand tons of pig iron and steel. Construction on the Lienyüan plant began during the Great Leap, but it is not believed to have reached its ultimate designed capacity of 850,000 tons of pig iron and 600,000 tons of steel ingots.

For its power supply, Hunan relies on a number of coal-burning steam-electric stations in the principal industrial centers as well as on the Cheki (or Toki) hydroelectric station on the Tze Shui, with a designed capacity of 435,000 kilowatts. Construction on the Cheki station, southwest of Anhwa, began in 1958, and the first of six 72,500-kilowatt generating units was installed in January, 1962. Three generators were reported in operation by the end of 1965, and the Cheki station was said to be feeding power to the industrial district of central Hunan over a 220-kilovolt transmission line.

It is in the central Hunan region that the main industrial cities (Table 39) are concentrated along the main north-south railroad and the navigable Siang Kiang. Three of these cities—Changsha, the capital, Chuchow, the

TABLE 39
CITIES OF HUNAN

City	City Level	Function	Population (*in thousands*)		
			1953	1957	1970 est.
Changsha	subprovincial	manuf.	651	703	800
Chuchow	subprovincial	manuf.	127	190	500
Siangtan	hsien	manuf.	184	250	400
Hengyang	hsien	manuf.	235	270	300
Shaoyang	hsien	trade	118		
Changteh	hsien	trade	95	120	
Yiyang	hsien	trade	50–100		
Former Cities	*Period*	*Function*	*1953 Population*		
Tsingshih	1953–62	trade	50–100		
Hungkiang	1953–62	trade	30–50		
Chenhsien	Chenchow, 1960–62	trade	30–50		
Tungkiang	1961–62	coal			
Lengshuitan	1961–62	timber			
Lowti	1961–62	rail jct.			
Lengshuikiang	Lengkiang, 1961–62	ore terminal			
Kienyang	Ankiang, 1961–62	trade	30–50		
Yoyang	1961–62	trade			

rapidly growing new industrial center, and Siangtan—are clustered close together and are virtually coalescing into a conurbation. The fourth central Hunan city, Hengyang, is situated farther south, where the main north-south railroad divides into lines running south to Kwangtung and southwest to Kwangsi.

Changsha, the provincial capital, had a population of 651,000 in the 1953 census and 703,000 in 1957. It is a major river port on the Siang Kiang, accessible to 500-ton vessels. Situated in the heart of Hunan's "rice bowl," Changsha is one of China's leading rice-marketing centers. It became accessible to foreign commerce in 1903 and rapidly developed as a supplier of tea, lumber, ramie, and nonferrous metals, processed at an old lead-zinc smelter from Shuikowshan ores. Economic development accelerated after the city was reached by the railroad in 1918. The city is noted for its handicrafts, including embroidery and porcelain. Modern manufacturing industries produce heavy machine tools and precision instruments. The availability of hydroelectric power from the Cheki station led to the construction of an aluminum reduction plant, reported in 1971. Changsha ("long sand") is named for the elongated sandy island of Shuiluchow in the Siang Kiang. An ancient literary and educational center, Changsha still is the seat of several educational institutions clustered around the hill of Yolushan on the left bank opposite the city proper.

Chuchow, in contrast to ancient Changsha, is entirely the product of the modern industrial and railroad era. The town arose at the turn of the twentieth century, when a railroad was built from the riverside terminal of Chuchow on the Siang Kiang to the Pingsiang coal mines, just across the Kiangsi border. With the construction of the Hankow-Canton railroad and the prolongation of the Pingsiang spur into the Kiangsi-Chekiang railroad, Chuchow became a major railroad junction. Its transport functions were to be further enhanced with the construction of the Hunan-Kweichow railroad westward. The eastern 200-mile segment of this line, as far as the Sikwangshan antimony-mining district on the Tze Shui, was in fact completed in 1937, but the rails were dismantled by the Japanese in World War II for construction of the Hunan-Kwangsi railroad. The dismantled segment was rebuilt in the late 1950's, opening to Lowti in 1959 and to the Kinchushan coal mine, near Sikwangshan, the following year. Chuchow's industrial development dates largely from the late 1950's. An old locomotive and rolling-stock plant was expanded in 1958. A coal-cleaning plant, with a capacity of 1.8 million tons a year, was inaugurated in 1959 to prepare high-ash coal from Tzehing, in southern Hunan, and from Pingsiang, in Kiangsi, for use as coking coal in blast furnaces at the nearby small iron and steel plant of Siangtan and partly at the Wuhan complex. In the early 1960's, a lead and zinc smelter is reported to have been completed at Chuchow, replacing the older refining installations of Changsha. A new superphosphate plant at Chuchow processes phosphate from the Yungho mine near Liuyang, northeast of Chuchow. A nitrogen fertilizer plant was under construction during the Great Leap. The growing industrial significance of Chuchow is reflected in its administrative status. Since 1959, it has been the only Hunan city, besides Changsha, at subprovincial level. Chuchow's population, which was 127,000 in the 1953 census and 190,000 in 1957, increased substantially subsequently, as the municipal area expanded from 100 square miles in 1957 to about 700 square miles, extending from the Changsha municipal center southward for more than 40 miles along the railroad. The estimated 1970 population of the Changsha urban district is 500,000.

Siangtan, the third city in this tri-city complex, is situated west of Chuchow on the left bank of the Siang Kiang. An early water-transport center serving as the outlet of the Lien Shui, a left tributary of the Siang Kiang, Siangtan declined after the construction of the Hankow-Canton railroad and the rise of Chuchow. An era of industrialization set in after World War II. An electric-motor plant, opened in 1947, became the core of a diversified electrical equipment industry. Beginning in the Great Leap, a small integrated iron and steel plant was established at Siangtan in the 1960's, presumably specializing in the production of ferromanganese in blast furnaces, using the manganese ore from the nearby Shaoshanchung mines to the west. The plant's biggest blast furnace (300 cubic meters) was opened in late 1968. A cement plant is reported to have been built in the 1960's at Siangsiang, west of Siangtan along the Hunan-Kweichow railroad. Siangtan's population was 184,000 in the 1953 census and 250,000 in 1957.

The southernmost of the cities along the railroad leading to Canton is Hengyang. This is the head of navigation of the Siang Kiang for large motorized junks. Above Hengyang only smaller junks can ascend the upper Siang Kiang and the Lei Shui, at whose mouth Hengyang is situated. The city is also a key rail hub, where the Hunan-Kwangsi line takes off toward the southwest. Several major roads meet at Hengyang, which was formerly called Hengchow. The city flourished briefly during World War II, when it was a center of Chinese Nationalist resistance from 1937 to 1943, but it declined after its fall to the Japanese in 1944. Although it has some manufacturing (rolled steel products, mining machinery, diesel engines, electric motors and small tractors), Hengyang has not matched the growth of Chuchow and Siangtan since the late 1950's. Formerly, Hunan's second-ranking city (235,000 in the 1953 census and 270,000 in 1957), Hengyang was presumably outdistanced in population size during the 1960's by both Chuchow and Siangtan.

Three of Hunan's cities are situated off the central transport axis formed by the Siang Kiang and the Canton-Hankow railroad. They are Shaoyang, Yiyang, and Changteh.

Shaoyang is the trade center of the upper Tze Shui valley at the point where a major highway crosses the stream. The city's transport situation was further enhanced in 1960, when it was reached by a 60-mile railroad branch from Lowti on the Hunan-Kweichow line. Shaoyang is the center of a bamboo region, which has supplied raw material for a traditional paper industry and bamboo handicrafts. Pine forests in the area provide the basis for a naval stores industry. Shaoyang had a population of 118,000 in the 1953 census. Its counterpart in the lower reaches of the Tze Shui basin is the city of Yiyang, which is primarily a timber trade and transport center, also with a traditional bamboo industry. Changteh, the trade center of the lower Yüan Kiang valley, flourished in the 1920's and 1930's as a shipping point for tung oil, timber, rice, and cotton. It was then Hunan's second largest city. Although it has retained significance as a regional marketing center in northwest Hunan, the industrialization program has bypassed Changteh and it has dropped behind the manufacturing centers of central Hunan. It had a population of 95,000 in the 1953 census and 120,000 in 1957.

Two regional centers acquired city status in 1953, but lost it in 1962, presumably because economic development did not justify a high administrative level. One was Tsingshih, a marketing and processing center for the Li Shui basin, north of Changteh. The other is Hungkiang, a tung oil and timber center in the upper reaches of the Yüan Kiang.

In an unusual flurry of administrative changes, seven other places were briefly elevated to the status of cities in the early 1960's but lost it again in 1962. In southern Hunan, the hsien town of Chenhsien, center of a tungsten and coal-mining region, was made a city in 1960 with the name of Chenchow but lost that status and name two years later. In the area of the Tzehing coal mines, the town of Tungkiang was briefly raised to the level of a city in 1961–62. On the Hunan-Kwangsi railroad, the lumber-milling town of Lengshuitan was a city during the same period. In western Hunan, the brief city-forming flurry affected Lowti, railroad junction on the planned Hunan-Kweichow railroad; Lengshuikiang (called Lengkiang while a city, 1961–62), the Tze Shui river terminal for antimony from the Sikwangshan mines; and Kienyang (called Ankiang while a city, 1961–62), a small textile town on the upper Yüan Kiang, where the stream is crossed by the main Hunan-Kweichow highway. Finally, in northeastern Hunan, the lumber-milling center of Yoyang was briefly a city in 1961–62.

Hunan is the only province of the Middle Yangtze plain with significant non-Chinese ethnic groups, totaling about 1 million in the 1953 census. They include 400,000 Tuchia of the Tibeto-Burman family, 380,000 Miao and 70,000 Yao of the Miao-Yao group, and 125,000 Tung of the Thai-language group. These groups form one autonomous chou and four autonomous hsien.

The West Hunan Tuchia-Miao Autonomous Chou takes in the uplands of northwestern Hunan. It has a population of 1.5 million, of whom about 25 per cent are Tuchia and 20 per cent Miao. The autonomous chou was established in 1952 as a Miao minority area, but after the Tuchia, who live in the northern half of the chou, were officially recognized as a separate ethnic group, the designation of the area was changed in 1957 to cover both minorities. The area produces timber, tung oil, and gallnuts used for tanning. It contains small coal and iron mines, as well as the mercury deposits near Fenghwang. Transportation with the rest of Hunan is maintained by junk traffic along the Li Shui and the Yüan Kiang, as well as by a highway from Changteh completed in 1954. The area's administrative center was established in a small Miao village called Soli, just north of the Chinese town of Kiencheng, a hsien seat. In connection with the establishment of the autonomous government, the administrative institutions of Kiencheng were transferred to Soli village and Soli was renamed Kishow, which means "auspicious beginning."

The Miao nationality, which numbered 380,000 in the province in 1953, also has an autonomous hsien, Chengpu, established in late 1956. The Tung, who number 125,000 in Hunan, are represented by two hsien in the southwest, adjoining the Sankiang Tung Autonomous Hsien in northern Kwangsi and the Southeast Kweichow Miao-Tung Autonomous Chou. One Tung hsien of Hunan was established in 1954 at Tungtao, whose population of 80,000 then included 50,000 of the Tung nationality, and the other was set up in 1956 at Hwanghsien, which was thereupon renamed Sinhwang ("new Hwang"). Finally the Yao have an autonomous hsien established in 1955 at Kianghwa as part of the Yao settlement area in the Hunan-Kwangtung-Kwangsi border region. The Kianghwa Autonomous Hsien had a population of 108,000, which included 39,000 Yao out of Hunan's total Yao population of 70,000.

KIANGSI PROVINCE

Capital: Nanchang; area: 64,000 sq. mi.; population: 25 million

Topographically, Kiangsi is very similar to Hunan. Like its western neighbor, Kiangsi consists of a central lowland, dominated by the Poyang lake basin in the north and by the Kan Kiang valley in the south, enclosed by uplands on the west, south, and east. Only in the north does the province open directly on the Yangtze valley proper.

Lake Poyang, which, like Lake Tungting, is a natural flood reservoir for the Yangtze River, has an area of about 1,000 square miles. Like Lake Tungting, Poyang has a high-water stage in the summer, when its depth reaches 60 to 70 feet. In the winter, the lake becomes quite shallow. It is connected with the Yangtze by a narrow arm that joins the stream at Hukow, east of Kiukiang. Again, like Tungting Lake, Poyang receives one major river, the Kan Kiang, and several minor ones. These are the Siu Shui, which enters Lake Poyang from the west, and the Sin Kiang and the combined Po Kiang and Chang Kiang, which enter the lake from the east.

The Kan Kiang traverses the province from south to north and serves as its major navigable waterway. Small junks can travel as far as Kanchow and even beyond that city up the two headstreams. Larger junks are prevented by rapids from going beyond Kian.

Most of Kiangsi falls in the conventional rice-tea area. The extreme south, adjoining Kwangtung, is part of the double-cropping rice area. The richest rice-growing region is the Poyang basin, with its trade center at Kiukiang. Tea is the hillside crop, with the best Kiangsi varieties originating in the Siu Shui basin on the southern slopes of the Mufow Mountains. It will be recalled that the high-grade Puchi tea of Hupei is produced on the northern slopes of the same hill range. Like rice, tea is marketed and processed at Kiukiang.

Cotton is a secondary crop, restricted largely to the northeastern shore of Lake Poyang near Tuchang and to the Siu Shui basin. Cotton is marketed and processed at Kiukiang.

Another fiber widely grown throughout Kiangsi is ramie. Production centers are at Wantsai, whose fiber is widely known throughout China, and Ichun in western Kiangsi, and at Ihwang and Fuchow in eastern Kiangsi.

In southernmost Kiangsi, where the long growing season permits the cultivation of two crops of rice, subtropical crops include sugar cane, tobacco, and tangerines. The surrounding uplands yield bamboo and other woods. These are floated down the Kan Kiang and its tributaries to mills at Nanchang.

Coal and tungsten dominate the province's mineral resources. The principal coal center is Pingsiang, situated near the Hunan border on the north slopes of the Wukung Mountains. Pingsiang, the largest coal-producer south of the Yangtze, produces a good coking coal. It has shared the fortunes of the iron and steel centers in the Wuhan area, flourishing from the turn of the century until the 1920's and virtually closing down thereafter. Production, now estimated at 5 to 10 million tons a year, was revived with the opening of the large Wuhan iron and steel plant in the late 1950's, and Pingsiang was raised to city status in 1960. Pingsiang coal is noted for its high ash content and requires cleaning before use as metallurgical coking coal. It is being shipped to a coal-washing plant opened in 1959 at Chuchow in neighboring Hunan. The coal mines proper are at Anyüan, on a rail spur southeast of Pingsiang, and at Kaokeng, on a four-mile rail spur from Chüankiang, east of Pingsiang.

A second coking-coal center began to be developed in 1959 near Fengcheng, south of Nanchang, with a designed capacity of more than 2 million tons a year. A 30-mile railroad to the new mine, at Shangtang, northwest of Fengcheng, was inaugurated in the early 1960's.

China's principal tungsten mines are concentrated in southern Kiangsi and yield copper, bismuth, molybdenum, and beryllium as byproducts. The leading mine is at Sihwashan, northwest of Tayü. Others are Pankushan, south of Yütu; Takishan, south of Chüannan; and Kweimeishan, south of Lungnan. The concentrates of tungsten and associated ores are shipped by truck to Shiukwan, in neighboring Kwangtung Province, or are sent from Kanchow downstream along the Kan Kiang. Elsewhere in Kiangsi, an important manganese deposit is found in the Loping area in the northeast, and kaolin, named for Kao Ling ("high hill"), provides the raw material for the porcelain center of Kingtehchen.

The industrial centers of the province rely for their power supply mainly on coal-burning thermal electric stations. However, the southern part of Kiangsi, including the regional center of Kanchow and the tungsten-mining industry, derives parts of its electricity requirements from the 60,000-kilo-

TABLE 40
CITIES OF KIANGSI

City	City Level	Function	Population (*in thousands*)		
			1953	1957	1970 est.
Nanchang	subprovincial	manuf.	398	508	
Kingtehchen	subprovincial	ceramics	92	150	270
Kanchow	hsien	trade	99	120	
Kiukiang	hsien	trade	65	80	
Kian	hsien	trade	53	60	
Pingsiang	hsien	coal		27	
Shangjao	hsien	trade			
Fuchow	hsien	trade			
Former City	*Period*				
Sinyü	1960–63				

watt hydroelectric station at Shangyu, 25 miles west of Kanchow. Construction on the Shangyu project began in 1954 and the first of four 15,000-kilowatt generating units was inaugurated in November, 1957.

The regional centers (Table 40) are situated either along the Kan Kiang in southern Kiangsi or along the two railroad lines in northern Kiangsi. The first stage of the 370-mile east-west railroad from Chekiang Province to Nanchang was completed by 1935. At that time, Pingsiang was also connected with the Hankow-Canton railroad at Chuchow. The gap between Nanchang and Pingsiang was closed in 1937. The 80-mile north-south railroad connects Nanchang with the Yangtze at Kiukiang. Long-range plans call for the continuation of this line southward along the Kan Kiang into Kwangtung. Kiangsi's railroad network was further expanded in the late 1950's with the construction of the line from Yingtan into Fukien Province. Ultimately, Yingtan is envisaged as a major railroad junction, when long-range plans for the construction of a railroad from Yingtan northward through Kingtehchen into southern Anhwei to Wuhu are realized.

Nanchang, the provincial capital, is situated on the right bank of the Kan Kiang, at the head of the river's delta on Lake Poyang. The city is an ancient waterway transport center on a traditional route linking northern and southern China. With the advent of modern, larger inland shipping and the construction of the Hankow-Canton railroad early in the twentieth century, Nanchang was partly supplanted in its transport functions by the Yangtze River port of Kiukiang. The city's economic position was strengthened once again by construction of the Chekiang-Kiangsi railroad in the late 1930's. A diversified manufacturing center, Nanchang has important cotton-textile, rice-milling, and oils and fats industries, as well as lumber and paper mills. Machinery manufacturing has specialized traditionally in the production of diesel engines, and this activity provided the basis for tractor manufacture in the late 1950's. A motor-vehicle repair plant was expanded in 1968–69 to assemble trucks. The city also has an aircraft plant. Nanchang had a population of 398,000 in the 1953 census and 508,000 in 1957.

Kiukiang, Kiangsi's port on the Yangtze River, is the traditional outlet for the province's agricultural products: rice, tea, tobacco, cotton, and ramie cloth. The city flourished for about seventy years after it was declared an open treaty port in 1858 and reached a population of 120,000 in 1930. But it declined after the completion of the Chekiang-Kiangsi railroad provided a new access route to the province in 1937. Kiukiang had a population of 65,000 in the 1953 census and 80,000 in 1957. Like many Chinese cities caught in the tempo of modern life, Kiukiang consists of an old town, in the east, and a commercial waterfront section, at the head of the railroad to Nanchang. South of Kiukiang is the popular hill resort of Kuling, in the Lu Shan.

In northeastern Kiangsi are the cities of Kingtehchen and Shangjao. Kingtehchen is the world-famous porcelain and ceramics center of China. It was based originally on the kaolin resources of Kao Ling, a hill to the east of the city, for which the white clay was named. The original deposit has been largely depleted through centuries of porcelain-making, but Kingtehchen still obtains most of its clay, feldspar (used as a flux), glazes, and coloring agents from the vicinity as well as from Kimen in adjoining southern Anhwei. The city had a population of 92,000 in the 1953 census, but subsequently the entire subsidiary region was included within its municipal boundaries directly under provincial jurisdiction, and the population within the expanded city limits rose to 270,000 by 1970. Shangjao, the regional agricultural center of northeastern Kiangsi, retained city status after the construction of the Kiangsi-Fukien railroad in the late 1950's but is likely to be superseded gradually by the new transport center of Yingtan to the west, especially when the Kiangsi-Anhwei railroad is completed northward from Yingtan.

Fuchow, an agricultural center of north central Kiangsi in the basin of the Fu Ho, a tributary of Lake Poyang, has alternated between the status of city and that of hsien known as Linchwan. It was a city from 1954 to 1964, reverted to hsien level under the name of Linchwan, and regained city status under the name of Fuchow in the late 1960's.

A former city is Sinyü, situated on the Chekiang-Kiangsi-Hunan railroad halfway between Nanchang and Pingsiang. Sinyü was raised to city status in 1960 in conjunction with plans to build a small integrated iron and steel plant. However, this project did not materialize, and Sinyü reverted to hsien status in 1963.

Southward along the Kan Kiang are the cities of Kian and Kanchow. Both are road and water transport centers along the historical north-south route from Kiangsi to Kwangtung. Kian, the center of south central Kiangsi, has rice mills and a camphor factory. It had a population of 53,000 in the 1953 census and 60,000 in 1957. Kanchow is the regional center of the southern Kiangsi tungsten-mining district. Its industries include the manufacture of mining equipment, paper, and farm implements. Kanchow had a population of 99,000 in 1953 and 120,000 in 1957.

7. The Southeast Coastal Uplands

The Southeast uplands include the coastal provinces of Chekiang and Fukien. The combined area of the two provinces is about 87,000 square miles and their population about 50 million. This amounts to more than 2 per cent of China's total area and 7 per cent of the nation's population, respectively. The average density of the Southeast uplands is 575 persons per square mile (see Map 6, p. 128).

In contrast to the predominantly low-lying regions considered thus far, the Southeast uplands, with the exception of a few coastal delta plains, have a rugged topography. Resistant rocks, such as granite, porphyry, and other hard formations, have withstood erosion over the years. In general, there is a distinct structural alignment from northeast to southwest. This trend parallels the coast and reflects the axis of the ancient rock folds of which today's ranges are the remnants.

Along the Chekiang-Anhwei border, the Tienmu Mountains rise to more than 5,000 feet in the highest points of Chekiang. These rugged border ranges are separated by the Tsientang River valley from a series of parallel coastal ranges. Near Linhai, the Kwotsang Mountains rise to more than 4,500 feet. The mountain ranges enclose a number of inland basins, such as those of Chühsien-Kinhwa, Chuki, and Chenghsien, and coastal plains, including those of Ningpo-Shaohing.

The southern part of the Southeast uplands includes two basic mountain ranges, trending northeast-southwest. They are the Wuyi Mountains along the Fukien-Kiangsi border, rising to 3,500 feet, and the Taiyün Mountains, nearer the coast. The principal plains along this part of the coast are those of Foochow, Chüanchow, and Changchow.

The rocky and intricately embayed coastline reflects the rugged inland topography. This is a coast of subsidence, with drowned valleys and offshore islands ranging in size from several miles to mere rocks. The coast offers many excellent natural harbors, but these long had poor connections with the hinterland and did not develop into major commercial ports. They do play a useful role in coastwise trade.

One of the most interesting coastal features is the large, funnel-shaped Hangchow Bay, at the extreme north of the region being considered here. The bay, which narrows from about sixty miles at its mouth to less than two miles near Hangchow, is famous for its tidal bore. The abrupt tidal front, caused by the rapid narrowing and shallowness of the channel, may reach 6 to 10 feet in height.

Outstanding coastal indentations south of Hangchow Bay are Siangshan Bay, which penetrates 30 miles inland; intricate Sanmen Bay, noted for fisheries and salines; Sansha Bay, virtually enclosed by two peninsulas; and Amoy Bay, with the Nationalist-occupied island of Quemoy. The most extensive island group is the Chushan Archipelago off Hangchow Bay.

The region is characterized by a typical trellis drainage pattern, in which the main streams have cut narrow valleys perpendicular to the trend of the mountain ranges, and tributaries follow the broad valleys between parallel ranges. The rivers divide the region into distinct economic subareas, each dominated by its rivermouth city. From north to south these cities are Hangchow, at the mouth of the Tsientang River, Ningpo, at the mouth of the Yung Kiang, Linhai, at the mouth of the Lin Kiang, Wenchow, at the mouth of the Wu Kiang, Foochow, at the mouth of the Min Kiang, Chüanchow, at the mouth of the Tsin Kiang, and Amoy, at the mouth of the combined Kiulung River and Lung Kiang.

The Southeast uplands have a hot and wet subtropical climate with some of the heaviest rainfall in China. The average rainfall is 60 inches along the coast and up to 80 inches in the inland mountains. The July temperature is uniformly high, averaging about 85° F (29° C). The averages in January, however, vary with latitude, being lowest in the north—about 40° F (5° C) —and highest in the south—about 60° F (15° C). In view of the mountain barrier against the Polar Continental air in the winter, cold air penetrates rarely into the region, and snow is all but unknown. The coast is especially exposed to typhoons, which occur most commonly in August and September. They are rare from January to April. As much as 4 to 8 inches of rain may fall in a single day.

Because of the predominantly mountainous relief, agriculture is restricted to narrow plains along the coast, river valleys, and inland basins. The principal areas are Ningpo-Shaohing, Wenchow, Kinhwa-Chühsien, Foochow, and Changchow. Terracing is practiced in the mountains wherever soil and climate conditions permit tilling.

In terms of distinct crop associations, most of the region falls in the rice-tea area, except the extreme south, where double-cropping of rice is possible. Irrigated rice takes about 60 per cent of the sown area. The first crop is usually sown in April and harvested in June. The second crop is sown either after the first harvest where the growing season is longest or between the rows of the first crop in June. In the second case, the new crop is harvested in October.

Chief among other food crops are sweet potatoes. Wheat, corn, and millet are cultivated on a small scale in the uplands. In view of the fact that rice can be grown only in plains and river valleys constituting only 5 per cent of the total area, sweet potatoes are a major local subsistence crop.

The warm, humid climate has made the Southeast uplands China's main tea-producer. Tea is grown especially in the Wuyi Mountains for export through Foochow. Well-known grades are also cultivated in Chekiang. Hangchow, Wenchow, and Foochow are all major tea-trade centers. Other characteristic agricultural products are subtropical fruit, sugar cane, and tobacco.

The Southeast uplands are favorably situated for the development of a forest industry. The extensive uplands are unusable for agriculture and are covered with luxuriant tree growth. Three main potential lumbering centers are the Tienmu Mountains and Tsientang valley, with outlet through Hangchow, the Wu Kiang valley, with outlet through Wenchow, and the Min Kiang and Tsin Kiang valleys, with outlets at Foochow and Amoy. In addition to construction timber, largely fir and pine, the region also produces camphor, tung oil, and lacquer.

Fishing is the most distinctive activity along the coast. The coastal margins are overcrowded with a population that cannot obtain its livelihood from the restricted agriculture. The surplus manpower together with the rocky indented character of the shore line, and the abundance of islands and coves have given the region a major place in China's fishing industry.

The Southeast uplands are generally poor in mineral resources, but coal and iron were evidently abundant enough to justify the construction of a medium-size integrated iron and steel plant in Fukien at Sanming during the Great Leap. Coal for the Sanming operation is mined in the Changping-Lungyen district and iron ore at nearby Hwaan. The region also has two distinctive mineral deposits in Chekiang: the fluorspar center of Wuyi, southeast of Kinhwa, and the alum mine at Fan Shan on the Fukien border near the sea. In connection with the fishing industry, salines have been developed along the coast, notably in the Antung salt district on the south shore of Hangchow Bay.

Industrialization of the region was also fostered by the start of development of its hydroelectric potential. One of China's largest hydroelectric plants in operation is the Sinan River complex, with a designed capacity of 650,000 kilowatts. The station, situated southwest of Hangchow, was inaugurated in 1960. Lesser hydroelectric installations are the 30,000-kilowatt Hwangtankow plant south of Chühsien in Chekiang, and the 62,000-kilowatt Kutien station northwest of Foochow in Fukien.

Except for the Chekiang-Kiangsi railroad, built in the 1930's through the inland basins of Chekiang, the Southeast uplands were long devoid of rail lines. A major share of transportation thus fell on waterways, and especially coastwise routes. Ningpo, Wenchow, Foochow, and Amoy developed as the main maritime ports. After 1949, maritime trade along the southeast coast suffered from hostilities between the Communists on the mainland and the

Nationalists on Taiwan. Foochow and Amoy, in particular, have been virtually interdicted by continuing Nationalist occupation of the offshore islands, notably Matsu off Foochow and Quemoy off Amoy. The situation of these two cities was alleviated in the late 1950's with completion of railroads linking them to the Chinese rail net at the junction of Yingtan in northeast Kiangsi. The Hangchow-Ningpo railroad, completed in 1937 and destroyed during World War II, was restored in 1955.

As might be expected, the greatest population density of more than 800 persons per square mile is found in the coastal agricultural lowlands. Inland river valleys have densities of about 300 to 400, and the upland areas 100 to 150. Although the region is virtually homogeneously Chinese from the ethnic viewpoint, it represents extraordinary linguistic diversity. The rugged relief and poor communications between valleys have resulted in a large number of local dialects. For example, Ningpo, Wenchow, Foochow, Chüanchow, and Amoy dominate linguistic subareas of their own. Language maps of China generalize the complex situation by grouping the Chekiang dialects under the Wu (Shanghai) speech, the northern Fukien dialects under the Min (Foochow) speech, and the southern Fukien dialects under the Amoy-Swatow speech.

Except for Kwangtung, Fukien has produced most of the Chinese overseas emigration. The ports of Ningpo, Wenchow, Chüanchow, and Changchow were early centers of China's foreign trade. Starting in the late Ming Dynasty and early Ch'ing Dynasty (seventeenth century), Chinese began to emigrate through these ports to seek their fortunes abroad—and to find them.

Two thousand years ago, most of the Southeast uplands were occupied by aboriginal tribes. As a result of the Chinese southward advance, these peoples were driven into the mountains. Today, most of their descendants have been assimilated. Only two small groups, neither of which has its own autonomous area, have retained distinguishing ethnic characteristics. They are the Tan people, who are largely boatmen along the lower Min Kiang, and the She (Yü) people, a branch of the Yao, settled in the uplands of the upper Wu Kiang in southern Chekiang and in northern Fukien.

CHEKIANG PROVINCE

Capital: Hangchow; area: 39,000 sq. mi.; population: 31 million

Northernmost Chekiang, north of Hangchow, is a continuation of the densely populated, intensively cultivated Lower Yangtze plain. The rest of the province is more typical of the Southeast uplands, with rugged mountain ranges enclosing coastal plains and inland basins.

Rice is cultivated throughout the province wherever water is available for irrigation and clay pans develop on the alluvial soils of flood plains and deltas. In the Lower Yangtze plain section of Chekiang, rice is associated with winter wheat and with silk and cotton. Cotton is also cultivated on the south shore of Hangchow Bay, chiefly around Yüyao, from where it is shipped to Shanghai and Ningpo. Mulberry for silkworms is also grown along the middle valley of the Tsientang River and along the Tsaongo River, which enters Hangchow Bay from the south. The towns of Tunglu, Siaoshan, and Shaohing are known for their silk production. Jute is an important bast fiber. Chekiang produces about half of China's jute.

Tea is a major crop in the uplands, where it is usually grown on hillside terraces. Several well-known leaf types are produced in Chekiang. They are the Lungtsing leaf, produced southwest of Hangchow, the Pingshui leaf, produced near Shaohing, and the Wenchow leaf, produced in the Wu Kiang valley. The province is a major green-tea producer but has increasingly shifted to black tea, an export variety.

Fruits make up an important part of the province's exports. Peaches, plums, and loquats are grown in the Ningpo-Fenghwa area. In the southern part of the province, near subtropical conditions make possible the production of citrus fruit, with centers in Tientai, Linhai, and Wenchow. Hwangyen, southeast of Linhai, is nationally known for its oranges.

Lumbering and fishing are major nonfarm occupations. Most of the lumber originates in the basins of the Tsientang River and the Wu Kiang and is exported via Hangchow and Wenchow. Tung oil is produced in the Tsientang valley and processed at Kienteh. The fishing industry is best developed in the Chushan Archipelago; other fishery areas are Sanmen Bay and the area around Yühwan Island. Chekiang has about 300,000 fishermen, many of whom are based at Tinghai, chief town of the Chushans. Other major fishing centers, not only of Chekiang but all China, are Puto (Shenkiamen), also in the Chushans, and Ningpo, on the mainland.

Chekiang's mineral resources are limited. Coal is mined northwest of Changhing, at the Kiangsu-Anhwei border, but this operation is only of local significance. However, the province plays a key role in the mining of two distinctive minerals: fluorspar, used as a flux in the iron and steel industry, as a source of fluorine compounds, and in the preparation of certain special glasses; and alum, an aluminum potassium sulfate that yields potash fertilizer, alumina (an intermediate product for the reduction of aluminum metal), and sulfuric acid. The fluorspar, at Wuyi, southeast of Kinhwa, has been mined since the 1930's, when it was first exported to Japan. The alum deposit is situated in the southeasternmost corner of Chekiang, where the Fukien border meets the sea south of Wenchow. The deposit, in a mountain known as Fan Shan, was incorporated in 1954 into a special mining district named Mingfan, the Chinese term for alum. Tsingtien, on the Wu Kiang upstream from Wenchow, produces a high-grade lithographic stone. Finally, Chekiang has a large salt production from coastal salines concentrated on the south shore of Hangchow Bay. The special Antung salt-producing district was set up there in the 1950's.

Though poor in fossil fuels, Chekiang is one of the leading Chinese producers of hydroelectric power. Development began with the start of construction in 1956 of a small station at Hwangtankow, 10 miles south of

TABLE 41
CITIES OF CHEKIANG

City	City Level	Function	Population (in thousands)		
			1953	1957	1970 est.
Hangchow	subprovince	manuf.	697	784	800
Ningpo	subprovince	port	238	280	300
Wenchow	subprovince	trade	202	210	250

Cities Abolished in 1963	1953 Population
Shaohing	131
Kashing	78
Huchow (now Wuhing)	63
Kinhwa	46

Chühsien, in southwestern Chekiang. The first of four 7,500-kilowatt turbines was installed in 1958, and the station reached its designed capacity of 30,000 kilowatts the following year. A far larger project began in 1957 on the Sinan River, farther north, where a hydroelectric station with a designed capacity of 650,000 kilowatts went into construction. An access railroad to the site was completed in 1958 by extending the old Kinhwa-Lanchi spur, and the first of nine planned 72,500-kilowatt units was installed in the Sinan River plant in 1960. By the middle 1960's, four such units were reported in operation. The power station has been linked by a 220-kilovolt line with Hangchow and Shanghai to feed electricity into the Chekiang-Kiangsu-Anhwei grid. Sinan is also linked by a transmission line with the smaller Hwangtankow power plant. A hydroelectric project was reported in 1969 to have been inaugurated on the Fuchun River, a section of the Tsientang River southwest of Hangchow, but neither exact location nor capacity has been disclosed.

Chekiang's regional centers (Table 41) are situated in the coastal plains and inland basins. They are served either by rivers navigable for large junks or by the Shanghai-Hangchow-Nanchang railroad, which traverses the northwestern half of the province. The chief navigable rivers are the Tsientang River, the Yung Kiang, the Lin Kiang, and the Wu Kiang. The Tsientang River is navigable from Hangchow to Tunglu and at high water as far as Lanchi.

The Yung Kiang is navigable for ocean-going vessels between Ningpo and Chinhai, its outer port. A navigable canal that can be regarded as an extension of the Grand Canal runs from Ningpo to Hangchow, paralleling the south shore of Hangchow Bay and serving the Ningpo-Shaohing agricultural lowland.

The Lin Kiang is navigable only for junks between Linhai and its outer port of Haimen. Haimen is a key harbor along Chekiang's coastwise shipping routes. Finally the Wu Kiang, a major timber-floating route in its upper reaches, is navigable for junks from Wenchow past Tsingtien to Lishui.

Hangchow, the provincial capital, was known as Linan under the southern Sung Dynasty (1127–1280), when it was the capital of South China. The city, which had a 1953 population of about 700,000, is situated on the north bank of the Tsientang River at the head of Hangchow Bay. Although the city is situated on the coast, shallow access rules out virtually all coastwise trade. Its port functions are restricted to navigation on the lower Tsientang River and the Grand Canal, which here reaches its southern terminus. Neither the Grand Canal nor the canal's extension to Ningpo is connected with the Tsientang, whose high tides would flood the canals. Hangchow, in a charming natural setting on the east shore of West Lake and at the foot of wooded hills, attracts tourists and vacationers. Modern commercial and industrial activities are centered in the northern suburb of Kungchenkiao, situated on both sides of the Grand Canal. Traditionally a center of light industry, notably silk fabrics, cotton textiles, paper, and tea-processing (the Lungtsing variety), Hangchow added substantial heavy industry under Communist rule. It includes a small steel plant, a chemical complex (nitrogen fertilizers, calcium carbide, soda ash), and some machinery (tea harvesting and processing equipment). Electric motors are manufactured in the southeast suburb of Siaoshan.

North and east of Hangchow are three subregional centers that lost their city status in 1963, presumably because of inadequate industrial development and because they were overshadowed by Hangchow. Two of these places, situated in the Lower Yangtze plain section of Chekiang, north of Hangchow, are the agricultural towns of Wuhing and Kashing. Wuhing, which was called Huchow while a city, is situated on the Nanking-Hangchow highway and south of the lake Tai Hu. Its population in 1953 was 63,000, and its chief products are silk and rice. Halfway between Hangchow and Wuhing is the noted hill resort of Mokanshan, situated in a spur of the Tienmu Mountains. Kashing, another silk and rice center of northern Chekiang, is situated at the junction of the Grand Canal and the Hangchow-Shanghai railroad. With a population of 78,000 in 1953, it later acquired manufacturing industries (metallurgical equipment, caustic-chlorine chemicals). East of Hangchow, on the south side of Hangchow Bay, is Shaohing, agricultural center of the Shaohing-Ningpo lowland. Shaohing, which had a population of 131,000 in 1953, is traditionally noted for its rice wine. A small steel plant arose here in the Great Leap.

A fourth subregional center that lost its city status in 1963 is Kinhwa, a transport hub of central Chekiang. It is situated in the Kinhwa-Chühsien basin, one of the province's rice-producing areas. The town, with a population of 46,000 in 1953, owes its regional importance to the Chekiang-Kiangsi railroad. A rail spur extending from Kinhwa to the old waterway town of Lanchi was extended in 1958 to the site of the Sinan River hydroelectric plant. The availability of cheap power from that project after 1960 is reported to have stimulated the construction of a small aluminum reduction plant at Lanchi. Kinhwa is also the outlet for fluorspar mined at Wuyi, to the southeast, and may regain city status after construction of a long-planned railroad to Wenchow on the coast. Another potential urban center in the southwest is Chühsien, where expansion of a small chemical plant (caustic soda and chlorine) has been contemplated. Limestone resources, which were intended to provide a raw-material base for the chemical complex, are already being used in cement manufacture at Kiangshan, on the railroad southwest of Chühsien.

Two other regional centers of some importance are situated on the Chekiang coast. Ningpo, a city of about 300,000 by 1970, is one of China's principal fishing ports. Situated on the Yung Kiang, it can be reached by ocean-going vessels from its outer harbor of Chinhai. Ningpo has been one of China's foreign-trade centers since the T'ang Dynasty (A.D. 618–907) and was one of the original treaty ports opened in 1842. The completion of the Hangchow-Ningpo Railroad in 1955 linked the port with the national rail net. Its textile and food-processing industries were supplemented in the 1950's by machinery manufacturing (diesel engines, farm equipment, shipbuilding).

Wenchow, with a population of 250,000 by 1970, is the trade center of southeast Chekiang. It is situated on the south bank of the Wu Kiang and exports tea, timber, paper products, and citrus fruits. Though linked by an all-weather highway with Kinhwa in the interior, Wenchow's industrial growth is still held back by the absence of a railroad into its hinterland.

FUKIEN PROVINCE
Capital: Foochow; area: 48,000 sq. mi.; population: 18 million

Fukien has no extensive lowlands comparable to the coastal plains of northern Chekiang. The southern province is essentially an upland region typical of the southeast coast. The uplands gradually descend in a series of parallel northeast-southwest ranges toward the sea. The main streams, cutting perpendicularly through the hill ranges, form small delta plains at their mouths. The principal coastal plains of Fukien are the lowlands around Foochow, Chüanchow, and Changchow and Amoy.

Rice is by far the principal food grain in Fukien, with double-cropping common in the south. Sweet potatoes are a major staple food in non-rice-growing areas. Total food crop production in Fukien is about 4 million tons a year. Tea is a hillside crop in the Min Kiang basin of northern Fukien. The province is noted for the bohea leaf, named for the Bohea Hills, a Western corruption of the name of the Wuyi Mountains. Bohea tea is exported through Foochow. Like Chekiang, Fukien is a major fruit producer. Its subtropical fruit includes citrus grown around Foochow, the longans of Putien, the pomelos of Changchow, and bananas south of the Tsin Kiang. Sugar cane is a characteristic crop of southern Fukien, particularly in the Chüanchow and Changchow areas. A large sugar mill is in operation in the Putien-Sienyu area. Another distinctive crop is tobacco, which is produced in the Engteng area. Engteng is situated in the upper reaches of the Han Kiang, here known as the Ting Kiang. The tobacco, which provides the livelihood for virtually the entire hsien of Engteng, is shipped to Swatow in Kwangtung.

Lumbering and fishing play a major role in the provincial economy. Before the construction of railroads in the 1950's, timber cut in the upper reaches of the Min Kiang and its tributaries was floated downstream to mills at Foochow on the coast. Improved transportation in the interior led to the development of a major lumbering center at Kiensi ("west of the Kien"), on the right bank of the Kien Ki. Nearby, at the confluence of the Kien Ki and the Min Kiang, the town of Nanping acquired one of China's largest newsprint mills in 1958, based on these expanded lumbering operations. Nanping, which was raised to the status of city in 1956, also has a medium-size cement plant.

The coastal fisheries of Fukien are concentrated around Santuao in Sansha Bay; off the mouth of the Min Kiang, at Pingtan Island; in Hinghwa Bay; and on Tungshan Island, near the Kwangtung border.

Railroad construction stimulated the development of the province's modest coal and iron resources during the Great Leap and led to the construction of a medium-size integrated iron and steel plant at Sanming. The first of two blast furnaces with a working volume of 250 cubic meters and an annual capacity of 120,000 tons was inaugurated in 1959, and the second the following year. Oxygen converters for steel production and rolling mills were added, and Sanming was given the status of a city in 1960. It kept that status even though the plant apparently became inoperative during the recession of the early 1960's. It was not restored to full operation until the reconstruction of blast furnaces and converters in 1969. Coal for the Sanming operation and other provincial needs is mined at Changping and nearby Lungyen, and iron ore at Hwaan.

Industrial development was fostered by the use of hydroelectric power in this hilly province. The Kutien station, on a left tributary of the Min Kiang, northwest of Foochow, was completed in 1959–60 with a capacity of 62,000 kilowatts and linked by a transmission line with Foochow and with Nanping and Sanming. The plant was designed as the first of a series of stations in the Kutien area, with a combined capacity of 250,000 kilowatts. A more ambitious project, proposed on the Kien Ki near Nanping, would have a capacity of 1.2 million kilowatts.

Aside from the two interior cities of Nanping and Sanming, which owe their growth to relative recent resource development, Fukien's regional centers are all situated on the coast. They are, from north to south, Foochow, Chüanchow, Amoy, and, Changchow (Table 42).

Foochow, the provincial capital, had a population of 553,000 in 1953, and 616,000 in 1957. The walled city is about two miles from the north bank of the lower Min Kiang. Its commercial riverside suburb is linked by the Wanshow ("ten thousand ages") and Kiangnan bridges with Nantai, former foreign settlement and business center located on a large island in the Min Kiang. Ocean-going vessels must anchor at the Pagoda, 9 miles

TABLE 42
CITIES OF FUKIEN

City	City Level	Function	Population (*in thousands*) 1953	1957	1970 est.
Coastal Cities					
Foochow	subprovince	manuf.	553	616	700
Amoy	subprovince	manuf.	224	310	350
Chüanchow	hsien	trade	108		
Changchow	hsien	trade	81		
Interior Cities					
Nanping	hsien	paper, cement			
Sanming	hsien	iron, steel			

downstream. Nearby Mamoi is a Chinese naval base and shipbuilding center. Foochow is the natural outlet of the Min Kiang basin and exports tea, timber, leather, and lacquerware. It was Foochow lacquerware that, together with porcelain and silk, became identified with the traditional Chinese export trade. Foochow's economic development, impeded by the Nationalists' continuing occupation of the offshore island of Matsu, was improved by the construction of the railroad linking it since late 1958 with the Chinese rail system. The principal industrial addition in the Great Leap was a chemical complex inaugurated in 1959. Based on the use of limestone, salt, and coke as raw materials, it produces caustic soda, chlorine, calcium carbide, and their derivatives, building up to the manufacture of polyvinyl resin (added in 1965). Foochow also produces acetate rayon, using the wood-pulp resources of the interior.

Chüanchow, formerly also called Tsinkiang, was one of China's leading ports during the Sung and Yüan (Mongol) dynasties (eleventh to thirteenth centuries). It lost its importance in connection with the silting of its port on the Tsin Kiang and the rise of Foochow and Amoy. However, Chüanchow is still the natural outlet for the Tsin Kiang basin. It has a population of more than 100,000. Its industry includes sugar-refining (on the basis of local sugar cane), oilseed-milling, and gunny-bag manufacture. Chüanchow is noted as the place of origin of a large overseas Chinese population.

Amoy is Fukien's second largest city, with a population of 224,000 in 1953, and 310,000 in 1957. It is situated in Amoy Bay on the southwest shore of Amoy Island, which is 10 miles across. West of the city, beyond the inner harbor, is the island of Kulangsu, a former foreign settlement and residential section. Both Amoy and Foochow are among the original treaty ports opened to foreign trade in 1842. Amoy has an excellent natural harbor, whose growth was limited by the lack of hinterland transportation until construction of the Yingtan-Amoy railroad. Amoy exports the products of the Lung Kiang and Kiulung River areas, including sugar, tobacco, and bamboo paper. Like Chüanchow, Amoy has yielded a large part of the Chinese overseas emigration. The arrival of the railroad in 1957, as in the case of Foochow, eased Amoy's economic situation, which had been hampered by the Nationalists' continued occupation of the offshore island of Quemoy.

Changchow, formerly also called Lungki, is located on the north bank of the Lung Kiang. It was the former commercial center of the Lung Kiang and Kiulung River basins but has been supplanted by Amoy. It is known for its satin and sugar production. Because of shallowness of the Lung Kiang, most vessels must anchor at the outer port of Lunghai (Shihma), 9 miles downstream from Changchow.

Legend:
A.C. AUTONOMOUS CHOU
⊚ Capital of Chou
+ Autonomous Hsien (Nationality)

FUKIEN
KIANGSI
KWANGTUNG
HUNAN
KWEICHOW
YÜNNAN
KWANGSI CHUANG A.R.
N. VIETNAM
HAINAN

Han Kiang
Namoa B.
Chaoan
Swatow
Kitchioh Bay
Meihsien
Chihing
Namyung
Hoyün
Waichow
Yungyün
Hong Kong
Shiukwan
Wushek
Whampoa
Canton
Macao
Litangkow
Punyü
Samshui
Sunfung Res.
Liangkow
Fatshan
Shuntak
Chungshan
Kongmoon
Shiuhing
Wuchow
Linnam (Yao)
Linshan (Chuang-Yao)
Chaoping (Yao)
Hohsien
Yeungchun
Mowming
Kwangchow Bay
Tuitung
Limkong
Kweiping
Kweihsien
Kwellin
Chüanchow
Lungsheng (Mixed)
Hingan
Luchai
Siwan
Tamiaoshan (Miao)
Sankiang (Tung)
Tayaoshan (Yao)
Mosun
Litang
Henghsien
Luichow
Hoppo
Pakhoi
Tsamkong
Luichow Peninsula
Hoihow
Kiungchow Strait
HAINAN
Gulf of Tonkin
Hochih
Nantan
Tuan (Yao)
Pama (Yao)
Shihlung
Laipin
Liuchow
Nanning
Pingyang
Poseh
Lunglin (Mixed)
Peipan
Hungshui K.
Yu Kiang
Tso Kiang
Tsi Kiang
Yamchow
Fangcheng
Tunghing (Mixed)
Lungchow
Pingsiang
Dongdang
Hanoi
Haiphong
N. VIETNAM
Siang Kiang
Chüanchow
Nan Shan
Ling Shan
Lokchong
Kwei Kiang
Yüan (Yao)
Si Kiang
Pei
Sunkiang
Jung Kiang
Kwei
South China Sea

HAINAN inset:
Luichow Pen.
Kiungchow Strait
Hoihow
Cheongkong (Shihlu)
Tungfang (Paso)
Tungshap
HAINAN LI-MIAO A.C.
Tientu
Yulin
Loktung
Hwangliu

Scale: 0 50 100 200 Miles

8. The Kwangtung-Kwangsi Hills

As the name implies, the region contains Kwangtung Province and the former Kwangsi Province, which was reconstituted in 1958 as the Kwangsi Chuang Autonomous Region on the basis of the indigenous ethnic minority. The Kwangtung-Kwangsi hills, which face the South China Sea, have a combined area of 174,000 square miles, which is more than 4 per cent of China's total area, and a population of 65 million, or about 9 per cent of the national total. The average population density is 370 per square mile. Kwangtung and Kwangsi have been known historically as Liangkwang ("the two Kwangs") or Lingnan ("south of the mountains"), a reference to the mountain divide along the northern boundary of the region. The offshore island of Hainan is administratively part of Kwangtung Province.

The northern mountain border plays a key role in shaping the physical geography of the region. The mountains, collectively known as the Nan Ling or Nan Shan ("southern mountains"), trend generally east-west and form a watershed between the tributaries of the Yangtze and the rivers flowing to the South China Sea. At the same time, the mountains are a major climatic divide, sheltering the region to the south from cold northern air masses in the winter.

South of the divide are the Kwangtung-Kwangsi hills proper, a hilly area with little level land and few well-defined ranges. In the west, the hills adjoin the Yünnan-Kweichow plateau, and, in the east, they continue in the Southeast uplands. The hills are dissected by the region's three main rivers and their tributaries—the Si Kiang (West River), Pei Kiang (North River), and Tung Kiang (East River). A characteristic feature of the northern Kwangsi hills is a mature karst topography in limestone, with deep sink holes, subterranean channelways, and weirdly dissected limestone pinnacles and spires.

Along the coast of the South China Sea, the hills enclose the Canton delta, the largest area of level land. The delta, built up by the alluvial sediments of the three main rivers, is also known as the Yüeh Kiang (Canton

River) or Chu Kiang (Pearl River) delta, for the names of the combined stream. The delta, similar in some respects to the Yangtze delta around Shanghai, is the economic focus and population center of the Kwangtung-Kwangsi region. Unlike the Shanghai area, however, the Canton area is not entirely level. Numerous low hills of red sandstone have been enveloped by the advancing alluvium of the delta.

Another subregion along the coast is the prominent Luichow (Leichow) Peninsula, frequently misspelled in English as Liuchow. The peninsula, which projects southward toward Hainan Island, is an ancient basaltic lava flow that has been eroded virtually to base level. With Hainan, the peninsula forms the eastern side of the Gulf of Tonkin, an embayment of the South China Sea.

Hainan itself is, next to Taiwan, the largest island off the Chinese coast. It was once connected with the Luichow Peninsula until faulting produced the present Kiungchow Strait. Hainan is low-lying in the north but mountainous in the south, where it rises to 5,000 feet in the Wuchi (Five Finger) Mountains.

The coastline of the Kwangtung-Kwangsi region is irregular, but less so than that of the southeast coast. Promontories, protected bays, and offshore islands abound. Ocean fishing has not developed extensively because of the warm water temperature, but some of China's most important harbors are along this coast: Swatow, Canton (with its outer port of Whampoa), Tsamkong, Pakhoi, and, on Hainan, Hoihow and Yülin.

The Kwangtung-Kwangsi region is bisected by the Tropic of Cancer, so that about half the region is situated in the tropics. Its climate is best described in terms of three seasons. The cool season, from November to February, is dominated by the northeast monsoon, which brings relatively dry, cool weather with pleasant days. This is followed by two months of relatively warm, muggy weather. The true summer lasts from June to October and is associated with considerable heat and excessive humidity. During this season, average July temperatures are about 85° F (29° C), the same as in the Southeast uplands. January temperatures, however, are considerably higher than along the southeastern coast, varying from 60° F (15° C) inland to 70° F (20° C) on Hainan. Winter is virtually absent, and snow is found only on the higher peaks. Vegetation grows luxuriantly all year round, producing a strikingly green landscape.

Rainfall exceeds 65 inches along the coastal ranges and in the higher inland hill ranges. Areas to the lee of the ranges are likely to receive only 45 to 50 inches. Rainfall is concentrated in the warm and hot seasons when the region is under the dominance of the southern and southwestern monsoon. Only about eight inches fall during the winter season from November through February. Part of the summer rainfall, especially from June through September, is associated with typhoons.

Soils fall in two categories: High-yield noncalcareous alluvium in flood plains and deltas, and humus-deficient reddish laterites in the uplands. In western Kwangsi, along the edge of the Yünnan-Kweichow plateau, yellowish laterites predominate.

Tillage agriculture is largely restricted to the level flood plains and delta land, or about 10 per cent of the total area. Terracing is practiced on the hill slopes. Thanks to the uniformly high temperatures and abundant precipitation, agriculture is virtually a year-round affair.

Irrigated rice is the dominant food grain, yielding two successive crops on the mainland and three crops on Hainan. The first sowing generally takes place in March, the first harvest and second sowing in July and the second harvest in November. In the northern part of the uplands, the second crop is generally planted between the rows of the first, about two months before the first harvest, to accommodate two crops within the shorter growing season. The principal rice areas are the lowlands of the Canton delta, the Luichow coastal plain, and the major river valleys.

The Canton delta is also an important silk-growing area. Sericulture is practiced in association with pond fisheries, the fish being fed on the by-products of silkworm breeding and fertile mud from the pond bottoms supplying fertilizer for the mulberry trees. In northern Hainan, silkworms are bred on the leaves of the camphor tree.

Characteristic subtropical crops are sugar cane and fruit. Bananas, pineapples, oranges and tangerines, litchi and betel nuts are produced. Other tree crops of interest are tung oil, as well as camellia, cassia, and anise oil. Lumbering, mainly for firewood, is of some importance in parts of Kwangsi.

The Kwangtung-Kwangsi region is moderately well endowed with mineral resources, but mining is still in its early stages. Some coal is found in scattered localities and is mined chiefly in the vicinity of railroads. Hainan has one of China's leading iron deposits. Mining was carried on here by the Japanese and has been resumed since World War II. Like the rest of South China, the Kwangtung-Kwangsi region is rich in nonferrous metals. Tungsten, in association with bismuth and molybdenum, is mined in northern Kwangtung in an extension of the Hunan-Kiangsi deposits. Kwangsi is China's second tin producer. The region's reserves of manganese are said to be the largest in China and are being exploited mainly in Kwangsi.

The region's dissected relief has offered considerable obstacles to railroad construction. Two main lines have been built. One is the southern section of the Hankow-Canton railroad, completed in 1936; the other, the Hunan-Kwangsi railroad, was completed to the Vietnamese border in 1951. Among major branch lines are the Kwangsi-Kweichow railroad, the Tsamkong branch, and the Canton-Kowloon railroad to Hong Kong.

Railroad transportation is supplemented by one of China's best highway nets, coastwise shipping lines, and inland waterways. The region's three main rivers are all navigable in their lower courses. River steamers can ascend the Si Kiang as far as Wuchow, and junks can penetrate deeply into Kwangsi. Three historic routes link the region with the north. They are the Meiling route linking Kwangtung and Kiangsi, the Cheling route between

Kwangtung and Hunan, and the Kweilin route between Kwangsi and Hunan. These routes are now used either by railroads or modern highways.

The population of the Kwangtung-Kwangsi region is distributed quite irregularly. The greatest concentration, 1,000 persons or more per square mile, is found in the Canton delta, the main river valleys and the coastal lowlands. A far more sparse settlement is found in the interior uplands. The inhospitable character of the uplands and the limited agricultural possibilities have long turned the attention of the people toward the sea. These early maritime interests resulted in mass overseas emigration after the seventeenth century. Most overseas Chinese are Cantonese.

Linguistically, the Kwangtung-Kwangsi region is rather complex. The upper Yangtze River (or southwestern) Mandarin dialect is spoken by the Chinese of northern Kwangsi. Southern Kwangsi, roughly south of the Tropic, is part of the Cantonese language area, which extends eastward to include the Canton delta. Northern Kwangtung is dominated by the Hakka dialect, while the Swatow dialect, akin to the Amoy, is spoken in eastern Kwangtung.

Non-Chinese minorities are most numerous in Kwangsi, where the large Chuang group, of Thai linguistic stock, has been constituted as the Kwangsi Autonomous Region since 1958, supplanting the former province. In addition to the Chuang, who number more than 6.5 million in Kwangsi, the principal ethnic minorities are the Yao, Miao, Tung, and, on Hainan, the Li. The non-Chinese population of the Kwangtung-Kwangsi region is about 9 million, or 14 per cent of the total population.

KWANGTUNG PROVINCE
Capital: Canton; area: 83,000 sq. mi.; population: 40 million

Traditionally, Kwangtung Province extended westward in a panhandle to the North Vietnamese border. Since 1950, this panhandle, with an area of 6,000 square miles and a population of about 2 million, including the administrative center of Yamchow (until 1963 called Yamhsien) and the port of Pakhoi, has changed hands several times between Kwangtung and Kwangsi. The area was ceded to Kwangsi in 1951, giving that land-locked region an outlet to the Gulf of Tonkin at Pakhoi, reverted to Kwangtung in 1955, and was again transferred to Kwangsi in 1965. The population of the smaller Kwangtung at the time of the 1953 census was 34.8 million (with its lost territory included, it would have been 36.7 million). The population of the larger Kwangtung, according to official estimates, rose to 38 million by the end of 1957 and to 40 million by 1964. The 1970 population of the larger Kwangtung is estimated at 42 million and of the smaller Kwangtung, the actual area of the province after 1965, at 40 million.

Kwangtung Province includes the drainage basins of the lower Si Kiang, the Pei Kiang, Tung Kiang, and, in the extreme east, the lower Han Kiang. The combined delta of the first three in the Canton area is the economic focus of the province. Unlike the deltas of the Yellow River and the Yangtze, this is not a broad plain but a fragmented area of alluvium cut by hills and wide distributaries. The population density on this restricted, hill-studded plain is truly amazing. About 10 million persons live on 3,000 square miles. The economic pressure for intense land use is such that parts of the delta have been diked off before the normal work of sedimentation is complete. Major embankment projects carried out after 1949 include the Sheklung-Shektan embankment along the lower Tung Kiang and the Kiupak dike on the lower Si Kiang south of Samshui.

Irrigated rice is the leading food crop and yields two harvests a year. In Hainan, where the area under rice is 140,000 hectares, three crops are produced on the same land during the year-round growing season. Kwangtung requires about 9 million tons of food crops for self-sufficiency. Before World War II, production was usually just short of that amount, and 500,000 tons of rice annually had to be imported from Thailand and South Vietnam. In 1949, only 6 million tons were produced, but production rose, and, by 1952, the province had become self-sufficient in food. Since that time, Kwangtung has generally been a rice-surplus area.

The Canton delta, which is the chief rice-growing area, is also a major silk-producer. In 1935, 2,840 tons of raw silk were produced, but, by 1949, output had dropped to 384 tons. By 1952, it was still only 50 per cent of prewar production. The most intensive breeding of silkworms is found in the areas of Fatshan and Shuntak, where cocoon crops are gathered six or seven times during the year. The provincial cocoon crop in the 1950's was about one-eighth of China's total.

Kwangtung is one of China's great sugar cane provinces. The total area planted in cane approached 100,000 hectares in the late 1950's, with a yield of about six tons per hectare. The principal producing areas are in the Canton delta near Punyü and Shuntak, in the Tung Kiang valley near Waichow, and on Hainan.

Oranges, tangerines, bananas, and pineapples are distinctive fruits in Kwangtung, which in 1954 had 30,000 hectares planted in fruit trees. Bananas are grown south of Canton in the delta. The banana crop was 45,000 tons in 1955.

Among other crops are tea, tobacco, and peanuts. Tea is grown on hillsides, both in the northern hills adjoining Hunan and in the Canton delta. Namyung, in northern Kwangtung, is noted for tobacco. The area under peanuts is to be expanded, chiefly in southwestern Kwangtung and on Hainan. The increase in acreage, from 12,000 hectares in 1952 to 33,000 hectares by 1957, was expected to triple the output of peanut oil to 100,000 tons.

Several tropical products are distinctive of Hainan, the only truly tropical part of China. They include coconuts, coffee, natural rubber, and figs.

Fisheries play a major role in the coastal economy. Fisheries are found in Kitchioh Bay, off the mouths of the delta distributaries, and Kwangchow

Bay. Three special fishing hsien have been set up in the main districts. They are Namoa, in eastern Kwangtung; Chuhoi (just north of Macao), in the Canton delta, and Luitung, on an island in Kwangchow Bay east of the Luichow Peninsula. Kwangtung's fishing population in the middle 1950's was 560,000, and the province contributed about one-fourth of China's total fish catch. One-fourth of the provincial catch consisted of fresh water fish and three-fourths of saltwater fish.

Kwangtung's principal fuel resource is the oil-shale deposit of Mowming in the southwest. This is China's second largest oil-shale source, after the Fushun deposit of Manchuria. Development of the deposit began in 1958 with construction of an open-cut mine having a capacity of 1.5 million tons of shale a year. The project was reached by a 40-mile rail spur from Limkong in early 1959, and the new city of Mowming was established on the site of the village of Kungkwan. A refining plant with two retort furnaces, producing gasoline, diesel fuel, and residual fuel oil, went into operation in 1961. A third retort was inaugurated in 1969 and a fourth in 1970. Shale oil, unlike petroleum, contains appreciable amounts of nitrogen compounds, and these yield ammonium sulfate as a byproduct of the Mowming oil-shale industry. The transport location of Mowming would be significantly improved with the completion of a railroad eastward to Canton, which has been reported under construction.

Kwangtung's small coal reserves are mined chiefly in northern Kwangtung around Shiukwan in the basin of the Wu Shui, a head stream of the Pei Kiang. The coal is used on the Wuhan-Canton railroad, which passes through the area, and in a heat and power plant at Wushek, which supplies electricity to the Shiukwan industrial district. Another coal-burning thermal power station is the Saitsun plant, in a northern suburb of Canton, with a generating capacity of 100,000 kilowatts.

Canton also derives a substantial share of its electric-power needs from hydroelectric stations. The largest project is the Sunfung River station on a tributary of the Tung Kiang near Hoyün. Construction began in 1958 on a dam 1,400 feet long and 300 feet high. The first of six proposed 35,000 kilowatt units, for a total designed capacity of 210,000 kilowatts, went into operation in 1960. The plant is linked by a 110-kilovolt power line with Canton. A smaller hydroelectric station, also linked with the Canton grid, is the Liangkow project on the Lowki River, about 50 miles northeast of Canton. Construction on the Liangkow station began in 1956, and the first generating unit was inaugurated in 1958. The Liangkow project consists of four 10,500-kilowatt units, for a total capacity of 42,000 kilowatts. A third project, reportedly even larger than the Sunfung River station, was reported under construction in the late 1960's on the Tung Kiang above Hoyün.

In northern Kwangtung, on the Hunan-Kiangsi line, is the continuation of the tungsten field of those two provinces. The principal mines are near Chihing, Lokchong, and Yungyün. Associated with the tungsten are bismuth, molybdenum, and tin.

TABLE 43
CITIES OF KWANGTUNG

City	City Level	Function	Population (*in thousands*)		
			1953	1957	1970 est.
Canton	subprovince	port, manuf.	1,599	1,840	3,000
Fatshan	hsien	manuf.	123		
Kongmoon	hsien	manuf.	85		
Shiukwan	hsien	manuf.	82		
Shiuhing	hsien	trade			
Waichow	hsien	trade			
Swatow	hsien	port	280		
Tsamkong	hsien	port	166		
Mowming	hsien	oil-shale			
Hoihow	hsien	port	135		

Former Cities

Chaochow (reverted to Chaoan hsien in 1958)
Shekki (reverted to Chungshan hsien in 1958)

With the exception of Shiukwan on the Canton-Hankow railroad, Kwangtung's regional centers (Table 43) have traditionally been situated along the coast, notably in the Canton delta. There, in addition to Canton, are the cities of Fatshan and Kongmoon. The metropolis of western Kwangtung is Tsamkong, and Swatow dominates the Han Kiang valley. Hoihow is the chief city of Hainan. Since the late 1950's, other cities have been established inland, either on the site of resource developments, as Mowming, or as subregional centers, as Shiuhing for the lower Si Kiang and Waichow for the lower Tung Kiang.

Canton, the metropolis of the province, had a population of 1.6 million in the 1953 census, rising to 1.8 million by the end of 1957. The Canton municipal area expanded substantially in 1961, extending about 35 miles north and 70 miles northeast to include the hsien of Fahsien and Tsungfa. The population of the enlarged urban district was about 3 million by 1970. The Chinese name of Canton is actually Kwangchow. Canton is a Western corruption of the name of Kwangtung Province.

The city was the first Chinese port opened for foreign trade. After early contacts with Hindu, Persian, and Arab traders, Canton was first visited by Portuguese in 1516, followed by the British, Dutch, and French. Its foreign trade prospered briefly after foreign concessions were granted in the mid-nineteenth century. But the phenomenal growth of British Hong Kong soon eclipsed Canton as a foreign-trade center. Since the completion of the railroad to Hankow in 1936, Canton has looked increasingly landward.

The city is the focal point of the river trade of the Kwangtung-Kwangsi region. From here, 2,000-ton vessels can travel up the Si Kiang as far as Wuchow. Junks can penetrate deeply into Kwangsi, using the wide-flung headstreams of the Si Kiang. Junks also travel up the Pei Kiang and the Tung Kiang and are the chief means of transportation within the combined delta itself. In addition to the trunk railroad going north, Canton is linked locally by rail with Samshui and with Kowloon in Hong Kong.

Canton is situated on both banks of a wide delta distributary. The main section of the city, on the north bank, includes the old city (walled until 1921) and the new sections of Saikwan (west), Namkwan (south), and Tungkwan (east). The former foreign residential and business concession was on an island in the river off Saikwan. Across the river are the industrial suburbs of Honam (south) and Fati (southwest). Other industries are concentrated at Saitsun, a northern suburb along the main line to Hankow.

Canton's principal modern industries are sugar-refining, newsprint-manufacturing, cement, shipbuilding, and chemicals. Canton's sugar refinery, one of the largest in China, processes raw cane sugar from the Canton delta and other cane-growing districts of Kwangtung. The newsprint mill, situated in the Honam industrial district, was renovated and expanded in the middle 1950's, producing about 75,000 tons in 1959. The Canton mill, which uses bagasse (sugar cane pulp) as raw material, is one of the important newsprint suppliers of China, rivaling the pulpwood-based plants at Kiamusze in Manchuria and Nanping in Fukien. The cement industry, located in the northern suburb of Saitsun near the city's thermal-power station, was expanded in 1963 with installation of a 400-foot kiln with an annual capacity of 100,000 tons, raising the cement mill's total capacity to 400,000 tons. Canton's chemical industry produces sulfuric acid and ammonia, used in an ammonium sulfate fertilizer plant of 100,000-ton capacity that was inaugurated in 1964. A legacy of the Great Leap is a small, integrated iron and steel plant that went into operation in 1958 and has a capacity of 50,000 tons a year. Canton also manufactures a wide range of machinery, textiles, and processed foods. There are also shipyards.

Still within Canton's eastern city limits is Whampoa, its outer port, accessible to ocean-going vessels of up to 10,000 tons. Dredging of the Pearl River upstream from Whampoa to Canton proper was completed in 1965, making the city accessible to vessels up to 4,000 tons. Transportation between the north and south banks of the Canton municipal area was further improved in 1967 with the completion of a second bridge across the Pearl River.

In the delta southwest of Canton are the cities of Fatshan and Kongmoon. Fatshan, which adjoins the Canton municipal area, was formerly also known as Namhoi. A traditional center of silk industry and porcelain handicrafts, Fatshan acquired a caustic-chlorine chemical plant in 1969. The city had a population of 123,000 in the 1953 census.

Kongmoon, another delta center, was formerly called Sunwui. It is situated on the west bank of the main delta arm of the Si Kiang. A city of 85,000 in the 1953 census, Kongmoon has a pulp and paperboard mill that may also use sugar cane bagasse as well as pulpwood shipped down the river. Another local trade center in the delta, Chungshan, south of Canton, existed as the city of Shekki from 1954 to 1958 but lost its municipal status because of lack of industrial development. It dominates the delta district north of the Portuguese territory of Macao.

The regional center of northern Kwangtung is Shiukwan, originally called Shiuchow and, under the Nationalists, Kükong. A major transportation center, Shiukwan is situated on the main railroad to Hankow, at the junction of two headstreams and head of navigation of the Pei Kiang, and on highways to Hunan and Kiangsi known, respectively, as the Cheling and Meiling roads. A major industrialization program has made Shiukwan a metallurgical and heavy-manufacturing city, with a population far in excess of the 82,000 recorded in the 1953 census. Shiukwan is a natural outlet for tungsten, tin, and antimony mines of southern Hunan and Kiangsi and around Shiukwan itself. In addition to nonferrous smelting facilities, the city is reported to manufacture heavy machine tools and other machinery, based in part on a small local iron and steel plant. Coal mined in the vicinity is burned at the Wushek thermal-power station south of the city.

West and east of Canton are the subregional cities of Shiuhing and Waichow, Shiuhing, a commercial center on the lower Si Kiang, was known as Koyiu when it had hsien status. It existed briefly as a city in 1958, then reverted to hsien, and was restored to municipal status in 1961. It manufactures electric motors and generators. Waichow, which occupies a similar position on the Tung Kiang east of Canton, was known as Waiyeung at hsien level. It also existed briefly as a city in 1958, reverted to hsien, and was restored to municipal status in 1964.

The port of Swatow in easternmost Kwangtung is the natural outlet of the Han Kiang basin. Its sphere of influence includes both eastern Kwangtung and southwest Fukien. Swatow was opened to foreign trade in 1858 and became a major port for Chinese overseas emigration. With a population of 280,000 in the 1953 census, the city has apparently not gone through a significant industrial development phase and remains largely a center of the surrounding agricultural area producing sugar cane and tropical fruit. The subsidiary trade center of Chaoan, to the north, existed as the city of Chaochow in the 1950's before it reverted to hsien level in 1958. It had a population of 101,000 in the 1953 census. Chaoan and Swatow are linked by a railroad, and construction was reported under way in the late 1960's on an extension to Meihsien and to the Fukien railhead of Lungyen.

Rapidly developing as the regional center of western Kwangtung is the city of Tsamkong, also spelled Chankiang according to the Mandarin. This city and its surrounding area were leased to France in 1898 and became the territory of Kwangchowwan (Kwangchow Bay). The city was returned to China after World War II, and its French name Fort-Bayard and former Chinese name Siying were changed to Tsamkong (Chankiang). With a population of 166,000 in the 1953 census, Tsamkong entered a period of expansion and industrial development after it was reached by a railroad from Litang (Kwangsi) in 1955. Beginning in the late 1950's, its port facilities were enlarged and modernized, now admitting ocean-going vessels of 10,000 tons. A superphosphate fertilizer plant, with a capacity of 100,000 tons, went into operation in 1962, and a nitrogenous fertilizer section was added in 1969. One of the largest Chinese saltworks was established on the tidal flats between Tsamkong and the island of Luitung, to the south.

The new oil-shale city of Mowming, which was given municipal status in 1959, is situated 45 miles northeast of Tsamkong, on the rail spur from Limkong on the Litang-Tsamkong line.

Kwangtung's minority peoples on the mainland are primarily the 41,000 Yao, with fewer numbers of the related Miao group and of the Chuang minority. They live mainly in the Nan Ling mountain area, where Kwangtung adjoins southern Hunan and northeastern Kwangsi.

Of the three autonomous hsien in this border district, the oldest is the Linnam Yao Autonomous Hsien, established in 1953. The hsien seat was located at Samkong, subsequently renamed Linnam, 10 miles southwest of Linhsien. The population included about 25,000 Yao in the mid-1950's. The area underwent repeated redesignations and transformations. In 1959–60, it existed as the Linyeung Multinational Autonomous Hsien, to reflect the presence of the Chuang and small elements of other minorities, and in 1961 as the Linnam Yao-Chuang Autonomous Hsien. Since early 1962, it has been split into the Linnam Yao Autonomous Hsien and the Linshan Chuang-Yao Autonomous Hsien, to the southwest. A third minority area was established in early 1963 as the Juyüan Yao Autonomous Hsien, with a population of about 100,000 Chinese and Yao.

The island of Hainan, which constitutes a separate administrative district under Kwangtung Province, is economically significant for its tropical agriculture in the northeastern lowland and in the elongated, narrow valleys descending from the Wuchi (Five Finger) Mountains. The northeastern plain yields three rice crops a year. Large areas are planted in sugar cane, and the central mountains yield timber. An attempt has been made to develop rubber and coffee plantations as well as coconuts and other tropical crops.

Hainan's principal mineral resource is iron ore. The main deposit at Cheongkong (the former Shihlu) is situated in western Hainan, 20 miles northeast of the port of Tungfang (the former Paso), which is linked by railroad with the mine. The iron deposit, largely hematite with a metal content of 55 per cent, was developed by the Japanese in World War II as an ore source for the Japanese iron and steel industry. The Japanese linked both Shihlu and a second iron mine, at Tientu (now depleted), by rail with the Yülin port area on the south coast. The Shihlu operation was reopened in 1958 and the short rail link to the seaside ore terminal of Paso was rebuilt. Much of the ore now moves by water to the mainland port of Tsamkong and on by rail to inland iron and steel mills. Some of the Hainan ore is smelted in a small local pig-iron plant that was built during the Great Leap, abandoned in the 1960's, and renovated in 1970. It has three blast furnaces.

On the south coast of Hainan, a segment of the old railroad was reopened in 1959 from the Yülin port area westward to Hwangliu and the nearby salt fields of Yingko.

The mountainous relief of Hainan's interior was used for the construction of the Sungtao hydroelectric station on the Nantu River, which flows northeast to Kiungchow Strait, separating the island from the Luichow Peninsula of the mainland. The Sungtao station was inaugurated in 1959. Its designed capacity has been reported as 50,000 to 60,000 kilowatts.

The main city of Hainan is Hoihow, on the north coast, with a population of 135,000 in the 1953 census. A shallow-water port, it has replaced the former island capital of Kiungchow or Kiungshan, south of the port.

The southwestern half of the island, including the mineral operations and the south-coast port of Yülin, is administratively part of the Hainan Li-Miao Autonomous Chou, originally set up in 1952, with its government seat at Loktung. The following year, the chou annexed the south coast, doubling its population to 540,000, and the capital was moved to a new site 25 miles east of Loktung. The new capital was at first called Chungchong and was renamed to its present designation of Tungshap. It had a population of 8,000 in the mid-1960's. The Li-Miao Chou includes all of China's Li minority of about 360,000, considered to be part of the Thai ethnic group. The Miao component on Hainan numbered 16,000 in the 1953 census.

In addition to Hainan, the provincial government of Kwangtung also administers the islands in the South China Sea claimed by China. These are the Tungsha, Sisha, Chungsha, and Nansha groups. The northernmost Tungsha group, also called Pratas, consists of an island at Lat. 21 degrees 42 minutes N. and Long. 116 degrees 43 minutes E., and two coral reefs to the northwest. The island has guano deposits and is the site of a meteorological station charged with the tracking of typhoon paths.

The Sisha group, also known as the Paracel Islands, extends from Lat. 15 degrees 46 minutes to 17 degrees 5 minutes N. and from Long. 110 degrees 14 minutes to 112 degrees 45 minutes E. These islands also have rich guano deposits. Twice a year, in the spring and fall, they are visited by fishermen from Hainan. The Chungsha group, also known as Macclesfield Bank, just southeast of the Sisha, consists merely of a group of underwater reefs and sandbanks.

Finally, the Nansha group, which has no collective Western designation, extends from Lat. 4 degrees to 11 degrees 30 minutes N. and from Long. 109 degrees 30 minutes to 117 degrees 50 minutes E. The main islands are Taiping (Itu Aba) and Nanwei (Spratly). The islands yield guano, tropical fruit, and fish. The Nansha group is also claimed by the Philippines.

KWANGSI CHUANG AUTONOMOUS REGION
Capital: Nanning; area: 91,000 sq. mi.; population: 25 million

Traditionally, Kwangsi was cut off from the Gulf of Tonkin by the western panhandle of Kwangtung, which extended to the boundary of North

Vietnam. Since 1950, this panhandle, with an area of 6,000 square miles and a population of about 2 million, including the administrative center of Yamchow (until 1963 called Yamhsien) and the port of Pakhoi, has changed hands several times between Kwangtung and Kwangsi. The area was ceded to Kwangsi in 1951, reverted to Kwangtung in 1955, and was again transferred to Kwangsi in 1965. The 1953 census population of the larger Kwangsi (at the time of the census) was 19.6 million and of the smaller Kwangsi (within the boundaries that existed from 1955 to 1965) was 17.6 million. Within the smaller territory, Kwangsi's population, according to official estimates, rose to 19.4 million by the end of 1957 and to 23 million by the late 1960's. The 1970 population of the larger Kwangsi, the actual area after 1965, is estimated at 25 million.

Kwangsi coincides essentially with the upper basin of the Si Kiang. The Si Kiang is the most important of the three rivers forming the combined Canton delta in Kwangtung. The Si Kiang is formed through the confluence of four main headstreams: the Hungshui River, the Liu Kiang, the Yü Kiang, and the Kwei Kiang.

The Hungshui River, the most important headstream, rises in two branches on the Yünnan plateau at an elevation of 6,000 feet. The branches, known as the Peipan and Nanpan (Northern Pan and Southern Pan), join on the Kwangsi-Kweichow border, and the combined stream flows through nonnavigable mountain gorges to a junction with the Liu Kiang at Shihlung. Although the Hungshui is the longest headstream of the Si Kiang system, precipitous limestone gorges render it unsuitable for navigation throughout its course.

The Liu Kiang, in turn, rises in two branches in southeastern Kweichow. The eastern branch, known as the Jung Kiang, is navigable for junks below Jungshui. Just before the Liu Kiang joins the Yü Kiang at Kweiping, it traverses the gorges variously known as Twantan and Tateng. This 20-mile stretch of rapids, formed where the Liu Kiang skirts the southern outliers of the Yao Shan, is a substantial hazard to navigation.

With both the Hungshui River and the Liu Kiang thus handicapped to a greater or lesser extent, the Yü Kiang is the headstream that carries most of the upriver navigation in the Si Kiang basin. The Yü Kiang also rises in two branches—the Yü Kiang or Siyang River, descending from southeastern Yünnan, and the Li Kiang or Tso Kiang, entering from North Vietnam. Although the Li Kiang is navigable for small junks as far as Lungchow near the Vietnamese border, it is the Yü Kiang that carries most of the traffic. The Yü Kiang is navigable in virtually its entire length to Poseh near the Yünnan border.

Finally, the Kwei Kiang, which joins the Si Kiang at Wuchow, is navigable for large junks as far as Kweilin. The Kwei Kiang has its source in the vicinity of the Siang Kiang, the chief river of Hunan. About 2,000 years ago, a canal was built across the low divide separating the two source streams. The canal, which at one time provided continuous navigation between South China and the central and northern parts of the country, has fallen into disuse.

The topography of the province of Kwangsi rises from the coastal lowlands in the south toward the Yünnan-Kweichow plateau in the northwest. Agriculture is favored in the south and east, where more level land is available. The southeastern half of Kwangsi is part of the double-cropping rice area. In the northwestern uplands, rice is the summer crop in the few valleys that offer sufficient level bottom land. In the mountains, the chief crops are corn, barley, and millet, and these form the staple diet of the non-Chinese minorities.

Sugar cane is a distinctive crop in the south, with production centered on Nanning, and sugar refineries located at Kweihsien and Kweiping, on the Yü Kiang east of Nanning. Subtropical fruits are raised in the warmer districts, and tea is grown on hillsides near the Hunan line.

Forestry is of considerable importance in the Yü Kiang basin. There is a large production of firewood. Sandalwood and cork are among the forest products. The northern limestone mountains are largely bare of any tree growth. Only in the extreme north near the Hunan border is there some lumbering activity. The wood is floated down the Liu Kiang and the Yü Kiang to the Si Kiang and markets in the Canton delta.

Other tree crops of interest are tung oil and cassia. The seeds, blossoms, and leaves of cassia, also known as Chinese cinnamon, yield an oil that is used in soaps and cosmetics. The Chinese word for cassia is "kwei," and the occurrence of this particle in such geographic names as Kweilin, Kwei Kiang, and Kweiping points to cassia production in the northeastern quadrant of Kwangsi. Another oil, that of the aniseed, is produced largely along the Yü Kiang between Lungchow and Poseh. Normal cassia-oil production in Kwangsi and adjoining parts of Kwangtung is 10,000 tons a year.

With the acquisition of the former Kwangtung panhandle along the coast of the Gulf of Tonkin, Kwangsi obtained a significant fishing industry around Yamchow Bay, at whose head is the administrative center of Yamchow. Fishing activities are also centered at the port of Pakhoi, the principal urban center of the Kwangsi coast.

Like Kwangtung, Kwangsi has moderately extensive mineral deposits, whose exploitation is dependent on improved transportation. Coal appears to be mined chiefly at Hoshan, north of Litang, where a deposit was opened up after construction of the railroad southward from Laipin in 1951. Other coal deposits are exploited in the Hingan-Chüanchow area near the Hunan border.

Most significant among metallic resources in Kwangsi is manganese. The principal mines are situated along the Si Kiang headstream between Kweiping and Mosün, where the river cutting through the Yao Shan has exposed marine sedimentary deposits of Devonian age. In 1959, Kwangsi reported a production of 735,000 tons of marketable manganese ore from this area. Manganese ore also occurs in the Yamchow-Fangcheng area on the coast.

Kwangsi is also one of China's leading tin-producers, second only to

Yünnan. In contrast to Yünnan's concentrated production in the Kokiu district, Kwangsi obtains its tin from a scattering of placer mines in the Hohsien district of eastern Kwangsi, near the Hunan-Kwangtung border. The tin-dredging operations yield ilmenite, monazite, and other heavy minerals as tailing products. A tin concentrator and refinery is in operation at Siwan, just northwest of Hohsien (the former Patpo).

For its electric-power supply, Kwangsi relies on coal-burning thermal-power stations at Liuchow and Nanning, each with a designed capacity of about 200,000 kilowatts. In 1959, two hydroelectric projects were reported to be under construction, one at Chaoping, on the Kwei Kiang northwest of Wuchow, with a designed capacity of 450,000 kilowatts; the other at Sitsin, on the Yü Kiang just west of Henghsien, with a designed capacity of 210,000 kilowatts. The first generating unit at the Sitsin plant, with a capacity of 72,500 kilowatts, was installed in October, 1964.

While east-west transportation in Kwangsi relies largely on the navigable headstreams of the Si Kiang, north-south connections are supplied by the Hunan-Kwangsi trunk railroad. The railroad was started in 1939 as a military line from Hengyang to Laipin. It was destroyed during the war and rehabilitated by 1947. The southern section from Laipin to the North Vietnamese border at Pingsiang was completed in 1951. Two major branches leave the railroad at Liuchow and at Litang. The Kwangsi-Kweichow railroad was originally built during World War II from Liuchow to Tuyün in Kweichow. It was rehabilitated after partial destruction and dismantlement, reaching Tuyün again in early 1958 and Kweiyang a year later. The second railroad branch, running from Litang to Tsamkong, the Kwangtung port, was inaugurated in 1955.

Kwangsi has six regional centers of importance (Table 44). Four are situated along the Hunan-Kwangsi railroad. They are Kweilin, Liuchow, Nanning, and the frontier town of Pingsiang on the North Vietnam border. The two others are Wuchow, on the Si Kiang, and Pakhoi, the seaport on the Gulf of Tonkin.

Nanning, the capital of Kwangsi, is the metropolis of the Yü Kiang basin, at the historical crossroads of routes to Yünnan through the Yü Kiang valley and to Vietnam through the Li Kiang valley. Since the early 1950's,

TABLE 44
CITIES OF KWANGSI

City	City Level	Function	Population (*in thousands*)		
			1953	1957	1970 est.
Nanning	subprovince	manuf.	195	260	400
Liuchow	subprovince	manuf.	159		
Kweilin	subprovince	trade	145		
Wuchow	subprovince	trade	111		
Pakhoi	subprovince	port			
Pingsiang	subprovince	border trade			

when it was reached by the railroad, its transport orientation has shifted increasingly from the traditional water routes to the rail line. Situated at the heart of Kwangsi's most fertile agricultural district, producing sugar cane and fruit, Nanning also has some modern industry. It produces metallurgical and mining machinery for Kwangsi's mineral industries, manufactures a wide range of industrial chemicals, and refines the locally grown sugar cane. The city's population was 195,000 in the 1953 census, rising to 260,000 by the end of 1957, and to about 400,000 in the late 1960's.

Northward along the railroad is Liuchow, the product of the railroad era with a more pronounced industrial orientation than Nanning. Liuchow is a transportation center at the junction of the railroad to Kweichow. It has an important cement industry, further expanded in 1964, and an electronics industry based on the manufacture of silicon rectifiers (since 1966) and transistors (since 1968). A small iron and steel plant rose during the Great Leap at Luchai, on the railroad northeast of Liuchow. The city had a population of 159,000 in the 1953 census and has probably matched Nanning's urban expansion since that time.

The northernmost railroad center in Kwangsi is Kweilin, at the point where the Hunan-Kwangsi rail line crosses the Kwei Kiang. The name of the city, meaning "cassia woods," reflects the character of the original vegetation in the area. Kweilin had a population of 145,000 in the 1953 census.

Pingsiang, the rail city on the North Vietnamese border, was raised to municipal status in 1956, reflecting the increasing rail traffic across the frontier. The actual border crossing, a pass (*kwan* in Chinese), has undergone several name changes. Originally known as Chennankwan, it was renamed Munankwan in 1953 and Yuyikwan in 1965. As the new rail transport center, Pingsiang has superseded the older border trade center of Lungchow, on the Li Kiang to the northeast.

The Si Kiang port of Wuchow on the Kwangtung border is the regional center of eastern Kwangsi. A city of 111,000 in the 1953 census, Wuchow is situated at the junction of the Si Kiang and the Kwei Kiang, serving as the eastward outlet for virtually the entire river trade of the Si Kiang basin. Tung oil and timber are among the principal commodities.

During the period 1951–55 and again since 1965, Kwangsi has had a seaward outlet to the Gulf of Tonkin at the port of Pakhoi. However, in contrast to the nearby Kwangtung port of Tsamkong, with its rail connection to the interior, the development of Pakhoi has been impeded by the absence of modern interior communications. Pakhoi was a city in the 1950's, briefly lost municipal status in 1959, but regained it in 1964.

The Kwangsi Chuang Autonomous Region is founded on the presence of the Chuang ethnic group, China's most numerous minority totaling about 7 million people, of whom about 6.5 million live in Kwangsi. The Chuang, a Thai linguistic group, were originally set up in the old Kwangsi Province as the West Kwangsi Chuang Autonomous Chou, established in December, 1952, and expanded in the autumn of 1953. The autonomous chou, with an area of 52,000 square miles and a population of 8.4 million, covered the more mountainous and relatively sparse settled western part of the province. Apparently, in view of the numerical strength of the Chuang people and a relatively high level of cultural development, the entire province was converted into the Chuang Autonomous Region in March, 1958. When Kwangsi annexed the Kwangtung panhandle in 1965, the Chuang Autonomous Region absorbed the Yamchow Chuang Autonomous Hsien, which had been established in Kwangtung in 1963. (A Yampei Chuang Autonomous Hsien existed briefly in 1958–59 north of Yamchow.)

Within the Chuang minority region, lesser ethnic groups, including about 470,000 Yao, 200,000 Miao, and 150,000 Tung, constitute eight autonomous hsien scattered through Kwangsi. The Yao are represented by three hsien and the Miao and Tung by one each, and there are three multinational hsien.

The oldest and most important Yao area is the Tayaoshan Yao Autonomous Hsien in the Ta Yao Shan (Great Yao Mountains), a hill range east of Liuchow. The hsien was formed in 1952 with its administrative seat at Kinsiu. Two Yao hsien were established in 1955 in the karst region of the middle Hungshui River basin, with their centers at Tuan and Pama. The Yao minority is also represented in the Lungsheng Multinational Hsien, established in 1951 in northern Kwangsi, and in the Tunghing Multinational Hsien, founded in 1958 on the North Vietnamese border in what was then the extremity of the western Kwangtung panhandle. The Tunghing area was first briefly called the Shihwanshan (Hundred Thousand Hills) Chuang-Yao Autonomous Hsien for the hill range in which these ethnic minorities lived. It received the multinational designation after about 4,000 Vietnamese had also been identified in the area.

The principal Miao community is the Tamiaoshan Miao Autonomous Hsien, formed in 1952 north of Liuchow. It is situated in the Ta Miao Shan (Great Miao Mountains), a hill range along the Kwangsi-Kweichow border. The hsien seat is at Jungshui, on the Jung Kiang. The Miao are also represented in two multinational hsien: the Lungsheng hsien, which they share with the Yao, and the Lunglin hsien, founded in 1953 in western Kwangsi.

Finally the Tung minority is constituted as the Sankiang Tung Autonomous Hsien, formed in 1952 in northern Kwangsi. The hsien, with its seat at Sankiang (the former Kuyi), represents a southern extension of the Tungtao Tung Autonomous Hsien of southwest Hunan.

9. The Yünnan-Kweichow Plateau

The region contains the provinces of Yünnan and Kweichow in southwestern China. The combined area is nearly 235,000 square miles, or 6 per cent of China, and the population 44 million, or 6 per cent of the nation's total. This yields an average density of 200 persons per square mile.

The plateau is a spur of the great Tibetan tableland. High, rugged surfaces dissected by deep valleys and crossed by mountains make up most of the region. The average elevation decreases from about 6,000 feet in Yünnan to 4,000 feet in Kweichow. The region may be divided into three related subregions: the plateau of Kweichow, the plateau of Yünnan, and the canyons of western Yünnan.

The Kweichow plateau consists of a high upland core dissected along its periphery by river valleys. The central core represents the undissected portion of an old plateau surface, serving as the divide between the Yangtze and Si Kiang drainage basins. Karst topography is found along the southern margins of the plateau bordering on Kwangsi.

The Yünnan plateau occupies the eastern part of the province and rises generally 2,000 feet above the Kweichow plateau. Here the westernmost headstreams of the Si Kiang rise. The plateau has in part been faulted into grabens, some of which are occupied by lakes. Karst topography is also present in wide tracts. Continuing geological activity is evidenced by occasional earthquakes.

The deep north-south canyons of western Yünnan are carved by some of the great rivers of southeast Asia. Here are the virtually inaccessible upper courses of the Salween, the Mekong, the upper Yangtze River, and the Red River of North Vietnam. The gorges are separated by narrow, abrupt mountain ranges. They are the Kaolikung Mountains along the Burmese border, separating the Irrawaddy from the Salween; the Nu Shan, between the Salween and the Mekong; and the Yünling Mountains between the Mekong and the upper Yangtze. Farther south, the Wuliang Mountains separate the Mekong and the Black River, a tributary of the Red River, while

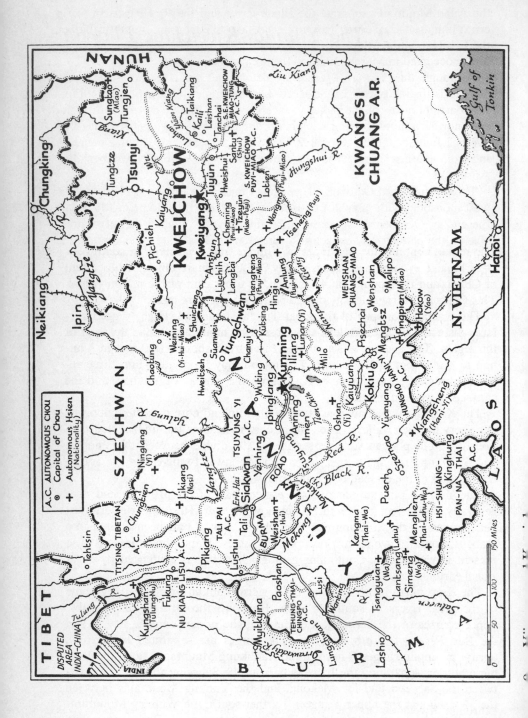

the Ailao Mountains separate the Black River and the Red River. In western Yünnan also, faulting has produced lake-filled basins, notably that of the Erh Hai, and earthquakes are a constant threat. The worst recent earthquake occurred in March, 1925, in the area of Tali.

—Although the Yünnan-Kweichow plateau lies next to the tropics, the climate is distinctly temperate because of the high altitude. Several mountain barriers north of the plateau place it beyond the effective reach of the cold northern monsoon and winters are largely devoid of major frosts. The average January temperature is 50° F (10° C), with temperatures decreasing from south to north. The dry winter season lasts from November until April.

From April until October, the region is under the influence of the southwest monsoon, with rains at frequent intervals from the middle of May until the end of October. Despite the high humidity, the climate is not oppressive on the plateau because temperatures remain moderate. The average for July is 77° F (25° C). Actually, the summer maximum does not occur in July but in May, just before the start of the rains. The May average may rise up to 80° F. Total annual rainfall is 50 to 60 inches.

Cultivation is confined to upland plains, locally called "pa-tzu" (literally, "dike, embankment"), a few open river valleys, and occasional terraced hillsides. Rice is the chief summer crop in irrigated land, while corn, barley, and millet are raised in the summer on nonirrigated fields. Wheat is the dominant winter grain. Other products of the region are sugar cane, tea, and oak-fed silk cocoons.

The region contains some of the richest timber reserves of China, but lack of transportation routes has limited lumbering operations to local needs. Tung oil is also a major forest product.

The chief mineral resources are nonferrous metals, notably tin and copper in Yünnan and mercury in Kweichow. Coal deposits are scattered through the region, with the principal mining centers at Ipinglang (west of Kunming) in Yünnan and in the Kweiyang area in Kweichow.

The rugged terrain has deprived the region of waterways, except on the northern margins of the Kweichow plateau. The terrain and relative remoteness of the region from the rest of China proper have also slowed the development of a railroad net, forcing reliance on road transportation. The principal railroad outlet has long been the French-built line from Kunming to the North Vietnam port of Haiphong, over which Yünnan's tin has been exported. A section of the railroad, between Pisechai and Hokow, was destroyed during World War II but was rebuilt by 1957, restoring traffic between Kunming and Hanoi and Haiphong.

While the Kunming-Haiphong line thus provides a direct outlet to the sea through allied North Vietnam, work on inland rail connections proceeded in the late 1950's and in the 1960's from Kwangsi and Szechwan through Kweichow to Yünnan. Kweiyang, the capital of Kweichow, was reached by the railroad from Kwangsi at the beginning of 1959 and from

Szechwan about 1966. Finally, the railroad link between Kweiyang and Kunming was reported to have been completed in the late 1960's. Direct rail connections between Szechwan and Yünnan are also planned. Construction between Neikiang (Szechwan) and Süanwei, a Yünnan town on the Kweiyang-Kunming line, began in 1956, and proceeded as far as Ipin in 1958. No subsequent progress on this rail project has been reported. Another proposed Szechwan-Yünnan rail link is planned to run south from Chengtu through the Liangshan Yi Autonomous Chou and Sichang to the Kunming area. Construction was reported to have proceeded by 1965 as far as Omei, 80 miles south-southwest of Chengtu.

Compared with other parts of China proper, the Yünnan-Kweichow plateau is sparsely populated. Population is concentrated chiefly in the upland plains along means of transportation, whether railroads or highways. The least settled sections are the peripheral parts of the Yünnan and Kweichow plateaus.

Chinese settlement of the region began 2,000 years ago, but the two provinces were not made an integral part of China until the fourteenth century. Chinese colonizers pushed the original tribal inhabitants into the mountains and occupied the best level land. The non-Chinese peoples thus retained their distinct languages and cultures, transforming the plateau region, and notably Yünnan, into one of China's most diverse ethnic areas.

The Chinese, who speak the southwestern variety of Mandarin, make up about 70 per cent of the population, the ratio being slightly larger in Kweichow and slightly smaller in Yünnan. Non-Chinese minorities, numbering about 10,000,000, are found around the periphery of the region. The principal minorities are the Puyi (Chungchia) and Tung and Shui peoples, all of Thai stock, in Kweichow Province, and the Yi (Lolo) and related peoples of the Tibeto-Burman ethnolinguistic family in Yünnan Province. The complex pattern of ethnic autonomous units, totaling ten autonomous chou and twenty-four autonomous hsien, is described in the provincial sections of this chapter.

KWEICHOW PROVINCE

Capital: Kweiyang; area: 67,000 sq. mi.; population: 20 million

Kweichow Province is drained in its northern half by the Wu Kiang, a right tributary of the Yangtze River, which traverses the province from west to east. The southwestern quadrant, characterized by karst topography, is drained by the Peipan Kiang, left headstream of the Hungshui River. The Yüan Kiang of Hunan Province and the Liu Kiang of Kwangsi both rise in southeastern Kweichow. None of these rivers is navigable. Only the lower Wu Kiang is accessible to small junks.

Rice, wheat, and corn are grown chiefly in the eastern part of the province, and their total production renders Kweichow virtually self-sufficient in food. The richest rice yields are obtained in the basins of the Wu Kiang and the Yüan Kiang. Silkworms are bred on oak leaves in the Tsunyi area. Tung oil is a distinctive forest product.

In the absence of navigable waterways, Kweichow long depended on highways for transportation, until it entered the railroad era in the late 1950's. The first railroad penetrated into Kweichow from Kwangsi in the southeast during World War II and reached the city of Tuyün, 90 miles from Kweiyang. The line was later partly destroyed and dismantled but was rehabilitated, reaching Tuyün again in early 1958 and completing the remaining segment to Kweiyang by the end of the year. The next phase of railroad construction focused on the Kweichow-Szechwan railroad linking Kweiyang northward through Tsunyi with Chungking. All tunneling and earthwork on the mountainous line was reported completed in early 1960. After an apparent interruption in construction during the early 1960's, work was resumed about 1964, and the Kweichow-Szechwan railroad was inaugurated about 1966. Construction crews then shifted their attention to the Kweichow-Yünnan railroad west from Kweiyang. Construction on this line began originally in 1958, and, by the early part of 1960, the roadbed was reported to have been completed as far as Anshun, 75 rail miles west of Kweiyang. This segment apparently went into operation in the early 1960's. Work resumed in earnest in 1964, and the entire Kweichow-Yünnan railroad was apparently completed in the late 1960's.

Coal deposits are scattered through the northern and central parts of the province, but lack of rail transportation long limited production potentialities. With the coming of the railroad, coal measures (mainly steam coals) extending from the area of Langtai and Anshun past Kweiyang to Tuyün began to be developed in the late 1950's. Plans were also made for development of a promising coking-coal deposit at Shuicheng in western Kweichow, but production was kept at a low level until the area was reached by the Kweichow-Yünnan railroad in the late 1960's.

Steam coals in the Kweiyang area serve as fuel for two thermal-power stations with designed capacities of about 100,000 kilowatts each. One is situated in Kweiyang, where the first generating unit went into operation in 1958, and the other in Tuyün.

Kweichow's noted mercury deposits extend in an arc-shaped belt from the southwestern part to the eastern part of the province. In the nineteenth century, Kweichow produced as much as 1,000 tons of metal, meeting China's demands and leaving a surplus for export. At that time, the largest mines were in the southwest at Paimatung, 10 miles west of Kaiyang, and at Nanmuchang, near Hingi. Since then, these producers have declined, and production has shifted to eastern Kweichow and adjoining Hunan. The main Kweichow mine is now at Wanshan, 15 miles south of Tungjen. Wanshan was formerly the seat of Shengki hsien.

Other potential mineral resources are bauxite and manganese. Bauxite reserves north of Kweiyang have been envisaged as the basis for an integrated aluminum industry, part of which was reported in operation at Kwei-

TABLE 45
CITIES OF KWEICHOW

City	City Level	Function	Population (*in thousands*)		
			1953	1957	1970 est.
Kweiyang	subprovince	manuf.	271	504	
Tsunyi	hsien	manuf.	98		
Tuyün	hsien	manuf.			
Anshun	hsien	manuf.			
Former City	*Period*				
Liuchih	1960–62				

yang in the late 1960's. The manganese deposits are found in the Tsunyi area and appear to be suitable for use in the iron and steel industry of Chungking, to the north.

Until 1958, only two urban centers—Kweiyang, the capital, and Tsunyi—had risen above the status of hsien towns, indicating Kweichow's relatively low level of urbanization and industrial development (Table 45). Two other centers—Anshun and Tuyün—became cities in 1958, were demoted in 1962, but reverted to municipal status in 1966. A fifth place, the rail town of Liuchih, also rose temporarily to city level from 1960 to 1962 but, unlike the two others, was not revived in later years.

Kweiyang, the provincial capital, is virtually at the geographical center of the province and has thus become its natural transportation focus. The city had a population of 271,000 in the 1953 census and expanded to 504,000 by the end of 1957. The arrival of the railroad a year later spurred industrial development. In addition to a small integrated iron and steel complex dating from the Great Leap, Kweiyang has machinery industries (machine tools, mining equipment, electrical equipment, diesel and steam engines), a rubber-tire factory, and a cement mill. Some elements of an aluminum industry are also reported in operation.

Tsunyi, Kweichow's second city, is situated on the railroad to Chungking and serves as the regional center of the northern part of the province. It had a population of 98,000 in the 1953 census. A phosphate fertilizer plant is in operation here. The city also manufactures general machinery and electric motors. Tsunyi is known in Chinese Communist history as the site of a meeting, held in January, 1935, during the Long March, at which Mao Tse-tung assumed the Party leadership.

Tuyün is a subregional city southeast of Kweiyang on the railroad to Kwangsi. It has coal mines and a coal-burning thermal-power station. Anshun is a subregional city west of Kweiyang on the railroad to Yünnan. It also has a small coal industry.

Kweichow's ethnic minorities are highly diversified and constitute a complex pattern of administrative autonomous units. The largest groups are the Puyi, a Thai linguistic group related to the Chuang people of Kwangsi; the

Tung and Shui peoples, also of Thai stock; the Yi, of Tibeto-Burman stock; the numerous, but scattered Miao, and the related Kolao (Gelao).

Most of China's Puyi minority (formerly known as the Chungchia), totaling 1.2 million people, is settled in the karst region of southern Kweichow, where it constitutes the South Kweichow Puyi-Miao Autonomous Chou and several autonomous hsien together with the Miao, who are interspersed in the main Puyi settlement area. The first Puyi autonomous units in southern Kweichow were the Hweishui Puyi-Miao Autonomous Hsien, established in 1953 at Hweishui (the former Tingfan), and the Lotien Puyi Autonomous Hsien, founded in 1954. These two hsien were absorbed by the South Kweichow Puyi-Miao Autonomous Chou, founded in early 1957, with its administrative center at Tuyün. The Puyi-Miao Autonomous Chou, which at first included virtually the entire Puyi settlement area, underwent repeated border changes in the late 1950's and early 1960's, in which the western margins of the Puyi region were detached and Chinese ethnic areas were attached in the north. The detached western Puyi areas were set up as separate autonomous hsien. They are the Chenning Puyi-Miao Autonomous Hsien, established in 1963, and five units founded in early 1966—Tseheng Puyi Autonomous Hsien, Anlung, Chenfeng, and Wangmo Puyi-Miao Autonomous Hsien, and Tzeyün Miao-Puyi Autonomous Hsien.

On the eastern margin of the Puyi region live the Shui people, also part of the Thai linguistic stock and numbering about 134,000. Most of them are constituted since early 1957 into the Santu Shui Autonomous Hsien, which is part of the South Kweichow Puyi-Miao Autonomous Chou.

The Tung people, who, with the Shui, form a separate Tung-Shui branch within the Thai-language family, are settled to the east of the Shui in southeast Kweichow, overlapping into Hunan (at Sinhwang and Tungtao) and into Kwangsi (at Sankiang). In Kweichow, where most of China's 713,000 Tung people live, they are joined with the Miao in the Southeast Kweichow Miao-Tung Autonomous Chou. This chou had its antecedents in four Miao autonomous hsien organized in a Miao settlement area centered at Kaili: the Kaili Autonomous Hsien, founded in 1950 and succeeded in 1953 by the Lushan Autonomous Hsien; Taikiang and Tanchai, established in 1953, and Leishan, created in 1954. All these Miao autonomous hsien were combined in 1957 with the Tung settlement area to the east to form the Southeast Kweichow Autonomous Chou.

The Miao people are also constituted into a separate autonomous hsien at Sungtao in northeast Kweichow. The Sungtao Miao Autonomous Hsien, which was founded in late 1956, has a population of 300,000, of whom about 30 per cent are Miao. It represents a western overlap into Kweichow of the Miao settlement area in the West Hunan Tuchia-Miao Autonomous Chou. Although the Miao, with 1.4 million, are the largest minority in Kweichow, they are widely scattered and are therefore less prominent than the more compactly settled 1.2 million Puyi.

Many of the 275,000 Yi people of western Kweichow are joined with local Hui and Miao elements into the triple-nationality Weining hsien, established in 1954.

Finally, the Kolao (Gelao), numbering 21,000, inhabit a small, compact area south of Pichieh, but without constituting a separate autonomous hsien.

YÜNNAN PROVINCE

Capital: Kunming; area: 168,000 sq. mi.; population: 24 million

Yünnan Province consists of two distinct sections: the eastern plateau, with small upland plains and a relatively dense population, and the western canyon section, inaccessible and sparsely settled.

Important crops are rice, grown mainly on the eastern plateau, wheat, barley, and corn. Sugar cane finds favorable conditions in southeastern Yünnan in the valley of the Nanpan Kiang. A well-known black tea is produced in the area of Puerh, formerly also called Ningerh.

Coal is distributed throughout the province. However, mining has reached significant development only at Ipinglang, 55 miles west of Kunming, particularly with the completion of an 85-mile railroad to the mines in 1959. Ipinglang is the source of coking coal for a small iron and steel industry developed at Anning, a southwestern suburb of Kunming, in the course of World War II, and expanded in the Great Leap. Smaller coal mines producing steam coals are situated in the Iliang area, east of Kunming along the railroad to North Vietnam, and provide fuel for thermal-power stations at Yangtsunghai, near Iliang, and Kaiyüan. The Yangtsunghai plant was inaugurated in 1959 with the first of five 12,000-kilowatt units, for a designed capacity of 60,000 kilowatts, and provides power for Kunming. The older Kaiyüan station is the electricity supplier for the Kokiu tin-mining and smelting complex.

The power of these coal-burning thermal plants is supplemented by a 25,000-kilowatt hydroelectric station inaugurated in late 1959 at Liulangtung, northeast of Kaiyüan on the upper Nanpan Kiang. Construction on a more ambitious hydroelectric project began in 1956 on the Yili River, near Tungchwan, where four proposed power plants on an 8-mile canal linking the Yili with the upper Yangtze River were to generate a total of 400,000 kilowatts. A diversion dam was reported completed in 1958, but work on the project was apparently interrupted in 1960 after the failure of the Great Leap.

Yünnan Province is one of China's leading producers of nonferrous metals, particularly tin and copper. Tin is mined and smelted at Kokiu, where primary lode deposits are associated with lead, zinc, and iron sulfides. Some of the associated minerals, especially lead, are recovered as byproducts. Kokiu, with a 1953 population of 160,000, has been producing a major share of China's tin output, which has been running at a level of 25,000 to 30,000 tons a year. The metal has been traditionally exported over the railroad to the North Vietnamese port of Haiphong.

Yünnan's copper center is the new city of Tungchwan, north of Kunming near the upper Yangtze River. Copper has been recovered in the area, near the old town of Hweitseh, for centuries. The mines flourished in the seventeenth century, when about 6,000 tons of metal a year were produced. But production dropped subsequently, as imported copper could be delivered more cheaply to market centers. After 1949, the Communists' policy of mineral self-sufficiency led to a revival of the old Yünnan mines. Reflecting a steady rise of production, a special Tungchwan mining district was established in 1954 and was raised to city level in 1958. Concentrate from the copper mines is sent by truck to a smelter at Kunming, 75 miles to the south.

Salt is obtained from brine wells in the Yenhing area (where the *yen* character means "salt"), west of Kunming. The principal producing center is Yüanyungtsing, north of the coal town of Ipinglang.

Iron ore for the Anning (Kunming) iron and steel complex is mined at Wuting, 40 miles northwest of the provincial capital, and at Imen, 45 miles southwest.

Transportation in Yünnan is heavily dependent on highways, the most important being the Burma Road, dating from World War II. The provincial rail net is still rudimentary and, with its center at Kunming, serves the southeast quadrant of Yünnan. The oldest rail line is the French-built access railroad from Haiphong, the North Vietnamese port, which has served as the traditional outlet for Yünnan's tin exports. The line was partly destroyed during World War II between the Vietnam border and the Kokiu district, but it was rehabilitated in 1957. Kunming is also linked by railroad with Kweiyang, the capital of Kweichow. Construction on the Yünnan-Kweichow railroad began in World War II from Kunming and proceeded as far as Chanyi. Work was renewed in 1958, and the entire line was reported completed in the late 1960's.

Four urban centers in Yünnan (Table 46) have been raised to the status of cities. Two are major regional centers, the provincial capital of Kunming and the western Yünnanese regional center of Siakwan; the two others are the mineral industry cities of Kokiu (tin) and Tungchwan (copper).

Kunming is situated at the north end of the lake Tien Chih. A major

TABLE 46
CITIES OF YÜNNAN

City	City Level	Function	Population (*in thousands*)		
			1953	1957	1970 est.
Kunming	subprovince	manuf.	699	880	
Kokiu	hsien	tin	160		
Tungchwan	subprovince	copper			
Siakwan	hsien	trade	26		
Former Cities	*Period*				
Hokow	1953–55				
Malipo	1953–55				

transportation center, it had a population of 699,000 in the 1953 census and 880,000 by late 1957. The city acquired a number of industries during World War II, including a copper smelter for the Tungchwan mines. During the Great Leap, a small iron and steel plant at the southwestern suburb of Anning was expanded with the addition of three blast furnaces, each with a capacity of about 100,000 tons of pig iron a year, and integrated steel-making facilities, including electric furnaces and rolling mills. The iron and steel complex uses coking coal from the Ipinglang mines to the west and iron ore from Wuting to the northwest. Manufacturing plants produce machine tools, electrical equipment, and, since 1969, trucks for the province's far-flung highway network. Kunming also has significant cement production. Industries used to depend for power on a 6,000-kilowatt hydroelectric plant at Shihlungpa, near Haikow, on the western shore of the lake Tien Chih. During the Great Leap, the city's power base was strengthened with inauguration of the coal-burning thermal station of Yangtsunghai east of Kunming, with a designed capacity of 60,000 kilowatts.

Siakwan, the transport center of western Yünnan, developed during World War II on the Burma Road and, because of its better situation at the junction of highways, supplanted the older city of Tali, situated to the north on the western shore of the lake Erh Hai. In an apparent attempt to preserve the historical importance of the name Tali, the city of Siakwan was briefly renamed Tali from 1960 to 1962, while the old town of Tali was called Chunghochen. However, the name Siakwan was restored after the two-year interval. Siakwan had a population of only 26,000 in the 1953 census, but is presumed to have grown significantly.

Yünnan is perhaps the most complex ethnographic province of China. Of the provincial population, estimated at 24 million in 1970, non-Chinese minorities made up 6 to 7 million. As many as 28 nationalities were represented in the provincial legislature in the 1950's, although only the fifteen most important groups sent delegates to the National People's Congress. In the late 1960's, the principal ethnic minorities were constituted into eight autonomous chou and fifteen autonomous hsien.

The most important ethnolinguistic group in Yünnan, outside of the Chinese majority, is the Tibeto-Burman ethnic family, particularly its Yi branch with several associated peoples (Pai, Hani, Lisu, Lahu, Nasi) as well as the Kachin (Chingpo) and Tibetan branches. Other language groups found in Yünnan are the Thai family, including the Chinese Shans of western Yünnan and the Lü-speaking Thais of the south, and the Mon-Khmer family, notably its Wa-Palaung branch.

The Yi people, who have been known traditionally as Lolo, and who designate themselves as Nosu, number more than 1.8 million in Yünnan, out of a total Yi population of 3.3 million in China. They are constituted into an autonomous chou in their main settlement area northwest of Kunming and into several autonomous hsien in smaller clusters elsewhere in Yünnan. The Tsuyung Yi Autonomous Chou, with its administrative seat at Tsuyung, on the Burma Road, was established in 1958. It then had a population of 1.67 million, of which 23 per cent, or 385,000, were of the Yi nationality. The autonomous chou represents a southern extension of the historical heartland of the Yi in Liangshan Yi Autonomous Chou and adjacent areas of southwestern Szechwan.

Of the six Yi autonomous hsien, two are shared with other ethnic groups. West of the Tsuyung Autonomous Chou, the Yi are associated with a Hui community south of Siakwan in the area of Weishan (known as Menghwa until 1954). In this area, the Weishan Yi Autonomous Hsien and, to the north, the Yungkien Hui Autonomous Hsien were established in 1956. They were combined in late 1960 into the Weishan Yi-Hui Autonomous Hsien. Finally, a new Nankien Yi Autonomous Hsien was established southeast of Weishan in late 1963, with a population of 113,000, including 49,000 Yi. Northwest of the Tsuyung Autonomous Chou is Ninglang Yi Autonomous Hsien, another portion of the Yi heartland adjoining Szechwan. The Ninglang hsien, which is situated north of the upper Yangtze (Kinsha) River, was established in late 1956. Its 56,000 Yi make up about half of the hsien population in this remote mountainous area. In southern Yünnan, in a wedge of territory bounded on the north by the Black River and on the south by Laos and North Vietnam, is the Kiangcheng Hani-Yi Autonomous Hsien, set up in 1954 with a population of about 40,000. The hsien lies just across the Black River from the Hungho Hani-Yi Autonomous Chou, the Hani heartland. Finally, there are two Yi autonomous hsien in the Kunming region, one at Oshan, established in 1953, south of the provincial capital, and the other at Lunan, southeast of Kunming. The Lunan Yi Autonomous Hsien was originally created in early 1958, was abolished three years later, but was restored in 1964. A third Yi autonomous hsien in the Kunming region was established in 1953 at Milo, south of Lunan, but was absorbed in 1958 by the Hungho Hani-Yi Autonomous Chou.

Second in size after the Yi in Yünnan is the Pai minority, also known as the Minchia (a Chinese term meaning "families of the people"). The Pai people, numbering 567,000 in 1953, are concentrated north of the Burma Road between the upper Mekong and Yangtze rivers. Although Western scholars consider their ethnic affiliation unclear, modern Chinese usage classifies them as Tibeto-Burman and related to the Yi group. In contrast to others in the Yi group, who are mainly mountain dwellers, the Pai people are traditional plains people and wet-rice growers. Since late 1956, they have been constituted into the Tali Pai Autonomous Chou, with its administrative center at Siakwan. Its population at the time of formation was 1.7 million, with Chinese in the majority. The Pai people occupy roughly the northwestern quadrant of the autonomous chou. Yi clusters in the southeast are represented by the Weishan and Nankien autonomous hsien mentioned earlier.

The Hani people, about 480,000 strong in Yünnan, are also known as Woni and Akha. Their heartland is situated in southern Yünnan between the Red and Black rivers on the border of North Vietnam. Under the Chinese Communists, the Hani people were first organized in 1953 as an autonomous hsien with its administrative seat at Hungho (formerly called Yisa), on the right bank of the Red River (Hung Ho is a Chinese rendering of Red River). In early 1954, the autonomous hsien was expanded into an autonomous chou with an area of 4,000 square miles and a population of 400,000, of whom 60 per cent were Hani. The capital of the chou was moved downstream from Hungho to Yüanyang (formerly called Sinkai). In a further expansion in 1958, the autonomous chou extended northward across the Red River to include the entire Kokiu tin district and reaching to within 50 miles southeast of Kunming. Since the annexed territory also had a substantial Yi population, including the Milo Yi Autonomous Hsien (formed in 1953), the ethnic area was renamed Hungho Hani-Yi Autonomous Chou. Its administrative center was established at Kokiu. The autonomous chou actually has a more complex ethnic make-up than is suggested by its name. This was reflected in part in 1958 with the establishment of the Pingpien Miao Autonomous Hsien and the Hokow Yao Autonomous Hsien in the southeast, along the railroad to North Vietnam. The two hsien were merged in 1960 into the Hokow Yao-Miao Autonomous Hsien, and separated again in 1963. The Pingpien hsien had a population of 68,000, including 35 per cent Miao, and the Hokow hsien a total population of 34,000.

The Lisu, another people of Tibeto-Burman stock related to the Yi, are concentrated in western Yünnan in the Salween-Mekong watershed, where they number 317,000. They live in villages perched high up on ridges and mountaintops along the Burmese frontier, which was finally delimited in 1960 after a long dispute. Ethnic administration under the Chinese Communists began in 1953, with the formation of four Lisu autonomous hsien along the upper Salween, at Kungshan, Fukung, Pikiang, and Lushui. The following year, the hsien were merged into the Nu Kiang Lisu Autonomous Chou, named for the Nu Kiang, the Chinese name of the Salween. The chou had a population of about 220,000, of whom half were Lisu. The administrative center was established at Pikiang. To accommodate two small minorities more closely related to the Tibetans, the Kungshan Tulung-Nu Autonomous Hsien was established in 1956 in the extreme north. The hsien includes Yünnan's 2,400 Tulung people, who live in an isolated valley of the Tulung River (eastern headstream of the Nmai Hka in Burma), and part of Yünnan's 13,000 Nu people (also known as the Lu people, both Nu and Lu being Chinese names of the Salween).

Yünnan's Lahu population, also related to the Yi, numbers 139,000 and is concentrated in the southern part of the province around Lantsang, between the Mekong River and the Wa settlement area on the Burmese border. In contrast to the other large minorities of Yünnan, the Lahu do not constitute an autonomous chou. They are represented by the Lantsang Lahu Autonomous Hsien, established in 1953, and share with two other ethnic groups in the Menglien Thai-Lahu-Wa Autonomous Hsien, formed the following year. The Lantsang hsien has a population of 200,000, of which 46 per cent is Lahu.

The Nasi people, totaling 143,000, occupy a compact area in northwestern Yünnan around Likiang, in the loop of the upper Yangtze (Kinsha) River gorge. The Nasi (another form of the name is Nakhi) were formerly known as the Moso. They live in settlements nestled in narrow valleys or built on terraces above river gorges and engage in subsistence sedentary agriculture and herding. They were established in 1958 as the Likiang Nasi Autonomous Hsien.

Yünnan has a relatively small number of Tibetans (67,000 in 1953) in the extreme northwestern portion, which is a southward extension of the Kantse Tibetan Autonomous Chou of western Szechwan. The Tibetan area, which adjoins the Nasi settlement region on the north, was first constituted in 1953 as the Tehtsin Tibetan Autonomous Hsien, with its seat at Tehtsin (the former Atuntze). In late 1956, the ethnic administration was expanded and converted into the Titsing Tibetan Autonomous Chou, with its capital at Chungtien. (Tehtsin and Titsing appear to represent variant Chinese renderings of Dechen, the Tibetan name of the region.)

Burma's Kachin and Shan minorities, which represent autonomous states in that country, overlap into China to form the Tehung Thai–Chingpo Autonomous Chou of western Yünnan. The chou was established in 1953 with an area of 8,000 square miles and a population of 400,000, including 175,000 Thai (or Chinese Shan), 100,000 Chingpo (Chingpaw, or Chinese Kachin), and 100,000 ethnic Chinese. The administrative seat was established in the Burma Road town of Mangshih, which was renamed Lusi. Another urban center in the autonomous chou is the Burma Road frontier town of Wanting, which has the distinction of being the only hsien-level *chen* (town) in the Chinese administrative structure (other *chen*-type towns are subordinate to hsien). In 1956, the Tehung Thai–Chingpo expanded eastward to absorb the entire Paoshan district with a predominantly Chinese population of 1.2 million. However, in late 1963, the autonomous chou reverted to its original territory, with a non-Chinese majority. Among the smaller ethnic groups within the autonomous chou are two minorities that are not reflected in the political-administrative structure. One is the Achang people of Tibeto-Burman stock, numbering 18,000 around Lungchwan. The other is the Penglung people, constituting a small community of 2,900 (1953 census) just northeast of Lungchwan.

In addition to the Western Thai, or Chinese Shans, of the Tehung Autonomous Chou, Yünnan's Thai population of 479,000 also includes the 150,000 Lü-speaking Thai in the southern part of the province. This Thai group, settled astride the Mekong River on the borders of Burma and Laos, constitutes the Hsi-shuang-pan-na Thai Autonomous Chou, whose name is the Chinese phonetic rendering of Sip Song Banna, the traditional Thai name of the area, meaning "twelve rice lands." The autonomous chou was set up in 1953 with an area of 7,000 square miles and a population of 200,000, of whom 70 per cent were Thai. The capital, Kinghung, is situ-ated on the right bank of the Mekong River, on a highway from Szemao, a Chinese administrative center to the north. Kinghung, originally known as Kenghung, later acquired the Chinese name of Cheli, and was called Yün-kinghung from 1954 to 1964. Like the other Thai autonomous chou in western Yünnan, the Hsi-shuang-pan-na Thai Autonomous Chou expanded substantially in 1958, annexing the Chinese administrative district of Sze-mao with a highly variegated ethnic composition. However, in 1964, the autonomous chou reverted to its original area.

Lesser settlement areas of the Thai ethnic group, situated along the Bur-mese border between the two autonomous chou, are represented by two autonomous hsien associated with the Wa nationality. They are the Meng-lien Thai–Lahu-Wa Autonomous Hsien, formed in 1954, and the Kengma Thai–Wa Autonomous Hsien, established in 1955.

The southeastern corner of Yünnan Province, adjoining the Kwangsi Chuang Autonomous Region, has a Chuang ethnic exclave associated with Miao, Chinese, and Yi population elements. In 1958, the area was set up as the Wenshan Chuang–Miao Autonomous Chou, with a population of 1.4 million. The administrative center was established in the old Chinese re-gional trade town of Wenshan.

The Wa-Palaung branch of the Mon-Khmer ethnolinguistic family is represented in Yünnan primarily by the Wa people, officially designated in China as the Kawa before 1963. A hill people practicing dry-field agricul-ture, the Wa are settled along the Chinese-Burmese border, with about 280,000 on the Chinese side and 50,000 on the Burmese side. They are rep-resented in four autonomous hsien, two Wa hsien and two hsien in which the Wa are associated with other ethnic groups. The two Wa hsien have their seats at Tsangyüan (formed in 1958) and at Simeng (established in 1963). The two others, previously mentioned, are Kengma and Menglien.

10. Szechwan Province

SZECHWAN PROVINCE

Capital: Chengtu; area: 220,000 sq. mi.; population: 75 million

Even before Szechwan's annexation of Sikang Province in 1955, Szechwan was the most populous province of China. The merger of Sikang almost doubled the area of Szechwan but added only 3,381,064 persons to the 62,303,999 already reported in the June, 1953, census. The enlarged Szechwan grew in population from 65.7 million in the 1953 census to 72.2 in the official estimate of late 1957. However, in the late 1960's, the Chinese Communists used consistently a round population figure of 70 million for Szechwan, suggesting the use of an old figure or extraordinary outmigration from Szechwan during the 1960's. We are estimating Szechwan's population, as of 1970, as at least 75 million, or about 10 per cent of the nation's total.

The Szechwan basin is so called largely in relation to the high encircling mountains. The detailed topography of the region is thoroughly hilly, and the basin as a whole lies at a higher elevation than the Middle Yangtze plain, though considerably below the Tibetan plateau to the west.

The high barrier ranges encircling the basin make isolation a distinctive aspect of the regional geography. The ranges are best defined in the west and north. In the northwest rises the 10,000-foot-high Min Shan, a spur of the Tibetan plateau that separates Szechwan from Kansu and Tsinghai to the north. The Min Shan is a meeting place of fold mountains trending both east-west and north-south and is subject to earthquakes. A destructive quake occurred here in August, 1933.

Eastward, the northern barrier of the Szechwan basin drops sharply to the upper Kialing valley, where the mountains are breached by the Chengtu-Paoki railroad. The ranges rise once again east of the valley in the Tapa Mountains, another rugged barrier on the Szechwan-Shensi border. The Tapa Mountains, made up largely of limestone, rise to more than 8,000 feet.

Along the eastern border with Hupei, a complex system of limestone up-

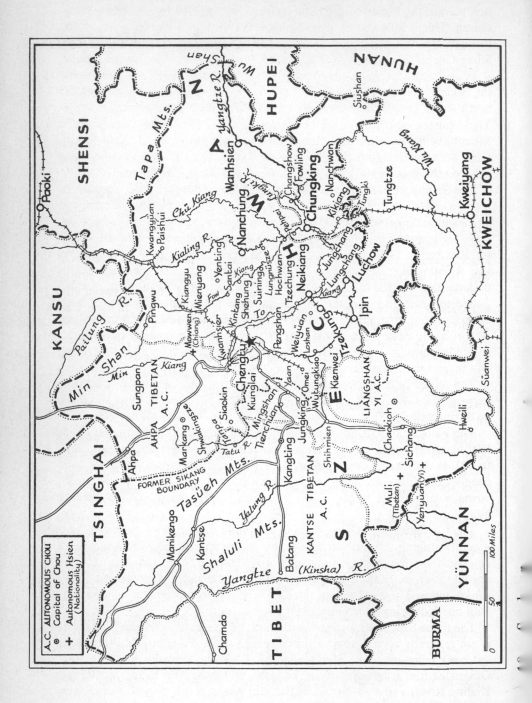

SHENSI

Paoki

Tapa Mts.

Wu Shan

Yangtze R.

HUPEI

HUNAN

Wanhsien

Kwangyuan
Paishui

Chü Kiang

NANCHUNG

Changshow
Fowling

Siushan

Kiukiang

Chungking

Nanchwan

KWEICHOW

Kweiyang

Wu Kiang

KANSU

Pingwu

Kiangyu
Mienyang

Pailung R.

Yenting
Santai
Fow

Mowwen
(Chiang)

Min Shan

Min Kiang

Kwanhsien

Kintang
Shahung
Hochwan

Suiningo

Lunganstze

Tzchung

Neikiang

Jungchang
Lungchang

Ipin

Luchow

Tungki

Tungtze

Kiang

To
Pengshan

Weiyüan

Kiang

Tzeliuching

LIANGSHAN YI A.C.

Süanwei

Sungpan

TIBETAN A.C.
AHPA

Markang

Ahpa

Shwakingtze

Tanpa

Siaokin

Tatu R.

Kiunglai
Mingshan

Tienchüan

Chengtu

Yaan

Omei

Loshan
Wutungkiao

Kienwei

Chaokioh

Shihmien

Jungking

FORMER SIKANG BOUNDARY

Manikengo

Tasüeh Mts.

Kantse

Kangting

Yalung R.

KANTSE TIBETAN A.C.

Shaluli Mts.

Batang

Yangtze (Kinsha) R.

TIBET

Chamdo

Muli
(Tibetan)

Yenyüan (Yi)

Sichang

Hweili

YÜNNAN

BURMA

A.C. AUTONOMOUS CHOU
⊛ Capital of Chou
+ Autonomous Hsien
   (Nationality)

TSINGHAI

100 Miles

50

0

lands is broken by the noted Yangtze gorges. These gorges, three in number, start in the 5-mile-long Chütang Gorge at Fengkieh in easternmost Szechwan. This is followed by the 30-mile-long Wu Hsia (Wu Gorge), cutting through the Wu Shan on the Szechwan-Hupei border. The easternmost Siling Gorge, 20 miles in length, lies in Hupei and ends just above Ichang.

In the west, the Kiunglai Mountains separate the Szechwan basin from the Sikang plateau and constitute the easternmost of a series of parallel north-south ranges that form the divides for deeply entrenched valleys. These ranges, which make up the dissected Sikang plateau, are the Kiunglai Mountains between the Min Kiang and the Tatu River, the Tasüeh Mountains between the Tatu and the Yalung River, and the Shaluli Mountains between the Yalung and the upper course of the Yangtze River itself.

The Szechwan basin proper thus lies enclosed by high barrier mountains rising to 8,000 and 10,000 feet. The central part of the basin, which lies at an elevation of 1,000 to 2,000 feet, can be described as an amphitheater descending toward the Yangtze valley. The Szechwan basin is also known as the Red basin. This term, first used by the German geographer Ferdinand von Richthofen, refers to the reddish coloring of the soft sandstones that underlie much of the region and to the predominantly reddish-purplish soils.

Erosion has dissected the central part of the Szechwan basin to such an extent that level land is confined to rounded hilltops and flood plains. Accordingly, three geomorphic subregions can be distinguished: the parallel folded hills of eastern Szechwan, the Fang Shan hills of central Szechwan, and the Chengtu plain of western Szechwan.

The folded hills of the eastern basin trend generally northeast-southwest between the Chü Kiang and the Yangtze River. Six parallel hill ranges can be distinguished in this area, extending about 125 miles in length.

The Fang Shan hills are separated from the folded hill area by the lower Kialing River. Unlike the uplands to the east, the Fang Shan has not been folded. It consists of horizontal strata of soft red sandstone that have been deeply eroded by streams. This has resulted in steep-sloped, level-topped, virtually square hill mesas. The name Fang Shan, in fact, means "square hills."

The Chengtu plain is the principal economic subregion of the basin. It is a gently sloping alluvial fan formed by the waters of the Min Kiang as it emerges from the western mountains at Kwanhsien. The plain has an average elevation of 2,000 feet. It slopes to the south and has an area of 1,700 square miles. The thickness of the alluvium has been estimated at 200 feet, with one foot being added every 100 years.

The name Szechwan means "four rivers." The identity of these four rivers is not generally agreed upon. Some sources list the Yangtze and three of its left bank tributaries—the Min Kiang, the To Kiang, and the Kialing River. Others list four tributaries of the Yangtze—either the Min Kiang, To Kiang, Kialing River, and Fow Kiang, or the Min Kiang, To Kiang, Kialing River, and Wu Kiang.

Since 1955, the upper Yangtze River (also called the Kinsha) forms the western border of enlarged Szechwan Province. Flowing in one of the deeply entrenched canyons of the Sikang plateau, the upper Yangtze flows south, briefly enters northern Yünnan, and receives the Yalung River, another north-south canyon stream. Throughout its encased course in the Sikang plateau, the Yangtze has a strong gradient, dropping from 10,000 feet to 1,000 feet at Ipin where it enters the Szechwan basin. Within the basin itself, the gradient is gentle and the river is navigable for 500-ton vessels. Only the gorges on the Hupei border present an obstacle to shipping, requiring careful navigation.

Upon entering the Szechwan basin at Ipin, the Yangtze River receives the Min Kiang. This tributary rises at 10,000 feet in the Min Shan, descends rapidly through canyon-like gorges, and emerges at Kwanhsien to form the Chengtu plain. The noted Tukiangyen irrigation system, devised in the third century B.C. and rebuilt in a mass-project in 1970–71, spreads the waters in channels over the Chengtu plain and reunites them into the main Min Kiang channel at Pengshan. At Loshan, where the Min Kiang receives the Tatu River, its main tributary, the river becomes navigable for large junks down to its mouth at Ipin.

The To Kiang, which joins the Yangtze at Luchow, is of less economic importance. It is linked in its upper course with the Chengtu plain irrigation system and is navigable only in its lower reaches for large junks.

The Kialing River, which joins the Yangtze at Chungking, rises in two main branches in southern Kansu. It receives its two main tributaries at Hochwan, the Chü Kiang on the left and the Fow Kiang on the right. Both the Kialing and its affluents are navigable for junks.

The only important right-bank Yangtze tributary is the Wu Kiang, which descends from the Kweichow plateau and enters the Yangtze at Fowling. Only the lower reaches below the plateau are navigable to any extent.

The topographic isolation of the Szechwan basin, in particular the presence of towering ranges along its northern margins, give the region a temperate, moist climate in spite of its inland position. The northern mountains are an effective barrier against the Polar Continental air in the winter. The average January temperature of 50° F (10° C) is several degrees above that of the Lower Yangtze plain, situated on the coast but exposed to the northern air. Severe frost and snow are uncommon.

Summers tend to become quite warm. The average for July is 85° F (29° C), or about five degrees above the July average of Shanghai. The high summer temperatures are partly explained by the adiabatic heating undergone by southern tropical air masses descending from the Kweichow plateau into the Szechwan basin.

These southern air masses bring abundant precipitation, the chief rainy months being June, July, and August. Total precipitation varies from 35 to 45 inches. Even the winter months are humid; fogs and mists are common. The characteristic frequency of near-surface condensation of moisture is partly explained by the enclosed situation of the basin, which limits the free circulation of air.

The mild and genial character of the climate is typical only of the basin proper. The surrounding mountains and, in particular, the 10,000-foot-high Sikang plateau, are characterized by altitudinal zonation typical of high-land climates.

The highly colored Tertiary sandstones that underlie the Szechwan basin have given rise to the characteristic purplish soils of the region. These soils, limy to neutral, are relatively immature, since the rate of erosion of the soft sandstones is quite rapid. South of the central basin, yellow lateritic soils predominate along the margins of Kweichow Province. The mixed coniferous and deciduous forests of the surrounding mountains are associated with podzolic soils, while the high plateau of the west bears a mantle of thin, immature highland soils.

In the Szechwan basin proper, the mild, humid climate and an eleven-month growing season produce favorable conditions for agriculture. Although relatively little land is available, more than 20 per cent of the total area is under cultivation. A large part of the land has been made arable through terracing of hillslopes.

The principal summer food crop in the lowland is rice, which yields in the Chengtu plain some of the highest outputs per unit of land. About 4 million hectares of Szechwan's land are in rice. During the winter, wheat is the dominant lowland crop. In the hills and other areas where irrigation water is not available, kaoliang, millet, and corn are grown, along with sweet potatoes. The total food crop ranges from 20 to 25 million tons, the largest of any province in China.

Rape is the leading oilseed of Szechwan and is cultivated chiefly along the banks of the Yangtze River. Soybeans and peanuts prosper in the basins of the Kialing River and the To Kiang.

Among the fibers, cotton, jute, and silk are produced. Cotton is limited to the Fow Kiang and To Kiang valleys. Shehung (formerly called Taiho-chen) is the leading cotton center of the Fow Kiang valley. About 300,000 hectares are planted in cotton. Lungchang and Jungchang on the Chung-king-Chengtu railroad are known for their jute production.

Szechwan is one of China's leading silk-producers, with four principal areas within the province itself. The largest output of cocoons is found in northern Szechwan around Nanchung and Santai. In second place is the Chungking area, which is the center of modern spinning mills. Weaving is developed principally at Chengtu and Mienyang, which have a small cocoon crop. The fourth area, around Loshan, has a large cocoon crop but uses largely handicraft processing methods. The raw silk is then shipped to weaving mills at Chengtu and Loshan.

Sugar cane and citrus fruit are distinctive subtropical crops. Szechwan is one of China's leading sugar-cane growers. Production is concentrated in the To Kiang valley, with mills at Neikiang and Tzechung. Citrus fruits, particularly oranges, are grown in extensive plantations in eastern Szechwan.

Tea and tobacco are hillside crops in the western margins of the basin. Most of the tea is grown in the area of Yaan, Mingshan, and Loshan and is shipped in pressed form from Yaan to eastern Tibet. Tobacco is produced near Hochwan in the Kialing River basin and near Kintang in the Chengtu plain.

One of the leading commodities of Szechwan is tung oil, which is one of the major export items of the province. The oil is concentrated for shipment at Chungking and Wanhsien, after having been collected at such local centers as Fowling, Hochwan, and Ipin. The tung oil of Siushan is well known. Other forestry products are mushrooms and medicinal herbs.

Goats and hogs are the principal livestock reared in the province's agricultural areas. Szechwan's hog bristles are well known as an export commodity, and goatskins originate chiefly in the northern part of the province. In the Tibetan highlands of the northwest and west, yak and sheep graze on the mountain pastures.

Szechwan is richly supplied with mineral resources. Coal underlies most of the province, and, in terms of reserves, Szechwan follows after Shansi and Shensi. The coal measures are usually at great depth and are accessible only where anticlines have raised them near the surface. A major mining district is at Pehpei on the Kialing River north of Chungking and still within the Chungking city limits. The coal is mined in the folded hill ranges east of the Kialing River and brought by narrow-gauge rail lines to riverside loading stations. The Kialing River coal is bituminous and of coking quality but contains much sulfur and requires washing before coking for use in blast furnaces. However, in the middle 1950's, higher-grade coking coal was discovered on the southern slopes of the Chungliangshan hills, about 10 miles west of Chungking, and two mines with a combined capacity of 1.8 million tons a year went into operation there in 1958–59. An older coking-coal basin has been worked since World War II south of Chungking near the Kweichow border. The Nantung basin, named for Nanchwan (Szechwan) and Tungtze (Kweichow), has its principal mines at Wanshengchang, on a spur of the Szechwan-Kweichow railroad. Like the Pehpei mines north of Chungking, the Chungliangshan and Nantung mining areas lie within the municipal district of greater Chungking. In 1959, the coal mines within the Chungking district accounted for more than one-half of Szechwan's total coal production.

Lesser coal-mining districts are situated along the Chungking-Chengtu railroad and, in northern Szechwan, near the Chengtu-Paoki railroad. Near the Chungking-Chengtu line are the Lungchang district, with a mine at Shihyen, north of Lungchang, and the Weiyüan district, with operations at Sungkiapu, on a spur from Tzechung. In the northern part of the province is the Wangtsang coal district, with a mine at Paishui, on a rail spur southeast of Kwangyüan.

Szechwan is a significant producer of petroleum and China's only im-

portant producer of natural gas. The main oil field, in upper Jurassic sandstones, is situated in the Lungnüsze area on the Kialing River between Nanchung and Hochwan. The field was discovered in 1956 and placed in
commercial production in 1958. The output, estimated in the late 1960's at
500,000 to 1 million tons, is refined in part at a small topping plant at
Nanchung, with a throughput capacity of 50,000 tons, and is shipped down
the Yangtze River to larger refineries at Nanking and Shanghai. A 300,000-
ton refinery was planned at Nanchung during the Great Leap but was apparently not completed.

Several natural-gas fields, in middle Triassic limestones, appear to be in
operation. The older Tzeliutsing field is associated with the salt brine wells
of the city of Tzekung and is used as a source of carbon black and as a fuel
for the city's important chemical industry. The newer gas fields, discovered
in the middle 1950's and put into operation in the early 1960's, are situated
south of Chungking along the railroad to Kweichow. Natural gas from these
fields, known as Shihyoukow and Tungki, is used in the Chungking iron
and steel industry. Total gas production in Szechwan in the late 1960's was
about 10 billion cubic meters.

Szechwan's electric-power industry is based both on coal-burning thermal
stations and on hydroelectric plants. The largest thermal-power stations are
at Chengtu, where a heat-and-power plant with a designed capacity of
100,000 kilowatts was put into operation in 1958, and at Chungking, with
a 112,000-kilowatt steam-electric plant. The Chungking station is connected
in a grid with a series of hydroelectric plants on the Lungki River, a left
tributary of the Yangtze northeast of Chungking. The largest of four stations on the Lungki River, the Shihtzetan plant, was inaugurated in late
1956, with a designed capacity of 48,000 kilowatts. Others were completed
in 1957 and 1958, for a combined generating capacity of 108,500 kilowatts.
A major hydroelectric project was begun during the Great Leap at Tze-
pingpu on the upper Min Kiang above Kwanhsien, but work on this project, with a designed capacity of 290,000 kilowatts, was apparently halted.

In addition to these fuel and energy resources, Szechwan also has deposits of iron ore, used in the Chungking iron and steel industry, copper,
gold, asbestos, mica, and salt. In contrast to nonmetallics, which are associated with the sedimentary rocks of the inner part of the Szechwan basin,
metallic ores occur in the surrounding mountain barriers and in the Sikang
Plateau to the west.

The principal iron-ore deposit for the Chungking iron and steel industry
is at Tutai, south of Kikiang, on the Szechwan-Kweichow railroad. Situated
in the same general area as the Nantung coking-coal field, the iron ore is
a high-grade hematite with an iron content of 55 per cent and is low in sulfur and phosphorus. Though exploited on a primitive level for centuries,
the deposit began modern commercial operation only in the late 1930's,
when the iron and steel industry was founded at Chungking. A narrow-
gauge railroad to the Kikiang mines was converted to standard gauge in the

1950's as part of the Szechwan-Kweichow railroad project, and ore production rose as the Chungking plant was expanded in the Great Leap. One million tons of usable ore was mined in 1959. A large magnetite deposit has been discovered in southwestern Szechwan near the confluence of the Yalung and upper Yangtze (Kinsha) rivers. However, development of this remote site, at Panchihhwa, west of Hweili, must await the construction of the Chengtu-Kunming railroad.

The Hweili area is also endowed with large copper deposits, which appear to be an extension of the reserves at Tungchwan, across the border in Yünnan Province. Gold deposits are also concentrated along the western mountain edge of the province. Lode deposits are found in former Sikang between Tienchüan and Mienning. Placers are mined in northern Szechwan along the upper reaches of left tributaries of the Yangtze River: at Pingwu on the upper Fow Kiang; at Sungpan and Mowwen on the upper Kin Kiang, and at Siaokin on the Siao Kin (Little Gold) River, a headstream of the Tatu River.

Szechwan is China's main producer of asbestos. The mine, situated at Shihmien on the Tatu River, southwest of Yaan, was opened in 1926, when the area was part of former Sikang. The Shihmien operation was substantially expanded in the 1950's and in the early 1960's, as China's demand for asbestos rose with industrialization. Szechwan's mica mine is farther upstream along the Tatu River, in the Tanpa area of former Sikang.

One of the most widespread mineral resources in Szechwan is salt, which is recovered from natural underground brines. The principal producing centers are Tzekung, which accounts for more than one-half of the province's salt production and has developed as a major salt-based chemical center; Wutungkiao, which has declined since the late 1950's; and along the Fow Kiang in the Shehung-Santai district.

Economic development of Szechwan was greatly speeded during World War II, when industrial enterprises from the east were evacuated in the path of the Japanese advance. Many of the industries were re-established in Szechwan, in particular at Chungking and Chengtu.

Before the war, transportation had to rely on the available navigable rivers and on roads. There were no railroads. The first rail construction during the war yielded the mining spurs in the Pehpei coal basin north of Chungking. In addition, the coking-coal basin of Nantung and the Kikiang iron ore were connected by rail with the river loading station of Miaoerhto, just east of Kiangtsingcheng on the Yangtze River.

Construction was also begun during the war on the long-planned and much-needed Chungking-Chengtu railroad, but, because of a shortage of steel, no rails were laid. Construction was pressed by the Communists after 1949, and the railroad was officially opened in July, 1952. The line, connecting the two great cities of Chungking and Chengtu, is of tremendous importance for the economic development of the province. Thanks to it, products from interior sections of the province can now be transported speedily to Chungking for trans-shipment to the Yangtze River.

The completion of the Chungking-Chengtu railroad established a major internal link within Szechwan but did not provide a railroad link to the rest of China. Soon after Chengtu had been reached, construction began on the line from Chengtu to Paoki. The railroad, after breaching the northern mountains in the upper reaches of the Kialing River, was inaugurated in July, 1956. It not only brought modern transportation to the Mienyang and Kwangyüan area of northern Szechwan but provided the first rail link between the province and the Chinese rail system. The construction crews next turned their attention to southward railroad connections between Szechwan and the adjoining provinces of Kweichow and Yünnan.

After the Kikiang mining railroad had been converted from narrow to standard gauge and a bridge was completed across the Yangtze River near Chungking in November, 1959, work proceeded southward to extend the railroad into Kweichow. After an apparent interruption in the early 1960's, construction was resumed about 1964, and the Chungking-Kweiyang main line was reported to have been completed two years later. Construction on a second southern line between Szechwan and Yünnan, connecting Neikiang, on the Chungking-Chengtu railroad, with Kunming, began in 1956 and reached Ipin in October, 1958. Designed to continue southward through Weining (Kweichow) to a junction with the Kweiyang-Kunming line at Süanwei, this railroad apparently had not been completed by 1970. A third major rail project is intended to open up the remote southwestern section of Szechwan, including the rich mineral resources around Sichang and Hweili. Construction on this line, which would ultimately connect Chengtu with Kunming, reached Omei, a distance of 80 miles south-southwest of Chengtu, in 1965.

In the meantime, road construction in the western mountains has improved transportation in the Tibetan-populated areas. A motor highway from Chengtu into the Ahpa Tibetan Autonomous Chou was inaugurated in 1955. It was extended later into Tsinghai and, through Langmusze, into southeastern Kansu. Farther south, the great Tibetan highway from Chengtu westward through Kangting, Kantse, and Chamdo was opened in 1954, followed by a branch from Tungolo (west of Kangting) to Batang in 1958. The southwestern part of Szechwan, ultimately to be opened up by the proposed Chengtu-Kunming railroad, is served for the time being by a highway running south through Yaan and Sichang to Hweili.

In keeping with its economic importance, Szechwan has eight cities that serve as regional and industrial centers (Table 47). Three of them are directly under provincial jurisdiction—Chungking, Chengtu, and Tzekung. The five others are at hsien level.

Chungking, Szechwan's largest city and the wartime capital of Nationalist China, is situated at the confluence of the Yangtze and Kialing rivers. The city proper is situated on a rocky, mile-wide promontory between the two rivers, but the city limits extend far from the city center. In a series of annexations, the Chungking municipal district incorporated the Pehpei coal mines north of the city in 1952, and the Kikiang iron and coking coal dis-

TABLE 47
CITIES OF SZECHWAN

City	City Level	Function	Population (in thousands) 1953	1957	1970 est.
Chungking	subprovince	manuf., iron-steel	1,773	2,121	4,400
Chengtu	subprovince	manuf.	857	1,107	1,700
Tzekung	subprovince	chemicals	291		400
Neikiang	hsien	sugar	190	220	
Ipin	hsien	trade	178	220	
Nanchung	hsien	petroleum	165	200	
Luchow	hsien	trade	289	170	
Wanhsien	hsien	trade		120	

Former Cities	Period	Function	1953 Population
Wutungkiao	until 1958	salt brines	199
Hochwan	until 1957	trade	
Yaan	until 1958	trade	55

trict to the south in 1959. Its territory, with an area of 4,000 square miles, now extends from the Yangtze River south to the Kweichow border.

The city population exceeded 1 million while Chungking was the wartime capital. Subsequently, it declined slightly. By the time of the 1953 census, it had risen again to 1.77 million, and the official estimate of late 1957 was 2.12 million. In the late 1960's, as a result of territorial annexations and industrial expansion, the population had grown to 4.4 million.

Situated in the southeastern part of the Szechwan basin, Chungking is a focal point of transportation routes. The Kialing River traffic joins the Yangtze here; and railroads go west to Chengtu and on toward Northwest China, and south to Kweiyang and on to Kwangsi and Yünnan. A heavy volume of goods is trans-shipped between the railroads and the Yangtze River, which provides a cheap water route eastward into the central provinces of China proper. Chungking's modern iron and steel industry arose in the late 1930's, when plants were dismantled in the Hanyang-Hwangshih area of the middle Yangtze valley and moved upstream out of the path of the Japanese advance. In 1940, an iron and steel plant, now called the No. 101, was set up at Tatukow, 10 miles southwest of the city center. The plant had a 100-ton blast furnace, two open-hearth furnaces, and rail mills. Until the completion of the heavy-rail mill at Anshan in 1953, the No. 101 plant was the nation's chief rail producer. Until the Great Leap, the Chungking steel mill was heavily dependent on long-haul pig iron, brought from as far away as Anshan. However, in the late 1950's, a series of small and medium-size blast furnaces were completed, the largest being a furnace with a working volume of 620 cubic meters (22,000 cubic feet), inaugurated in 1960. Since the Great Leap, Chungking's iron and steel complex has been fully integrated, with open-hearth furnaces, oxygen converters, and rolling mills. Steel output is estimated at 1 million tons.

The city's diversified manufacturing industries include machine-building (machine tools and electrical equipment), shipyards, and rolling-stock shops. A growing chemical industry includes an old plastics factory, based on phenol derived from gallnuts, and a synthetic rubber and tire complex, inaugurated in 1958–59 at Changshow, an industrial satellite town at the junction of the Lungki and Yangtze rivers. The Changshow chemical complex uses cheap power supplied by the hydroelectric stations on the Lungki River. An old cement mill, with a capacity of 55,000 tons, was supplemented in 1959 by a 450,000–ton plant.

Szechwan's capital and second city, Chengtu, is an old-style walled town that has developed into a major industrial center as a result of wartime construction and postwar expansion. It had a population of 857,000 in the 1953 census, rising to 1.1 million in 1957 and an estimated 1.7 million in the late 1960's. Chengtu proper is primarily a manufacturing center, with an emphasis on electronics and radio industries, instrument manufacturing (measuring and cutting tools), and the processing of timber brought down from the lumbering region of northwestern Szechwan in the Ahpa Tibetan Autonomous Chou. A loosely constituted industrial district extending northeast along the Chengtu-Paoki railroad includes the chemical center of Kintang and the cement town of Kiangyu. Both gained their industries during the Great Leap, but apparently did not reach a level of development to qualify as cities. Kintang acquired a nitrogen fertilizer plant supplied with Czechoslovak equipment. It hás a designed capacity of 300,000 tons of ammonium sulfate and was inaugurated in 1959–60. Kiangyu is the site of one of China's largest cement mills with a designed capacity of 1 million tons. Provided with East German equipment, the mill went into operation in late 1959. Kiangyu is also reported to have maintained a small iron and steel complex since the days of the Great Leap, using nearby iron-ore and coking-coal resources.

Tzekung, the third Szechwan city directly under provincial jurisdiction, is a major chemical center based on the rich local salt-brine wells. The city was formed in 1939, when two salt-producing towns—Tzeliutsing ("self-flowing wells") and Kungtsing ("pumped wells")—were merged to constitute the city of Tzekung. Although the wells had been producing for 2,000 years, using bamboo tubes and other primitive equipment, Tzekung did not become a major industrial complex until it was reached by the Neikiang-Ipin railroad in 1958. The recovery of salt was modernized through the use of natural gas associated with the salt deposits. Brine by-products (borax, potash, bromine, iodine) were extracted in increasing amounts. The basic chemical complex is a caustic-chlorine plant that derives caustic soda and chlorine through electrolysis of brine. Chlorine, in turn, is used for a wide range of derivatives. Carbon black is obtained from natural gas before it is used as a fuel in the evaporation of the brines. Tzekung had a population of 291,000 in the 1953 census and had probably grown to 400,000 by the late 1960's. Its rapid development overshadowed another historical salt-brine center, Wutungkiao (1953 population: 199,000), which was deprived of its municipal status in 1958.

Northeast of Tzekung, at the junction of the Chungking-Chengtu railroad and the branch line to Ipin, is the city of Neikiang, Szechwan's sugar capital. The city is situated in a major sugar-cane-growing district that at one time produced half of China's cane sugar. Its share has steadily declined since the 1920's, as sugar-cane production shifted to the climatically more favorable subtropical provinces of Fukien, Kwangtung, and Kwangsi. Neikiang has maintained its position through the development of sugar-based industries (refining, distilling), the manufacturing of agricultural machines, and its role as a rail transport center. Neikiang had a population of 190,000 in the 1953 census, rising to 220,000 in 1957.

At the end of the railroad branch from Neikiang is the city of Ipin, head of navigation for Yangtze steamers at the mouth of the Min Kiang. Its historical significance as a water transport center and gateway to Yünnan from the north was further enhanced by arrival of the railroad from Neikiang in 1958. Ipin has a small chemical industry based on salt from the brine wells of Wutungkiao, upstream on the Min Kiang. The city's population was 178,000 in 1953 and rose to 220,000 by the end of 1957.

In contrast to the growing transport function of Ipin, another old waterway center, Luchow, situated a short distance downstream along the Yangtze, has been declining because of railroad construction. Luchow was the historical transport outlet for the To Kiang, handling both the salt of Tzekung and the sugar of Neikiang. However, the construction of the Chungking-Chengtu railroad diverted this trade and reduced Luchow's functions. This has been reflected in the population, which declined from 289,000 in the 1953 census to 170,000 in 1957. The trend may have been reversed by the reported construction of an ammonia fertilizer plant in the 1960's.

The last Yangtze port city, in eastern Szechwan, is Wanhsien, where the river enters the gorges leading to Hupei. Wanhsien, which had a population of 120,000 in 1957, is a collecting center for tung oil, goatskins, hog bristles, and other traditional products of its region. It has been largely bypassed by industrialization.

The central Szechwan city of Nanchung, on the Kialing River north of Chungking, underwent rapid industrial development in the 1950's in conjunction with discovery of the Lungnüsze oil field south of Nanchung. Although most of the crude oil moves southward to Chungking for transshipment to Yangtze River tankers, Nanchung acquired a small topping plant and the supply and administrative services for the oil field. It is also a traditional silk textile center. Its population rose from 165,000 in 1953 to 200,000 by the late 1950's.

Yaan was the principal city and former capital of the Sikang section incorporated into Szechwan in 1955. Situated in a Chinese settlement area of the largely Tibetan-inhabited Sikang, Yaan succeeded Kangting in 1950 as the Sikang capital. It is a tea center and a major highway hub on the eastern margins of the Tibetan plateau, with a population of 55,000 in the 1953 census. However, because of a low level of industrial development, it lost its city status in 1958.

Szechwan's predominantly Chinese population speaks the southwestern variety of the Mandarin. The greatest population density of 1,000 persons per square mile is found in the Chengtu plain and a lesser concentration in the central part of the Szechwan Basin. Sparse settlement is characteristic of the surrounding mountains, with the lowest population density on the margins of the Tibetan plateau.

The province has a non-Chinese ethnic population of about 2.5 million, settled entirely in the western mountains of Szechwan and the adjoining margins of the Tibetan plateau. Tibetans, occupying by far the larger territory, number 713,000 (1953 census), constituted in two autonomous chou, Ahpa and Kantse, and in the Muli Tibetan Autonomous Hsien in the Sichang region. The Yi (Lolo) minority, with a population of about 1.1 million, is areally more concentrated in the Liang Shan, the historical Yi heartland, which is an autonomous chou, and in the adjoining Sichang region, where a Yi autonomous hsien has been established at Yenyüan. Smaller ethnic groups are the 36,000 Chiang of Tibetan stock, who occupy a compact area around Mowwen; about 80,000 Miao, who are settled south of Ipin along the Yünnan and Kweichow borders, and scattered communities of Hui (Chinese Moslems).

Prior to the annexation of Sikang, Szechwan had only one minority region, the Ahpa Tibetan Autonomous Chou, in the northwestern part of the province. This Tibetan chou was set up in December, 1952, with headquarters at Mowhsien. In 1954, the chou capital was moved to Shwakingsze, a Tibetan lamasery on the Chengtu-Ahpa highway. Finally, in 1958, the administrative seat shifted to Markang. The chou has a population of 500,000, of whom about 250,000 are Tibetans. The Chinese, who make up most of the non-Tibetan component, have been developing the virgin forests (fir, spruce) of the Ahpa chou into a major lumbering region since the 1950's. The timber is floated down the Min Kiang for processing at mills in the Chengtu area.

The Ahpa autonomous chou contains most of the Chiang minority, established in 1958 as an autonomous hsien, with its seat at Mowwen (the former Mowhsien).

With the addition of Sikang in 1955, Szechwan gained three additional autonomous areas: the Kantse Tibetan Autonomous Chou, the Liangshan Yi Autonomous Chou, and the Muli Tibetan Autonomous Hsien.

The Kantse Tibetan Autonomous Chou was set up in November, 1950, one of the earliest nationality areas established by the Communist regime, apparently as a gesture toward Tibet, which was not yet under Peking's control. The capital of the chou was set up in Kangting, the former administrative center of Sikang, rather than at the Kantse lamasery, for which the chou was named. The chou, with an area of 70,000 square miles and a population of about 500,000, covers almost the entire Tibetan plateau section of western Szechwan. About 95 per cent of the population is Tibetan, but only one-fourth are herders.

The Liangshan Yi Autonomous Chou was established in October, 1952, in the Ta Liang Shan (Great Liang Mountains), the historical homeland of the Yi people, on the left bank of the upper Yangtze (Kinsha) River. After the annexation of Sikang to Szechwan, the Yi autonomous chou absorbed adjacent Yi minority areas of southwest Szechwan, reaching an area of 9,000 square miles and a total population of about 1 million, of whom 80 per cent were Yi tribesmen. The administrative center is Chaokioh, meaning "bright awakening."

Two autonomous hsien have been established in the Sichang region, in which a Yi population of about 300,000 is associated with Chinese and has not achieved over-all autonomous status. A Tibetan concentration around Muli was established as an autonomous hsien in 1953, and an isolated Yi settlement area west of the Yalung River was set up as the Yenyüan Yi Autonomous Hsien in 1963.

11. The Loesslands

The loesslands are taken to include the two provinces of Shansi and Shensi. Their combined population is 42 million, or 5.5 per cent of China, and their total area is 137,000 square miles, or 3.5 per cent of the nation. The average population density thus is 320 per square mile.

The region is essentially a dissected plateau, varying in elevation from 1,500 to 6,000 feet. It is covered by a mantle of yellow wind-laid silt, known as loess. The thickness of the loess cover averages 500 feet and ranges to a maximum of 1,000 feet. The greatest deposits are found in northern Shensi and in the adjoining parts of eastern Kansu. The source of the loess is generally thought to lie in the Ordos Desert of Inner Mongolia, outside the Great Wall and just north of the area of greatest loess accumulation. From there the northerly winter monsoon winds are thought to have blown the fine lake and river sediments over the bordering region.

Both Shensi and Shansi, which are separated by the middle course of the Yellow River, can be divided topographically into a number of subdivisions. The economic and population center of Shensi is the Wei Ho valley. This narrow, elongated plain lies at an average elevation of 1,000 to 1,300 feet along the north foot of the Tsin Ling divide. The Wei Ho valley, also known as the Kwanchung plain, extends from Paoki in the west to Tungkwan on the Honan border. It is about 170 miles long, 40 miles wide, and covers an area of 6,000 square miles.

In the north, the relief gradually rises to the North Shensi plateau, which is a structural basin buried in loess. The plateau here lies at an average elevation of 2,600 to 3,300 feet between the Liupan Mountains of eastern Kansu and the Yellow River. In the north, the Great Wall separates the plateau from the Ordos Desert of Inner Mongolia. A series of hill ranges crowned by the Great Wall rise to 5,500 feet in the Paiyü Mountains. Streams descending from these heights have deeply dissected the loess plateau of northern Shensi.

South of the Wei Ho valley, the great Tsin Ling divide separates that

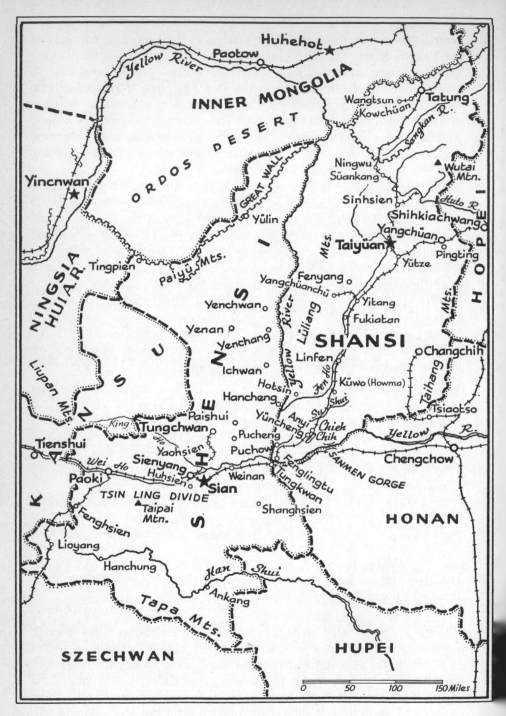

11.   Loesslands (Shansi and Shensi)

central Shensi plain from the upper reaches of the Han Shui, tributary of the Yangtze River. The Tsin Ling divide rises abruptly above the Wei Ho valley, reaching an elevation of 13,500 feet in the Taipai Mountains. Its gentler southern slopes descend to the Han Shui valley. The upper Han Shui valley, which centers on Hanchung, is in sharp contrast to the parts of Shensi north of the Tsin Ling divide. The barrier range prevents the cold winter monsoon from penetrating into the upper Han Shui valley. This produces conditions similar to those of northern Szechwan, from which the Han Shui is separated by the Tapa Mountains.

The Shansi plateau lies between the Yellow River in the west and the Taihang Mountains, which separate it from Hopei Province and the North China plain. The plateau is traversed by the valley of the Fen Ho, which flows south-southwest to the Yellow River. The Fen Ho valley widens into a number of small basins, including the basins of Taiyüan and Linfen. The Taiyüan basin, 100 miles long and 30 miles wide, is the economic heart of Shansi Province. It lies at an elevation of 2,500 feet. On both sides of the Fen Ho valley lies the dissected Shansi plateau. The eastern plateau rises to 10,000 feet in the Wutai Mountains, while the western plateau is dominated by the Lüliang Mountains between the Fen Ho and the Yellow River. North of the Fen Ho valley, between inner and outer sections of the Great Wall, lies the Sangkan basin, drained by a headstream of the Yungting River of Hopei Province. The center of the Sangkan basin is Tatung.

The Yellow River flows in precipitous gorges along the border between Shensi and Shansi. The stream enters the loesslands from Inner Mongolia at an elevation of about 3,000 feet and leaves it at an altitude of 650 feet. In the interval, the river bed drops steeply in rapids-strewn gorges that render the stream unsuitable for navigation. The long-range plan for improvement of the Yellow River, adopted in 1955, called for the construction of dams along this section of the river, notably at the Sanmen Gorge. But the program has not been realized.

The Wei Ho in Shensi and the Fen Ho in Shansi, the principal tributaries of the Yellow River within loesslands, are the economic and population centers of the two provinces. The King Ho, a major left tributary of the Wei Ho, gives rise to an important irrigation system known as Kinghweichü at the confluence of the two rivers.

In climate, the loesslands are intermediate between the aridity of Inner Mongolia and the barely adequate rainfall of the North China plain. Because of the greater average elevation, both winter and summer temperatures on the plateau are lower than in the North China plain. January temperatures are about 15 to 20° F (—9 to —7° C), lower in the north and higher in the south. The city of Sian, which occupies a sheltered site in the Wei Ho valley in the lee of the North Shensi plateau, has an average January temperature of barely under 32° F (—0.5° C). Freezing temperatures occur during four winter months. Summer temperatures vary from 70° F (20° C) in the north to 80° F (27° C) in the south. They are generally somewhat lower than North China plain temperatures taken at the same latitudes. Summer days are quite hot, but mornings and nights are cool.

The bordering Taihang Mountains and the Tsin Ling divide offer an effective barrier to the moisture-laden southeasterly summer monsoon. The average rainfall is about 15 inches, considerably less than in the North China plain. Virtually all the precipitation occurs in the summer; two-thirds is concentrated in the months of June, July, and August. Rain falls frequently in heavy downpours, a major factor in the strong erosion of the regional loess mantle.

The typical soil of the plateau is a light-colored chestnut soil, high in lime content and subject to renewal by wind work. Darker chestnut soils and even black earth have developed on more humid mountain slopes. Podzols predominate in the Tsin Ling divide and the upper Han Shui valley, while true alluvial soils occur in the Wei Ho plain.

Except for their northern margins, the loesslands are part of the winter wheat–millet crop association area. Spring wheat is the dominant crop along the northern fringes on the Inner Mongolian frontier. In the main agricultural area, the chief plains are the valleys of the Wei Ho in Shensi and the Fen Ho in Shansi. More than one-third of the cropland is found on terraced hillsides. The principal food grains are millet, kaoliang, barley, and wheat. Kaoliang and wheat are cultivated in the plains and valleys, millet on the drier hillsides. Oats are associated with spring wheat in the north.

Cotton prospers in the warmer valleys of the Wei Ho and the Fen Ho, which have become among the major cotton producers of China, accounting for about one-sixth of the nation's crop. The cotton used to be shipped largely to mills on the coast, but regional cotton-milling capacity was substantially expanded in the 1950's, notably in the Sian-Sienyang area of the Wei Ho valley. Other irrigated specialty crops are tobacco, melons, and grapes.

The raising of livestock assumes increasingly greater importance toward the north as rainfall decreases and more areas are used for pasture. This is the spring-wheat zone where a mixed economy of crop tilling and herding prevails. Horses, sheepskins, and wool are exported.

The region is well endowed with minerals. Coal is by far the most important mineral resource, with Shansi accounting for 47 per cent and Shensi for 29 per cent of the nation's reserves. However, production has not developed to any great extent because of the region's remoteness from industrial centers. The most important coal-mining centers are Tatung and Yangchüan in Shansi, and Tungchwan in Shensi.

The region is served by railroads connecting the North China plain with Inner Mongolia and Northwest China. Foremost in Shensi is the east-west Lung-Hai railroad, while Shensi is traversed from north to south by the Tatung-Taiyüan-Puchow line. A rail project announced during the Great Leap called for a connection between the two provinces through a line from

Howma (Shansi) across the Yellow River to Sian, but construction of this transport link has been shelved.

The major regional industrial and manufacturing cities are Taiyüan in Shansi, and Sian, Sienyang, and Paoki in Shensi.

The loesslands are one of the earliest seats of Chinese culture. According to ancient chronicles, Chinese tribes were settled here as early as the Shang Dynasty (1766–1122 B.C.). Sian was China's capital under the important Han Dynasty (206 B.C. to A.D. 220). The present population is almost entirely Chinese, speaking the northern (Peking) Mandarin. The Upper Yangtze (Szechwan) variety of Mandarin is used south of the Tsin Ling divide in the upper Han Shui valley.

The population is concentrated in the agricultural valleys of the Fen Ho and the Wei Ho, where the density reaches 500 per square mile. The loess uplands are more sparsely settled, the average density being 50 to 60 per square mile. It was in these sparsely populated uplands that the Chinese Communists consolidated their power after 1935, having established their center at Yenan in the northern Shensi plateau.

SHENSI PROVINCE

Capital: Sian; area: 76,000 sq. mi.; population: 22 million

Shensi falls into four clearly differentiated natural subdivisions. They are the northern loess plateau, the alluvial Wei Ho plain in the south central part of the province, the great Tsin Ling divide, and the upper Han Shui valley, which has more in common with adjoining Szechwan than with the rest of Shensi.

The Wei Ho valley, also known as the Kwanchung plain, is the economic heart of the province. Here is concentrated most of the agricultural production; here passes the Lung-Hai railroad, and here are the major provincial cities of Sian, Sienyang, and Paoki. The alluvial plain produces winter wheat and summer millet as the chief food grains, cotton being the principal cash crop.

The province produces about 5 million tons of grain on 4.5 million hectares of land, for an average yield of 1.1 tons per hectare. About 35 per cent of the grain crop is in winter wheat. The cotton harvest ranges around 100,000 tons, or 8 per cent of the nation's total cotton lint output, with about 300,000 hectares planted in cotton.

Shensi's mineral resources are limited to coal (with the principal mining center at Tungchwan), some crude oil (in the old Yenchang field), and salt, recovered from salt lakes in the semi-arid north and from brine wells in the south.

Although Shensi has some of China's most extensive coal reserves, most of them are in the northern part of the province, remote from transportation, and are difficult to mine because of the thinness of seams and the heavy dissection of the loessland surface. The most accessible reserves are in the so-called Weipei ("north of the Wei [Ho]") basin, with the mining center at Tungchwan. Large-scale production began in 1940, when a branch of the Lung-Hai railroad was completed from Sienyang to Tungchwan, previously called Tungkwan. Mining was further expanded in the late 1950's and early 1960's, and may be approaching the 5-million ton level. Tungchwan's growing importance as an urban center was underlined in 1958, when it was raised to city status.

The Yenchang oil field was discovered in 1907 in Upper Triassic sandstones at a depth of 500 to 600 feet. Well-flow, at first significant, dropped rapidly to the level of 30 to 50 kilograms of crude oil a day per well. The field is therefore a negligible element in the Chinese petroleum industry, accounting for 11,000 tons of crude oil in 1958.

Salt is obtained both from salt lakes near Tingpien in the semi-arid north, near the Great Wall, separating Shensi from Inner Mongolia's Ordos Desert, and from brine wells. The wells, in the Pucheng-Paishui area, are linked by a narrow-gauge railroad with the Lung-Hai main line at Weinan.

Until 1934, the Lung-Hai railroad stopped at Tungkwan, a gateway town on the Shensi-Honan border. Thereafter, the railroad was gradually extended westward across Shensi, opening up the Wei Ho valley to modern transportation. Sian was reached in 1935, Paoki in 1937, and Tienshui, just across the border in Kansu, in 1945. The only other railroad serving Shensi is the newer Paoki-Chengtu line, but it passes only through the southwesternmost corner of the province and has not significantly affected its development. The Han Shui valley in the extreme south, with the sub-regional towns of Hanchung and Ankang, and the entire northern section of Shensi remain without rail transportation.

Aside from railroads, highways play the major transportation role in Shensi. The Sienyang-Yülin highway is the main route through the northern plateau, connecting the Wei Ho valley with the spring wheat belt adjoining the Great Wall. River navigation is negligible. Pending the completion of major improvement projects, the Yellow River course is entirely unusable for navigation. Small junks can navigate on the Wei Ho below Sienyang and on the Han Shui below Hanchung.

Industrial development in Shensi has been marked since 1949 by the construction of new cotton mills to process the locally grown cotton, most of which used to be sent to textile centers on the coast. The new mills, completed at Sian and Sienyang, raised the province's cotton textile capacity to 600,000 spindles and 4,000 looms by the late 1950's.

Electric power for the compact Sian-Sienyang-Tungchwan industrial district and the separate urban area of Paoki to the west is provided by thermal electric stations burning bituminous coal from Tungchwan. The power plants are interconnected by 110-kilovolt lines.

The principal industrial cities (Table 48) are Sian, the capital, Sienyang and Paoki, all manufacturing centers, and the coal-mining city of Tungchwan. A fifth center, Hanchung, lost its city status in 1964, evidently be-

TABLE 48

CITIES OF SHENSI

| City | City Level | Function | Population (*in thousands*) | | |
			1953	1957	1970 est.
Sian	subprovince	manuf.	787	1,310	
Sienyang	hsien	textiles			
Tungchwan	hsien	coal			
Paoki	hsien	transport	130	180	

Former City

Hanchung (demoted to hsien town in 1964)

cause of its poor transport accessibility and limited prospects for industrial development.

Sian, one of China's oldest capitals, lies in the center of the Wei Ho plain. It owes its administrative and industrial importance largely to its location at the focus of major overland routes linking the North China plain with the Northwest. The development of industries since 1949 has included several large cotton mills, chinaware, agricultural machines, mining equipment, and flour-milling. The city has two large steam electric stations, each with a capacity of about 200,000 kilowatts; one is situated in the southwestern suburb of Huhsien. Recent industrial construction included a large woolen textile mill, opened in 1966 with a capacity of 1.6 million meters of fabric, and an electronics and electrical-engineering industry, producing automatic-control instrumentation, electrical goods, and power-generating equipment. Industrialization has resulted in substantial population growth. The city grew from 787,000 in the 1953 census to 1.3 million by 1957, partly through incorporation of surrounding territory. The central city was built in a walled rectangle (2.5 by 1.5 miles), with small walled suburbs adjoining the four main gates. Industrial expansion has affected primarily the western suburbs since 1949. The city was the capital of China under the Han Dynasty and was then called Changan ("long peace"). It flourished again under the T'ang Dynasty (A.D. 618–906) as the western capital of the empire and was known as Siking ("western capital"). In modern times, it became known as Sian ("western peace") under the Manchu Dynasty, reverted to Changan from 1913 to 1932, to Siking from 1932 to 1943, and has been known as Sian since 1943.

About 10 miles northwest of Sian, across the Wei Ho, is the city of Sienyang. Formerly a simple hsien town, Sienyang was raised to the status of city in December, 1952, in connection with the construction of large cotton mills. Sienyang receives its power from the Sian plant, with which it is connected by a transmission line. Sienyang is the junction for the coal-carrying railroad from the Tungchwan mines and the nearby cement-producing town of Yaohsien.

Paoki, the westernmost city in the Wei Ho valley, is a major transportation center of the Northwest. It developed at the junction of the Lung-Hai

railroad and the Shensi-Szechwan highway, superseding Fenghsien, an old
road hub in the Shensi-Kansu-Szechwan tri-state border area. Its significance was further enhanced with the completion of the railroad from
Chengtu across the Tsin Ling mountain barrier. Paoki thus became the
modern transportation gateway to Szechwan from the north. The city has
railroad shops and other service facilities, handling transit traffic both westward toward Lanchow and southward into Szechwan.

Somewhat isolated from the rest of Shensi Province is the subregional
center of Hanchung, economic heart of the Han Shui valley south of the
Tsin Ling divide. Hanchung serves a distinctive agricultural region of
southern crops, including rice, tea, and citrus fruit. Known as Nancheng
until 1953, Hanchung lost its city status in 1964, presumably because of
its economic stagnancy away from major transport routes.

SHANSI PROVINCE

Capital: Taiyüan; area: 61,000 sq. mi.; population: 20 million

Shansi Province is bordered by the Yellow River on the west and south,
the Taihang Mountains on the east, and the outer section of the Great Wall
on the north. In the early years of Communist rule, the northern section of
Shansi was detached from the province and annexed to Chahar. The detached area, situated between the outer and inner sections of the Great
Wall, was restored to Shansi in 1952, when Chahar was abolished.

The Shansi plateau, which lies at an elevation of 3,000 to 6,000 feet, is
traversed from north to south by a longitudinal depression occupied in part
by the Fen Ho, the province's principal river. The depression widens in a
few places to form rather extensive upland plains. In the extreme north, between the outer and inner sections of the Great Wall is the Sangkan basin,
with its center at Tatung. This basin is drained toward the northeast by the
Sangkan River, a headstream of the Yungting River. The central part of the
Sangkan basin lies at an elevation of 2,000 to 2,500 feet.

The next upland plain to the south is that of Sinhsien. The Sinhsien
basin is drained toward the east by the Huto River, a headstream of the Hai
Ho of Hopei Province. The Fen Ho valley proper widens into the Taiyüan
basin, in the geographical center of Shansi, and the Linfen plain to the southwest. The Taiyüan basin, 100 miles by 30 miles, is the economic heart of the
province. It lies at an elevation of 2,500 feet. The lowest basin of Shansi is
the Anyi plain in the extreme southwest at an elevation of 1,300 feet. The
area between the lower Fen Ho and the Su Shui, which traverses the Anyi
basin, is one of the most important agricultural areas of the province.

In addition to the lower Fen Ho valley and the other basins of the longitudinal depression, agriculture is also of some importance in the Changchih basin on the eastern plateau. Among the food grains, millet and kaoliang are the chief summer crops and wheat the winter crop. Spring wheat
and oats are cultivated in the Sangkan basin, where winter temperatures are
lower than in the rest of the province.

Cash crops include cotton and tobacco. Vineyards are found in the sheltered Taiyüan basin near Fenyang and are used in the production of "fen-chiu" (Fen liquor), for which Shansi is famous. Each of the cash crops requires irrigation. About one-third of the total cultivated area of 3.5 million hectares is under irrigation. About 250,000 hectares under cotton yield 100,000 tons of cotton lint. The total grain area is about 3 million hectares, one-third in wheat, and yields 4 million tons of grains.

Shansi greatly exceeds Shensi in the exploitation of mineral resources, particularly coal. The province has extensive reserves of a wide variety of coals, from anthracite to bituminous coal of both coking grades and steam-raising qualities and ranks among China's principal coal-producers. The most important coal basin is Tatung, in the extreme north of the province, where good bituminous coal, partly suitable for coking, is mined. The modern development of Tatung began in the early 1920's, after the coal basin had been reached by the railroad from Peking. The early mines were situated at Kowchüan, 10 miles southwest of Tatung. As development proceeded in the early 1960's, the railroad spur serving the coal mines advanced 35 miles farther southwest to Wangtsun. Coal output rose to more than 6 million tons in 1957 and is estimated to have exceeded 10 million tons a year in the 1960's. Though used mostly for power generation and on the railroads, Tatung coal has been adapted increasingly to coking mixes, particularly at the iron and steel center of Paotow in Inner Mongolia.

Proceeding south along the Tatung-Taiyüan railroad, completed by the Japanese during World War II, coking coal is mined at Süankang, southeast of Ningwu. Plans were announced during the Great Leap for expansion of this coking-coal site, but they do not appear to have materialized. On a spur leading northeast from Sinhsien are the small mines of Kiangtsun and Hopientsun.

A more important coal basin is the so-called Sishan ("western mountain") district, in the upland west of the city of Taiyüan. The district, with a production of close to 5 million tons a year, yields both steam coals and coking coals. Rail spurs extend to the mines at Paikiachwang, southwest of Taiyüan, and Shanglantsun, to the northwest.

South of Taiyüan, the Yitang coal basin was developed in the early 1960's, with a railroad spur extending from Yitang, on the Taiyüan-Puchow main line, westward to the mining town of Yangchüanchü. Beyond the Yitang district is the Fensi ("west of the Fen [Ho]") coal basin, with the principal mining center at Fukiatun. This area also produces coking coal.

Somewhat isolated from the rest of Shansi is the Luan coal basin in the southeastern section of the province. This mining district is separated by a mountain range from the economic centers of the Fen Ho valley and has been traditionally oriented toward Honan. This southeastward orientation was strengthened with the arrival of a railroad from Honan in 1961. The Luan mines have their center in the regional city of Changchih.

Shansi also contains one of China's most important anthracite mining districts at Yangchüan on the Taiyüan-Shihkiachwang railroad. An excellent low-sulfur fuel, the anthracite has been sent out of the province to the urban centers of southern Hopei, and even as far away as Shanghai. Production in the 1960's is believed to have ranged between 5 and 10 million tons a year.

Iron resources are widespread in Shansi and, in conjunction with the equally widely distributed coal resources, have provided the basis for an iron craft industry, with production centers clustered around Yangchüan in the east and Changchih in the southeast. However, iron deposits are too small to support modern iron and steel plants, and the integrated plant at Taiyüan has had to rely on long-haul ore, principally from the Lungyen district of northwestern Hopei.

Shansi has one of China's major inland salt sources. Salt is obtained from the salt lake Chieh Chih in the Anyi basin. The lake, which is 15 miles long and 2 miles wide, yields 600,000 tons of salt a year. The producing center is Yüncheng, just southwest of Anyi. In addition to the salt, which is consumed largely for household uses, the Yüncheng saltworks yield Glauber's salt (the natural sodium sulfate) as a byproduct for the chemical industry. During the Great Leap, a small caustic-chlorine plant was built at Yüncheng, making use of some of the salt output for chemical purposes.

Shansi is relatively well supplied with railroad lines. The backbone of the province is the Tatung-Puchow railroad, which traverses Shansi from north to south. In the north, the line connects at Tatung with the Peking-Paotow railroad. In the south, the line originally ended at Puchow (formerly called Yungtsi). Subsequently, it was extended 20 miles to Fenglingtu, in the southwestern corner of Shansi, on the Yellow River opposite Tungkwan (Shensi). The Tatung-Puchow railroad was originally a narrow-gauge line built by Yen Hsi-shan, a Shansi warlord. During World War II, the Japanese converted the northern section (north of Yütze) to standard gauge to provide direct access to the northern coal mines. The entire line was reconstructed, and the southern section was converted to standard gauge in 1955–56. The usefulness of the Tatung-Puchow Railroad was further increased in 1958 with the completion of a bridge across the Yellow River between Fenglingtu and Tungkwan, connecting the Shansi rail network with the Lung-Hai railroad. Plans were announced during the Great Leap for construction of a second connection linking the Tatung-Puchow line with Sian in Shensi. The connection was to run from Küwo (Howma), on the Tatung-Puchow line, along the right bank of the lower Fen Ho, cross the Yellow River between Hotsin and Hancheng, at the upper end of the Sanmen reservoir, and continue southwest toward Sian. In anticipation of the construction, the town of Howma was elevated in 1958 to the status of city. However, in view of the failure to complete the Sanmen project, the railroad construction plans were also shelved, and Howma reverted to the level of town and became the seat of Küwo hsien.

The province's chief east-west link is the Taiyüan-Yütze-Shihkiachwang

TABLE 49
CITIES OF SHANSI

City	City Level	Function	Population (*in thousands*)		
			1953	1957	1970 est.
Taiyüan	subprovince	iron-steel, manuf.	721	1,020	
Tatung	subprovince	coal	229		
Yangchüan	subprovince	anthracite	177		
Changchih	hsien	coal	98		
Former Cities					
Yütze (1954–63)			60		
Howma (1958–63)					

railroad. The line, originally built with narrow-gauge track, was also converted to standard gauge by the Japanese during the war.

Except for small-junk traffic on the lower Fen Ho, Shansi's rivers are not navigable. An adequate highway network supplements the railroad system.

Shansi has three industrial cities at the subprovince level—Taiyüan, the capital, Tatung, and Yangchüan—and a fourth at hsien level, Changchih, in the southeastern part of the province. (Table 49).

Taiyüan occupies a central position in Shansi. It is situated at the northern end of the Taiyüan basin, a major agricultural area producing wheat and cotton. The city acquired modern industries, such as cotton mills and agricultural implement factories, before World War II, under the rule of Yen Hsi-shan. Industrialization and territorial expansion raised the city's population from 270,000 at the time of the Communist takeover in 1949 to 721,000 in the 1953 census and 1.02 million in 1957. Industrial growth was achieved in particular through expansion of an iron and steel plant and machine-building and chemical industries, making Taiyüan a major diversified center of heavy industry in China. The iron and steel plant, situated in the northern suburbs of Taiyüan, is an integrated operation with a capacity of about 700,000 tons. It includes coke ovens using coking coal from the Sishan mines west of the city; five blast furnaces, the largest with a working volume of 900 cubic meters, three open-hearth furnaces, with capacities of 30 to 50 tons each, electric furnaces, oxygen converters, and finishing mills. Taiyüan, which uses iron ore mainly from the Lungyen mine of northwestern Hopei, was China's second largest integrated iron and steel producer (after Anshan in Manchuria) in the middle 1950's, but it was surpassed during the Great Leap by the construction of the new integrated plants at Wuhan and Paotow and expansion of the iron and steel industry at Shanghai. Taiyüan's chemical industry, which included originally a small chlorine-caustic plant and a coke byproducts shop, was expanded through the addition of superphosphate production in 1958, a nitrogenous fertilizer plant in 1963–64, and a polyvinyl-chloride unit in 1965. A heavy-machinery plant in the western outskirts manufactures rolling-mill equipment, forging presses, and coke ovens.

Yütze, a southeastern suburb of Taiyüan, situated at the junction of the main Shansi north-south railroad and the Taiyüan-Shihkiachwang line, achieved city status in 1954, when a large textile-machinery plant was inaugurated there. The plant, originally situated in Shanghai, was dismantled and moved to Shansi as part of the policy of industrialization of the interior. It produces spindles for spinning mills set up in the cotton areas of Hopei and Shensi. Despite its transport function as a major rail junction and the presence of industry, Yütze lost its city status in 1963, reverting to a hsien town. It had a population of 60,000 in the 1953 census. The Taiyüan-Yütze industrial district obtains its electric power from two thermal-power plants, an older installation of less than 100,000-kilowatt capacity, and a new plant, built in the late 1950's, with a designed capacity of more than 100,000 kilowatts.

The industrial center of northern Shansi is the city of Tatung. A rail center of considerable importance, Tatung is situated at the junction of the Shansi main line and the Peking-Paotow railroad. In addition to its coal mines, served by a rail spur to the southwest, the city has a large cement industry, railroad shops, and a mining-machinery repair plant. Power is provided by a 50,000-kilowatt thermal electric plant fed by local coal. Tatung had a population of 229,000 in the 1953 census, making it Shansi's second largest city.

East of Taiyüan, on the railroad leading to Shihkiachwang, is the anthracite-mining center of Yangchüan, situated in the heart of a traditional iron-crafts district of Shansi. Just to the south is the ancient ironworking town of Pingting. This town was superseded in the early twentieth century by Yangchüan, where the Paochin company erected a small blast furnace during World War I, with a capacity of about 100,000 tons of pig iron. Yangchüan obtains its electric-power supply over a 110-kilovolt transmission line from Taiyüan, built in the 1950's. Yangchüan had a population of 177,000 in the 1953 census. An aluminum-ore mine was reported at Yangchüan in 1970.

Another ancient ironworking center is Changchih, in southeastern Shansi. Formerly called Luan, this city lies at the heart of an agricultural region oriented toward the adjoining province of Honan. This link was further emphasized with the completion of a railroad from Honan in 1961. With a population of 98,000 in the 1953 census, Changchih has a small iron and steel plant and ships coal from nearby mines over the rail line to Honan. Light manufacturing includes a rubber products factory.

12. Manchuria

Manchuria has traditionally consisted of the three provinces of Heilung-kiang, Kirin, and Liaoning (formerly also known as Fengtien) and is treated within that framework in the present chapter. However, over the years, the boundaries of the three provinces—and at times the entire provincial structure of Manchuria—have undergone substantial changes, which need to be briefly reviewed.

In 1928, the original three provinces were supplemented by newly created Jehol Province, and these four provinces were included in the Japanese-sponsored state of Manchukuo proclaimed in March, 1932. In a gesture toward the Mongol minority in the western reaches of Manchuria, the Manchukuo authorities set aside the Mongol territory as an autonomous province known as Hsingan, the Chinese rendering of the name of the Greater Khingan Range, which formed the backbone of the province from north to south. In subsequent provincial reorganizations, beginning in 1934, Hsingan was broken up into four provinces—North, East, South, and West Hsingan—and the rest of Manchukuo was also divided into smaller provincial units, but the separation of the Mongol areas was basically maintained.

The Hsingan concept was preserved after the abolition of the state of Manchukuo at the end of World War II. A Chinese Nationalist provincial structure, announced in June, 1947, divided Manchuria into nine provinces (Liaoning, Antung, Liaopei, Kirin, Sungkiang, Hokiang, Heilungkiang, Nunkiang, and Hsingan), plus Jehol. However, this pattern was not fully implemented, because the Nationalists failed to gain complete control of Manchuria in the civil war then under way. Their provincial structure was superseded by five Communist provinces (Liaotung, Liaosi, Kirin, Sungkiang, and Heilungkiang), plus Jehol. In 1954, Sungkiang was incorporated into Heilungkiang, and Liaotung and Liaosi (meaning, respectively, "east of the Liao" and "west of the Liao") were merged to form Liaoning, thus restoring the traditional three-province structure of Manchuria plus Jehol. The latter province was abolished in 1955.

237

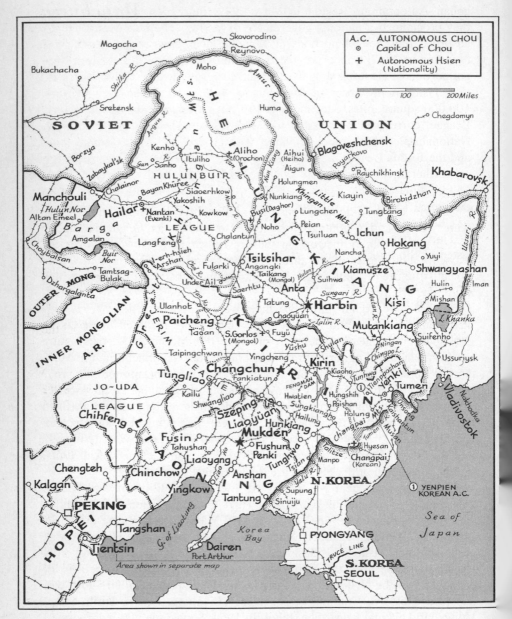

12. Manchuria

In the meantime, the territorial separation of the Mongols of Manchuria, begun with the creation of Hsingan Province under Manchukuo in 1932, was maintained when the Chinese Communists established the Inner Mongolian Autonomous Region in May, 1947, more than two years before they proclaimed a national government in Peking. The new Mongol region absorbed the Mongol portions of Manchuria in three stages. First, at its founding in 1947, it incorporated the Hulunbuir League, the western Mongol portion of Heilungkiang. This league corresponded to the old North and East Hsingan provinces of Manchukuo, with a combined area of about 100,000 square miles. Second, in 1949, Inner Mongolia absorbed the Jerim League, corresponding roughly to the old South Hsingan Province or the Nationalists' 1947 Liaopei Province, with an area of 40,000 square miles, and the Jo-uda League, corresponding to the former West Hsingan Province or northernmost Jehol, north of the Shara Muren, with an area of about 15,000 square miles. Third, in 1955, following the abolition of Jehol, an additional 15,000 square miles south of the Shara Muren, including the city of Chihfeng, was incorporated into Inner Mongolia's Jo-uda League.

Thus, after the middle 1950's, the traditional Manchurian region consisted of the three provinces of Heilungkiang, Kirin, and Liaoning, with a combined area of 310,000 square miles, and a population of 51.5 million in 1957, and the Inner Mongolian portion, with an area of 170,000 square miles and a population of about 3 million in 1957. Natural increase and heavy in-migration raised the population of the three provinces to 71 million and of the Inner Mongolian portion to 4 million by the late 1960's.

In late 1969, there were indications that the former Manchurian portions of Inner Mongolia had been returned to the traditional three provinces in an effort to place the entire Manchurian border zone with the Soviet Union under unified military command. The territorial transfers were not formally announced but became evident when local radio stations began to relay material from Heilungkiang, Kirin, and Liaoning instead of the usual Inner Mongolian service. The provincial readjustment violated the principle of € inic integration that had led to the establishment of Inner Mongolia, but it made economic sense in view of the linkages between the Mongol areas and the rest of Manchuria and the virtual absence of lateral communications within the Manchurian portion of Inner Mongolia. In late 1969, the Hulunbuir League was thus returned to Heilungkiang Province, with which it has natural linkages through the old Chinese Eastern railroad and other transport routes. Jerim League was incorporated into Kirin Province and Jo-uda League into Liaoning, again on the basis of feeder rail connections. The reabsorption of the western Mongol territories increased the area of Manchuria by 50 per cent, to about 480,000 square miles, and added perhaps 4 million people, including 400,000 Mongols, to Manchuria's population, for a new estimated total of more than 75 million.

Manchuria is the northeastern region of China and is known to the Chinese simply as "the Northeast." The region borders on the Soviet Union along the Amur and Ussuri rivers and on Korea along the Tumen and Yalu rivers. It consists essentially of a central lowland enclosed by mountains. The major subregions are: the Liaotung peninsula, the East Manchurian uplands, the Manchurian plain, the Khingan mountains, and the eastern Jehol uplands.

The Liaotung peninsula, in southernmost Manchuria, juts out into the Po Hai toward Shantung, with which it has much in common physically. The two peninsulas have a common geological structure interrupted by the downfaulted Po Hai Strait; both have a hilly topography, the eroded remains of mountain masses, covered by the identical mantle of brown podzolic forest soils. The Liaotung peninsula has an average elevation of 600 to 1,000 feet. Its eroded mountain backbone, the Tsien Shan, an extension of the East Manchurian uplands, rises to 1,850 feet south of Penki. At the extremity of the peninsula is the Port Arthur–Dairen municipal district.

The East Manchurian uplands extend in a series of ranges northeast-southwest along the Korean border. They rise to 9,000 feet in the Changpai (Long White) Mountains. The culminating volcanic peak of Paitow Shan contains the crater lake of Tien Chih. The East Manchurian uplands have some of China's most important timber reserves and hydroelectric potential. In addition to the Korean border rivers—the Yalu and the Tumen—the Sungari and its right tributary, the Mutan River, rise in these uplands.

The Manchurian plain is also known as the Sungari-Liao plain, for its two main rivers. It is bounded by the East Manchurian uplands in the east, the Little Khingan Mountains in the north, the Great Khingan Mountains in the west, and terminates in the south in the Liaotung peninsula. Its average elevation ranges between 150 and 600 feet. A low watershed of 800 feet separates the plain into the Sungari lowland in the north and the Liao lowland in the south. Unlike the North China plain, which is of depositional origin, the Manchurian plain is a structural lowland with rolling topography. The Sungari, known in Chinese as the Sunghwa, flows northwest until it meets the Nun Kiang (Nonni). It then turns sharply northeast and receives the Mutan River before joining the Amur. In the southern part of the Manchurian plain, the Liao Ho flows east and south to the Gulf of Liaotung, west of the Liaotung peninsula. A narrow strip of coastal lowland, the so-called Liaosi ("west of the Liao") corridor, joins the Manchurian plain at Shanhaikwan with the North China plain and constitutes the only natural link between the two regions.

The Khingan mountain complex includes two distinctive parts: the Greater Khingan range, extending roughly north-south on the western margins of the Manchurian plain, separating it from the Mongolian plateau, and the Little Khingan range, which trends northwest-southeast along the northeastern margin of the Manchurian plain, separating it from the Amur valley. The Greater Khingan rises to about 6,000 feet in its middle section, sloping steeply on its Manchurian side and merging more gently westward into the Mongolian plateau. The Little Khingan is of lower elevation, rising to about 3,000 feet. Both mountain ranges are heavily forested, except for the southern portion of the Greater Khingan, which passes gradually into wooded steppe with increasing aridity. The region is China's principal timber-producing area, with the Dahurian larch the principal tree species in the Greater Khingan and the Korean pine in the Little Khingan.

The Jehol uplands are separated from the Greater Khingan by the Shara Muren, the west branch of the Liao Ho. A transition zone between the arid Mongolian plateau and the monsoon country of Manchuria and North China, the Jehol uplands were originally wooded steppe in which much of the woodland has been cut over and much of the steppe has been put under cultivation. It is a deeply dissected region, with the highest points rising to 3,000 feet or more, and the valley floors at elevations of 1,000 to 2,000 feet.

Manchuria lies mainly between Lat. 40 and 50 degrees N., corresponding to the northern United States and southern Canada. This suggests similar climatic conditions, but the greater continentality of Asia results in sharper seasonal contrasts. Winters are long and bitter, summers short and hot. Average January temperatures range from 21° F (−6° C) in the extreme southern Liaotung peninsula to −13° F (−25° C) in the extreme north on the Amur River. Nowhere else in the world are such low winter temperatures found in these latitudes. Snow falls during six to seven months and temperatures are below freezing for four to five months.

By contrast, in the summer temperatures are high throughout the region. July averages range from 80° F (27° C) in the south to 70° F (21° C) in the north. The growing season is 200 days in the south and 150 days in the north, making it possible to raise only one crop a year. Winter crops are excluded not only by the low temperatures but also by the thin snow cover, which results in the ground's freezing to a depth of six feet or more.

Precipitation is in effect seasonal, with light winter snowfall, a dry spring and fall, and a summer maximum of rainfall. The total amount of precipitation decreases from the southeast (40 inches at Tantung) toward the northwest (10 inches in the Barga plateau at the west foot of the Greater Khingan range), where agriculture becomes precarious without irrigation.

Owing to a natural grass-cover in the Manchurian plain, the soils there are among the most fertile in China. There is an extensive development of chernozem in the Sungari plain, passing into chestnut soils toward the south. These are steppe soils corresponding to similar soils in European Russia. Along the drier western margins of the plain, gray steppe soils with saline and alkali patches predominate. Podzolic soils and brown forest soils cover the mountains enclosing the central Manchurian plain.

Manchurian agriculture is characterized by the soybean-kaoliang crop association. Millet, spring wheat, corn, barley, and some rice are other crops. Soybeans are by far the most important crop in value of production, in percentage of sown area, and as an export product. It covers 25 to 30 per cent of the sown acreage. In recent times, soybean production has been gradually concentrated in northern Manchuria as more land in the south was being sown in kaoliang and other grains to feed the growing population. Manchuria accounts for about 40 per cent of China's soybean crop. Of this, 30 per cent is exported in the form of oil and beancake.

Kaoliang predominates among the Manchurian grains. Not only does it constitute the chief food crop of the Manchurian peasant, but it is also used for the distilling of the local alcoholic beverage. Kaoliang occupies close to 25 per cent of the Manchurian crop area, being concentrated in the Liao plain. South of Mukden, kaoliang takes up 30 to 40 per cent of the sown acreage. Manchuria's share in China's total kaoliang output is about 35 per cent.

Another major Manchurian grain is millet. The most common among several varieties is the Italian millet or spiked foxtail millet, known as "ku-tzu" in Chinese. The husked millet grain, an important Manchurian food, is known in Chinese as "hsiao-mi-tzu"; this term has been corrupted by the Russians into "chumiza" and is used to designate the millet grown in the Soviet Far East. A less common millet variety grown in Manchuria is the glutinous millet, known in Chinese as "shu-tzu," which grows in more humid soils than the Italian millet. Millet is widespread throughout Manchuria, but predominates in the southwestern part of the central plain.

Corn is grown primarily in the more humid southeastern part of the Manchurian plain. Unlike millet, which is also exported, corn is consumed entirely within Manchuria. In the southeast, it takes up as much as 40 per cent of the sown area. Another grain crop of the southeast is rice, which is grown predominantly by Koreans in the valleys of the East Manchurian uplands. In 1954, Manchuria produced 1.4 million tons of rice.

Spring wheat is associated with soybeans in northern Manchuria. Almost all of Manchuria's wheat crop comes from the chernozem of the Sungari basin, where Harbin is the major milling center. Barley and oats are also grown.

Taking all food crops together, Manchuria produces about 12 per cent of the Chinese total output. Because of decreasing population density from south to north, the northern farming areas, notably in Heilungkiang Province, tend to produce a larger food surplus, which is then shipped southward to more densely settled Liaoning Province, a food deficit region.

Among industrial crops are fibers, such as cotton, hemp, and flax, tobacco and sugar beets, and a number of oil-bearing plants, particularly peanuts, castor beans, sunflowers, perilla, sesame, and rape.

Peanuts are grown chiefly in the extreme south of the Liaotung peninsula, on sandy forest soils similar to those of Shantung, another important peanut-growing province. In the 1950's, Manchuria contributed about 6 per cent of China's peanut crop and was second to Shantung in exports. Sunflowers are cultivated on the drier western margins of Heilungkiang and Kirin.

Among the fibers, cotton is grown in Liaoning, with the principal districts in the Liaotung peninsula, in the lower Liao Ho valley around Liaoyang, and near Chinchow. The cotton crop tends to fluctuate from year to year because of spring drought and late summer rains. Hemp is grown for both its seed and its fiber, which is made into sacks for soybeans. The production of flax has been expanded in northern Manchuria, both in Heilungkiang and in adjoining portions of Kirin.

Tobacco is grown chiefly in central Manchuria and sugar beets in the north. The sugar-beet area was expanded significantly during the 1950's, resulting in a tenfold increase of production to more than 1 million tons of beets a year.

Institutionally, Manchuria's agriculture differs considerably from that of most of China. The Communists carried through their land-reform program in Manchuria earlier than in the rest of the nation. This fact plus the lower population density per unit of cultivated land have led to a relatively high degree of mechanization in Manchuria. Unlike China proper, Manchuria also offers the possibility of expansion of the cultivated area. It has been calculated that about 30 million hectares, or one fourth of Manchuria's total area, is suitable for cultivation. At present only 20 million hectares are actually in crops. Most of the unused acreage is in the northern province of Heilungkiang, where efforts are being made to bring more land under cultivation. Mechanization plays a major part in this expansion program.

Manchuria's mountains have China's most extensive forest reserves. Lumbering plays a major role in the economy of the Greater Khingan in the northwest, the Little Khingan in the northeast, and the East Manchurian uplands. Transport facilities for timber from the Greater Khingan were improved in the 1950's and early 1960's by construction of a special lumbering railroad into the mountains and the development of timber centers in the Ituliho district. In the Little Khingan, timber operations began earlier, around 1950, in the Ichun district. The oldest lumbering industry is associated with the East Manchurian uplands, where timber has been floated down the Yalu River to Tantung, the upper Sungari to Kirin, the Tumen River to the Tumen district, and the Mutan River to the Mutankiang district.

In most of the Manchurian plain, livestock-raising is subsidiary to the tilling of crops. The herds include mainly hogs, draft animals, and cows. They are fed on the byproducts of agriculture. However, in the western Mongol margins, herding is a major part of the economy. Sheep, goats, horses, and beef cattle predominate and are fed on steppe pastures.

Fisheries are of some importance along the Yellow Sea coast of Manchuria, where the indented coastline, an abundance of offshore islands, and shallow coastal waters offer favorable conditions for fishing. Liaoning Province, the only Manchurian province with a coastline, accounts for about 10 per cent of the Chinese catch. The principal species are croaker, cutlass fish (hairtail), shrimp, and lobster. Fishing fleets are based in the Dairen–Port Arthur district.

A distinctive occupation in the mountains of Manchuria is the hunting of fur-bearing animals. Fox, sable, and squirrel are hunted in the East Manchurian uplands and in the Khingan mountains.

The mineral resources of Manchuria are more limited than those of some other parts of China, but mining developments, particularly under the Japanese, have made Manchuria one of the most important mineral-industry regions of China. The discrepancy between reserves and production is particularly pronounced in the case of coal. Manchuria had only about 7 per cent of China's coal reserves in 1957, but accounted for one-third of the national output. Manchuria's share in Chinese coal production has been declining with the development of new fields in other parts of the country. The largest producers, with annual output of more than 10 million tons a year each, are Fushun and Fusin in Liaoning, and Kisi and Hokang in Heilungkiang. All yield good coking coals, except Fusin, which produces low-ash steam coals. Associated with the Fushun coal field is a major oil-shale deposit, which is part of the overburden of the coal seams. Since 1929, the deposit has been supplying a shale-oil industry at Fushun. It yielded 600,000 tons of crude oil in 1957.

Since 1960, Manchuria has also become China's leading producer of natural petroleum with the development of the so-called Taching ("Great Celebration") field in the Anta district of Heilungkiang Province. The first indications of crude oil were found in the Manchurian plain in 1958, and the discovery well of the Taching field was completed in September, 1959, just about the time a curtain of secrecy descended on Chinese economic developments. The field has therefore not been precisely located in official publications and continues to be referred to by the code name Taching. By the late 1960's, Taching contributed at least one-half of China's total petroleum production of 20 million tons.

In keeping with its high level of industrial development, Manchuria is also the leading regional producer of electric power. In 1957, it contributed about 8 billion kilowatt-hours, or more than 40 per cent of China's total power generation of 19 billion kilowatt-hours. Most of the electric power is generated by coal-burning steam electric stations, notably at Mukden, the principal manufacturing city, and the coal-producing centers of Fushun and Fusin. But a substantial share is contributed by the 560,000-kilowatt Fengman hydroelectric station on the Sungari River in Kirin Province, which transmits surplus power over a 220-kilovolt grid northward to Heilungkiang and particularly southward to power-short Liaoning Province. The Manchurian grid also derives some power from the 700,000-kilowatt Supung hydroelectric station on the Yalu River, which China shares with North Korea.

Aside from its pre-eminent position in fuels and energy, Manchuria is also a significant producer of metals, particularly iron ore, magnesite, manganese, and molybdenum, all associated with the Anshan iron and steel industry. The region accounted for two-thirds of China's iron-ore production in 1957, roughly the same proportion that the Anshan iron and steel industry represented in the processing sector. With the development of other iron and steel industries elsewhere in China, Manchuria's share has steadily declined to about one-half. The principal iron mines are in the immediate vicinity of Anshan and at Kungchangling, 25 miles to the east; other mines are at Miaoerhkow and Waitowshan, in the Penki district, and at Talitze, in the Tunghwa district of Kirin Province. One of the world's greatest magnesite deposits is favorably located in the Tashihkiao district as a source of refractories for the Anshan furnaces. The magnesite was also used by the Japanese during World War II for the production of magnesium metal at Yingkow. Manganese, an essential element in steel production, is mined at Wafangtze in the Chaoyang area of the Jehol uplands, and molybdenum, used in alloy steels, is derived from the Yangkiachangtze mine, west of Chinsi, which used to be operated mainly for lead and zinc. The ores of scattered lead, zinc, and copper mines are processed at smelters in Mukden.

Aluminum-bearing shale, a rock associated with coal deposits east of Penki (Niusintai, Siaoshih, Tienshihfu) and near Yentai, is a potential low-grade material for aluminum production. Beginning in 1938, the Japanese used a hydrochloric acid process to produce alumina, which was then reduced electrolytically to aluminum metal. The plant at Fushun used power from the local coal burning power station. The aluminum plant was reported to have been rehabilitated in the middle 1950's.

The Liaoning coast is a significant producer of sea salt, which is used as a raw material of the chemical industry, particularly at Dairen and at Chinsi, in food-processing and as table salt. In 1957, Liaoning produced 1.7 million tons of salt, or 21 per cent of national output of sea salt. The principal salines are at Fuchowwan, just north of the Dairen–Port Arthur municipal district, and near Yingkow.

Gold is another mineral resource of Manchuria, with placers predominating in the north along the Amur River, and lode deposits in the East Manchurian uplands, notably at Kiapikow near Hwatien, and in the Tumen district.

On the basis of existing mineral resources, Manchuria became China's leading center of heavy industry during the Japanese occupation before and during World War II. After 1949, many of the Japanese-built enterprises were gradually restored and expanded. Manchuria continues to dominate in China's heavy industry, despite the build-up of iron and steel and associated enterprises elsewhere in China. Manchuria's industry includes iron and steel enterprises, notably at Anshan and Penki, machinery industries at Mukden, Dairen, Changhun, and Harbin, and food-processing and consumer industries in these and other cities.

Manchuria's industrial centers are served by a relatively dense rail network, including about a third of China's total track mileage. The main lines are the historic Chinese Eastern and South Manchuria railroads, whose T-shaped system formed the only Soviet-Chinese rail link prior to 1955. In that year, the completion of the Tsining–Ulan-Bator line through the Mongolian People's Republic offered a second and shorter connection between the two countries.

The Chinese Eastern and South Manchuria railroads were administered jointly by the Soviet Union and China as the Chinese Changchun railroad from 1945 to 1952. Thereafter, the system passed into Chinese hands. The system consists of four main sections: the Harbin-Manchouli line, the Harbin-Suifenho line, the Harbin-Changchun line, and the Changchun-Dairen line. Major branches lead from Mukden to Tientsin and Peking and from Mukden to Tantung on the Korean border.

Of Manchuria's two principal rivers, only the Sungari plays a role as a significant waterway during the ice-free season, which lasts about six months. Traffic on the Sungari is particularly heavy between Harbin and Kiamusze. The Liao Ho, once the chief transport route of southern Manchuria before the coming of the railroads, is no longer a significant waterway, having been silted up over most of its course. The Amur and Ussuri rivers, which form the border with the Soviet Union, were little used along the sparsely settled Chinese bank even before Soviet-Chinese relations cooled in the early 1960's. The Yalu River, on the Chinese–North Korean border, has some limited use below the Supung dam.

Dairen, at the tip of the Liaotung peninsula, is Manchuria's chief seaport. Of much lesser importance are Hulutao and Yingkow on the Gulf of Liaotung, and Tungkow, outer port of Tantung.

Manchuria's population density is low by Chinese standards. There are about 400 persons per square mile in the relatively closely settled Liaotung peninsula and the Mukden industrial area, but the region's over-all average is 160. Parts of the northern Manchurian plain have as few as 25 persons per square mile. Migration from overpopulated parts of China to Manchuria has been a continuing process in recent decades. Even under the Japanese occupation, Chinese workers were recruited for Manchuria's growing industries. The Peking regime is stimulating migration from such provinces as Shantung, Hopei, and Honan to put Manchuria's virgin lands under the plow.

More than 90 per cent of Manchuria's population is Chinese, speaking the northern (Peking) variety of Mandarin. Among the region's minorities are most of China's 1.1 million Koreans, of whom about one-half live in the Yenpien Korean Autonomous Chou of Kirin Province.

Even before the incorporation of the Inner Mongolian portion into Manchuria in 1969, the region had a Mongol minority population of 320,000 along the western margins of the Manchurian plain. They were organized in several autonomous banners: The Kharachin East Wing banner and the Fusin (Tumet) banner in Liaoning; the South Gorlos banner in Kirin; and the Durbet (Taikang) banner in Heilungkiang. The territorial transfer of the Inner Mongolian areas is estimated to have added 400,000 Mongols to Manchuria, for a total Mongol minority population of about 750,000. At least initially, the Mongol leagues of the annexed areas were preserved within the three Manchurian provinces.

Manchuria also contains virtually China's entire Manchu minority population, or 2.1 million out of a national total of 2.4 million. The descendants of the original Manchu population of Manchuria, these people no longer represent a separate cultural group and have been almost fully assimilated into Chinese life. Half of the Manchus live in Liaoning, one-third in Heilungkiang, and one-sixth in Kirin. Another group closely integrated with the ethnic Chinese and residing mainly in cities are the Hui (Chinese Moslems), who number 230,000.

In northern Manchuria, according to the 1953 census, were 44,000 Daghors, an ethnic group closely related to the Mongols; small Tungusic tribes, including 5,000 Evenki (Solun), 2,300 Orochon (Oronchon), and 500 Golds (Fishskin Tatars); and about 23,000 ethnic Russians, members of a community that settled in Manchuria at the turn of the twentieth century. As a result of repatriation to the Soviet Union, the number of Russians was reduced to about 9,800 by 1957.

LIAONING PROVINCE
Capital: Mukden; area: 90,000 sq. mi.; population: 29 million

From 1949 until August, 1954, Liaoning Province consisted of the two provinces of Liaosi and Liaotung, respectively west and east of the Liao Ho, and the independent cities of Mukden, Fushun, Anshan, Penki, and Port Arthur–Dairen. At the time of consolidation of these areas into Liaoning Province, a strip of territory along the province's northern border, including the cities of Tunghwa, Liaoyüan, and Szeping, was ceded to Kirin Province. Within the resulting territory, Liaoning had a population of 18.6 million according to the 1953 census.

In 1956, Liaoning Province acquired the eastern section of partitioned Jehol, with a 1953 population of 2 million. Within this enlarged territory, with an area of 58,000 square miles, Liaoning thus had a 1953 population of 20.6 million, rising to 24.1 million in the 1957 estimate and perhaps to 28 million by 1969. As constituted from 1956 until late 1969, Liaoning included the Liaotung peninsula and part of the East Manchurian uplands in the east, the Liao plain, and the Liaosi corridor in the southwest. In the west, the province reached into the Jehol uplands.

It appeared in late 1969, in conjunction with the realignment of military district boundaries, that one of the eastern Inner Mongolian leagues—Jo-uda, with the city of Chihfeng—had been incorporated into Liaoning Province. The annexation increased the provincial area by about 50 per cent and added perhaps 1 million people, including more than 100,000 Mongols, to the population.

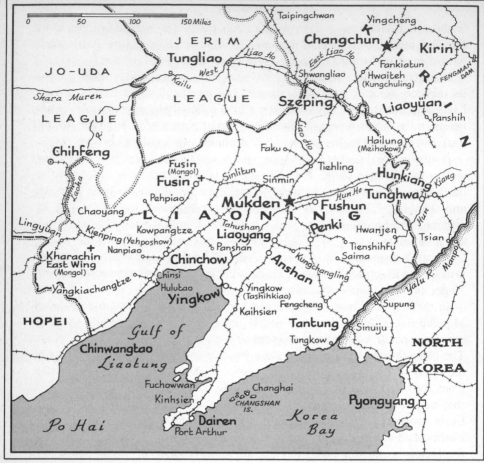

13. Southern Manchuria

Liaoning is the part of Manchuria that is closest to the rest of China and as such was settled by the Chinese earlier than the rest of the region. Its seaboard location and the early construction of a rail net played a major part in the rapid development of the province. During World War II, the area was a key base of war industries of the Japanese.

Agriculture is concentrated in the Liao plain, which extends largely west of the river. Almost all available land has been put under cultivation. Because of the relatively high population pressure, agriculture is largely of the subsistence type, unlike the commercial surplus farming typical of northern Manchuria. As a result, soybeans occupy less than one-sixth of the sown area, while food crops, such as kaoliang and millet, take up more than one-half, particularly in the western part of the province. Soybeans become more important toward the north. Corn is a leading crop in the southeast, where it covers 40 to 50 per cent of the sown area. The limited cultivation of rice in the same area must also be noted. The production of food crops is about 6 million tons a year, with kaoliang and corn accounting for more than 1.5 million tons each. Substantial amounts of food grains, particularly wheat, must be brought into Liaoning from northern Manchuria.

Liaoning produces nearly all of Manchuria's cotton and a large part of its tobacco, sesame, and castor beans. Cotton is cultivated chiefly around Liaoyang and toward the southwest, tobacco in the northeast, and castor beans in the west and southwest. The normal cotton crop is about 60,000 tons, but spring droughts and wet late summers often reduce the harvest.

A distinctive product of the province is wild silk, which is spun and woven into pongee cloth. The silk, which is produced by a worm feeding on oak leaves, is produced chiefly on the Liaotung peninsula near Kaihsien and Tantung. The oak-fed silkworm was introduced into Liaoning by settlers from Shantung, a province with which southeastern Liaoning has much in common.

Another distinctive crop is fruit, especially apples and pears. The apple area on the Liaotung peninsula, again centered on Kaihsien, produces about 70 per cent of China's apple crop.

In the realm of mineral resources, Liaoning leads in the production of Manchurian coal and produces nearly the region's entire iron output. Coal resources occur both on the western and eastern edges of the Liao plain. The two principal mining centers are Fushun and Fusin, each producing of the order of 15 to 20 million tons a year. Fushun yields both steam coals, from the western part of the 10-mile-long basin, and coking coals, from the eastern section, for use in the Anshan and Penki iron and steel mills. Fusin produces high-grade steam coals not suitable for coking. Both Fushun and Fusin have both underground mines and open pits, including the Haichow pit at Fusin, China's largest surface mine, opened in 1953. Liaoning's third largest producer is the Pehpiao district, a southwestern extension of the Fusin basin, with an output of the order of 5 to 10 million tons, mainly coking coal. Finally, there is the Penki district, with relatively small reserves, where underground mines produce about 5 million tons of good coking coal.

In addition to these four principal districts, at least two others were developed in the Great Leap and the 1960's. One is the Nanpiao area, south of Pehpiao, with its center at Tayaokow. The Nanpiao coal deposit, originally tapped by the Japanese, is linked by a rail spur with the Chinchow area. The other new coal development is the so-called Tiehfa basin, between Tiehling and Faku, north of Mukden. A railroad linking Tiehling, on the Mukden-Changchun main line, with Faku was built in the middle 1960's, and a 600,000-ton coal mine was inaugurated in the Tiehfa field in 1968. The development of the so-called Shenpei field ("north of Shenyang [Mukden]"), which appears to be a westward extension of the Fushun basin, was also reported under way during the Great Leap, but no further progress has been reported.

The coal seams at Fushun are overlain by large reserves of oil shale, which is being stripped as part of the overburden and is used for the production of shale oil and its derivatives at a refinery at Fushun. The oil shale reserves are estimated at 2.5 billion tons, and the mean content of organic matter at 5 to 6 per cent.

Some of China's greatest concentrations of iron ore are found in Liaoning, and have given rise to the great iron and steel industry of Anshan as well as the lesser complex of Penki. Relatively small reserves of high-grade ore in the immediate vicinity of Anshan (Takushan, Sianshan, Tunganshan) were the first to supply the iron and steel plant after its inauguration in 1917. Later the larger reserves of low-grade ore (35 per cent iron content) were developed at Kungchangling, 25 miles east of Anshan. The Kungchangling underground operation was expanded during the Great Leap, and a new concentrator was completed in 1959. Another low-grade ore deposit, at Chitashan, was developed in 1968–69 with construction of an open-pit mine and concentrator. The total usable-ore output of the Anshan district is about 10 million tons. Some ore is also mined in more limited reserves of the Penki district, notably at Miaoerhkow, 15 miles south of Penki, and Waitowshan, 15 miles north.

Large magnesite reserves in the Liaotung peninsula offer a potential source of refractory materials and metallic magnesium. The deposit, which extends for 20 miles and has a thickness of up to 2,000 feet, is situated between the towns of Haicheng and Kaihsien along the Mukden-Dairen railroad. The rail junction of Tashihkiao (now called Yingkow hsien), from which a rail spur goes to the port of Yingkow, is in the area of the magnesite deposit, whose reserves are estimated at 1.4 billion tons.

Another source of refractory materials and light metal is low-grade aluminous shale found with coal deposits at Penki (Niusintai, Siaoshih, Tienshihfu) and near Yentai. The shale was used by the Japanese after 1938 in an alumina-aluminum plant at Fushun. The plant was rehabilitated in the middle 1950's.

Among nonferrous metals, copper, lead, and zinc are mined in a number of scattered small deposits throughout the province, particularly the East Manchurian uplands and the Liaosi corridor. A copper mine at Hungtaoshan, in the Fushun area, was reported to have been expanded to a major operation in 1968–69.

In conjunction with the requirements of the iron and steel industry, Liaoning has developed manganese and molybdenum deposits in the Liaosi corridor. The molybdenum mine is at Yangkiachangtze, on a rail spur west of Chinsi. The deposit is estimated at 30 to 40 million tons, with a metal content of 0.5 per cent. The manganese deposits, with a metal content of 20 to 30 per cent, are mined at Wafangtze in the Chaoyang area. This was once China's largest manganese producer, now surpassed by the mining operation near Siangtan in Hunan.

Electric power for Liaoning's highly industrialized economy relies both on large steam-electric stations, based on the province's coal resources, and on several hydroelectric plants. The largest thermal-power complex is the so-called Liaoning steam-electric station in Mukden, with a designed capacity of 600,000 kilowatts. The station was inaugurated in 1959 with the installation of the first two 50,000-kilowatt units. They burn steam coals from the nearby Fushun mines. Large thermal-power complexes are also in operation at the two principal coal-mining centers, Fushun and Fusin. The designed capacity at Fusin is 300,000 kilowatts, with 150,000 kilowatts installed by the end of 1957; at Fushun, it is 248,000 kilowatts, with 187,000 installed by the end of 1957. Other heat and power stations are situated at Anshan, Chinchow, and Dairen. The largest hydroelectric project is the Shuifeng (Supung) station on the Yalu River, with a generating capacity of 700,000 kilowatts, which China shares with North Korea, though most of its output appears to feed into the North Korean power grid. Within Liaoning itself is the relatively small Tahwofang hydroelectric station, on the Hun Ho, just east of Fushun. The reservoir for this station was inaugurated in 1958 after five years' construction, and the designed capacity of 32,000 kilowatts (two 16,000-kilowatt units) was installed in 1959. During the Great Leap, construction was reported to have been started on a 290,000-kilowatt hydroelectric project on the Hun Kiang, a Yalu tributary, near Hwanjen, but, like similar projects in China, it appears to have been shelved. All the major power-producing centers of Liaoning are interconnected by a 220-kilovolt transmission grid. Since electric-power consumption in highly industrialized Liaoning exceeds production, substantial amounts of power are fed into the Liaoning grid from the Fengman hydroelectric station in adjoining Kirin Province.

Modern industry first penetrated into Liaoning Province at the turn of the century, with the construction of railroads. Initially light industry was dominant. Soybeans produced both in Liaoning and farther north were shipped here for processing into oil and beancake for export. Other factories processed tobacco, grain, and other agricultural products. Cotton and silk textiles were produced in the leading cities. But it was the development of heavy industry, notably under Japanese impetus, that gave the province its distinctive economy.

The development of the industrial focus of Mukden-Fushun-Anshan-Penki was greatly aided by the construction of a dense rail net. The Dairen-Mukden-Changchun railroad is the main line crossing the economically most important parts of the province along the eastern margin of the Liao plain. From Mukden, leading rail hub, lines radiate toward the North China plain, Korea, and northern Manchuria.

Liaoning Province is one of the most urbanized parts of China (Table 50). In addition to the five cities that were under the jurisdiction of the central government until 1954, Mukden, Fushun, Anshan, Penki, and Port Arthur–Dairen, the province includes five other cities under provincial jurisdiction. They are Tantung, Liaoyang, Yingkow, Fusin, and Chinchow. The municipal districts of these ten cities include large rural portions of the

TABLE 50
CITIES OF LIAONING

City	City Level	Function	Population (*in thousands*)		
			1953	1957	1970 est.
Mukden	subprovince	manuf.	2,299	2,411	3,000
Dairen–Port					
Arthur	subprovince	manuf., port	1,200	1,508	
(Dairen proper			766	800)	
(Port Arthur			126)		
Fushun	subprovince	coal, oil shale,			
		aluminum	679	985	
Anshan	subprovince	iron-steel	549	805	
Penki	subprovince	iron-steel	449		
Tantung	subprovince	manuf.	360	420	
Chinchow	subprovince	manuf.	352		
Fusin	subprovince	coal, power	189	330	
Liaoyang	subprovince	manuf.	168	200	
Yingkow	subprovince	manuf.	131	200	
Chihfeng	hsien	trade	50		
Former Cities	*Period*				
Chaoyang	1959–64				
Hulutao	1956–57				

province, far beyond the urbanized cores. For example, the city of Tantung in the late 1960's had under its jurisdiction five rural hsien covering an area nearly 200 miles long, along the Yalu River frontier with North Korea and the coast of Korea Bay and extending up to 75 miles inland.

Mukden, the capital of the province and its largest city, is situated on the right bank of the Hun Ho, a tributary of the Liao Ho. The Manchus had their capital here in the seventeenth century prior to their conquest of China. After the capital was moved to Peking in 1644, Mukden (which is the city's Manchu name, preserved in Western usage) was given the Chinese names of Shengking and, later, Fengtien. Its present Chinese name of Shenyang, first used under the Mongol Yüan Dynasty, was restored in 1928. Situated in the southern part of the Manchurian plain and well supplied with transportation routes, Mukden was in a natural position to become the political and economic hub of Manchuria. The city developed particularly under Japanese rule, when its population quadrupled from 421,000 in 1931 to 1,891,000 in 1945. Its population dropped during the Chinese civil war to 1,021,057 in 1948. Under the Communist regime and its emphasis on industrialization and urbanization, Mukden's population doubled to 2,299,000 in the 1953 census. By the end of 1957, it was reported to have risen to 2,411,000, and an estimate for 1970 was 3 million. It is China's fifth largest city.

Favorably situated near the iron and steel centers of Anshan and Penki, Mukden has developed into one of China's principal metal-fabricating and machinery-manufacturing centers. It produces about one-fourth of China's machinery, and this industrial sector makes up 45 per cent of Mukden's total output by value. The city is a leading maker of machine tools, heavy machinery for the iron and steel industry (beneficiation equipment, blast furnaces, forging presses), electrical equipment (transformers, electric cable, electric motors), and transportation equipment (tractors, trolley cars, bicycles, aircraft). Part of the metal requirements for these industries are furnished by a local steel plant, which uses pig iron from Penki and Anshan as well as scrap. Mukden also has a nonferrous-metals industry, smelting and refining copper, lead, and zinc from mines of Liaoning Province. The city's chemical industry produces soda ash, chlorine and its derivatives, as well as pharmaceuticals. Textiles, paper, glass, and processed foods are also produced here.

Mukden consisted originally of the old Chinese city in the east and the new city in the former Japanese railway concession zone. The Chinese city, bounded by a ten-mile-long earthwall now largely in disrepair, contains the inner city with the former Manchu imperial palace and administrative offices. East of the Chinese city is the old Chinese industrial area known as the arsenal district. West of the Chinese city and extending in rectilinear fashion to the railroad station is the new city, which was developed by the Japanese after 1905. Finally, beyond the railroad, in the extreme western part of the city, is the Tiehsi district, known to the Japanese as Tetsunishi. Both Tiehsi, the Chinese name, and Tetsunishi mean "west of the railroad." Tiehsi, which was largely developed after 1937, houses the factories and workers' residences of Mukden's heavy and metal-fabricating industries.

East and south of Mukden, whose municipal district covers an area of 1,200 square miles, are the satellite cities of Fushun, Penki, Anshan, and Liaoyang.

Fushun adjoins the Mukden city limits on the east, although the distance between the two city centers is 25 miles. Fushun's urban limits were expanded in late 1953 from 40 square miles to an area virtually equal to that of Mukden. The population of the expanded city was 679,000 in the 1953 census, of whom about 500,000 lived in the central city. By the end of 1957, greater Fushun had a population of 985,000. Fushun was first developed as a coal-mining center by the Russians in 1902 in connection with railroad construction. In 1905, it passed to the Japanese. The Fushun coal deposit, which occupies an area of 25 square miles, consists largely of one inclined bed, 130 to 165 feet thick, compressed between granites and gneisses. At the point where the coal measures outcrop, they are overlain by more than 300 feet of oil shale. The coal reserves have been estimated at nearly 1 billion tons and the oil shale at 2.5 billion tons. Fushun's steam coals are mined mainly in open pits at the western end of the deposit, and coking coals in underground mines in the east. The largest underground mine is at Laohutai. Fushun has been Manchuria's leading coal-producer since its beginnings, but its share in total output has steadily declined as other mines developed. In the late 1950's, production exceeded the previous peak of close to 10 million tons achieved under the Japanese, and output in the 1960's was estimated at 15 to 20 million tons. The mining and distilling of oil shale began in 1929. The Chinese Communists rehabilitated two shale-oil plants in the 1950's; one of them yields ammonium sulfate fertilizer as a byproduct. A shale-based petrochemical industry added in the middle 1960's is reported to produce synthetic rubber, resins, and plastics. Fushun's coal has been used for the hydrogenation of synthetic fuel, and the methane gas associated with the coal deposit has yielded carbon black. Other industries at Fushun are special steels for ball bearings, produced from Penki pig iron; mining equipment and other heavy machinery, cement and refractories. However, two-thirds of the city's employment is in coal and oil-shale mining, related fuel industries, and power generation. A Japanese-built aluminum plant deriving alumina from shale was rehabilitated in early 1955. Fushun extends more than 20 miles along the south bank of the Hun Ho, with the coal basin adjoining the built-up section on the south. The Tahwofang flood-control and hydroelectric project, with a generating capacity of 32,000 kilowatts, was inaugurated on the Hun Ho east of Fushun in 1958–59. A copper mine was developed in the 1960's at Hungtaoshan, within the Fushun municipal area.

Southeast of Mukden, on the railroad to Tantung and North Korea, is the iron and steel center of Penki. Its municipal district, which exceeds that of Mukden or Fushun, had an area of almost 2,000 square miles and a population of 449,000 in the 1953 census. In late 1958, the Penki municipal district expanded eastward to include Hwanjen and reached an area of more than 3,000 square miles. Penki is Manchuria's second iron and steel producer, after Anshan. In contrast to Anshan's bulk of production of ordinary carbon steels, the small Penki plant uses its local resources of high-grade coking coal and low-phosphorus iron ore to produce low-phosphorus pig iron for use in stainless alloy steels. Only half of Penki's total pig-iron output, estimated at about 600,000 tons, is converted into steel locally in electric furnaces and basic oxygen converters. Penki arose as a metallurgical center in World War I, when two 200-ton blast furnaces went into operation. Two larger blast furnaces, each of 500-ton capacity, were added by the Japanese in 1939 in the southern suburb of Penki, called Miyanohara in Japanese and Kungyüan in Chinese. One of the large furnaces was restored in 1948, the other in 1955. Most of Penki's iron ore comes from the Miaoerhkow open-cut mine, near Nanfen rail station, 15 miles south of Penki. Another mine is at Waitowshan, 15 miles north of the city. The coal mines, including Niusintai and Tienshihfu, are along a rail spur running east from Penki. The city is also a major cement-producer, with two large mills.

West of Penki, on the Mukden-Dairen railroad, is Anshan, Manchuria's and China's leading iron and steel center. Like Penki, Anshan had its beginnings in World War I, when the first two blast furnaces were built, followed by a third in 1930. Initially, high-grade ore, containing 50 to 60 per cent iron, was mined in the immediate vicinity of the plant. However, reserves were limited, and mining operations moved to Kungchangling, 25 miles east of Anshan, where 35-per cent ore, requiring beneficiation, was available in larger reserves. Until 1933, Anshan produced only pig iron. Under the Japanese-dominated Manchukuo regime, the Anshan works were expanded with the addition of steel-making capacity (open-hearth furnaces) and six more blast furnaces. During World War II, Anshan made a significant contribution to the Japanese war effort, and, at the end of the war, in 1945, the plant had a pig-iron capacity of 2 million tons and a steel capacity of 1.4 million tons. The Soviet Union dismantled the Anshan iron and steel plant, and, by the time of the Communist take-over in 1949, pig iron and steel output was of the order of 100,000 tons. During the 1950's, reconstruction proceeded at a rapid pace. The two oldest blast furnaces were the first to be restored in 1949, to a working volume of 600 cubic meters each, followed in 1950 by the No. 4 furnace, with a working volume of 900 cubic meters. At the same time, one steel plant with nine open-hearth furnaces was put back into operation. In 1952, Anshan produced 1.46 million tons of pig iron and 900,000 tons of crude steel. During the first five-year plan (1953–57), six more blast furnaces, each with a working volume of 900 cubic meters, were reopened (Nos. 7 and 8 in 1953, No. 6 in 1954, No. 5 in 1955, No. 9 in 1956, and No. 3 in 1957). During the same period, a second steel plant was rebuilt and expanded. In 1957, Anshan produced 3.38 million tons of pig iron and 2.95 million tons of crude steel. Finishing mills produced a variety of finished steel products, including heavy rails, shapes, and seamless tubing. During the Great Leap, Anshan's iron and steel capacity was further expanded through the construction of a tenth blast furnace, with a working volume of 1,513 cubic meters (inaugurated in 1958), and a third steel plant, which includes two 660-ton open-hearth furnaces, each with a daily output of 1,300 to 1,500 tons. The increase in iron and steel capacity outstripped ore-mining capacity, and, in the 1960's, additional open-pit mines and concentrators for the beneficiation of low-grade ore were completed. Anshan's ten blast furnaces were believed to be producing 5 million tons of pig iron in the 1960's, and the three steel plants about 6 million tons of crude steel annually. Anshan's development as China's leading iron and steel center has been reflected in its population growth. The 1953 census recorded 549,000, and the 1957 estimate was 805,000.

North of Anshan, along the railroad to Mukden, is the fifth provincial city of the Mukden complex, Liaoyang, one of the oldest of Manchuria's cities. Liaoyang has been by-passed by the modern industrialization effort and is significant mainly for its light industries (cotton textiles, food-processing). The city was administratively subordinated to Anshan in 1959 but regained independent municipal status in 1965. Liaoyang had a population of 168,000 in the 1953 census, rising to about 200,000 by the end of 1957.

In the southeastern part of Liaoyang Province lies Tantung, gateway to North Korea. The city was known as Antung in the past but was renamed in 1965, presumably because its former name, meaning "peaceful or pacified East," could lend itself to derogatory interpretation by North Korea. The new name, Tantung, may be translated as "sincere or honorable East." The city owes its development to the construction (1907) of the railroad from Mukden to North Korea, which here crosses the Yalu River to the North Korean frontier city of Sinuiju. One of the earliest industries of Tantung was the milling of the wild silk, produced by the oak-leaf-feeding silkworm of the East Manchurian uplands. This was followed by the establishment of a pulp-and-paper mill and other wood-processing facilities using timber floated down the Yalu River. A viscose rayon plant, originally built by the Japanese in 1939, was restored in 1958, adding a modern component to the old natural-silk industry. The city had a population of 360,000 in 1953, expanding to 420,000 by the end of 1957. Since 1959, Tantung's municipal administration has had a large hinterland area under its jurisdiction. Though situated near the mouth of the Yalu River on Korea Bay, Tantung has not developed into a major seaport. It can be reached by ocean-going vessels of 10-foot draft at high tide. At other times, ships anchor off Tantung's outer harbor, Tungkow (originally known as Tatungkow and later, until 1965, as Antung hsien). Upstream from Tantung is the Shuifeng (Supung) hydroelectric station on the Yalu River. Originally built by the Japanese in 1941 and dismantled by the Russians after the war, the hydroelectric plant was restored in the 1950's to a capacity of 700,000 kilowatts (seven 100,000-kilowatt units). Most of its electric power is used by North Korea, but some is probably allocated to the Manchurian grid.

Three provincial cities in the western part of Liaoning are Fusin, Chinchow, and Yingkow.

Fusin is a rapidly developing coal-mining and power-producing center, founded in the late 1930's and now rivaling the older producer of Fushun. Large-scale coal production began in 1937, when Fusin was reached by the railroad. By the late 1950's, Fusin was mining coal in ten underground mines and four open pits. The Haichow strip mine, largest in China, was inaugurated in 1953. Fusin reached Fushun's production level of 10 million tons in 1958 and was believed to be producing 15 to 20 million tons a year in the late 1960's. Fusin's coal is not of coking grade and is being used mainly as a power-station fuel, both at a local steam-electric station, with a designed capacity of 300,000 kilowatts, and elsewhere in Manchuria. Fusin's rapid development is reflected in population growth: It had a population of 189,000 in the 1953 census and 330,000 at the end of 1957.

Chinchow, at the entrance to the Liaosi corridor leading to Shanhaikwan and the North China plain, is an old Manchurian city. It is situated on the Peking-Mukden railroad at the junction of branch lines from the Jehol uplands and the Fusin coal mines. The Chinchow industrial district, originally developed by the Japanese in the 1930's, extends 30 miles southwest to Chinsi (the former Lienshan) and its port, Hulutao. Early industrial construction, mainly in the Chinsi area, focused on the use of Fusin coal for the extraction of synthetic fuel and other chemicals. Chinchow acquired a heavy machinery plant, manufacturing mining equipment, and Chinsi a chemical equipment plant. Under the Communists, most of these industries were rehabilitated in the 1950's, with Chinsi continuing primarily as a chemical center. It has a chlorine-caustic plant, based on the electrolysis of sea salt and, since 1960, manufactures polyamide fibers via the caprolactam route. Chinsi is also reported to have an oil refinery with a throughput capacity of 500,000 tons. Since the Great Leap, the Chinchow industrial district has acquired an important electronics industry, including the manufacture of quartz glass, transistors, electronic tubes, and rare-earth elements, some of which have electronic applications. In addition to Fusin coal, Chinchow also obtains coal from the Nanpiao mines, at the end of a rail spur 20 miles west of Chinchow. Another rail spur leads west from Chinsi to the molybdenum mine of Yangkiachangtze. Despite the industrial character of Chinsi, it has not been raised to municipal status and has not been included in the city limits of Chinchow. The 1953 population of Chinchow was reported as 352,000. The port of Hulutao is an artificial ice-free harbor built by the Japanese in the early 1930's. It also had a lead smelter for the processing of ore from lead mines near the molybdenum site of Yangkiachangtze. Because of its sheltered site and year-round accessibility, Hulutao was envisaged as Manchuria's port of the future, rivaling even Dairen. These plans may have been revived briefly in 1956–57, when Hulutao existed temporarily as a city, but no such development has occurred.

Another Manchurian port whose traffic lags far behind that of Dairen is Yingkow, at the mouth of the Liao Ho. However, unlike Hulutao, Yingkow once was Manchuria's leading seaport prior to the coming of the railroads. From 1836, when Yingkow replaced the original silted Liao port of Newchwang, until the turn of the century, when Dairen became the chief Manchurian outlet, Yingkow was the gateway to Manchuria. It handled the growing agricultural production of the Liao plain and received the increasing numbers of Chinese settlers. It declined not only because of the rise of Dairen, but also because of its own inadequacies as a port. It is frozen three to four months of the year. The Liao Ho is navigable only for small vessels, and its sediments moreover silt up the approaches to Yingkow. The city maintained some importance as a local trade port and industrial center. Rail spurs approach it from Tashihkiao (officially Yingkow hsien), on the Dairen-Mukden railroad, and from Kowpangtze, on the Peking-Mukden line. The spur from Tashihkiao was again in operation after World War II, but the other rail approach to Yingkow has not been rebuilt in its entirety. A rail spur from Kowpangtze to Panshan opened in 1969 to provide access to an agricultural reclamation project in the southern reaches of the Liao Ho plain. Yingkow is now a relatively minor industrial city, with cotton-milling, knitwear, paper, and food-canning establishments. It is situated in a rice-growing area and has fisheries and saltworks along the coast. The 1953 population was 131,000, rising to about 200,000 by 1957. The Japanese operated a magnesium metal plant at Yingkow after 1939, using magnesite from Tashihkiao. It is believed to be in production.

A fourth subregional center in the western part of Liaoning is Chaoyang, which had municipal status from 1959 to 1964. Situated in a cotton and kaoliang area, it has textile mills and a food-processing industry. It evidently lost its position as a city because of limited industrial prospects for a city that is off the main transport routes up in the Jehol upland.

At the southernmost tip of the Liaotung peninsula is the Port Arthur–Dairen municipal district. It is known as Lüta in its Chinese abbreviation, for the Chinese names of Port Arthur (Lüshun) and Dairen (Talien). The successor of the Japanese-leased Kwantung territory, the district was set up in 1945 as a joint Soviet–Chinese Nationalist naval base area. After the Communist take-over, Soviet forces were withdrawn in 1955. The district had an area of 1,300 square miles, including not only the two cities of Port Arthur and Dairen on the tip of the peninsula, but Kinhsien to the north and Changhai, in the Changshan Islands to the east. In the 1953 census, the district had a population of 1.2 million, including 766,000 in Dairen proper, 126,000 in Port Arthur proper, and the rest in rural areas. The 1957 population estimate for the district was 1.5 million. The district area expanded further in 1959 to include additional areas of the Liaotung peninsula, but since 1965 it has been limited to the Port Arthur–Dairen area and the offshore Changshan Islands.

Dairen began to be developed in 1898 by the Russians, who called it Dal'niy. It passed to the Japanese in 1905. As the southern terminus of the Manchurian main line and the principal outlet for Manchuria's agricultural products, Dairen boomed under Japanese rule, its population rising from 386,000 in 1931 to 873,000 in 1945. The city is Manchuria's leading soybean-processing center and rivals Mukden as a machinery manufacturer, with emphasis on shipbuilding and locomotives and rolling stock. The city's shipyards build ocean-going vessels, including 5,000-ton oil tankers and 10,000-ton freighters. Dairen's machinery industries also produce machine tools, cranes, and electric motors. Metal needs are furnished in part by a local steel plant, producing tool and alloy steels from scrap and Penki low-phosphorus pig iron. The Dairen steel plant produced 230,000 tons in 1958. Chemicals rank second to machinery in the city's industrial structure. Dairen produces a wide range of basic chemicals based both on sea salt, via the caustic-chlorine route, and on byproducts of a major oil refinery. Most of the salt is harvested in the Fuchowwan salines, north of the Port Arthur–Dairen urban district. The Dairen refinery, which used to receive crude oil by tanker and now processes oil from the Taching field, yields hydrogen for ammonia synthesis and nitrogen fertilizer derivatives. Dairen also produces cement, textiles, and canned foods. Situated on the sheltered south shore of the Bay of Dairen, the city consists of the modern former Japanese administrative and commercial Chungshan section adjoining the port and the former Chinese residential Sikang quarter in the west. The port, sheltered by a 2.5-mile-long mole, can accommodate vessels up to 20,000 tons along a total of 3 miles of piers. South of the city are the residential resort towns of Laohutan and Singpu.

Port Arthur is 25 miles southwest of Dairen at the very tip of the Liaotung peninsula. The city is situated on the north shore of a landlocked bay accessible through a 1,000-foot-wide strait. The old Chinese city and the new section are respectively east and west of the railroad station. Port Arthur is a major naval base dominating the entrance to the Po Hai.

The incorporation of the Inner Mongolian league of Jo-uda in 1969 added one more municipality to the province. Unlike the other Liaoning cities, this municipality, Chihfeng, is at hsien level.

Chihfeng, the administrative center of Jo-uda League, is situated in an agricultural Chinese settlement area extending northward into the Jehol uplands. It is primarily a trade center at the end of a feeder railroad completed in 1935 from Yehposhow (since 1956, the seat of Kienping hsien). Chihfeng had a population of about 50,000 in the 1950's and achieved municipal status in 1958.

Before the incorporation of Inner Mongolia's Jo-uda League in 1969, Liaoning's ethnic minority population was about 1.6 million, or 5 per cent of the total. The largest group is the Manchu minority, numbering 1.1 million, or nearly half of China's Manchu population. The Manchus are assimilated with the Chinese and are concentrated in large cities (110,000 in Mukden alone) and along railroad lines. Before the 1969 annexation, Mongols numbered 235,000, concentrated in two Mongol autonomous hsien—Fusin hsien (the old Tumet banner), just east of the coal-mining center of Fusin, and the Kharachin East Wing hsien (the old Tachengtze), 20 miles south of the Yehposhow rail junction. The annexation may have added more than 100,000 Mongols in Jo-uda League, including the Barin, Aru-Khorchin, Ongniut, Kheshikten, and Kharachin West Wing banners.

Finally, Liaoning's population includes 125,000 Hui (Chinese Moslems), who live mainly in cities, and 116,000 Koreans, settled along the Yalu River frontier.

KIRIN PROVINCE

Capital: Changchun; area: 110,000 sq. mi.; population: 21 million

Kirin has undergone a number of boundary changes in the Communist provincial structure. As one of the five Manchurian provinces in the early 1950's, it had an area of about 47,000 square miles and a population of 7 million. In 1954, Kirin annexed territory from northern Liaoning, including the cities of Szeping, Liaoyüan, and Tunghwa, and a western steppe district around Paicheng from Heilungkiang Province. Within this enlarged territory of 72,000 square miles, Kirin had a population of 11.3 million in the 1953 census, rising to 1,206 million by the end of 1957. As a result of intensive migration to new agricultural settlement areas and to industrial cities, Kirin's population rose to 20 million by the late 1960's. As a result of the dismemberment of Inner Mongolia's eastern wing in late 1969, Kirin absorbed the entire Jerim League, with its headquarters at Tungliao, which is connected by rail with the Kirin railroad system. In addition, Kirin gained the southernmost banner of Hulunbuir League, the rest of the league going to Heilungkiang. The southern banner, known as the Khorchin West Wing's South banner, with its administrative seat at Ulanhot, was detached because it is served by the Paicheng-Arshan railroad penetrating into the banner from Kirin. These annexations of former Inner Mongolian territory raised the total area of Kirin Province to about 110,000 square miles and added about 1 million people, including more than 200,000 Mongols, for a 1970 population of 21 million.

Like Liaoning Province, Kirin also falls into a western lowland section and eastern uplands, each occupying roughly one-half of the total area. The lowland, the most important agricultural part of the province, lies astride the low divide separating the Liao and Sungari plains. The eastern hills, extending as far as the borders of Korea and the U.S.S.R., are part of the East Manchurian uplands. They include the Changpai Mountains with the lake-topped volcanic peak Paitow Shan culminating at 9,000 feet. Lumbering and mining are the principal branches of the upland economy.

Soybeans occupy about 30 per cent of the sown area and constitute the leading commercial crop, especially in the valleys of the east branch of the Liao Ho and the upper Sungari River. Among the food grains, kaoliang and corn predominate in the western lowland, with wheat increasing northward. In the eastern upland valleys, rice and millet are cultivated chiefly by the Korean population. Total food production in Kirin, including soybeans, is 6 to 7 million tons a year. The most important industrial crop is sugar beet, whose cultivated area and production expanded roughly tenfold during the 1950's. Sugar beet is grown mainly along the railroads in the center and west of the province, for easy transportation to mills at Fankiatun, just southwest of Changchun, and at Kirin.

Lumbering has assumed two specialized aspects in Kirin Province. In the upper Sungari basin, the emphasis is on construction timber, with the principal sawmills at Kirin city. In the extreme eastern part of the province, timber of the upper Mutan and Tumen valleys is largely converted into pulp and paper. The principal paper mills are in the Tumen River valley at Kaishantun, south of Tumen city, and at Shihhsien, just north of Tumen. A third major pulp and paper mill is in the city of Kirin.

Kirin's mineral resources include coal, consumed mainly within the province; iron ore, which is shipped to the Anshan steel plant; and copper and associated lead, zinc, and silver ores, which are sent to Mukden for refining. There are also gold deposits in the upper reaches of the Sungari River.

As in Liaoning, coal in Kirin is found in the zone separating the Liao-Sungari lowland from the eastern uplands. About half of Kirin's coal output stems from the Liaoyüan district, which yields mainly steam coals. Its mining capacity was substantially expanded in 1955 with completion of the so-called Sian shaft mine, which bears a former name of Liaoyüan. In the late 1950's, the Liaoyüan coal district contributed about 3 million tons of the province's total output of 6 million tons.

Kirin's second largest coal-producer, which may have approached Liaoyüan's output level in the 1960's, is the Hunkiang district, northeast of Tunghwa, near North Korea's Yalu River boundary. This area yields good bituminous coking coal, which is being shipped to the Anshan steel mill. The mines are situated at Hunkiang proper and along a rail spur running 50 miles northeast past Wankow and Sungshuchen (the so-called Sung-wan sector) to Sungkiangho. The Hunkiang area produced 1.2 million tons in 1957 but apparently expanded considerably in the late 1950's and early 1960's. This is suggested both by extension of the coal-carrying railroad and by the elevation of the old coal-mining town of Pataokiang to city status in 1959, when the name was changed to Hunkiang.

Other mines, yielding lower-grade subbituminous coal, are operated in the Changchun-Kirin urbanized area, where they supply both power station fuel and chemical raw material. The Kiaoho mine, east of Kirin, is the largest of this group, with a production of 1.1 million tons in 1957. It is consumed by power stations and industrial establishments along the Changchun-Tumen railroad. Between Kirin and Changchun is the Ying-cheng mine, with an annual output of 1 million tons, which is used both as a power station fuel in the Changchun heat and power plant and as a chemical raw material by Kirin industries. Coal is also mined in the newly developed Shulan basin, northeast of Kirin, where production activity is suggested by the construction of a railroad spur southwest from Shulan in the 1960's. There is also a small oil-shale mine in the Hwatien area.

The principal power plants burning coal are the old 50,000-kilowatt station at Changchun, dating from the Japanese period, and the new Kirin heat and power plant, with a designed capacity of 400,000 kilowatts. Construction of the Kirin facility began in 1955. Four 25,000-kilowatt units were installed in 1956–57, and two 50,000-kilowatt units were added in 1959, for a total capacity of 200,000 kilowatts. Other coal-burning power stations are at Liaoyüan, with about 30,000-kilowatt capacity, and at Erh-taokiang, eastern suburb of Tunghwa, with a capacity of 37,500 kilowatts.

However, Kirin's thermal-electric generating capacity is overshadowed by the presence of the Fengman hydroelectric station on the upper Sungari River, 15 miles southeast of Kirin. The station, built during World War II by the Japanese at the point where the Sungari leaves the East Manchurian uplands in a rapids-strewn section, has a dam 0.7 mile long and 300 feet high. Originally designed for a capacity of 560,000 kilowatts (eight units of 70,000 kilowatts each), the plant was partly dismantled by the Russians at the end of the war and had only two units in operation in the late 1940's. By the end of 1957, seven generators were installed, and the eighth was added in 1959. The Fengman station is linked by 220-kilovolt transmission lines with Kirin, Changchun, Harbin, Mukden, and Fushun. The plant is also known as Siaofengman (Little Fengman), for a settlement on the left bank of the Sungari River, and as Tafengman (Big Fengman), for one on the right bank linked by a rail spur with Kirin.

In an attempt to utilize other potential hydroelectric sites in the East Manchurian uplands, additional power projects were planned in the late 1950's on the upper Sungari River above the Fengman reservoir (in the Paishan-Lungwangmiao area) and on the Yalu River at Yungfeng near Tsian. Construction on the Yungfeng project, with a designed capacity of 400,000 kilowatts, was reported begun in 1959 in cooperation with North Korea. A concrete dam, half a mile long, was reported completed in 1962 at the station, known in Korean as Unbong, but there has been no reliable information on installed capacity.

Foremost among the province's metallic minerals is iron ore in the Tunghwa-Hunkiang district. The principal mines are at Talitze, on a rail spur running southeast from Hunkiang to the Yalu River, and at Tsitaokow, on the Tunghwa-Tsian railroad. These mines, particularly the Talitze operation, with significant reserves of 60 per cent iron ore, are major suppliers of the Anshan iron and steel plant.

Kirin has two old copper mines, which also yield lead, zinc, and silver as coproducts. One is Tienpaoshan, 25 miles west of Yenki and linked by a rail spur with Laotowkow station on the Changchun-Tumen line; the other is Shihtsuitze, north of Panshih. Both mines have been in operation since the late nineteenth century and are near depletion. Concentrates are shipped for refining at Mukden.

The principal gold mine in the upper reaches of the Sungari River is Kiapikow, southeast of Hungshih. The mine, which yields silver as a by-product, has been in operation since the early nineteenth century and is also approaching depletion.

Transportation in Kirin relies mainly on the Mukden-Changchun-Harbin railroad and its branches. Most important among these are the Mukden-Kirin line, running roughly parallel to the main railroad in the east, and the Szeping-Tsitsihar railroad, in the west. Two transverse lines supplement these north-south railroads. One runs from Changchun via Kirin city to the Yenpien Korean Autonomous Chou, where it crosses into North Korea in the Tumen area. The other crosses virtually all of Kirin Province, from the North Korean border at Tsian through Tunghwa, Meihokow (Hailung hsien), Szeping, and Shwangliao, and proceeding through Paicheng into the Great Khingan Mountains at Arshan. The Paicheng-Arshan railroad, built in 1936, taps a timber district in the southern Great Khingan. An-

TABLE 51
CITIES OF KIRIN

City	City Level	Function	Population (*in thousands*)		
			1953	1957	1970 est.
Changchun	subprovince	manuf.	855	975	
Kirin	subprovince	chemicals, ferroalloys	435	568	
Liaoyüan	hsien	coal	120	170	
Szeping	hsien	manuf., transportation	126	150	
Tunghwa	hsien	timber, power	129		
Hunkiang	hsien	coal			
Paicheng	hsien	farm trade		70	
Tungliao	hsien	farm trade	50		
Yenki	hsien	farm trade	73	83	
Tumen	hsien	paper, transport			
Former City	*Period*				
Kungchuling	1956–59			60	
Ulanhot	1947–64			51	

other branch line from Paicheng runs east to South Gorlos Mongol Hsien. Under the Japanese, it extended on to Changchun, but this section was dismantled in 1947–48 and has not been rebuilt. Finally, the western part of Kirin Province is also crossed by the special railroad built from Anta southward to Tungliao in the early 1960's to provide a direct outlet for the new Taching oil field of Heilungkiang. Waterways are of no significance in Kirin Province, except for the Fengman reservoir on the upper Sungari River, where small vessels ply local routes.

Kirin Province has ten industrial and regional centers of city status (Table 51), two being at the subprovince level (Changchun, the capital, and Kirin, the chemical center) and eight at hsien level. They are Liaoyüan, Szeping, Tunghwa, Hunkiang, Paicheng, Tungliao, and, in the Yenpien Korean Autonomous Chou, Yenki and Tumen.

Changchun ("long spring") occupies a central position in Manchuria, and, under the Manchukuo regime, it was selected as the country's capital under the name of Hsinking ("new capital"). The city's development was closely tied to the railroad construction program. As the junction (after 1905) of the then wide-gauge Chinese Eastern and standard-gauge South Manchuria railroads, Changchun became a major trans-shipment point between northern Manchuria and the southern port cities. The city's first industries were concerned with the processing of the agricultural products of central Manchuria. In 1912, the Changchun-Kirin railroad linked the city with the lumbering areas of the East Manchurian uplands, and Changchun acquired a sawmilling and match making industry. As the capital of Manchukuo from 1932 to 1945, Changchun was greatly enlarged and reconstructed, gaining broad avenues, parks, and modern public buildings. As the administrative and educational center of Manchuria, the city expanded from 133,000 persons in 1931 to 862,600 in 1945. The city suffered a sharp decline after World War II with the departure of the Japanese, who had made up about one-third of the population, and the effects of the civil war. But the city had again recovered by the time of the 1953 census, with a population of 855,000, and reached 975,000 by the end of 1957. During the 1950's, the city's industrial structure shifted from the previous emphasis on agricultural processing to metal fabricating and machinery manufacturing. The most prominent industrial project of that period was an automotive plant, which was inaugurated in July, 1956, and produces both trucks (about 30,000 a year) and some passenger cars. A railroad equipment plant, manufacturing passenger cars and locomotives, began operations in 1959. During this period, a diesel motor plant was also converted into a tractor factory. In addition to its predominant machinery industries, Changchun also produces pharmaceuticals, rubber footwear, and tobacco products.

Kirin, the province's second largest city, has had a much longer history than Changchun, which is basically the product of the railroad era. Kirin arose as a Chinese fortress in 1673 on the upper Sungari River and long performed political-administrative, commercial, and transport functions. It was therefore a natural provincial seat when Kirin Province was first established in 1907, but it lost its political pre-eminence to Changchun when that city became the capital of Manchukuo in 1931. After World War II, Kirin briefly regained its political position in an apparent reaction against the Japanese sponsorship of Changchun's rise, but Changchun's advantageous central location and facilities prevailed, and it became the provincial capital in 1954. Economically, Kirin developed in the early twentieth century as a lumber center, collecting and processing timber floated down the tributaries of the upper Sungari from the East Manchurian uplands. But, under Japanese rule, the construction of the nearby Fengman hydroelectric project resulted in a dramatic shift of the city's economic functions to chemicals, ferroalloys, and other power-oriented industries. The chemical industry, restored and expanded by 1957, consists of three basic complexes: calcium carbide, dyestuffs, and nitrogen chemicals. Calcium carbide, a big power-user, is derived by heating lime and coke in electric furnaces, and provides the basis for the generation of acetylene and its derivatives as well as calcium cyanamide, a fertilizer, weed-killer, and defoliant. Ammonia for the nitrogenous fertilizer complex was originally derived from calcium cyanamide, but this process was later replaced by ammonia synthesis, for which hydrogen could be obtained from coal by the water-gas reaction or from water by electrolysis (a power-consuming process made economical by the presence of the Fengman station). The dyestuff industry, in turn, was also related technologically to the nitrogen complex. The ferroalloys plant, operating with electric furnaces, was also located at Kirin because of the presence of cheap hydroelectricity. In addition to these basic-power oriented industries, Kirin is an important producer of paper (90,000 tons a year), sugar (with a capacity of 300,000 tons of beets a year), and cement. The city had a population of 435,000 in the 1953 census, rising to 568,000 by the end of 1957.

Szeping, formerly called Szepingkai, arose early in the twentieth century as a major railroad center of Manchuria and developed as an agricultural collecting and processing hub for the surrounding soybean and kaoliang region. Its farm orientation accounts for the presence of a large agricultural-equipment plant among machinery industries. Szeping had a population of 126,000 in the 1953 census, increasing to about 150,000 in 1957. To the northeast, halfway between Szeping and Changchun, is the subregional center of Hwaiteh, which under the name of Kungchuling briefly existed as a city from 1956 to 1959. However, with limited agricultural processing functions and a population estimated at only 60,000 in 1957, it reverted to hsien status.

Southeast of Szeping is the coal-mining center of Liaoyüan, in the upper reaches of the east branch of the Liao Ho. Before 1950, this city was known as Sian, and the name Liaoyüan was applied to a rail junction on the west branch of the Liao Ho, northwest of Szeping. (That rail hub, originally called Chengkiatun, has been known as Shwangliao since 1950.) Liaoyüan's steam coals are used in part in a local 30,000-kilowatt power plant, connected to the Manchurian electric grid. The city's basic fuel and energy functions are supplemented by some manufacturing (ore-concentrating equipment, mineral fertilizer, paper products). Liaoyüan had a population of 120,000 in 1953, increasing to an estimate of 170,000 in 1957.

Tunghwa is situated in the East Manchurian uplands on the upper reaches of the Hun Kiang (tributary of the Yalu). Because of its riverside location, Tunghwa developed relatively early (1870's) as a local timber and soybean trading center, but its modern growth dates from 1937, when it was reached by the railroad. The presence of coking-coal deposits at nearby Hunkiang (called Pataokiang until 1959) and of high-grade iron ore at Talitze and Tsitaokow make the Tunghwa area a potential iron and steel district. The Japanese made plans for the development of heavy industry in the district, which they called Tungpientao (eastern frontier area). During the Great Leap, the Chinese disclosed plans for the construction of an iron and steel plant with a capacity of 1 million tons of pig iron and 600,000 tons of crude steel, but these plans do not appear to have been realized. Both the coking coal and the iron ore continue to move to the iron and steel plant of Anshan. In the absence of this development, Tunghwa's functions continue to focus on the shipment of timber, coal, and iron ore from the surrounding area. It also has a 37,500-kilowatt coal-burning power station in the eastern suburb of Erhtaokiang, the proposed site for an iron and steel plant. Tunghwa's population was 129,000 in the 1953 census. The coal-mining center of Hunkiang, 25 miles northeast of

Tunghwa, was raised to the status of city in 1959, suggesting expansion of mining activities in the area.

Somewhat isolated from the economically developed central and eastern sections of Kirin Province are the western cities of Paicheng and Tungliao, subregional centers of Chinese settlement areas in Mongol grazing lands.

Paicheng, whose Chinese name means "white city," became a colonization center in the Mongol steppe around the turn of the twentieth century. Development intensified after it was reached by the railroad in 1926, and the acreage in corn, sorghum, kaoliang, and sugar beets expanded. The railroad was extended in 1931 to the Mongol lamasery town of Wangyehmiao (now Ulanhot) and in 1936 on to the Arshan mineral springs, where it opened up a lumbering district in the Great Khingan Mountains. Another railroad was completed in 1935 from Paicheng southeastward to the South Gorlos Mongol Hsien, an area of rice cultivation and fisheries in the floodplain of the Nun Kiang and Sungari river confluence. (This railroad initially extended to Changchun, but that segment was dismantled in 1947–48 and has not been restored.) Paicheng's growing population (70,000 in 1957) and its regional dominance were reflected in its elevation to city status in November, 1958. In the 1930's and 1940's, the town was known as Taoan, meaning "peace of the Tao," in reference to the Tao River valley, in which Chinese colonization was centered. Since late 1958, the name Taoan applies to the hsien town formerly known as Taonan ("south of the Tao"), on the south side of the valley.

Tungliao, the administrative center of the Jerim League, annexed from Inner Mongolia in 1969, is also situated in a Chinese colonization district dating from the early twentieth century. The original settlement was known as Bayan Tala, a Mongol name meaning "rich plain," in allusion to the fertile land of the west branch of the Liao Ho. The name Tungliao ("penetration of the Liao"), which was adopted in 1918, refers to Chinese colonization of the area. Development of the western Liao valley was promoted when the first railroad arrived in 1921 (from Shwangliao, the former Chengkiatun), followed in 1927 by a line from Tahushan (on the Peking-Mukden main railroad). The city's transport function was further enhanced in the early 1960's with construction of a special rail outlet for the Taching oil field in the Anta area. The oil railroad runs southward through Tungliao to the main southern Manchurian rail system at Tahushan. Tungliao, with agricultural-processing industries (hides, wool), has been a municipality since the early 1950's, when it had a population of about 50,000.

The transferred portion of Inner Mongolia contains still another urban center, Ulanhot, which had city status from 1947 to 1964, and regained it in 1970. Formerly known as Wangyehmiao, (miao means "temple" in Chinese), it became the first capital of Inner Mongolia when the autonomous region was first established in 1947. Served by a railroad running from Paicheng to the hot-springs resort of Arshan, Ulanhot (meaning "red town") developed rapidly while it was the administrative seat of Inner Mongolia and reached a population of 51,400 in 1953. By that time, the capital had been moved to Kalgan (in 1950), but Ulanhot remained the center of Khingan League until 1954, when this league was incorporated into Hulunbuir League, and the administrative functions passed to Hailar. Despite its loss of regional government functions, Ulanhot retained city status until 1964 and regained it about 1970 because of industrial development in the city. It remained the headquarters of one of the banners of the Khorchin Mongols, the Khorchin West Wing's South Banner, known historically as Jasakto Khan Banner. In late 1969, when Hulunbuir League was detached from Inner Mongolia and annexed to Heilungkiang Province, this Khorchin banner was given to Kirin Province, with which it has economic and transport links via the Arshan-Paicheng railroad. It is assumed that the banner was incorporated into the Jerim League, which already contained other banners of the Khorchin Mongols.

Before Kirin's annexation of the Jerim League, the Paicheng district contained virtually all of the province's Mongol population of 47,000, concentrated in the South Gorlos Banner, which became an autonomous hsien in 1955. Also within this Mongol hsien, and across the Sungari River at Fuyü, are a few hundred members of the Sibo ethnic group, descendants of a Mongol tribe used by the Manchu rulers as military guardsmen, as well as Daghor Mongols.

The acquisition of Jerim League is believed to have added more than 200,000 Mongols to Kirin, mainly members of the Khorchin tribe tending their herds in the steppes north and south of the Chinese-colonized valley of the Liao Ho's west branch.

Like the rest of Manchuria, Kirin Province also has substantial minorities of Manchus and Hui (Chinese Moslems). The Manchus, who numbered 333,000 in the 1953 census, are settled in the central part of the province, between Kirin city and Liaoyüan. The 56,000 Hui live primarily in cities, half of them in Kirin and Changchun.

But the most distinctive ethnic minority is the Koreans, who migrated across the Tumen River into Kirin Province in the second half of the nineteenth century. They are constituted mainly into the Yenpien Korean Autonomous Chou in the easternmost section of the province, with 17,000 square miles and a population of 1.2 million, including 600,000 Koreans (out of Kirin's total Korean population of 765,000). The chou, which borders on North Korea and the Soviet Union, was established in 1952 and expanded westward in 1958 to include the Tunhwa area. A wooded, heavily dissected upland, the Yenpien chou is significant mainly as a supplier of timber, both in the form of roundwood and sawnwood and of processed products (wood pulp, paper). Timber and wood products are shipped over the railroads running from Tumen westward to Changchun and northwest to Mutankiang in Heilungkiang Province. Two large pulp-and-paper mills are at Kaishantun, south of Tumen, and at Shihhsien, just northwest of Tumen. The Korean chou contains the Tienpaoshan copper mine, which also yields lead, zinc and silver. The mine is linked by a rail spur with Laotowkow station (coal mine), on the Tumen-Changchun main line.

Yenki, the capital of the Yenpien chou, had a population of 72,800 in 1953, rising to 83,100 in 1957. (The name Yenpien consists of the characters for "yen," meaning "extended, prolonged," as in Yenki, and "pien," meaning "frontier.") The city is the center of an agricultural district producing soybeans, tobacco, and flax. Southwest of the city is the hsien town of Yenki (the former Lungtsing), with a 20,000-kilowatt thermal-power station burning coal from the nearby Holung mine.

The Yenpien chou's second city, Tumen, was raised to that status only in 1965, when the rail town of Tumen was combined with the paper-milling town of Shihhsien to form the city. Tumen is a transportation hub on the Tumen River border, where a major railroad crosses over to the North Korean frontier town of Onsong.

In addition to the autonomous chou, Kirin's Korean minority also has a second autonomous unit, the Changpai Korean Autonomous Hsien, established in 1958. Changpai is a lumbering town on the upper Yalu River, opposite the industrial city of Hyesan in North Korea.

HEILUNGKIANG PROVINCE
Capital: Harbin; area: 280,000 sq. mi.; population: 25 million

Manchuria's northernmost province bears the Chinese name—Heilung Kiang (Black Dragon River)—of the Amur River, which forms its northern border with the Soviet Union. The earliest administrative headquarters of the region, the present Old Aigun on the Amur River at Lat. 50 degrees N, was originally known as Heilungkiang Cheng (Heilungkiang Town) and gave its name to the entire province. The name was retained even after the provincial capital moved to Tsitsihar in the second half of the nineteenth century and to Harbin in 1954.

The boundaries of the province have also changed from time to time through the twentieth century. Under Nationalist rule, before the Japanese occupation of Manchuria in the early 1930's, Heilungkiang lay astride the Great Khingan Mountains, extending from the border of Outer Mongolia in the west to the Sungari River in the east. Under the state of Manchukuo, the western Mongol areas were detached from Heilungkiang and set aside as an autonomous Mongol province known as Hsingan (another form of Khingan). After World War II, this Mongol section became the core of the Inner Mongolian Autonomous Region established by the Chinese Communists in 1947. The truncated Heilungkiang Province had an area of about 70,000 square miles and a population of 6 million in the early 1950's. It expanded eastward across the Sungari River to the Ussuri frontier of the Soviet Union in 1954, with the incorporation of the short-lived Sungkiang Province, reaching an area of 180,000 square miles and a population of 11.9 million in the 1953 census. As a result of a high rate of natural increase and migration from other parts of China, the population of Heilungkiang rose to 14.9 million in 1957, 21 million in 1964, and 23 million in 1969.

In late 1969, when the former Manchurian portions of Inner Mongolia were returned to provinces with which they had close economic and transport links, Heilungkiang absorbed most of the Hulunbuir League. (The League had been formed in 1954 and named for two lakes of the Barga region—Hulun Nor and Buir Nor.) However, the southernmost banner of the League, the Khorchin West Wing's South Banner with headquarters at Ulanhot, was detached and annexed to Kirin Province with which the banner has a direct rail link. The annexation of Hulunbuir League expanded the area of Heilungkiang Province to about 280,000 square miles and added around 2 million people, for an estimated total population of 25 million in 1970.

Within these expanded boundaries, Heilungkiang Province includes the sparsely populated Barga section of the Mongolian plateau in the extreme west, the forested Great Khingan Mountains, the lowlands of the Sungari River and its tributary, the Nun Kiang, where most of the population and economic activities are concentrated, the forested Little Khingan Mountains in the northeast, the East Manchurian uplands, and the swampy, virtually unpopulated lower Sungari-Ussuri interfluve in the east.

The cultivation of spring wheat plays a far more important role in Heilungkiang than in southern Manchuria. Both soils (largely chernozem and dark chestnut) and climate (relatively cool summers) favor wheat growth. The leading areas are the lowlands of the Sungari and its tributaries, the Lalin and Hulan Rivers, south and north of Harbin, and the Nun Kiang. Harbin itself is the center of the flour-milling industry. Oats and barley have been traditionally concentrated in the northwestern part of the province, along the old cattle trail from Tsitsihar to Old Aigun on the Amur River. The total food crop is about 6 to 7 million tons, with significant fluctuations from year to year, but a generally large marketable surplus.

Soybeans are a major crop along the Sungari River and its left tributary, the Hulan, where they take up 20 to 40 per cent of the sown area. One of China's principal soybean-producers, Heilungkiang supplies roughly one-sixth of the national crop.

Significant industrial crops are sugar beets, flax, and sunflowers. Heilungkiang accounts for roughly 70 per cent of the Chinese area in sugar beets, which are grown mainly near sugar refineries in the area of Harbin and Kiamusze. Flax was introduced into the province by Russian settlers after the construction of the Chinese Eastern railroad. The crop is grown mainly around Harbin, supplying a linen mill in that city. Heilungkiang accounts also for about 30 per cent of China's acreage in sunflowers, which are grown widely as an oilseed.

Heilungkiang's virgin lands have been viewed as a major potential for agricultural expansion. In the early 1950's, the province's cropped area was about 6 million hectares, and about 3.5 million hectares more were considered suitable for cultivation. During the first five-year plan (1953–57), 1.1 million hectares were added to the cropped area in Heilungkiang, raising the total to 7.1 million hectares. The additional land put under cultivation in the five-year period represented about 20 per cent of all the land added to the cultivated area in China. The new land, which has been organized as state farms (Heilungkiang had thirty-six in 1957), is situated mainly in the swampy interfluve between the Sungari and Ussuri rivers. One of the largest state-farm reclamation projects, at Santaokang, 70 miles east of Kiamusze, was raised in 1959 to the status of a hsien named Yuyi, meaning "friendship," in allusion to the Soviet-Chinese amity of that period. The Heilungkiang state farms are among the more highly mechanized agricultural establishments of China, and many of them are operated by military units.

Lumbering plays a major role in the Heilungkiang, which accounted for nearly one-fourth of China's timber reserves even before the annexation in 1969 of the Great Khingan lumbering region. If the western timber region is included, Heilungkiang produces about one-half of China's roundwood. In the Great Khingan, the most significant tree species is the Dahurian larch, which covers about 70 per cent of the forest area, with particularly dense stands in the northern section of the mountain range. This timber region was opened up in the 1950's with the construction of a lumber railroad north from the mill town of Yakoshih on the Hailar-Harbin main line. By 1957, the spur line had advanced 160 miles north along the west slope of the Great Khingan to the area of Ituliho, on the Ituli River. Construction proceeded eastward, across the divide, and in 1962 reached Aliho, administrative seat of the Orochon Autonomous Hsien, situated where the Ali River joins the Kan Ho. A rail circuit through the Great Khingan was completed in the middle 1960's, when the timber railroad was extended from Aliho southeastward along the Kan Ho to Nunkiang. A shorter timber-carrying spur was built in the 1950's into the Great Khingan south of the Hailar-Harbin main railroad. This spur taps forest stands in the upper reaches of the Chol (Ch'o-erh) River, a right tributary of the Nun Kiang. This southern timber railroad runs 77 miles from the mainline junction of Kowkow, just southeast of Pokotu, to Langfeng (Kilometer 125) at Lat. 48 degrees N. Finally, the southernmost section of the Great Khingan, tapped by the Paicheng-Arshan railroad, has been under the jurisdiction of Kirin Province since late 1969. In the drier south, the northern larch is replaced by Japanese white birch as the principal commercial species.

In addition to the Great Khingan, Heilungkiang Province has extensive lumbering operations in the Little Khingan Mountains and in the Wanta Shan and Laoyeh Ling, northern outliers of the East Manchurian uplands. In contrast to the predominance of larch in the Great Khingan, the Korean pine is the principal commercial species in the Little Khingan, followed by Okhotsk fir and Japanese birch. The Little Khingan lumbering district has been exploited since the early 1950's by constructing a timber railroad up the valley of the Tangwang River, a left tributary of the Sungari. The first section of the forest spur extended from Nancha, on the Kiamusze-Harbin railroad, to the new lumber center of Ichun, which was raised to the status of city in 1957. From Ichun, the timber railroad was extended in a short spur westward up the Ichun River to Tsuiluan, meaning appropriately "green summits," and in a longer extension northward along the Tangwang valley past Wuying and Sintsing to Tungtang, only 30 miles across a narrow divide from the Amur River. Kiamusze is the principal processing center for the timber resources of the Little Khingan. Mutankiang performs the same functions in the East Manchurian uplands.

Until the development of the Taching oil field in the 1960's, Heilungkiang's mineral resources were limited largely to good bituminous coal as well as gold. The principal coal centers are Kisi, northeast of Mutankiang, and Hokang and Shwangyashan, in the Kiamusze area, all producing coal of coking quality. Hokang, the most important coal field, has 5 billion tons of Jurassic coal, part of which is accessible to strip-mining operations. Development of the Hokang basin began in 1936 with construction of a rail spur southward to the riverside coal terminal of Lienkiangkow on the Sungari River, opposite Kiamusze. Production was further expanded in subsequent years as Kiamusze was linked by rail with the rest of Manchuria, and reached 2.5 million tons in 1943. Output was still increased under Communist rule, to 4.9 million tons in 1957. It may now be near 10 million tons.

The Shwangyashan coal-mining district, on a rail branch going 50 miles east from Kiamusze, was developed later than Hokang, dating from the end of World War II and the postwar period. It yielded 2.3 million tons in 1957 and probably exceeded 5 million tons in the late 1960's.

The third major coal basin around Kisi, with reserves of 1.4 billion tons, also dates from the middle 1930's, when the deposit was first reached by a rail spur running north from Siachengtze junction on the Harbin-Vladivostok railroad. The coal mines are situated at Lifuchen, the oldest mining town, southwest of Kisi; Titao, west; Pingyang, east; and Hengshan, southeast. The Kisi district yielded 5.8 million tons in 1957 and had probably passed the 10-million-ton level by the late 1960's.

A coal-producing center now largely of historical importance is the low-grade brown-coal deposit of Chalainor, just southeast of the border city of Manchouli in what was northern Inner Mongolia. The Chalainor deposit was discovered in 1901 during construction of the Chinese Eastern railroad and has been used mainly for coal-burning locomotives on the railroad.

Gold is mined predominantly in placer deposits along left-bank tributaries of the Amur River on the northern slopes of the Great Khingan and the Little Khingan. Gold-mining began in the 1880's in the Moho district, which flourished in the early years of the twentieth century. Other placers are still being mined in the areas of Huma, Aihui (particularly Handatsi, 60 miles to the west), and Kiayin (where Ulaga, 35 miles to the southwest, is the province's principal producer).

Heilungkiang's traditional resource orientation was dramatically modified by the development of large petroleum reserves in the 1960's in the so-called Taching district. The discovery well was completed in September, 1959, at about 4,000 feet in Lower Cretaceous sandstones in the Tatung area, 30 miles southwest of Anta. Because of the secrecy on economic developments that was then imposed, Peking has never officially disclosed the precise location of the oil field, referring to it publicly only by the code name Taching, meaning "great celebration." However, the elevation of the hsien town of Anta to the status of city in early 1960 indirectly pinpointed the center of production. Regular commercial output began in 1962, and, by 1965, the Taching field was producing 3.5 million tons, or nearly one-half of China's total crude-oil output. Part of the oil is refined at a local diesel-oil plant opened in 1963, with a throughput capacity of about 600,000 tons. The rest is shipped both by pipeline and by rail to refineries at Dairen and Chinchow and, by coastal tanker, to Shanghai. To move the crude oil southward by rail without adding to the load of the Harbin-Mukden main line, a new railroad was completed in the middle 1960's from the Tsitsihar-Harbin line just west of Anta 250 miles south to Tungliao, where it joins the existing network.

The power supply for Heilungkiang's industries stems mainly from coal-burning steam-electric stations. The largest generating capacity is at Harbin, the main manufacturing city, where about 40,000 kilowatts dating from the Japanese period were supplemented in 1959 with a new heat and power plant with a designed capacity of 200,000 kilowatts. The first two 25,000-kilowatt units inaugurated in 1959 were followed by two more in 1963, for a total installed capacity of 100,000 kilowatts, or half of the ultimate design. Other significant power plants are at Fularki (50,000 kilowatts in 1957) for the Tsitsihar industrial district, Kiamusze (12,000 kilowatts in 1957), Mutankiang, and Kisi. Harbin is linked by a 220-kilovolt line with the main Manchurian power grid based on the Fengman hydroelectric station. Heilungkiang has a small water-power producer of its own, at Lake Chingpo, south of Mutankiang. The station, with a capacity of 36,000 kilowatts, was built by the Japanese, destroyed in the war, and reopened in 1947.

For transportation, Heilungkiang relies primarily on the old Chinese Eastern and its branch lines. It traverses the southern part of the province from northwest to southeast, entering from the Soviet Union at the border city of Manchouli, crossing the Nun Kiang in the Tsitsihar area and the Sungari River at Harbin, and passing through the Mutankiang lumbering district to the Soviet border at Suifenho. From Harbin, the main Manchurian north-south railroad runs through Changchun and Mukden to Dairen. Among the more significant branch lines is the Harbin-Kiamusze railroad (completed in 1939), which handles much of the timber traffic out of the Little Khingan Mountains, and the Tsitsihar-Szeping railroad (opened

TABLE 52

CITIES OF HEILUNGKIANG

City	City Level	Function	Population (*in thousands*) 1953	1957	1970 est.
Harbin	subprovincial	manuf.	1,163	1,552	2,000
Tsitsihar	subprovincial	manuf.	345	668	
Mutankiang	subprovincial	manuf.	151	252	
Kisi	subprovincial	coal		262	
Kiamusze	subprovincial	manuf.	146	250	
Hokang	subprovincial	coal	90	210	
Shwangyashan	subprovincial	coal		100	
Ichun	subprovincial	timber		278	
Anta	hsien	petroleum			100+
Hailar	hsien	trade	43		
Manchouli	hsien	trade		50	
Former Cities	*Period*				
Peian	1960–63				

in 1920), which serves as a direct outlet from the Tsitsihar industrial district to southern Manchuria, bypassing Harbin.

During the ice-free navigation season, the Sungari River has an active traffic between Harbin and Kiamusze for river vessels of up to 500 tons. This section of the Sungari handles more than 80 per cent of the goods transported by waterways within the province. Small vessels may ascend the Sungari above Harbin and the Nun Kiang as far as Tsitsihar, but water traffic along this stretch is negligible, as is the movement of goods along the boundary rivers with the Soviet Union, the Amur and the Ussuri. The navigation season is about six months, from April to October.

Eight industrial cities are under the direct control of the provincial government (Table 52). They are Harbin, the capital; Tsitsihar, manufacturing city; the regional center of Mutankiang with the nearby coal city of Kisi; the regional center of Kiamusze, with the coal cities of Hokang and Shwangyashan; and the timber center of Ichun. A ninth city, Anta, the center of the Taching oil field, is at hsien level. Two additional places in the Hulunbuir League of Inner Mongolia have city status at hsien level—Manchouli and Hailar.

Harbin, a city of nearly 2 million, is the product of the railroads, as are most of the urban centers of Manchuria. Prior to the start of construction of the Chinese Eastern by the Russians, it was a fishing village on the Sungari River. It became the transportation hub of northern Manchuria and rose to second position among Manchuria's cities, after Mukden. Traditionally, Harbin has been Manchuria's leading food-processing center, with a complex of flour mills, tobacco and soybean-processing plants, meat-dairy and sugar-refining industries. Expanding on an industrial base started under Japanese rule, Harbin has become one of China's principal producers of power-generating equipment (steam turbines, boilers), electric motors, bearings, and machine tools. The city has a measuring and cutting instruments plant, opened in 1956, and a cement plant that produced 300,000 tons in 1957. Of marked Russian appearance, Harbin has long had a substantial Russian minority population. The city consists of several functional sections. Along the Sungari bank and opposite the left-bank winter harbor are the commercial Taoli district, the industrial and port district at the foot of the Sungari bridge, and the old Chinese residential Fukia section with consumer industries. Farther inland and adjoining these riverside districts is the new city of Harbin, which developed largely after World War I. The population of the city increased eightfold from 40,500 in 1911 to 332,000 in 1931, then doubled to 661,000 by 1940. Under Chinese Communist rule, the population was reported as 1.16 million in the 1953 census and 1.55 million in late 1957. The city was officially called Pinkiang under Manchukuo rule. Its present official Chinese name is Harbin, which is rendered phonetically by the characters Ha-erh-pin.

Tsitsihar, the province's second largest city, is the metropolis of the Nun Kiang valley at the foot of the Great Khingan Mountains. It is one of the earliest Chinese settlements in Manchuria, having been founded in 1691 as a strongpoint in Daghor Mongol country in the Chinese northward drive to the Amur River. The name Tsitsihar means "natural pasture" in Daghor. The city became the capital of Heilungkiang Province as it grew in a loosely spread-out Mongol settlement pattern around the central walled Chinese city. Tsitsihar underwent an industrial rebirth after the construction of the Chinese Eastern railroad, which passed through the southern suburb of Angangki in 1903. The completion of the Tsitsihar-Szeping railroad in 1926 provided a direct outlet to southern Manchuria, and the construction of the Tsitsihar-Peian railroad (by 1932) opened up an agricultural hinterland to the northeast. Traditional agricultural processing industries (soybeans, grain, sugar, paper) have been supplemented by modern machinery manufacturing, mainly at the rail junction of Angangki and at the southwestern industrial suburb of Fularki, where the Chinese Eastern crosses the Nun Kiang. The Tsitsihar industrial district produces locomotives and rolling stock (freight cars), heavy machine tools, and mining and metallurgical equipment. Part of the crude-steel needs are being met by a small special steel plant at Fularki. The city of Tsitsihar had a 1953 census population of 345,000. After incorporation of the industrial suburbs of Angangki and Fularki, a population of 668,000 was reported in late 1957.

The town of Peian, an agricultural center 135 miles northeast of Tsitsihar, functioned temporarily as a city from 1960 to 1963. Under the Japanese, a railroad led northward from Peian to the Amur River at Heiho or the New Aigun (known as Aihui since 1956), opposite Blagoveshchensk, but this line was destroyed and has not been rebuilt.

Mutankiang is the regional center of the East Manchurian uplands. It developed in the early twentieth century on the newly built Chinese Eastern, supplanting the older regional center of Ningan (Ninguta) in a small agricultural basin to the south. The position of Mutankiang at the junction of railroads and the Mutan River has made it a center of the lumbering industry of the surrounding forested uplands and of the farming of inter-montane basins. Modern industries include tire-manufacturing for the automotive industry of Changchun. A small iron and steel plant project, with a capacity of 300,000 tons, was completed in 1969–70 after having been abandoned after the Great Leap. Mutankiang had a population of 151,000 in the 1953 census, rising to 252,000 in late 1957.

Nearby is the coal-mining center of Kisi, which was raised to city status in late 1956. The municipal district of 850 square miles includes suburban mining settlements and had a population of 262,000 in late 1957.

Kiamusze is the regional center of the lower Sungari valley and developed originally on the basis of river trade. By 1933, it had a population of 22,500. The completion of railroads from Mutankiang in 1937 and from Harbin in 1939 stimulated further development, including the opening up of the nearby coal mines of Hokang and Shwangyashan. By 1940, the city had a population of 128,000. Under Chinese Communist rule, Kiamusze reported a population of 146,000 in the 1953 census, rising to 250,000 in 1957. The city has a diversified industrial structure, including food-processing (soy-beans, grains, sugar) based on the surrounding farm area, a large paper mill (using pulpwood from the nearby Ichun lumbering district of the Little Khingan), and agricultural equipment manufacturing. The city also handles coal movements from Hokang and Shwangyashan and timber shipments from Ichun.

The coal-mining center of Hokang, formerly called Hingshan, has had municipal status since the early 1950's. It had a population of 90,000 in the 1953 census, and 210,000 (presumably after some areal expansion) in late 1957.

Shwangyashan, whose development began after that of Hokang, was given city status in 1956, and reported a population of 100,000 the following year.

The lumbering center of Ichun, which achieved municipal status in 1957, probably has the largest area of any of the north Manchurian cities, including virtually the entire valley of the Tangwang River in the Little Khingan. A population of 278,000 was reported within this municipal district in 1957.

The petroleum center of Anta, in the Taching oil field, was a small agricultural town on the Chinese Eastern, 80 miles northwest of Harbin, before the oil strike in 1959, and was raised to city status the following year. Through the 1960's, it developed as the management and supply center of the oil field. It acquired a small oil refinery in 1963, specializing in the production of diesel fuel. The population is believed to exceed 100,000.

Hailar, capital of the Hulunbuir League of Inner Mongolia, was formerly also known by the Chinese name of Hulun. It consists of an old Chinese city, founded in the early eighteenth century, and a new city of rectilinear street pattern that developed after construction of the Chinese Eastern railroad. As the center of a Mongol herding region, Hailar is engaged primarily in the processing of hides and dairy and meat products. Its population was reported as 43,200 in the 1953 census, with subsequent expansion to 129,000 by 1961.

Manchouli, the other Inner Mongolian city affected by the 1969 incorporation, is a transport center on the Soviet border. Formerly also known as Lupin, it flourished in the late 1940's and early 1950's as the principal railroad border-station handling heavy overland trade between China and the Soviet Union. Its importance declined after the opening of the Trans-Mongolian railroad through Ulan-Bator in 1955 and particularly with the virtual cessation of Soviet-Chinese trade in the 1960's. Manchouli had a population of about 50,000 in 1956. The name Manchouli is a phonetic Chinese rendering of the original Russian name Manchuria.

Heilungkiang's ethnic composition was altered significantly by the 1969 changes. The largest minority, the Manchus, numbered 630,000 in the 1950's in the old Heilungkiang area, with perhaps 20,000 added by the Inner Mongolian shift. Largely assimilated with the Chinese, the Manchus are settled in the early agricultural colonization districts of Ningan, around Harbin, and near Peian.

The Korean minority, of 240,000 in the 1950's, is settled in southeastern Heilungkiang, adjoining the Yenpien Korean Chou of Kirin Province. Koreans, who are largely rice-growers, are particularly numerous in the belt extending from the old Ningan farming district northeast through Mutankiang and Kisi to Mishan. Perhaps an additional 10,000 were living in the former Inner Mongolian territory.

Before the 1969 territorial annexation, there were 38,000 Mongols in Heilungkiang, of whom about a third lived in a Durbet Mongol autonomous hsien, with headquarters at Taikang, on the Chinese Eastern between Tsitsihar and Anta. A second autonomous unit, the North Gorlos hsien, with headquarters at Chaoyüan, on the Sungari River, 80 miles west-southwest of Harbin, was abolished in 1956, presumably because of increasingly heavy Chinese settlement.

The 1969 incorporation added more than 100,000 Mongols of the Hulunbuir League to Heilungkiang, making a total of perhaps 150,000 Mongols. They were the Barga Mongols around Hailar, and the Jalait Mongols southwest of Tsitsihar.

The Barga Mongols are constituted in three banners: the Old Barga banner, with headquarters at Bayan Khüree, the old Chipchin Sume (lamasery), just northwest of Hailar; the New Barga West banner, with headquarters at Altan Emeel, near the southwest end of Hulun Lake; and the New Barga East banner, with headquarters at Amgalan, 60 miles southwest of Hailar. To the north of Hailar is the fertile agricultural Three Rivers district, formed by the Gan River (in Chinese, Ken Ho) and the lesser Derbul and Khaul rivers, tributaries of the Argun. Russian settlers had farmed the dark chestnut soils of this area since the early twentieth century, but they appear to have been largely replaced by Chinese farmers since the late 1940's, with Mongols grazing their stock in the untilled pasture lands. Administratively, the Three Rivers district (Trekhrech'ye in Russian) was then constituted as the Argun banner, with its seat in the old Russian village of Dragotsenka, which the Chinese renamed Sanho (Three Rivers). After the wooded upper reaches of the Gan River (Ken Ho) were reached by the timber railroad from Yakoshih about 1960, the seat of Argun banner was moved upstream to the new lumber town of Kenho. In 1966, the Argun banner was split, with the Argun West banner centered at Sanho and the Argun East banner at Kenho.

Outside of the dominant Barga Mongol component, the Hulunbuir League of Heilungkiang Province contains the Jalait Mongols. This group is settled in the valley of the lower Chol River, a right tributary of the Nun Kiang, and has its seat at Under Ail, 60 miles southwest of Tsitsihar.

The 1969 administrative shift would appear to have merged most of China's Daghor minority within Heilungkiang. This group, related to the Mongols, is settled primarily in the valley of the Nun Kiang. Of the 40,000 Daghors, half were settled in the Heilungkiang portion of the valley around Tsitsihar and half on the western slopes in Inner Mongolia. The Daghors of Inner Mongolia were constituted as the Morindava (Mo-li-ta-wa) Daghor Autonomous Banner, with headquarters at Pusi (Busi), 18 miles west of Noho. The autonomous hsien had a population of 64,000, including 16,000 Daghors, when it was founded in 1958.

Heilungkiang also includes three small Tungusic minorities—the Evenki (also known in Chinese as Solun) and the Orochon (or Oronchon) in the Great Khingan Mountains, and the Gold people, or Fishskin Tatars, in the lower Sungari marshes.

The Evenki include a small, purely Tungusic component of forest hunters in the northwest section of the Great Khingan, near the Argun-Shilka confluence, and a larger Mongolized component of herders in the Barga steppe south of Hailar. The steppe group was organized in Inner Mongolia as the Solun banner, renamed in 1958 the Evenki Autonomous Banner, with its headquarters at Nantun, about 5 miles south of Hailar. Its population of 10,000 included 3,400 Evenki (out of a total of 5,000 in the region), as well as Mongols and Daghors.

The Orochon (Oronchon) people number about 2,300, about evenly divided between Heilungkiang and the Inner Mongolian section before the 1969 merger. They are engaged in hunting and herding on the eastern slopes of the Great Khingan, where they are also known as the Manegir, and in smaller numbers in the Little Khingan, where they are also called the Birar. The Great Khingan component was set up as the Orochon Autonomous Banner in the early 1950's, with its first headquarters at Siaoerhkow on the Nomin River, a headstream of the Nun Kiang, 150 miles north of Tsitsihar. After the Great Khingan timber railroad crossed the divide in 1962, the Orochon headquarters was moved 75 miles farther north to Aliho, a new lumber railroad town, on the Kan Ho, another headstream of the Nun Kiang.

The Gold people of the lower Sungari, with 500 members, is one of the smallest distinctive minorities of China. Called traditionally the Fishskin Tatars in English, they are known as the Nanay in the Soviet Union and as the Hoche in China. They derive their livelihood from fishing in the marshy lowland between the lower Sungari and the lower Ussuri.

Before the 1969 administrative enlargement, Heilungkiang also had 42,000 Hui (Chinese Moslems), who lived mainly in the province's bigger cities. Perhaps 5,000 of Inner Mongolia's 52,000 Hui may have been added to Heilungkiang with the transfer of the Hulunbuir League.

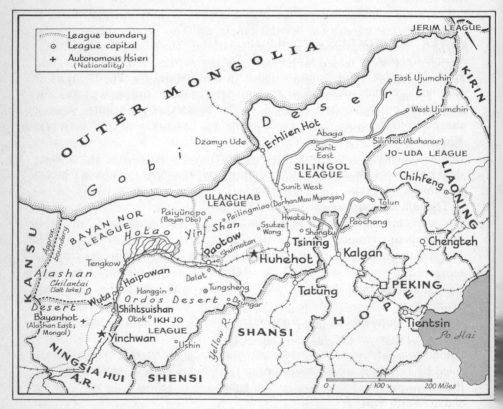

14.   Inner Mongolia

INNER MONGOLIAN AUTONOMOUS REGION

Capital: Huhehot; area: 225,000 sq. mi.; population: 9 million

Inner Mongolia is not being treated here as a natural region with more or less homogeneous physical characteristics. In fact, the region was distinguished by great physical diversity during part of its history, when it ranged from the Gobi desert lands to the coniferous forests of the Greater Khingan Range. The region's political boundaries have also undergone frequent alteration, and it is therefore discussed here as a major political division, one of the important autonomous regions of the Chinese People's Republic.

The autonomous region of Inner Mongolia had its immediate origins in the autonomous Mongol province of Hsingan, established in 1932 within the Japanese-sponsored state of Manchukuo. Hsingan was broken up into four provinces—North, East, South, and West Hsingan—in a provincial reorganization of 1934, but the principle of Mongol autonomy was essentially preserved until the abolition of the state of Manchukuo at the end of World War II. Inner Mongolia also had its antecedents in a Japanese-sponsored autonomous government established in Chahar and Suiyüan after the Japanese war against China began in 1937. The Inner Mongolian autonomous government, known as Mengkiang (Mongol Territory), was ruled by Te Wang, a Mongol prince of the Silingol League, from 1939 until it was overrun by Soviet–Outer Mongolian forces in August, 1945, at the end of World War II.

The Chinese Communists, who promptly gained control of the region, established the Inner Mongolian Autonomous Region in May, 1947, more than two years before they set up their national government in Peking in October, 1949. Inner Mongolia consisted at first of the Hulunbuir League, the western Mongol portion of traditional Heilungkiang that formed North and East Hsingan provinces in Manchukuo, and of the Silingol and Chahar leagues, the northern Mongol portions of Chahar, which had been part of

279

Mengkiang during World War II. The original capital of the autonomous region was Wangyehmiao ("prince's temple"), which was renamed more appropriately Ulanhot ("red town") by the Communists.

In 1949, this original area of Inner Mongolia was expanded through the incorporation of the Jerim League from Manchuria's former Liaopei Province (corresponding to Manchukuo's South Hsingan) and the Jo-uda League from northern Jehol (corresponding to Manchukuo's West Hsingan). In 1952, the region was further enlarged through the addition of the three hsien of Hwateh, Paochang, and Tolun from partitioned Chahar. In the meantime, as Inner Mongolian territory expanded westward, the capital was moved in 1950 to Kalgan (Chahar Province) and in 1952 to Kweisui (Suiyüan Province). At this stage, Inner Mongolia had an area of 250,000 square miles and a population of 2.5 million, of whom 800,000 were Mongols.

In March, 1954, Inner Mongolia absorbed Suiyüan Province. The merger expanded the autonomous region's area to 370,000 square miles and its population to 6.1 million in the 1953 census, including about a million Mongols. The regional capital, now again situated within Inner Mongolian territory, was renamed from Kweisui to Huhehot ("blue town"). The annexation of Suiyüan added two traditional Inner Mongolian leagues to the autonomous region: the Ulanchab League, north of the Yellow River bend, and the Ikh Jo League of the Ordos Mongols, south of the bend.

In a further annexation, in late 1955, Inner Mongolia absorbed another portion of partitioned Jehol Province, with the city of Chihfeng, which was incorporated into the Jo-uda League. This section, with an area of about 15,000 square miles and a population of 1.2 million in the 1953 census, brought the total population of Inner Mongolia to 7.3 million. Finally, in 1956, the autonomous region absorbed its westernmost territory from Kansu Province. This territory, consisting of the Alashan and Edsin banners in the Alashan desert, became the new Bayan Nor League.

Inner Mongolia retained this maximum extent of 460,000 square miles from 1956 until late 1969. During this period, natural increase and a high rate of Chinese in-migration brought the population to 13 million. At that point the former Manchurian wing was returned to the Manchurian provinces and the Alashan desert region in the west was annexed by Kansu Province and Ningsia Hui Autonomous Region. Although the dismemberment, reportedly related to an alignment of military district boundaries, violated the principle of Inner Mongolian ethnic integrity on which the autonomous region had been founded, it made economic sense by reconnecting Inner Mongolian areas with adjacent provinces along lines of established transport routes and other economic linkages. In economic terms, Inner Mongolia had been an artificial creation within its maximum extent from the Alashan desert in the southwest to the forested Great Khingan Mountains in the northeast. The outlying Mongol leagues related to adjoining provinces through feeder railroads and highways; internal lateral communications within Inner Mongolia had remained virtually undeveloped.

Under the 1969 territorial adjustment, the former Manchurian section of Inner Mongolia, corresponding to Manchukuo's Hsingan Province, was reincorporated into the three traditional Manchurian provinces. Heilungkiang obtained the Hulunbuir League, except for the Khorchin West Wing's South Banner (with headquarters at Ulanhot), which is connected by rail with Kirin Province and was therefore incorporated into this province. Kirin also obtained the Jerim League, and the Jo-uda League went to Liaoning. Initially, at least, the league structure, equivalent to autonomous chou, was preserved within the Manchurian provinces.

At the western end, the Alashan desert region, which had been annexed by Inner Mongolia in 1956 after having been originally part of the old Ningsia Province and, from 1954 to 1956, in Kansu, was now divided between Kansu Province and the Ningsia Hui Autonomous Region, established in 1958. The Alashan East banner, with headquarters at Bayanhot (Alashan was divided into West and East banners in 1961), was annexed to Ningsia Hui Autonomous Region, with which it has close economic ties. The Alashan West banner and the Edsin banner had road connections with Kansu, and were therefore incorporated into this province.

The territorial transfers of 1969 returned an area of about 170,000 square miles with a population of 4 million to Manchuria, and an area of about 63,000 square miles with a sparse desert population of several ten thousands to Ningsia and Kansu. Inner Mongolia's territory was thus reduced to about 240,000 square miles with a population of 9 million in 1970, including perhaps 600,000 Mongols.

Topographically, Inner Mongolia represents essentially part of the Mongolian plateau, at an average elevation of 3,000 feet. Three major physical divisions may be distinguished: the plateau, bounded by the Great Khingan on the eastern side and the Yin Shan in the south; the Yin Shan, a mountain range trending east-west on the northern side of the Yellow River, and the Ordos Desert within the great river bend.

The Yin Shan system, a continuation of the Holan (Alashan) Mountains in Kansu Province, trends generally east-west on the northern side of the Yellow River bend. Its ranges enclose the Hotao irrigated plain north of the Yellow River and the Huhehot plain, an eastern continuation. The Yin Shan has an average elevation of about 4,500 feet, with individual heights rising to nearly 9,000 feet. Like the Great Khingan, the Yin Shan has one steep-sloped side (on the south) and gentle slopes on the plateau side.

The Yellow River on entering Inner Mongolia describes a vast rectilinear bend. Irrigated plains along the river are major agricultural districts. They include the Hotao plain and the Huhehot plain, to the east. The Hotao plain is an alluvial lowland of clayey soils of high fertility. About 100 miles long and 40 miles wide, the Hotao plain is crisscrossed by a dense network of irrigation canals dating from the late Manchu Dynasty. The Huhehot plain, between Paotow and Huhehot, is irrigated in part by the Minsheng Canal, originally built in 1918. The canal subsequently fell into disuse and was rehabilitated in the 1950's. South of these irrigated lowlands lies the Ordos plateau, enclosed west, north, and east by the Yellow River bend and sloping gently from south to north. In the south, hill ranges crowned by the Great Wall separate the Ordos from the loess uplands of northern Shensi. It is a desert covered with a veneer of gravel or small stones that rest directly on the hard eroded rock floor.

North of the Yin Shan and west of the Great Khingan is the Mongolian plateau proper. The plateau, at an average elevation of 3,000 feet, is underlain by a complex of hard rock formations eroded to an essentially flat surface and covered with a gravel veneer. It ranges from the Gobi Desert to steppes along the foothills of the enclosing mountains, with steppe and semidesert landscapes most prominent. Major physical subdivisions of the Mongolian plateau are dry Silingol steppe in the east and the Ulanchab semidesert passing into the Alashan Desert in the west.

Climatically, Inner Mongolia is distinguished by extreme continentality, which expresses itself in a wide annual temperature range and low precipitation. During the winter, the region is under the influence of the Siberian high, which produces dry, cold, and windy weather. Mean January temperatures vary from 11°F (-12°C) in the north to 18°F (-8°C) in the south. Average temperatures in July are 68° to 72°F (20 to 22°C). About 80 to 90 per cent of the precipitation occurs from May to September, when the region comes under the influence of a Central Asian low-pressure area. The Greater Khingan range in the east and the Yin Shan in the south constitute an effective barrier against the southeasterly summer monsoon. Through most of the region, rainfall is inadequate for farming, and irrigation is essential. Furthermore, precipitation is highly variable from year to year, a typical aspect of continental climate. For example, Huhehot, with a long-range mean annual precipitation of 16 inches, received 33 inches in 1919 (a record year) and only 2 inches in 1928.

Climate and topography combine to restrict agriculture to a few areas of available irrigation, mainly in the Hotao and Huhehot plains on the Yellow River. Irrigation of the Hotao plain was expanded in the 1960's by the construction of a new diversion dam on the Yellow River at Sanshengkung. Work on the project began in 1959, and completion of a 120-mile irrigation canal with a drainage outlet was reported in 1970. Sanshengkung, an old missionary center, expanded considerably after it became the seat of Tengkow hsien in the early 1950's and the headquarters of the Bayan Nor League in 1958, succeeding Bayanhot. (Under the Nationalists, the seat of Tengkow hsien was 25 miles farther south, at a place now called Tingkow.) The population influx associated with the new administrative functions and the irrigation project led in 1960 to the formation of a city at Tengkow (Sanshengkung), with the Mongol name Bayangol, meaning "abundant river." Its municipal district had a population of 70,000, including 52,000 urban. However, in 1964, Bayangol lost its city status in the absence of sustained economic growth and reverted to the status of hsien under the name of Tengkow.

The leading agricultural crops in the irrigation districts along the Yellow River bend are grains (oats, spring wheat), which are sown in April and harvested in August. Millet and kaoliang, which are more drought-resistant, are planted on dry land in early May and harvested in early September. Linseed is cultivated mainly for its oil, used for lighting. Sugar beets, favored by the local climate and irrigated soil, were introduced in the 1950's, and a refinery, with a capacity of 22,000 tons of sugar a year, was inaugurated at Paotow in 1955. The average annual food crop in the 1950's was a little better than 3 million tons, mainly in millet and kaoliang. Oil-seeds covered about 300,000 hectares. In addition to linseed, they included sesame, rapeseed, castorbeans, and sunflower.

Outside of the limited farming areas, livestock-herding is the leading economic activity on the Mongolian plateau. There are three types of animal husbandry in Inner Mongolia: (1) nomadic herding with year-round maintenance of the livestock on the open range, as practiced by the Mongols; (2) summer herding and winter stall-feeding, common in livestock and crop-raising areas with mixed Chinese-Mongol population; and (3) stall-feeding of livestock, chiefly draft animals, in Chinese agricultural areas. About half the herds in the pasture areas are made up of sheep and goats, one fourth of cattle, and the rest of horses, camels, and other stock. The total livestock population rose above 20 million head in the middle 1950's, but may have declined during the subsequent collectivization.

Inner Mongolia's mineral resources, virtually undeveloped before the 1950's, were explored and developed particularly in conjunction with the construction of the Paotow iron and steel plant. The first coking-coal deposit was developed in the Tatsing Mountains, an outlier of the Yin Shan, in the Shihkwaikow area, 20 miles northeast of Paotow. A 300,000-ton shaft mine was inaugurated in 1957, and a rail spur linked the new mining town of Shuimotan with the Paotow iron and steel plant. Two more shaft mines, with a capacity of 600,000 tons each, were reported under construction in the late 1950's, for a total capacity of 1.5 million tons. However, a lag in development forced the Paotow plant to rely mainly on Shansi and Hopei coking coals, pending the opening up of new deposits in Inner Mongolia in the early 1960's.

The additional coal deposits were discovered in the Shihtsuishan basin straddling the border between Inner Mongolia and the Ningsia Hui Autonomous Region on the Yellow River. Development of these resources was made possible by the completion of the Paotow-Lanchow railroad in 1958. In addition to mines at Shihtsuishan proper, within the Ningsia Hui Autonomous Region, two coking-coal centers developed on the railroad to the north across the border in Inner Mongolia. The two new centers, Haipowan and Wuta, were raised to the status of cities in 1961 in recognition of their economic significance. Haipowan, on the east bank of the Yellow River, developed on the basis of coal mines in the Chotze Shan hill range, to the east of the city. Wuta, on the west bank, was reported to have a capacity of 1 million tons of coking coal in 1962 and continued to expand in the 1960's.

The iron-ore source for the Paotow steel mill is Paiyünopo, 80 miles north of Paotow, on the northern (plateau) side of the Yin Shan. Paiyünopo is the Chinese phonetic rendering of the Mongol name Bayan Obo, meaning "rich cairn." The ore, containing 60 per cent iron, lies close to the surface and can be mined in open pits. A railroad running north from Paotow across the Yin Shan was completed in 1959, and the first ore began moving to the Paotow blast furnace inaugurated in that year. The mine is believed to yield close to 4 million tons of usable ore a year.

Seasonal lakes of the Mongolian plateau and the Ordos plateau abound in salt and soda deposits. The principal commercial operation is located at the Chilantai (Jalatai) salt lake, 50 miles west of the coal city of Wuta on the Yellow River. A narrow-gauge rail spur was reported in 1963 to have been built from the Paotow-Lanchow railroad to the salt lake, for the expansion of natural soda ash recovery. Asbestos, talc, and mica have been mined in small amounts in the Yin Shan near Huhehot, with processing plants in the city itself.

The modern economic development of Inner Mongolia dates essentially from the construction of the Peking-Paotow railroad. This line, on which construction began in 1905, reached Paotow in 1923. Railroad development was resumed in the 1950's with the construction of the Trans-Mongolian railroad and the Paotow-Lanchow railroad.

The Trans-Mongolian line, inaugurated in 1955, runs from Tsining, junction town on the Peking-Paotow railroad, to the Outer Mongolian frontier at Erhlien and on to Ulan-Bator and the Soviet Union. As originally constructed, the Soviet-gauge track (five feet) extended to Tsining, where wheel-change operations were located for conversion to the standard gauge (4 feet 8½ inches) of the Chinese system. The location of trans-shipment operations at Tsining at a time when freight traffic was heavy between the Soviet Union and China led to its elevation to city status in 1956. As Soviet-Chinese relations cooled in the early 1960's, the Chinese converted the Tsining-Erhlien segment of the Trans-Mongolian railroad to standard gauge and transferred wheel-change and trans-shipment activities from Tsining to the border station of Erhlien. The new transportation functions of Erhlien were reflected in turn in its elevation to city status in early 1966. It was named Erhlien Hot, a hybrid name consisting of the Chinese element Erhlien, meaning "second link," perhaps an allusion to the new connection with the Soviet Union, and the Mongol element Hot, meaning "town."

The extension of the Peking-Paotow railroad to Lanchow, completed in 1958 after difficult construction through the shifting sands of the Alashan

Desert, was economically highly significant. It provided a rail link between two growing industrial centers, Paotow and Lanchow; opened up the intervening segment of the Yellow River, including the Ningsia plain, for modern transportation, and made possible the commercial exploitation of mineral resources, particularly coal, along the way. In its Inner Mongolian portion, the new railroad improved access to the Hotao irrigation district, one of the region's principal farming areas, and made possible the development of the coking-coal reserves at Haipowan and Wuta.

The rail lines are supplemented by motor roads, notably the Kalgan–Ulan-Bator highway, which parallels the Trans-Mongolian railroad. Kalgan, though situated in Hopei Province outside Inner Mongolia, is a hub of motor roads serving adjoining sections of the Silingol League. As noted earlier, the Manchurian section of Inner Mongolia between 1956 and 1969 had virtually no lateral communications with the developed central areas between Tsining and Paotow and was served by the Chinese Eastern railroad and by feeder rail lines and motor roads from the Manchurian transport net.

The territorial changes that Inner Mongolia has undergone since its creation as an autonomous region have been reflected in its distinctive system of internal administration. In contrast to the subprovincial special districts (areas) elsewhere in China, the Inner Mongolian Autonomous Region is divided into subprovincial units known as "leagues" (Chinese *meng,* Mongol *chuulgan* or *aymug*), which in turn are broken down into hsien in Chinese-populated areas and into "banners" (Chinese *ch'i,* Mongol *hushuu[n]*) in Mongol areas. The Chinese hsien, in keeping with the practice elsewhere in China, are named for the administrative seat. The Mongol banners usually bear the names of tribes or, in the case of large tribes, the names of tribal subdivisions designated by directions or points of the compass. (In Mongol, some locational terms designate both points of the compass and directions from the point of view of an observer facing south, so that, for example, south is front and west is right; the principal locational terms used in the names of banners appear in Table 53.)

After the separation of the three Manchurian leagues (Hulunbuir, Jerim, and Jo-uda) in 1969, Inner Mongolia consisted of four leagues and two cities of subprovincial level, Huhehot and Paotow. Following are brief administrative descriptions of the leagues:

Silingol League (Chinese phonetics Hsi-lin-kuo-lo), covering the steppe lands in the far north of former Chahar Province, adjoining the Mongolian People's Republic, absorbed the Chahar League to the south in late 1958. The Silingol League proper has consisted traditionally of the following tribes: Ujumchin (Wu-chu-mu-ch'in), Abaga (A-pa-ka), Abahanar (A-pa-ha-na-erh), and Sunit (Su-ni-t'e). With virtually no Chinese colonization or agriculture, Silingol has remained a stronghold of the old Mongol nomadic society. It was the heart of the autonomy movement of the 1930's that led to the establishment of the Japanese-sponsored Mengkiang terri-

TABLE 53

GLOSSARY OF GENERIC TERMS IN MONGOL BANNER NAMES

Chinese Term	Mongol Term	English Equivalent
Ch'en	Huuchin	Old
Ch'i	Hushuu(n)	Banner
Ch'ien	Ömnö	South, front
Chung	Dund(a)	Center
Hsi	Örnö	West
Hsin	Shine	New
Hou	Ar(a)	North, rear
I	Gar	Wing
Meng	Chuulgan or aymag	League
Tso	Dzüün	East, left
Tung	Dorno	East
Yu	Baruun	West, right

tory. The headquarters of the Silingol banners are at former lamaseries whose Chinese names contain the word "miao," meaning lamasery. The administrative seat of the entire league is at the headquarters of the Aba-hanar banner. Known as Peitzemiao until 1953, it was renamed Silinhot (Hsi-lin-hao-t'e) in 1953. Silinhot functions as the principal collecting and processing center for the animal products of the surrounding steppe region and has a population of about 30,000. The former Chahar League, adjoining Hopei Province, has been heavily colonized by Chinese agriculturists and consists of both Mongol banners (the Chahar Mongols' east wing) and Chinese hsien. The territorial banners of the Chahar Mongols, who were organized along military rather than tribal lines under the Manchu Dynasty, are named for the colors of their regimental banners: All Blue (Cheng-lan), All [White] and Bordered White (Cheng-hsiang-pai), Bordered Yellow (Hsiang-huang), as well as the tribal banner Taipus (T'ai-p'u-ssu), with its seat in the town of Paochang. The Chinese hsien are Tolun and Hwateh.

Ulanchab League (Wu-lan-ch'a-pu), formerly part of Suiyüan Province, is economically the most highly developed section of Inner Mongolia. It has been heavily colonized by the Chinese and contains geographically, if not administratively, the two subprovincial cities of Huhehot and Paotow. As might be expected, pastoral Mongols are in a small minority, in the northern arid steppe, with Chinese (and some Mongol) agriculturists dominating farther south in the area served by the Tsining-Paotow railroad.

The pastoral Mongols of northern Suiyüan are constituted into two banners: the Darhan Muu-Myangan (Ta-erh-han-mao-ming-an) and the Dörvön Hüühet. The Darhan Muu-Myangan banner resulted from the merger of the Darhan, a Khalkha banner that migrated from Outer Mongolia in the seventeenth century, and the Muu-Myangan, or Bad Thousand, so named because, according to tradition, the tribe once fought against Genghis Khan. The combined banner has its headquarters at the old lamasery town of Pailingmiao, about 25 miles east of the new iron-mining center of Bayan Obo. The Dörvön Hüühet banner, whose name means "four children," unlike most other Mongol banners is rendered in Chinese not through phonetics but through translation, as Ssu-tze or Ssu-tze Wang, if the title of a former ruling prince (wang) is used. This banner has its headquarters 50 miles north of Huhehot.

In the eastern part of the Ulanchab League, north and south of the league capital, Tsining, are three banners of the west wing of the Chahar Mongols. (The west wing, which used to be under Suiyüan Province, became part of Ulanchab League, while the east wing, in former Chahar Province, was merged with Silingol League.) Finally, the Ulanchab League contains two banners of the Tumet (T'u-mo-t'e) tribe along the railroad between Huhehot and Paotow. These Tumets, related to another Tumet banner at Fusin in Manchuria's Liaoning Province, are descendants of a Mongol tribe that flourished in the sixteenth century under Anda, the Altan Khan (Golden Khan), who built the town of Huhehot. Most of the Tumets are agricultural. The Chinese hsien in the southern part of the league, as well as the Chahar and Tumet banners, were administered separately until 1958 as Pingtichüan District (for the old name of Tsining).

Ikh Jo League (I-k'o-chao), within the great bend of the Yellow River, was also part of Suiyüan Province until its incorporation into the Inner Mongolian Autonomous Region in 1954. The league, whose name means "great temple" in Mongol, corresponds in area to the Ordos Desert and is inhabited by the Ordos Mongols, a largely pastoral tribe. The Ordos Mongols, separated by the Great Wall from the Chinese settlement area of northern Shensi, are traditionally descended from the palace guard of Genghis Khan (the name Ordos is derived from the Mongol word "ord," meaning "palace"). The Ordos are divided into several banners, which used to bear directional designations but have been identified on Chinese maps by proper names. They are: Otok (O-t'o-k'o) and Hanggin (Hangchin) in the center; Ushin (Wu-shen) in the southeast; Dalat (Ta-la-t'e); Dzungar (Chun-ko-erh); and Dzasak (superseded by a banner rendered in Chinese as I-chin-huo-lo). The principal Chinese settlement and headquarters of the league is Tungsheng, 50 miles south of Paotow.

Bayan Nor League (Pa-yen-nao-erh) is the westernmost Inner Mongolian league, having been formed in 1956 as a result of the annexation of the Alashan Desert from Kansu Province. The most sparsely populated of the Inner Mongolian leagues, Bayan Nor, which means "rich lake," was apparently named for the Chilantai salt lake, 50 miles west of the coal-mining center of Wuta. The boundaries of this league have undergone repeated changes, reflecting the instability of the administrative structure in the Alashan Desert region. At first, the league included only the Mongol banners of Edsin (O-chi-na) in the west and Alashan in the east. (Alashan had existed briefly as the Kansu Mongol Autonomous Chou while in Kansu Province, from 1954 to 1956.) During this early period, the league had its administrative seat at Bayanhot (the former Tingyüanying), which was given city status. In 1958, the league acquired additional territory, including the Hotao irrigation district and the adjoining steppe land north of the Yellow River bend. In conjunction with this areal expansion, the league's administrative seat moved from Bayanhot, which lost its city status, to Tengkow, which functioned temporarily as a city from 1960 to 1964 under the name of Bayangol. Before its incorporation into the Bayan Nor League, the Hotao irrigation district, with a substantial Chinese agricultural population, had been administered as a separate area, with its seat at Shenpa. The principal Mongol element in this area, including both pastoral nomads in the northern steppe and settled agriculturists in the Hotao, is the Urat (Wu-la-t'e) tribe, whose name may be related to that of the Oirat, a major western Mongol division. In the 1969 dismemberment, Bayan Nor League lost Edsin Banner and Alashan Banner, which in 1961 had been divided into east and west wings. Alashan East Banner, with headquarters at Bayanhot, passed to Ningsia Hui Autonomous Region, and Alashan West and Edsin were ceded to Kansu Province. These territorial changes reduced Bayan Nor League to the coal-mining and salt-processing centers of Wuta and Lake Chilantai, the Hotao irrigation district, and adjoining steppe lands.

Ethnically, the population of the Inner Mongolian Autonomous Region is heavily dominated by Chinese, who account for about 8 million of the region's estimated 9 million people (after separation of the Manchurian leagues in 1969). Mongols number 600,000, including 400,000 in agricultural pursuits and 200,000 in pastoral activities. The settled population of Chinese and ethnic minorities is concentrated in the southern belt served by the railroad through Tsining, Huhehot, Paotow to Lanchow, including both industrial and mining centers and densely inhabited irrigation districts, such as the Hotao area. Mongol stock-herders are founded mainly in the Silingol League, with the best grasslands, the northern part of the more arid Ulanchab League, and in the Ikh Jo League of the Ordos Desert.

TABLE 54
CITIES OF INNER MONGOLIA

City	City Level	Function	Population (*in thousands*)		
			1953	1957	1970 est.
Huhehot	subprovincial	administration, manuf.	148	320	
Paotow	subprovincial	iron-steel	149	500	
Tsining	hsien	rail center	30	80	
Erhlien Hot	hsien	border town			
Haipowan	hsien	coal			
Wuta	hsien	coal			
Former City	*Period*				
Bayangol	1960–64				

Inner Mongolia's urban centers (Table 54) include six cities, two at subprovincial level—Huhehot, the capital, and Paotow, the iron and steel center—and four at hsien level—the two railroad towns of Tsining and Erhlien Hot, and the coal-mining centers of Haipowan and Wuta.

Huhehot, the regional capital since 1952, was founded in the sixteenth century by the Tumet ruler Anda, known as the Altan Khan, and was initially known by its present Mongol name, which means "blue town." Upon conquest under the Manchu dynasty, the Mongol town was renamed by the Chinese as Kweihwa, meaning "return to civilization." While Kweihwa developed as a trade center, a new walled Chinese administrative city named Suiyüan ("pacified remote place") arose about a mile to the northeast. Ultimately, the two communities were joined under the name Kweisui, which was used until the traditional Mongol name Huhehot was restored officially in 1954. The city's significance as a commercial center for the surrounding Mongol herding lands was enhanced in 1921, when it was reached by the railroad from Peking. A second period of growth began in the middle 1950's in conjunction with its functions as the Inner Mongolian capital and with industrial development. Huhehot has a sugar refinery serving nearby irrigated sugar-beet lands. Its manufacturing industries include a diesel-engine factory, opened in 1966. The city's population rose from 148,000 in the 1953 census to 320,000 by late 1957.

Paotow, another old Mongol trade center, surpassed Huhehot in population and economic significance in the 1950's, when it was selected as the site of one of China's new iron and steel centers. Its development as a commercial town dates from the arrival of the railroad from Peking in 1923, and for more than three decades, Paotow performed a major regional trade role as a railhead in the Mongol grasslands and near the Hotao irrigation district on the Yellow River. Its iron and steel phase began in the middle 1950's, with the development of the iron mine at Paiyünopo, 80 miles to the north, and a coking-coal deposit in the Shihhwaikow area, 20 miles to the northeast. The iron and steel complex arose on the Yellow River plain west of the old trade town. A heat and power station and a coking plant were the first facilities to be completed in 1958, followed in September, 1959, by the inauguration of the No. 1 blast furnace with a working volume of 1,513 cubic meters and an annual pig-iron capacity of about 900,000 metric tons. The first 500-ton open-hearth steel furnace went into operation in May, 1960, and a second steel furnace is reported to have been completed subsequently. Work on the No. 2 blast furnace, of the same capacity as the first, was interrupted by the failure of the Great Leap. It appears to have been completed in 1970. A rail and girder rolling mill, also delayed by the economic crisis of the 1960's, opened for production in early 1969 and was followed by an oxygen converter in 1970. The development of the iron and steel complex brought about an influx of workers that raised Paotow's population from its 1953 census of 149,000 to nearly 500,000 in 1957 and about 700,000 by the end of the 1950's. The municipal area expanded to 50 miles in length, including the coal mines in the east and the iron and steel plant in the west.

Tsining, long an obscure stop on the Peking-Paotow railroad, gained in significance in the early 1950's in conjunction with the construction of the Trans-Mongolian railroad, which was opened in 1955. Tsining became the point where the wheel trucks of rail cars were changed between the 5-foot gauge of the Outer Mongolian and Soviet rail systems for the standard Chinese gauge of 4 feet 8½ inches. The enhanced transport functions, which raised Tsining's population from 30,000 in 1953 to 80,000 by 1956, also led to its elevation to city status in 1956. Its significance declined in the early 1960's, when the Chinese gauge was extended to the actual border station of Erhlien, which thus became the wheel-change point. It was raised to city status in early 1966 and named Erhlien Hot, even though by this time the decline of Soviet-Chinese trade had reduced traffic to a small fraction of its level in the late 1950's.

The two coal cities of Wuta and Haipowan were given city status in 1961 in conjunction with development of local coking-coal deposits. The two cities, on opposite sides of the Yellow River, are part of a coal field that extends southward across the border of Ningsia Hui Autonomous Region to the coal city of Shihtsuishan. The development of this coal-producing district, made possible by the construction of the Paotow-Lanchow railroad (opened in 1958), strengthened Inner Mongolia's coking-coal supply for the Paotow iron and steel complex. Until the opening up of the Wuta-Haipowan mines, Inner Mongolia had to obtain most of its coking coal from Hopei and Shansi because of the limited capacity of the mines near Paotow.

14. The Kansu Corridor

Like Inner Mongolia, the Kansu corridor cannot be considered a physically homogeneous region. It is treated as a separate division, partly because of its political unity during certain periods, partly because of its traditional importance as a routeway linking China proper with central Asia between the Gobi Desert on the north and the Tibetan high plateau on the south.

Politically, this region has undergone a number of administrative changes. Until 1928, the region consisted of a single province, Kansu. In that year, Ningsia Province was carved out of Kansu Province, combining the irrigated Ningsia plain on the Yellow River around Yiuchwan with the Alashan section of the Gobi Desert, which was inhabited by a sparse population of Alashan and Edsin Mongols. In September, 1954, Kansu again absorbed Ningsia, reverting to its pre-1928 area of 250,000 square miles, with a population of 12.9 million in the 1953 census. In 1956, the Mongol-inhabited Alashan Desert portion of about 80,000 square miles, with a population of a few tens of thousands, was transferred to the Inner Mongolian Autonomous Region. In June, 1958, the Ningsia plain and nearby districts with a significant Hui (Chinese Moslem) population were separated from Kansu Province to form the Ningsia Hui Autonomous Region, with an area of 25,000 square miles and a 1957 population of 1.8 million. This left Kansu Province with an area of about 140,000 square miles and a 1957 population of 12.8 million. In the 1969 dismemberment of Inner Mongolia, an Alashan Desert area of about 50,000 square miles reverted to Kansu, raising its area to 190,000 square miles. At the same time, a 15,000-square-mile portion of the Alashan Desert passed to Ningsia Hui Autonomous Region, increasing its area to about 40,000 square miles.

The region can be divided into five physical subregions: the Ningsia irrigated plain, the eastern Kansu loesslands, the Lanchow basin, the Kansu corridor proper, and the Alashan Desert.

The eastern Kansu loesslands are actually part of the northern Shensi loess plateau, which adjoins on the east. The loess area, which is drained

291

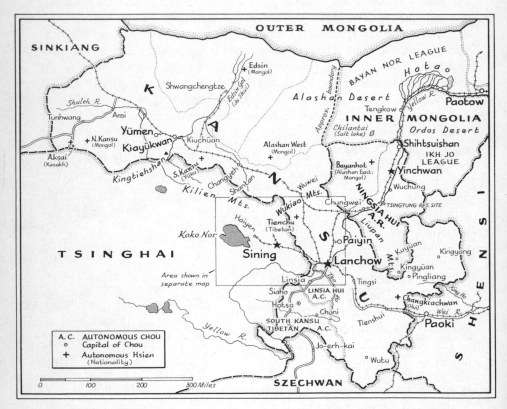

15. Kansu and Ningsia

by the King Ho, a tributary of the Wei Ho in Shensi, lies at an average elevation of 2,500 to 3,000 feet. Pingliang is the chief town of the loesslands, which are bounded in the west by the Liupan Mountains.

West of the Liupan Mountains lies the Lanchow basin, a mountain-ringed region situated at the focal point of transportation routes. From this heartland of Kansu, historic routeways lead west onto the Tibetan high plateau, northwest through the Kansu corridor to Sinkiang, northeast along the Yellow River to the Ningsia plain and Inner Mongolia, and southeast to China proper. The basin is traversed by the upper Yellow River, which descends from the Tibetan high plateau in the west and receives here the Tao Ho, on the right. The Lanchow basin is the leading agricultural area of Kansu Province. It is also known as the Lungsi basin ("west of the Lung Shan"), named for the Lung Shan, another name of the Liupan Mountains. The main cities of this subregion are Lanchow and Tienshui.

Northwest of the Lanchow basin, and separated from it by the Wukiao Mountains, is the 600-mile-long Kansu corridor, historic routeway to central Asia. The corridor extends along the northern foot of the towering Kilien Mountains, a section of the great Nan Shan system. From these mountains, rising to nearly 20,000 feet, streams feed water to oases before disappearing in the Alashan Desert sands of the Mongolian plateau. The principal oases, serving as centers of population, administration, and transportation along the corridor, are those of Wuwei, Changyeh (the former Kanchow), and Kiuchüan (the former Suchow). (The old names of the last two places gave rise to the name Kansu.) The Changyeh and Kiuchüan oases are watered by headstreams of the Jo Shui (known in Mongol as the Edsin Gol). The Jo Shui penetrates deep into the Alashan Desert, terminating in two salt lakes near the border of Outer Mongolia. Another mountain stream, the Shuleh (Sulo) River, waters northwestern Kansu.

The Alashan Desert, extending from the Kansu corridor north to the border of Outer Mongolia, is part of the Gobi Desert. Its sandy expanses are virtually lifeless, except for pastures along the lower Jo Shui (Edsin Gol).

Northeast of the Lanchow basin lies the irrigated Ningsia plain, the heart of the Ningsia Hui Autonomous Region. Separated by the Alashan Mountains from the desert to the west, the Ningsia plain extends along the Yellow River between Chungwei (in the south) and the coal-mining center of Shihtsuishan (in the north). Irrigation canals from the Yellow River bring much-needed water to the plain, which has its economic center in the city of Yinchwan.

Kansu's climate, like that of Inner Mongolia, is classified as a middle-latitude dry climate, including both the steppe and desert varieties. It is characterized by interior continental location, far from oceans, resulting in lower precipitation and a wide annual temperature range. Monthly mean temperatures range from 15° to 20°F (−10° to −6°C) in January to 70° to 80°F (21° to 26°C) in July. January temperatures generally increase from north to south, while summer averages are more or less uniform through the region. Although most of the precipitation occurs in summer, it is inadequate for the growing of crops without irrigation. Annual totals range from 20 inches in the southeast (Lanchow basin) to less than two inches in the northwestern desert.

Irrigation is developed especially in the Ningsia plain along the Yellow River and along streams descending from the Kilien Mountains into the Kansu corridor. The water supply for the Ningsia plain was to be regulated through the construction of dams in the Yenkuo, Liukia, and Tsingtung gorges upstream. Work on these projects, for power generation and flood control, was begun in 1958, but they have not been completed.

In accordance with its physical differentiation, Kansu Province falls into three distinct agricultural regions: the winter wheat–millet area, the spring wheat area, and the area of oasis agriculture. The winter wheat–millet area coincides with the loesslands of easternmost Kansu. Here, January temperatures just below freezing still permit the cultivation of winter wheat, while millet leads kaoliang as the summer grain. Cotton and tobacco are the chief cash crops. The spring wheat area includes the Lanchow basin, while irrigated agriculture is the rule in the Ningsia plain and the oases of the Kansu corridor. The total food crop in the middle 1950's was 4 to 5 million tons, of which about 30 per cent was in wheat.

The region's mineral resources include coal and petroleum, copper and iron ore. The principal coal-mining center is Shihtsuishan, in the Ningsia Hui Autonomous Region on the Inner Mongolian border. The development of Shihtsuishan, which yields coking coal, began in 1958, after construction of the Lanchow-Paotow railroad provided access to the deposit. Lesser coal mines are being operated in the Lanchow area—at Akanchen, south of Lanchow, and at Yaochieh, to the west, on the Tsinghai border. There is also coal production at Shantan, in the Kansu corridor proper.

Petroleum production is centered at Yümen. The Laochünmiao field in this district has been in commercial operation since 1939, with the large Yaerhsia deposit following after its discovery in 1957 just west of Laochünmiao. The crude oil was refined at a small local topping plant, until a large refinery was inaugurated at Lanchow in 1958.

Metallic minerals are associated mainly with the copper-mining center of Paiyin, 45 miles northeast of Lanchow. Paiyin was raised to the status of city in 1958, after construction of the Lanchow-Paotow railroad had provided access to the deposit. In 1963, the mining district was placed under the direct jurisdiction of Lanchow, indicating its growing significance.

The iron-ore deposit of Kingtiehshan in the Kilien Mountains bordering on the Kansu corridor has been described as a potential ore base for a new iron and steel center in the Kiuchüan area. Plans for the development of the ore and steel project were announced in 1958 but appear to have been dormant until 1965, when the urban district of Kiayükwan was established just west of Kiuchüan.

Resource development in the region was greatly promoted by railroad construction during the 1950's. Lanchow, the regional metropolis, was reached by the railroad from China proper in 1952, and, by the late 1950's, the railroad had traversed the entire Kansu corridor on its way to Sinkiang. Transportation was further improved by the completion of the Lanchow-Paotow railroad in 1958, and the following year a line was opened from Lanchow westward to Sining in neighboring Tsinghai Province. The Yellow River, Kansu's only potential waterway, is not navigable under present conditions because of its steep gradient and rapid flow as it cascades down from the Tibetan high plateau. However, 'the long-range Yellow River reclamation project was expected to make Lanchow accessible to 500-ton vessels after completion of dams and locks.

Chinese, speaking northern Mandarin, constitute about 90 per cent of the region's population. They are settled in the agricultural areas of the southeast, including the loesslands and the Lanchow basin, and in the irrigated oases of the corridor and the Ningsia plain.

Among the ethnic minorities of the region are mainly the Hui (Chinese Moslems), as well as small communities of Tibetans, in the highlands; Mongols, in the desert margins; and the Tungsiang, Yüku, and Kazakhs. About 577,000 of the region's 1.1 million Hui live in the Ningsia Hui Autonomous Region, carved out of Kansu Province in 1958. Another significant Hui concentration, in the Linsia area, southwest of Lanchow, was established as the Linsia Hui Autonomous Chou in 1956. The Tibetans have autonomous units in the South Kansu Autonomous Chou, in the highlands southwest of Lanchow, and in the Tienchu Autonomous Hsien occupying a mountain spur enclosing the Lanchow basin on the northwest. Kazakhs, Yüku, and Tungsiang have an autonomous hsien each. The small Mongol population of the region was increased in 1969 by the incorporation of Inner Mongolia's Alashan Desert region. In addition to an autonomous hsien in northwest Kansu, the Mongols are now represented in the province by two additional former Inner Mongolian banners (Edsin and Alashan West), while a third banner, Alashan East, was annexed by Ningsia Hui Autonomous Region.

KANSU PROVINCE

Capital: Lanchow; area: 190,000 sq. mi.; population: 16 million

Since ancient times, Kansu has been the routeway between China proper and central Asia. The Silk Road, used by caravans loaded with silk, tea, and other Chinese goods, passed through the Kansu corridor, known traditionally by the Chinese as Hosi ("west of the [Yellow] river"). The trade route skirted the foot of the Kilien Mountains, at the northern margins of the Tibetan highlands, and was protected against inroads of desert and steppe nomads to the north by a wall originally built about 100 B.C. under the Han Dynasty. It was restored in the sixteenth century under the Ming Dynasty, and ruins still remain. In modern times, the Silk Road became

TABLE 55
CITIES OF KANSU AND NINGSIA

City	City Level	Function	Population (*in thousands*)		
			1953	1957	1970 est.
KANSU PROVINCE					
Lanchow	subprovincial	industrial, trans- portation	397	699	
Kiayükwan	subprovincial	iron-steel project (?)			
Tienshui	hsien	trade	63		
Yümen	hsien	petroleum		60 (in 1956)	
Former Cities					
Linsia (until 1964)			63		
Pingliang (until 1964)					
Paiyin (1958 until absorbed by Lanchow in 1963)					
Changyeh (1958–61)					
Kiuchüan (1958–64)					
Tewulu (name of Hotso while a city, 1958–61)					
NINGSIA HUI AUTONOMOUS REGION					
Yinchwan	subprovincial	trade	84		
Shihtsuishan	subprovincial	coal		60	
Former Cities					
Bayanhot (1956–58)					
Tsingtungsia (1960–63)					
Wuchung (until 1963)					

a motor road that played a particularly important role during World War II as one of China's lifelines. Finally, in the mid-1950's, the railroad came, as construction crews pushed northwestward from Lanchow toward Sinkiang, opening up the ancient oasis towns of Wuwei, Changyeh, and Kiuchüan to modern transportation.

Rail construction, improving access to the province's mineral resources, in turn resulted in substantial urbanization and industrial development, in what had long been an economic backwater producing mainly wool, felt, hides, and skins from sheep and camel herds. As resources were put into production, new cities arose on the extraction sites, while older subregional centers bypassed by the industrialization program lost their municipal status.

In the late 1960's, Kansu Province had four cities (Table 55). Two were under provincial jurisdiction: Lanchow, the provincial capital and outstanding new industrial complex, and Kiayükwan, a presumed iron and steel center; and two were at hsien level: Tienshui, subregional center of the southeast agricultural region of Kansu, and Yümen, the petroleum city. Other subregional centers in the agricultural southeast, such as Pingliang and Linsia, were cities during the 1950's and early 1960's but lost their municipal status in 1964, presumably because of inadequate industrial development. Still other towns, such as Changyeh and Kiuchüan in the Kansu corridor, were raised to the status of city after the arrival of the railroad but were again demoted to hsien town in the early 1960's, in the absence of industrial construction.

Lanchow, the provincial capital, is an old regional center of northwest China that entered a modern era of industrial development in the 1950's. Situated on the south bank of the Yellow River, it is a natural focus of transport routes from the loesslands in the east, the Kansu corridor in the northwest, the Ningsia plain in the northeast, and the Tsinghai and Tibetan highlands in the west. Historically the chief crossing of the upper Yellow River on the way from China proper to central Asia, Lanchow thus developed into a major overland transport center even before the arrival of the railroad from China proper in 1952. The Yellow River, here 700 feet wide, was bridged in 1910 for road traffic and again in 1954, when work began on the railroad extension through the Kansu corridor to Sinkiang. Its excellent transport situation has made Lanchow the natural supply and distribution center for China's Northwest.

Before the railroad era of the 1950's, local industry was concerned mainly with the processing of regional animal products (wool and hides, woolen textiles, and leather goods). After Lanchow had been designated as one of the future industrial hubs of inland China in the proposed shift away from the industrial concentration in Manchuria and coastal cities, construction began in the middle 1950's on a number of modern industrial projects, including an oil refinery for the Yümen oil fields, a nitrogenous fertilizer plant, a synthetic-rubber factory, and an aluminum reduction plant. The oil refinery, inaugurated in late 1958, was further expanded into a petrochemical complex during the 1960's. It supplies byproduct hydrogen for ammonia synthesis at the nitrogenous fertilizer plant, which also began operations in late 1958. It is also assumed to provide the basic ingredients, butadiene and styrene, for general-purpose synthetic-rubber manufacture, which began in 1959. (According to some reports, the plant was originally designed for the production of neoprene, or chloroprene, rubber by the acetylene route.) The aluminum-reduction plant, whose source of alumina is unclear, began production in November, 1959. In addition to the primary industries, Lanchow has also acquired a range of machinery manufacturing, including a locomotive repair shop for the northwestern rail network, machine tools, ball bearings, and oil-field equipment for the Yümen and Karamai producing districts.

At least part of Lanchow's industrial development, notably power-oriented activities, such as aluminum reduction, was based on plans for the construction of major hydroelectric projects nearby on the Yellow River. These projects, located in Yellow River gorges upstream from Lanchow, where the river descends from the Tsinghai plateau, were the 595,000-kilowatt Yenkuo hydroelectric plant, 30 miles west of Lanchow, and the 1.05-million-kilowatt Liukia station (five units of 210,000 kilowatts), 45 miles southwest of Lanchow. Construction on both the Liukia project, which was listed in the original Yellow River development plan announced in 1955, and the Yenkuo site, added later, began in September, 1958. Cofferdams diverting the stream flow from the dam sites were completed at Yenkuo in April, 1959, and at Liukia in January, 1960. There has been no further announcement on progress, and the two hydroelectric sites are presumed to be incomplete.

In the absence of the proposed low-cost hydroelectric power supply, Lanchow's industries have been dependent on thermal-power generation. A modern heat and power station, burning coal from nearby mines, was inaugurated in November, 1957, with installation of a 25,000-kilowatt unit. A second unit was added in 1959. The ultimate capacity of the station was at least 300,000 kilowatts. Coal for the Lanchow power plant is supplied partly by the nearby Akanchen and Yaochieh mines. The older Akanchen mine, about 10 miles south of Lanchow, was reached by a rail spur in 1955 and expanded in conjunction with the city's industrialization program. The Yaochieh operation, situated on the Tsinghai border 60 miles northwest of Lanchow, developed in the late 1950's and early 1960's. Each is believed to yield more than a million tons of coal a year. Residual fuel oil from the Lanchow refinery may also serve as a local power-station fuel.

The Lanchow industrial district also includes the cement-manufacturing town of Yungteng and the copper-mining center of Paiyin. Yungteng, 60 miles northwest of Lanchow, on the railroad through the Kansu corridor, developed in the middle 1950's as a cement-producer for Lanchow's industrial construction program.

The development of the Paiyin copper site, which was discovered in the middle 1950's, began in 1958 when a spur was completed from the newly opened Lanchow-Paotow railroad. In that year, Paiyin (also known as Paiyinchang, or "white silver place") was established as a city, with its center at Haokiachwan, the mining settlement at the railhead. The unusual significance of Paiyin was highlighted in late 1961, when it was placed directly under provincial administration. Except for Lanchow, Paiyin was then the only Kansu city enjoying such high status. In 1963, the importance of activities at Paiyin was further accentuated, when its status as a separate city was abolished and its territory was merged with Lanchow as an exclave of the Lanchow municipal district.

In the early 1960's, the construction of a uranium-enrichment plant was reported in the Lanchow area. The plant, believed to have been inaugurated in 1963, separates the fissionable U-235 isotope from natural uranium by what is presumed to be a sequence of gaseous diffusion and electromagnetic methods. The highly enriched weapons-grade U-235 produced by the Lanchow facility is thought to have been used in Chinese nuclear-weapons tests beginning in 1964.

The industrial development of Lanchow since the early 1950's has been reflected in population growth and in expansion of the municipal district.

Its population increased from 397,000 in the 1953 census to an estimated 699,000 at the end of 1957. Since 1959, the municipal boundaries extend in a 70-mile-long ribbon from Lanchow proper westward along the railroad to Sining as far as the Tsinghai border. The urban area thus includes both the coal mines of Akanchen, south of Lanchow, and of Yaochieh, to the west. As noted earlier, since 1963 the old Paiyin municipal area has also been under the jurisdiction of Lanchow. Territorial expansion was reflected in an increase of the population of the Lanchow municipal area to 1.2 million by September, 1959, including 900,000 urban.

Tienshui, in the eastern loesslands, was the head of the Lung-Hai railroad from 1945 until 1952, when the line was extended to Lanchow. During this period, the city flourished as a trans-shipment center from truck transport of the Northwest to the Chinese rail system. Since the extension of the railroad, the city has been relatively stagnant as an agricultural-processing center (flour milling, burlap sacks, textiles) for the upper Wei Ho valley. The city was originally planned to be the junction of the railroad to Szechwan before revised route alignments made Paoki, in Shensi, the new rail hub. Tienshui's population is believed to have grown little above the 1953 census figure of 63,000.

Another loessland center, Pingliang, is situated northeast of Tienshui in the upper valley of the King Ho, a left tributary of the Wei Ho. Pingliang is a road-transport town on the Sian-Lanchow highway, but its significance as a subregional center has declined since the completion of the railroad to Lanchow. Pingliang, with an estimated population of about 50,000, was therefore deprived of its city status in 1964.

After the railroad from Lanchow to Sinkiang had penetrated into the Kansu corridor, two corridor towns, situated in oases of irrigated agriculture and serving as distribution points for nearby nomadic districts, were raised to the status of cities in late 1958. They were Changyeh (the old Kanchow) and Kiuchüan (the old Suchow), whose former names had given Kansu Province its name. A third corridor town, Wuwei (the former Liangchow), was not given municipal status. However, no significant industrial development followed to back up the enhanced urban position of the corridor cities. Changyeh reverted to hsien town status in late 1961. Kiuchüan retained its municipal position for three additional years, presumably because of announced plans to develop an iron and steel center in the Kiuchüan area based on the Kingtiehshan ore deposit in the Kilien Mountains to the southwest. But in 1964, Kiuchüan was also demoted to hsien town, suggesting indefinite postponement of the iron and steel project.

However, an unusual development a year later indicated that the development plans for this area had not been abandoned. In the second half of 1965, virtually on the eve of the Cultural Revolution, a new municipal district was established just west of Kiuchüan, with its urban center at the town of Kiayükwan, just across the river Lin Shui from Kiuchüan. Kiayükwan was an ancient gateway town on the historic Silk Road, at the westernmost sixteenth-century extension of the Great Wall. The configuration of the municipal limits of Kiayükwan, extending deep into the uninhabited Kilien Mountains up to 50 miles southwest of the urban center, indicates that the city may have been established in connection with a resource-development project, possibly the Kingtiehshan ore site. When plans for the exploitation of this iron deposit were first announced in 1958, they called for construction of a 60-mile railroad linking the ore site with the projected iron and steel plant. Reserves were said to be adequate to supply a 1.5-million-ton steel plant for half a century. Mention of a "Kansu metallurgical plant" in 1971 news reports may have been connected with the Kiayükwan iron and steel project.

About 140 miles northeast of Kiayükwan, across the former provincial border of Inner Mongolia, is the desert missile proving ground of Shwangchengtze. The launching center is served by a rail spur running north into the desert from Tsingshuipao, a station southeast of Kiuchüan on the Lanchow-Sinkiang main line. It is from Shwangchengtze that China's first medium-range missile was launched in October, 1966, for a 500-mile flight southwest into the Lop Nor impact area. The missile center was also used for launching China's first artificial earth satellite in 1970, and the second in 1971. The proving ground is situated approximately at Lat. 41 degrees N, Long. 100 degrees E.

Adjoining the Kiayükwan municipal district on the west is the petroleum center of Yümen, one of China's principal producers of crude oil. Operations began here in 1939 in the Laochünmiao field, and during World War II, a small topping plant was built, producing gasoline, kerosene, and diesel fuel for China's wartime needs. Yümen was then China's only major petroleum-producer, but poor transportation facilities (with the nearest railhead 700 miles away) kept annual output to about 100,000 tons. After the Communist take-over, crude-oil production expanded, and the refinery was modernized and enlarged to yield additional refined products, such as lubricants, wax, and asphalt. The expansion was reflected administratively in December, 1955, when Yümen was established as a city. Its prospects were further enhanced when it was reached by the railroad in 1956 via a 20-mile spur from the Lanchow-Sinkiang main line. The following year the promising Yaerhsia field was discovered just west of Laochünmiao, with daily well flows of up to 200 tons. By 1958, when a pipeline was completed to the new Lanchow refinery, Yümen yielded about 1 million tons of crude oil. During the 1960's, its output was believed to range between 1.5 and 2 million tons a year. Yümen's population, estimated at 60,000 in 1956, probably has exceeded 100,000 since then.

In northwestern Kansu are the two road towns of Ansi and Tunhwang. Ansi, a road junction on the main highway to Sinkiang, was bypassed by the Lanchow-Sinkiang railroad and did not develop into a significant subregional center. It is situated on a road running across the Kilien Mountains into the Tsaidam Basin in Tsinghai and passed through a flurry of activity in the late 1950's, when an abortive attempt was made to develop the mineral resources of Tsaidam with the help of truck transport. Tunhwang is noted chiefly for the locality of Tsienfotung, 10 miles southeast, site of ancient caves with stone Buddhas, murals, and writings of the T'ang and Sung dynasties.

The ethnic minorities of Kansu Province—the 535,000 Hui (Chinese Moslems), 205,000 Tibetans, 156,000 Tungsiang, about 15,000 Mongols, 3,900 Yüku and a few thousand Kazakhs—are constituted into two autonomous chou and six autonomous hsien.

The most populous of these autonomous areas is the Linsia Hui Autonomous Chou, southwest of Lanchow, in the relatively densely settled agricultural belt of southeastern Kansu, with its capital at Linsia. The Hui minority in this area was first constituted in 1953 as an autonomous hsien at Kwangtung (called Kwangho since 1958). In 1956, Hui autonomy was extended to the entire Linsia district, which was established as an autonomous chou. Linsia itself is an old subregional center at the gateway to the Tibetan minority area of southeastern Kansu and a concentration point for the area's animal products, such as hides and wool. It had a population of 63,300 in the 1953 census and had city status through the 1950's, but in the absence of significant industrial projects was demoted to hsien town in 1964.

Within the Linsia Hui Autonomous Chou, in hilly country east of the town of Linsia, lies the autonomous hsien of the Tungsiang, a Moslem Mongolic minority, whose Chinese name means "eastern village" (with reference to Linsia). The Tungsiang Autonomous Hsien was established in 1950, with its seat at Sonanpa, 15 miles east of Linsia on the main road to Lanchow. The hsien has a population of about 160,000, including perhaps 100,000 Tungsiang (two-thirds of the total Tungsiang population).

In addition to its autonomous chou, the Hui minority of Kansu has an autonomous hsien at Changkiachwan, northeast of Tienshui on the Shensi border. The hsien was set up in 1953 with a population of 134,000, including 77 per cent Moslems. It was temporarily known as Tsingshui in 1959–61.

The second most numerous minority in Kansu are the Tibetans, who are settled primarily in highland areas southwest of Lanchow on the Tsinghai and Szechwan borders. The first Tibetan autonomous unit to be established there was the Choni autonomous hsien, set up in 1951 on the river Tao Ho, south of Lintan (the old Chinese subregional town of Taochow). Other Tibetan autonomous units were established subsequently, notably at Siaho, site of the great Labrang lamasery. These minor units were merged in 1953 to form the Kannan (South Kansu) Tibetan Autonomous Chou. The chou had a population of 300,000, including about 50 per cent Tibetans, 43 per cent Chinese, and 6 per cent Hui. The administrative seat of the Tibetan chou, first established at Siaho, was moved in 1954 to a more isolated lamasery, 35 miles southeast of Siaho. The lamasery is known in

the Chinese rendering as Tohusze, "sze" being the Chinese character of
lamasery. The presumably Tibetan name of the settlement at the lamasery
was initially rendered phonetically by Chinese characters as Heitso, meaning
"black error," but was soon renamed Hotso ("cooperation"). In an apparent attempt to give the Tibetan administrative center added stature, it
was raised to the level of city in 1958, with the name Tewulu, apparently
another Chinese rendering of the lamasery name. However, city status was
abrogated in 1961, and the name Hotso was restored. In addition to
traditional Tibetan activities, such as stock-herding and limited raising of
crops, the autonomous chou has a small lumbering industry on the slopes
of the Min Shan, which forms the southern boundary of the chou with
Szechwan's Ahpa Tibetan Autonomous Chou.

Kansu's Tibetan minority also has the Tienchu Autonomous Hsien,
which represents an extension of Tsinghai's Haipei Tibetan Autonomous
Chou across the Nan Shan into the Wukiao Mountains. This upland spur is
crossed by the Lanchow-Sinkiang railroad about 100 miles northwest of
Lanchow. The hsien, founded in 1950 with a population of 120,000, has
its headquarters at Tienchu (the former railroad station of Anyüanyi),
just outside the Great Wall, which extends along the crest of the Wukiao
Mountains.

Proceeding northwestward along the Kansu corridor, we find three other
ethnic autonomous areas along the foothills of the Nan Shan, representing
the Yüku, Mongol, and Kazakh minorities.

The Sunan (South Kansu) Yüku Autonomous Hsien was established in
1954 for the Yüku people, a Turkic-language group of Lamaist religion
that is also known as the Sary-Uigur (Yüku is a Chinese phonetic rendering
of Uigur). The hsien has its seat at a lamasery known as Hungwansze, 50
miles southeast of Kiuchüan, near the Tsinghai border. When the municipal district of Kiayükwan was established in 1965, it absorbed part of the
Yüku territory, presumably including the iron deposits of Kingtiehshan.
The Yüku hsien has a population of 17,000, which includes 3,500 Yüku,
or 90 per cent of the entire Yüku minority.

In northwestern Kansu are the Kazakhs of the Aksai Kazakh Autonomous Hsien, established in 1954 at the junction of the Tsinghai and
Sinkiang borders. The hsien, with a population of 2,500, which is half
Kazakh, has its administrative seat at the former Changtsaokow, now
known by a Kazakh name rendered in Chinese phonetics as Pu-lo-chuan-
ching. It is situated just north of the Tsinghai border, on a motor road leading from Kansu into the Tsaidam basin.

The Mongols of Kansu are represented by three administrative units:
the Supei (North Kansu) Mongol Autonomous Hsien and two banners in
the Alashan Desert that passed from old Ningsia Province to Kansu in
1954, then to Inner Mongolia in 1956, and reverted to Kansu in 1969.

The Supei hsien, established in 1951, had its nomadic headquarters
originally at Tsiangküntai, about 100 miles north of the oil-field city of

Yümen. In 1953, the administrative seat was reported at Chihkinpao, just northwest of Yümen, and, since early 1955, it has been 150 miles west of Yümen, at Tangchengwan, in the upper reaches of the Tang Ho. The Mongols of Supei hsien belong to the historical Torgut division.

The Edsin (O-chi-na) banner, one of the Alashan Desert units that reverted to Kansu in 1969, is situated in the lower reaches of the Jo Shui (Edsin Gol) on the western margins of the desert. The Edsin Mongols, also a branch of the Torgut division, have moved their headquarters repeatedly within the Edsin Gol plain as channel shifts altered the sources of water supply. Since about 1960, it has been at Dalan Huv (Ta-lan-k'u-pu), on the eastern branch of the Edsin Gol and a few miles west of the ruins of Karakhoto, a desert fortress of uncertain origin that was discovered in 1908–9 by Pyotr Kozlov, the Russian explorer.

The other Alashan Desert banner that reverted to Kansu in 1969 is Alashan West, the western section of the combined Alashan banner, which was divided in 1960. Alashan West has its administrative seat at a well, 35 miles northeast of the Kansu corridor town of Shantan. The name of the well is rendered phonetically in Chinese as O-k'en-hu-tu-ko, possibly standing for the Mongol name Ohin Hudag, which means "daughter's well." Unlike the other Kansu Mongols, the Alashan group belongs to the historical Ölöt division of the Mongols.

NINGSIA HUI AUTONOMOUS REGION

Capital: Yinchwan; area: 40,000 sq. mi.; population. 2.5 million

The name Ningsia was applied from 1928 to 1954 to a Chinese province that combined the relatively densely settled Ningsia plain, with a significant Hui (Chinese Moslem) minority, and the sparsely Mongol-inhabited Alashan Desert to the northwest. This province, with an area of 115,000 square miles, mostly desert, and a population of 1.5 million, concentrated in the irrigated plain, was absorbed in 1954 by Kansu, from which it had been originally detached.

Under the Chinese Communists' ethnic autonomy policy, the Hui minority of this region was originally organized into two autonomous chou and one autonomous hsien. Within former Ningsia Province was the Wuchung Hui Autonomous Chou, established in April, 1954, east of the Yellow River and known initially as the Hotung ("east of the river") chou until it was renamed in April, 1955, for its capital Wuchung. The chou had a population of 230,000, 62 per cent of whom were Chinese Moslems. It occupied the east-bank section of the Ningsia irrigated plain, adjoining the Ordos Desert and passing southeast into the loesslands.

Adjoining it to the south, within Kansu Province, was the Kuyüan Hui Autonomous Chou, established in October, 1953, with a population of 220,000. Until 1956 this chou was called Sihaiku, for the initial characters of the names of its three hsien—Siki, Haiyüan, and Kuyüan, the capital. Its territory was situated astride the Liupan Mountains on the western edge of the loesslands. Finally, there was the Kingyüan Hui Autonomous Hsien, established in 1953 on the southern border of the Sihaiku chou, with its seat in the former hsien town of Hwaping.

In 1958, the two autonomous chou and the Kingyüan hsien were combined with the west-bank section of the Ningsia plain to form the Ningsia Hui Autonomous Region. At the time of its formation, the region had a population of about 1.8 million, including 577,000 Hui. The Hui element was concentrated mainly in the Kuyüan district, which was preserved as a special district (area) within the autonomous region.

In yet another territorial change, Ningsia Hui Autonomous Region acquired a Mongol banner, Alashan East, in the dismemberment of Inner Mongolia's Alashan Desert portion in late 1969. The annexation of the desert banner, with its headquarters at Bayanhot, added only a few tens of thousands to the regional population but increased the area by about 15,000 square miles, from the original 25,000 to about 40,000.

The economic heart of the region is the Ningsia plain, an elongated oasis along the Yellow River, which is said to have been first irrigated about 220 B.C. under the Ch'in Dynasty, when a wall protected the plain against steppe nomads to the northwest. The principal crops are rice, wheat, millet, cotton, and sugar beets as well as melons and apricots. The supply of irrigation water was to be improved under the Chinese Communists by the construction of the Tsingtung storage reservoir in a gorge 60 miles south of Yinchwan. Construction of the project, which also called for a 260,000-kilowatt hydroelectric plant, began in 1958. Its significance was pointed up two years later by the establishment of the city of Tsingtungsia ("sia," "hsia" = gorge) at the site. However, the project was apparently abandoned after the failure of the Great Leap, and Tsingtungsia reverted in 1963 to a hsien whose seat was moreover moved away from the construction site into the irrigated plain to the north.

Mineral resources of the Ningsia autonomous region are limited to coking-coal reserves in the Pinglo area, at the northern end of the plain adjoining the Inner Mongolian border. Coal was mined on a small scale in the past, but modern development of the deposit was made possible only by the construction of the Paotow-Lanchow railroad in 1958, providing a stimulus to the Ningsia plain economy in general. The coal-mining area of Shihtsuishan, north of Pinglo, yielded 1.2 million tons in 1958, and two modern mines with a capacity of 500,000 tons each were inaugurated the following year. The importance of the new coal district was indicated by the elevation of the old mining town of Shihtsuishan in early 1960 to the status of city. The coal-mining center, which was reported to have a population of 60,000 in 1959, is part of a growing mining district that also includes the Inner Mongolian coal cities of Wuta and Haipowan, just across the regional boundary.

The principal urban center of the Ningsia Hui Autonomous Region is its capital, Yinchwan, with a population of 84,000 in the 1953 census. The city, also known as Ningsia in the past, was a processing center for wool and hides of the nearby desert herds and for grains and other agricultural products of the irrigated oasis. Additional industry followed the arrival of the railroad in 1958. It included a modern linen mill, whose completion in 1970 suggested an expansion of the cultivation of flax in the region. Yinchwan's position as a local transport center improved after construction of a highway bridge across the Yellow River nearby.

Yinchwan is the supply center for Bayanhot, administrative seat of the Alashan Mongols' East Banner, on the western slopes of the Holan (Alashan) Mountains, which separate the Ningsia irrigated plain on the Yellow River from the Alashan Desert to the west. It was because of this close economic link that the banner was incorporated into Ningsia in the 1969 dismemberment of Inner Mongolia. A modern highway linking Yinchwan with Bayanhot has been in existence since 1955. Bayanhot, a Mongol name meaning "prosperous town," was originally known by the Chinese name Tingyüanying and later as Tzehu, before acquiring the Mongol name officially in the early 1950's. It is the traditional headquarters of the Mongols' Alashan banner, which existed briefly as the Kansu Mongol Autonomous Chou from 1954 to 1956, after the Alashan Mongols had passed from the jurisdiction of the old Ningsia Province to Kansu. In 1956, when the Alashan Mongols joined Inner Mongolia, Bayanhot became the administrative seat of the new Bayan Nor League and was given city status until the league capital moved to Tengkow in 1958. After the Alashan banner was divided into East and West banners in 1961, Bayanhot remained the headquarters of the eastern banner.

Another urban center of the Ningsia plain, Wuchung, acquired the status of city in the early 1950's and functioned as the eastern-bank capital of the Wuchung Hui Autonomous Chou from 1954 until the formation of the Hui autonomous region in 1958. But the absence of significant industrial development deprived Wuchung of city status in early 1963.

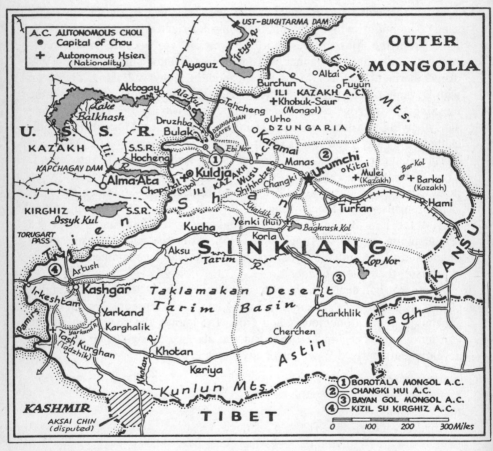

16. Sinkiang

15. Sinkiang

SINKIANG UIGUR AUTONOMOUS REGION

Capital: Urumchi; area: 640,000 sq. mi.; population: 10 million

Sinkiang is China's largest political unit. It is situated north of the Tibetan highlands and borders on three Central Asian republics of the Soviet Union—Kazakhstan, Kirghizia, and Tadzhikistan. Aside from the highland margins that penetrate into Sinkiang from the south, the region can be divided into three major subregions: the rugged Tien Shan mountain system in the center, separating the Dzungaria basin in the north from the larger Tarim basin in the south.

The Tarim basin is bounded in the north by the Tien Shan, in the south by the Kunlun system, and extends from the Pamirs in the west to Kansu in the east. With a length of 850 miles from west to east and a width of 350 miles, the basin occupies about 45 per cent of all of Sinkiang. The oval-shaped basin can be visualized in the form of a series of concentric belts, proceeding from the outer mountain barriers, past the foothills and alluvial fans, a string of oases, the sandy desert, and the playa lakes at the center.

The Kunlun system, which towers at 20,000 feet above the Tarim basin, is the northern edge of the Tibetan highlands. It extends from the Pamir mountain knot, branching out eastward where subsidiary ranges enclose the Tsaidam basin of Tsinghai. Beyond the zone of foothills, rising to an average elevation of 3,000 feet, semipermanent mountain streams spread their water in irrigation ditches over their alluvial fans. Each oasis thus formed commands a piece of Sinkiang, including a bit of desert, some irrigated land with a chief town, and the well-watered mountain valleys upstream. The principal oases of the Tarim basin are Khotan, Yarkand, Kashgar, and Aksu. Between the oases and beyond stretches the desert, taking up about half the area of the entire Tarim basin. This is the nearly rainless Taklamakan, filled with great sand dunes, more developed here than anywhere else in China. Sinkiang's main river, the Tarim, is fed by major mountain streams, such as the Khotan, Yarkand, Kashgar, and Aksu rivers. These rivers have the greatest flow in the late spring and early summer, when they are fed by the melting snow and glacier ice. A large part of their

307

water evaporates, is used for irrigation, or disappears in the desert sands before reaching the Tarim. Having skirted the northern edge of the Takla-makan, the Tarim River in turn reaches its terminal lake, the Lop Nor, a salt lake with a unique history. According to ancient Chinese sources, the lake was at Lat. 41 degrees N and Long. 90 degrees E 2,000 years ago. Alternate sedimentation and wind deflation gradually diverted the lake basin southward and the Russian explorer Przhevalsky found it at Lat. 40 degrees N in 1876. The Swedish explorer Sven Hedin found subsequently that the Tarim had returned to its earlier course and that the Lop Nor oc-cupied its original site. That is where the lake is shown on current Chinese maps. The desolate desert land around the Lop Nor has been used as a nuclear testing ground since China's first atomic test in 1964.

The Tien Shan mountain system consists of a series of parallel ranges extending from Soviet Central Asia eastward into Sinkiang for 1,000 miles. Elevations reach 24,500 feet on the Soviet-Chinese border in the Pobeda (Victory) Peak and 23,600 feet in the Khan Tengri, just to the north. The ranges of the Tien Shan system enclose intermontane basins and val-leys, where population and economic activities are concentrated. In the extreme west, the Borokhoro and Ketmen ranges enclose the Ili River valley, centered on the city of Kuldja and oriented toward the Soviet Union. Between the main Tien Shan and the Kuruk Tag lies the Yenki (Kara-shahr) depression occupied by the salt lake Baghrash Kol. Between the Bogdo Ula and the Chol Tag lies the Turfan depression. The bottom of the depression, at 427 feet below sea level, is the lowest point in China. At the eastern end of the Tien Shan are the twin Hami and Barkol depres-sions, respectively south and north of the Barkol Tag.

The Dzungarian basin, situated north of the Tien Shan, extends to the Altai Mountains on the Soviet and Mongolian borders. West of the Dzun-garian basin, the Tarbagatai and Dzungarian Ala-Tau ranges enclose the Dzungarian Gates, main routeway between Dzungaria and the steppes of Kazakhstan. Like the Tarim basin, the Dzungarian subregion includes a zone of oases at the foot of the enclosing mountains and a steppe and desert belt in the center of the depression. Major oases along the north foot of the Tien Shan are Kitai, Urumchi, and the Manas and Wusu oases; on the northern side of the Dzungarian basin are Tahcheng (Chuguchak) and Altai (Sharasume). Unlike the Tarim basin, Dzungaria has no unifying river. Dzungaria is slightly less arid than its neighbor to the south, its sand dunes are less developed, and its grassland belt more ample. The main rivers are the intermittent Manas River, which sometimes reaches its ter-minal lake, the Telli Nor, and the upper Irtysh River, which flows west into the Soviet Union.

No part of China is as far removed from the moderating influence of oceans as is Sinkiang. The high mountains that enclose the region on all sides cut off maritime air masses and produce a continental arid steppe and desert climate throughout the region. Internal climatic differences are largely caused by the Tien Shan, which separates the exceptionally dry Tarim basin from less arid Dzungaria. The Tien Shan acts, in particular, as a climatic barrier against the continental polar air that enters Dzungaria from Siberia during the winter. As a result, average January temperatures in the Tarim basin are about 20° F (—7° C) compared with 5° F (—15° C) in many parts of Dzungaria. In the summer, too, average temperatures north of the Tien Shan are generally lower than south of the mountains. In Dzungaria, July averages vary from 70° F (20° C) in the north to 75° F (24° C) in the south. In the Tarim basin, July averages in the neighborhood of 80° F (27° C) are more typical. The hottest point is the Turfan depression where adiabatically heated air descending from the surrounding mountains produces a July average of 93° F (33.7° C).

While Dzungaria is exposed to the northern air masses, it is also accessible to Atlantic maritime polar air, especially during the spring. At that time of the year, weak cyclonic storms occasionally reach Dzungaria from the west. These storms, to be sure, have lost most of their moisture in their long overland route, but they are the major factor in the slightly moister climate of northern Sinkiang. Urumchi, in the steppe belt along the northern foot of the Tien Shan, has an annual precipitation of nearly 10 inches. The Tarim basin, by contrast, is effectively barred from most moisture sources. It receives less than 4 inches a year. Charkhlik (Jochiang), near the lower reaches of the Tarim River, has the reputation of being the driest point in China. Its average annual precipitation is one-fifth of an inch. In contrast to the spring storms in Dzungaria, whatever little moisture reaches the Tarim basin is of Pacific origin and occurs during the summer.

The mountain climate of the Tien Shan reflects the conditions of the adjoining basins. Greater precipitation and generally lower temperatures are characteristic of the northern slopes, where the snow line is at 11,500 feet. Forests and alpine meadows are well developed. Higher temperature and greater aridity are typical of the south slopes, where the snow line is at 13,000 feet and vegetation is sparse.

In accordance with the moister climate, chestnut soils are developed on the fringes of the central Dzungarian desert. The associated steppe vegetation constitutes an important belt of grazing land. The Tarim basin has no such grasslands, and the population and economic activity are limited to the oases.

Climatic differences between north and south continue to be evident in the distribution of the rural economy. Widespread oasis agriculture in the Tarim basin occupies about 40 per cent of the population, while only 2 per cent are engaged in animal husbandry. North of the Tien Shan, the grasslands support about 35 to 40 per cent of the population through the grazing of herds.

A seven-month growing season in the south makes possible the raising of two crops, provided ample irrigation water is available. The first crop is usually sown in February and harvested in June, the second planted in

July and harvested in October. Only one crop is harvested in Dzungaria, which has a five-month season.

The semicircular oasis belt of the Tarim basin, west of a line linking Kucha and Keriya (Yütien), contains about 95 per cent of all oasis land and 97 per cent of the population of southern Sinkiang. There are concentrated the major towns of the Tarim basin, including Khotan, Yarkand, Kashgar, and Aksu.

Efforts have been made during the 1950's and 1960's to expand the area under cultivation through the construction of new irrigation systems and the expansion of old projects. In the first five-year plan, the only period for which actual figures are available, the cultivated area expanded from 1.1 million hectares in 1952 to 1.6 million in 1957. Most of the new land (almost 60 per cent of the total) was developed on the northern slopes of the Tien Shan in Dzungaria, particularly in the Manas River basin west of Urumchi. The southern piedmont of the Tien Shan and the intermontane basins were developed to a lesser extent. According to the second five-year plan (1958–62), which collapsed in the Great Leap experiment, further irrigation development was to be focused on the Aksu area on the middle course of the Tarim River and in the Yenki area on the lake Baghrash Kol. A distinctive aspect of the agricultural development of Sinkiang has been the role of the army in reclamation work and in the actual operation of the newly reclaimed land. As in other desert lands, reclamation through irrigation has encountered such problems as a rise of the water table, producing dense reed-growths in cultivated fields, and secondary accumulation of salt in the soil, requiring frequent soil leaching and the provision of drainage installations for the used irrigation water.

About 80 per cent of the total cultivated area is in grains, and half of the grain acreage is in wheat. Before the Communist take-over in 1949, spring wheat predominated heavily, with about 32 per cent of the total cultivated area, compared with 8 per cent in winter wheat. During the 1950's, the area in the higher-yield winter wheat varieties was expanded significantly, and, by 1955, the winter wheat crop already exceeded the spring wheat harvest. The cultivation of winter wheat is most reliable in the oases of the Tarim basin, where winters are less severe than in Dzungaria. The principal wheat producing areas are the Ili River basin, where exposure to the severe winter temperatures of Soviet Central Asia requires the cultivation mainly of spring varieties; the northern piedmont of the Tien Shan, and the oases of the upper Tarim basin. Corn, accounting for about 20 to 30 per cent of the grain crop, is limited largely to the Tarim basin, as is rice, which represents about 10 per cent of the crop. Total grain production in the late 1950's was close to 2 million tons.

Cotton production, which was close to 50,000 tons in 1957, or 3 per cent of China's total crop, is concentrated in the Tarim basin, particularly the oases of Kashgar and Yarkand. Aside from the longer growing-season in this region, cotton-growing is also favored by the high population density of the oases. Cotton-growing is likely to remain at a relatively low level because of the area's remoteness from textile centers and the absence of railroad transportation in the Tarim basin. The need for long-distance truck hauls was reduced to some extent with the construction of a cotton mill at Kashgar in 1960.

A significant new industrial crop in Sinkiang is sugar beets, introduced in the late 1950's in the newly irrigated Manas basin, west of Urumchi. A sugar refinery with a capacity of 25,000 tons of sugar was opened in late 1959 at Shihhotze, center of the Manas irrigation district, about 10 miles west of the hsien seat of Manas. Traditional products of the oases in the Tarim basin are natural silk and dried fruit, including raisins, pears, and apricots. Hami is noted for its melons.

About 600,000 nomads, or 6 per cent of the total population, are stockherders, the great majority in the Dzungarian steppe where pasture lands are superior to those of the Tarim basin. The herders are predominantly Kazakhs and Mongols in Dzungaria, and Kirghiz and Tadzhiks on the western mountain margins of the Tarim basin. As elsewhere in central Asia, transhumance is practiced, with herds moving to summer pastures in the mountains and to winter pastures in the plain. About 60 per cent of the Sinkiang herds are sheep, with cattle, camels, and horses making up the balance of the livestock holdings, which were about 20 million in the middle 1950's. Subsequent collectivization probably reduced these holdings somewhat. Sheep and camel wool, hides, and horse hair are major export items.

The nature of Sinkiang's mineral resources was stressed in 1950 and 1951, when Soviet-Chinese joint stock companies were set up to exploit petroleum and nonferrous and rare metals. Mineral production sharply increased during the subsequent years and, as of January 1, 1955, control over mineral exploitation passed entirely into Chinese hands.

Petroleum is by far the principal fuel resource. Commercial production dates from about 1940, when the relatively small Tushantze field was developed 15 miles southeast of Wusu, a highway junction in the northern piedmont of the Tien Shan. The crude oil, produced at the rate of about 100 tons a day, was refined at a small local topping plant. Refined products were transported eastward by tanker trucks.

In 1955, geological exploration in the northwestern part of Dzungaria disclosed the existence of a larger field about 80 miles north of the Wusu-Tushantze district. The new field was called Karamai, a Uigur name meaning "black oil." Its discovery was followed by that of the Urho field, 60 miles northeast of Karamai. Commercial production in the Karamai district began in 1958. In that year, Karamai was established as a city, with a municipal area extending from the Urho field 150 miles south to Tushantze. A crude-oil pipeline linking the Karamai field with the Tushantze refinery was inaugurated at the beginning of 1959, with a capacity of 400,000 tons a year. A second line was reported to have been added in the early 1960's.

In the meantime, refining capacity at Wusu-Tushantze was expanded with a second refinery going into operation in 1959. Total refining capacity was estimated at 1.5 million tons, and the total crude-oil output in the middle 1960's at about 2 million tons. Further development of the Karamai field was slowed by two factors: first, the discovery of the large Taching oil field of Manchuria in 1959 provided an ample petroleum source in a more accessible region of the country that was closer to markets; second, failure to complete the Sinkiang railroad between Urumchi and the Soviet border deprived the Karamai operation of cheap transportation and required continued trucking of refined products and surplus crude oil to the Urumchi railhead, more than 100 miles to the east.

In contrast to petroleum, which serves national needs, Sinkiang's coal industry has been developed for local consumption. Mines were built in the late 1950's and early 1960's near Hami and Urumchi in conjunction with the construction of the Sinkiang railroad and the expansion of a small iron and steel plant at Urumchi. What was described as Sinkiang's first modern coal mine was under construction in 1958 in the Urumchi coal field, which yields bituminous coal of coking quality. A modern strip mine opened at Hami in 1970. In addition to supplying the railroad, Urumchi coal is burned in a local power station and serves for the production of coke at the Urumchi steel plant. The power station, with an ultimate designed capacity of 400,000 kilowatts, was inaugurated in 1959 with a 25,000-kilowatt generating unit. The so-called First of August iron and steel plant, dating from the early 1950's, was expanded in 1958–59 to a capacity of about 200,000 tons. The Urumchi steel operation is based on nearby iron-ore deposits in the eastern Tien Shan.

Sinkiang is a significant gold-producer from placer and lode deposits in the Altai district on the southern slopes of the Mongolian Altai Mountains. The richest placers have been reported in this area along the right tributaries of the upper Irtysh River. It is also in the Altai-Fuyün area that uranium is believed to have been mined, first by the joint Soviet-Chinese rare metals company, from 1951 to 1954, and later by the Chinese themselves. Deposits of nonferrous metals, including lead, zinc, copper, molybdenum, and tungsten have also been found in the eastern Tien Shan, but few are of industrial significance.

Before the construction of the Sinkiang railroad in the early 1960's, transportation in Sinkiang had been dependent mainly on two major motor roads. They were the so-called North Road (north of the Tien Shan) and the South Road, along the south foot of the mountain system. The North Road passes from Kansu through Hami and Urumchi to Wusu, where it bifurcates into two routes going to the Soviet Union. The northern branch crosses the border in the Tahcheng-Bakhty area, and the southern branch, after having entered the upper Ili valley, crosses in the Hocheng-Panfilov area. These are the two principal low-level highway routes across the Soviet border, much of which follows high mountain ranges. The South Road skirts the south foot of the Tien Shan, serving the major oases of the Tarim basin. It circles the Taklamakan desert and joins the North Kunlun road along the north foot of the Kunlun mountain system.

In the late 1950's, the Chinese rebuilt and improved a 200-mile road running from Urumchi southward across the eastern Tien Shan to Yenki and Korla, on the South Road. The Urumchi-Korla highway is the only route linking the North and South roads across this major mountain system. In another significant road project, the South Road at Karghalik was linked in 1957 with Rudog (Tibet). This strategic link between Sinkiang and Tibet crosses the Aksai Chin area, disputed between India and China. In 1971, a motor road was inaugurated between Sinkiang and Pakistan across Khunjerab Pass of the Karakorum Mountains.

The Sinkiang railroad, on which surveys began in 1955, was originally conceived as a major overland transport link between China and the Soviet Union, running through Lanchow and the Kansu corridor, Hami, Urumchi, and through the Dzungarian Gate, a historic routeway on the Soviet-Chinese border, to join the Soviet rail system at the Turksib railroad town of Aktogay. The 190-mile Soviet segment, from Aktogay to a new border town named Druzhba ("friendship"), in the Dzungarian Gate, was completed in 1960, just as Soviet technical and material assistance to China was curtailed. By that time, the Chinese segment, after rapid progress through the Kansu corridor, had reached Hami, the first major Sinkiang town. In the economic depression that followed the failure of the Great Leap, railroad construction was sharply reduced, and Urumchi was reached only in 1963, completing a 1,175-mile railroad from Lanchow. The missing 480-mile segment, between Urumchi and the Soviet border, has remained incomplete.

Four places in Sinkiang have the status of city (Table 56). They are Urumchi, the regional capital, Karamai, the petroleum center, and two subregional centers near the Soviet border, Kuldja and Kashgar. A fifth place, Hami, briefly held municipal status in 1961–62, after the arrival of the railroad had held out promise of industrial growth, which did not materialize.

Urumchi, known officially by its Chinese name, Tihwa, until 1954, is

TABLE 56

CITIES OF SINKIANG

| City | City Level | Function | Population (in thousands) | | |
			1953	1957	1970 est.
Urumchi	subprovince	manuf.	141	320	
Karamai	subprovince	petroleum		40	
Kuldja (Ining)	hsien	trade	108		
Kashgar	hsien	trade	91	140	

Former Cities	Period
Yarkand	1953–54
Hami	1961–62

situated at the north foot of the Tien Shan in an agricultural district on the southern margins of the Dzungarian steppe. In the 1950's, an industrial district developed outside the old walled city on the right bank of the Urumchi River, which flows northward from the Tien Shan into the desert. The industries include the First of August iron and steel plant, founded in 1951 and expanded to a capacity of about 200,000 tons in the late 1950's, cement, agricultural machinery, textiles, and food products. Power for the industries was derived from a small coal-burning thermal station and the 2,400-kilowatt Ulabai (Wulapo) hydroelectric station on the Urumchi River above the city. A larger steam-electric station, with an ultimate designed capacity of 400,000 kilowatts, was inaugurated in 1959. The population of Urumchi increased as a result of the industrialization program and territorial expansion from 80,000 in 1949, to 141,000 in the 1953 census, and to 320,000 by the end of 1957. The population was reported to have risen further, to 400,000 by the time the railroad arrived in 1963. Employment in industry was 50,000. Urumchi's municipal district includes the Liutaowan coal mine, to the east of the city, and the iron mine of Motosala, off the highway to Korla, to the southwest.

Karamai, the petroleum center (discussed earlier), was established as a municipal district in 1958 with a population of more than 40,000. Both Urumchi and Karamai are cities at the subprovince level, directly under the Sinkiang administration.

Kuldja, the urban center of the upper Ili valley and capital of the Ili Kazakh Autonomous Chou, is officially known by its Chinese name, Ining. Its population, 108,000 in the 1953 census, has been relatively stable because of its isolation from the rest of Sinkiang in an area that is oriented physically westward toward the Soviet Union. Kuldja has a small processing industry for the agricultural products (grains, fruit) of the Ili valley and for the animal products (wool, hides) of the nearby stock-herding areas.

Kashgar, the largest center of the Tarim basin, is another subregional city near the Soviet border and is relatively isolated by sheer distance from the rest of China. Its official Chinese name is K'a-shih, an abbreviated form of K'a-shih-ka-erh, the phonetic rendering of Kashgar. It consists of two towns about 3 miles apart: the older Uigur town (to the northwest) of Kashgar proper, known in Chinese as Shufu or Sufu, and the newer Chinese town (to the southeast), known in Chinese as Shuleh or Sulo, and in Uigur as Yangishahr ("new town"). By analogy, the Uigurs apply the name Konashahr ("old town") to Kashgar proper. Kashgar is an ancient crafts center (textiles, rug-weaving, tanning) with some modern industries, such as cement and agricultural machinery. A cotton mill was opened in 1960, but Kashgar has not been greatly affected by industrial development. Its population, 91,000 in the 1953 census, rose to 140,000 in the early 1960's.

Sinkiang's population underwent substantial growth in the late 1950's and through the 1960's mainly because of the influx of Chinese from China proper. This in-migration had the effect of substantially reducing the Uigur majority. In the 1953 census, out of a total population of 4.9 million, the Uigurs numbered 3.6 million, or about 75 per cent of the total; other non-Chinese ethnic groups (Kazakhs, Hui, Kirghiz, Mongols, Tadzhiks, Sibo) about 1 million, and the Chinese only 300,000. It was on the basis of the predominant Uigur population, settled primarily south of the Tien Shan in the oases of the Tarim basin, that Sinkiang Province was transformed into the Sinkiang Uigur Autonomous Region in September, 1955. By the mid-1960's, Chinese in-migration was reported to have increased the Chinese component to 2.6 million, or one-third of the total population of 8 million, compared with 4 million Uigurs. By 1970, the Chinese may have been close to matching the Uigur component in a population approaching 10 million. The Chinese influx also had the effect of substantially altering the distribution of population within Sinkiang. In the 1953 census, about 1.3 million people lived in the Dzungarian section of Sinkiang, north of the Tien Shan, and 3.6 million, or three-fourths of the population, in the great oases of the Tarim basin, south of the Tien Shan. The Chinese influx was directed primarily into Dzungaria, where resource development spurred urbanization, as in the new petroleum center of Karamai, and many of the new land reclamation and irrigation projects were concentrated along the northern piedmont of the Tien Shan. By 1970, the population of Sinkiang was believed to be roughly evenly divided between the northern and southern sections, with a significant Uigur majority in the Tarim basin and a predominant Chinese component in the urbanized areas and new land projects of Dzungaria.

Ethnic minorities include about 500,000 Kazakhs, 134,000 Hui (Chinese Moslems), 71,000 Kirghiz, 58,000 Mongols, 19,000 Sibo, and 14,-000 Tadzhiks. These groups are constituted into five autonomous chou and six autonomous hsien. In Dzungaria are the Ili Autonomous Chou and the Mulei and Barkol autonomous hsien of the Kazakhs, the Changki Autonomous Chou of the Hui, the Borotala Autonomous Chou and the Khobuk-Saur Autonomous Hsien of the Mongols, and the Chapchal Autonomous Hsien of the Sibo nationality. The Tarim basin contains the Kizil-Su Autonomous Chou of the Kirghiz, the Bayan Gol Autonomous Chou of the Mongols, the Tash Kurghan Autonomous Hsien of the Tadzhiks, and the Yenki Autonomous Hsien of the Hui.

The Kazakhs, the third largest ethnic group in Sinkiang, after the Uigurs and Chinese, are mainly nomadic herdsmen in the steppes of Dzungaria. The greatest Kazakh concentrations, in the upper Ili valley, the Tahcheng area, and the upper Irtysh valley south of the Mongolian Altai, have been included in the Ili Kazakh Autonomous Chou set up in 1954, with its capital at Kuldja, in the Ili valley. The population of the chou in the middle 1960's was 1 million, half of them Kazakhs. Total livestock-holdings during that period were reported as 10 million head, of which 2.7 million were in the upper Irtysh valley. The Irtysh basin, constituted administratively as the Altai district of the autonomous chou, had a population of 140,000, of whom 80 per cent were Kazakhs.

The two Kazakh hsien, situated in southeastern Dzungaria, on the northern slopes of the easternmost outliers of the Tien Shan, were also created in 1954. The western hsien is Mulei Kazakh Autonomous Hsien, with its headquarters at Muleiho, 130 miles east of Urumchi. It is administratively part of the Changki Hui Autonomous Chou. The eastern Kazakh hsien is the Barkol Kazakh Autonomous Hsien, also known by its Chinese phonetic rendering, Pa-li-k'un. It has its administrative seat at Barkol (the former Chensi), situated northwest of Hami across the Barkol range and east of the lake Bar Kol. The hsien has a population of about 10,000 nomadic herdsmen.

The Ili Kazakh Autonomous Chou has under its jurisdiction the Chapchal Sibo hsien and the Khobuk-Saur Mongol hsien and encloses the Borotala Mongol Autonomous Chou as an enclave.

The Chapchal hsien, established in 1954, is situated on the south bank of the Ili River at the Soviet border and is named for the Chapchal Pass in the Ketmen range, which bounds the autonomous area on the south. The hsien has a population of 50,000, including 12,000 Sibo, descendants of a Manchurian Mongol tribe recruited by the Manchus for use as frontier guards on the Russian border. The hsien has its seat at Ningsi ("west of Ningyüan," a former Chinese name of Kuldja). Similarly, members of another Manchurian Mongol tribe, the Daghors, were used by the Manchus as guards, and 3,000 of them are still settled on the Soviet frontier north of Tahcheng.

The Khobuk-Saur Mongol Autonomous Hsien, east of Tahcheng, occupies the grassy Khobuk valley at the south foot of the Saur mountains, a small Soviet-Chinese border range. The hsien was established in 1954 with its seat at Hofeng. The Khobuk-Saur Mongols are members of the Torgut tribe.

The Borotala Mongol Autonomous Chou occupies the valley of the Borotala River, wedged in between the Dzungarian Alatau in the north and the Borokhoro range separating the Borotala from the Ili valley in the south. The grassy character of the valley is suggested by the Mongol meaning of its name, "rainy steppe." The chou was formed in 1954 and has a population of 50,000, of whom half are Mongol herders. The administrative seat is Bulak (with the Chinese phonetic rendering Po-lo), west of the lake Ebi Nor. The Borotala Mongols are Chahar Mongols who were moved from the Chahar region in the eighteenth century.

Outside of the Kazakh chou, in the Urumchi agricultural district, is the Changki Hui Autonomous Chou, with its administrative seat at Changki, northwest of Urumchi. The population of the chou is highly mixed and includes Chinese and Uigurs in addition to the Hui (Chinese Moslems), who are concentrated around Changki. Expansion of the cultivated area, including part of the Manas reclamation project, and Chinese in-migration are believed to have raised the population of the autonomous chou far above the 100,000 it had at the time of its formation in 1954.

South of the Tien Shan, in the eastern section of the Tarim basin, lies the Bayan Gol Mongol Autonomous Chou, set up in 1954. The name Bayan Gol, rendered phonetically in Chinese as Pa-yin Kuo-leng, means "abundant water" and refers to the Khaidik River, whose valley on the southern slopes of the Tien Shan is settled by the Mongol component of the population. The 20,000 Mongol herdsmen in the valley are members both of the Hoshut tribe, in the Yulduz plateau in the upper reaches of the Khaidik, and of the Torgut tribe, in the lower reaches near Yenki (Karashahr). The irrigated piedmont around Yenki and Korla, west of the lake Baghrash Kol, is settled by Hui and Uigurs. The Hui, numbering about 15,000 in the Yenki area, were constituted in 1954 as the Yenki Hui Autonomous Hsien, with a total population of 40,000. For the first seven years, the Bayan Gol Autonomous Chou was limited to the Mongol-inhabited mountain section and the irrigated piedmont area of Yenki, where it had its capital. But, in early 1961, the chou absorbed the entire southeast desert quadrant of Sinkiang, which had been administered from Korla, southwest of Yenki. The administrative seat of the expanded autonomous chou moved in that year from Yenki to Korla.

The southwestern section of Sinkiang, corresponding to the western half of the Tarim basin, contains the great oases of Aksu, Kashgar, Yarkand, and Khotan, as well as the bulk of the region's Uigur population. Because of its remoteness from Urumchi, this section, roughly west of Long. 84 degrees E, was temporarily administered as a special South Sinkiang District from 1954 to 1956, when it was broken up into the Aksu, Kashgar, and Khotan districts in addition to the Kizil-Su Kirghiz Autonomous Chou.

The Kirghiz chou lies along the south slopes of the Tien Shan, which here forms the frontier between Sinkiang and the Kirghiz S.S.R. of the Soviet Union. It is named for the Kizil Su, rendered phonetically in Chinese as K'o-tzu-le-su, the Kirghiz designation of the Kashgar River. The chou, which was established in 1954, has its headquarters at Artush (rendered in Chinese as A-t'u-shih), in the foothills 20 miles north of Kashgar. The total population is 150,000, of whom one-third are Kirghiz nomadic herdsmen.

The Tash Kurghan Tadzhik Autonomous Hsien, also established in 1954, lies at an elevation of 10,000 feet on the eastern fringes of the Pamir highland. It is situated on the Tash Kurghan, a left headstream of the Yarkand River. The total population is 12,000, of whom 80 per cent are Sarikoli Tadzhiks. The hsien seat is Puli, known by the Tadzhiks as Tash Kurghan ("stone fort").

Several Turkic minority groups of Sinkiang—the Kazakhs, Kirghiz, and Tadzhiks—have counterparts on the Soviet side of the border. In fact, the settlement areas of these minorities within China may be considered extensions of Soviet republics established for each of these ethnic groups. Despite the ethnic affinity of the Soviet and Chinese branches of the minorities, the international frontier has been an effective barrier against close contact, even in the years of the Soviet-Chinese alliance. There were tentative plans in the mid-1950's, to convert the Arabic script used by the Chinese minorities into the Cyrillic used on the Soviet side of the border since the late 1930's. But these plans were abandoned as a result of the Soviet-Chinese split. During the 1960's, as relations between the two countries worsened, some elements of the Turkic minorities of Sinkiang crossed into the Soviet Union. The Uigur population of the Soviet Union rose from 95,000 to 173,000 in the intercensal period 1959–70, suggesting an in-migration from Sinkiang of about 30,000 to 40,000. Most of the Chinese Uigurs apparently settled in Kazakhstan's Alma-Ata Oblast (including the city of Alma-Ata), where the Uigur population more than doubled, from 42,000 in 1959 to 92,000 in 1970. An unusual increase was also recorded in the Soviet Union's Hui (Chinese Moslem or Dungan) population—from 22,000 in 1959 to 39,000 in 1970. This suggested an in-migration of perhaps 5,000 to 6,000, divided between Kazakhstan and Kirghizia.

16. The Tibetan Highlands

The Tibetan highlands are a unique part of China. Extending over an area of 750,000 square miles in the heart of Asia, this region lies for the most part above 10,000 feet. Within its largely desolate highland plains live 4 million persons who carry on a precarious existence with animal husbandry and marginal agriculture. As treated in this chapter, the Tibetan highlands are taken to include the province of Tsinghai and Tibet proper.

In broad strokes, the Tibetan highlands can be divided into four major regions bounded on the north by the Kunlun and Nan Shan mountain systems, on the south by the Himalayas, and on the east by the longitudinal ranges of western Szechwan. The four regions are: the Tsinghai plateau, the Tsinghai-Sikang canyon country, the Chang Tang plateau of northern Tibet, and the great valley of southern Tibet.

The Tsinghai plateau lies between the Nan Shan in the north and the Bayan Kara Mountains in the south. On the eastern side of the plateau, which takes up the northern part of Tsinghai Province, rises the Yellow River. Rising at an elevation of 13,000 feet, this great northern Chinese stream flows through the two lakes Kyaring and Ngoring and then describes a zigzag course between the Bayan Kara, Amne Machin (Kishih), and Tasurkai (Sitsing) mountains. In the northern part of the plateau are the Tsaidam and Koko Nor basins. The former is an oval-shaped, mountain-ringed desert and salt swamp at an elevation of 9,000 feet. The latter is occupied by the lake Koko Nor or Tsing Hai, Mongol and Chinese designations that mean "blue sea." The lake, which lies at an elevation of 10,000 feet, is the largest of the Tibetan highlands, with an area of 1,600 square miles.

The Tsinghai-Sikang canyon country lies south of the Bayan Kara Mountains. This land of great valleys and intervening high ranges is the source area of some of Asia's greatest rivers—the Yangtze, the Mekong, the Salween, and the Irrawaddy. The valleys of these rivers, which have a general southeasterly trend, offer so little level land that most people live on the

A.C. AUTONOMOUS CHOU
⊙ Capital of Chou
+ Autonomous Hsien
(Nationality)

① HAIPEI TIBETAN A.C.
② HWANGNAN TIBETAN A.C.

0   100   200 Miles

INNER MONG.

KANSU

Nan Shan
Kilien Mts.
Wenyuan (Hui)

Lanchow
★ Sining
②
Tungjen
Tasinkai Mts.
Yellow R.
Honan (Mongol)
Chalang

HAINAN TIBETAN A.C.
Haiyen
Koko Nor
Kungho
①

Machin Mts.
Amne Machin Mts.
Manikengo

SZECHWAN

Yangtze R.   Mekong R.

Tienchün
Tachaitan
Mahai
Tulan (Tsagan Usu)
Chaka
Golmo

Tienching
Telingha
Lenghu

HAISI MONGOL – TIBETAN – KAZAKH A.C.

Yüchüantze

Yushashan
Mangyai
Kansen

Tsaidam Basin

TSINGHAI

Hwanghoyen
NGOLOG TIBETAN A.C.
Tajih
Bayan
Kara Mts.
Yüshu

Chamdo
Bomda
Salween R.

CHAMDO

BURMA

YÜSHU TIBETAN A.C.

Khetinsiring

Tanglha Shan
part of HAISI A.C.

Tanglha Range

Manikengo
Taichao
OLD CHAMDO AREA
BORDER
Tsetang

L H A S A

Nagchu
Nagchu

Kunlun Mountains

Chang Tang

NGARI

NAGCHU

T I B E T

Nam Tso
Nyenchen Tanglha

Lhasa ★
Gyangtse
Shigatse
Lhatse

SHANNAN (Disputed)

BHUTAN

Rudog
Shihchüanho
Gartok

Indus R.

Dongba
Saka

Brahmaputra R.
SHIGATSE
Nyalam
Phari
Yatung
Kalimpong

Pulan (Taklakhar)

Tashigong
Sutlej R.

N G A R I

AKSAI CHIN (disputed)

KASHMIR

Kodari
Kabmandu ★

N E P A L

INDIA

SINKIANG

Area shown in separate map

mountainsides between 9,000 and 13,000 feet. The westernmost range of the canyon country is the Nyenchen Tanglha, separating the Brahmaputra and Salween valleys and continued southward by the Kaolikung Mountains on the Yünnan-Burma border. Toward the east follow in succession the Nu Shan, between the Salween and the Mekong, and the Ningtsing Mountains, between the Mekong and the upper Yangtze River. Beyond the Yangtze are the canyons and ranges of the dissected Sikang plateau, since 1955 part of western Szechwan.

The Chang Tang plateau forms the largest part of Tibet proper. Situated between the Kunlun system in the north and the Trans-Himalayan ranges in the south, this desolate upland consists of a series of desert playa basins and massive, low mountains, trending generally east-west. Situated at an average elevation of 15,000 feet, the Chang Tang is too cold and dry for grass or cultivated crops. Among the hundreds of lakes, both fresh and salt, the largest is the Tengri Nor, known as Nam Tso in Tibetan. The southern margin of the Chang Tang is formed by the massive Trans-Himalayan ranges, so described by the Swedish explorer Sven Hedin, but variously known as the Kailas in the west and the Nyenchen Tanglha in the east. On Chinese maps, the Trans-Himalayan ranges are designated as Kang-ti-szu Shan.

The great valley of southern Tibet extends for more than 1,000 miles between the Trans-Himalaya and the Himalaya. It is occupied by the upper Indus River in the west and the upper Brahmaputra in the east. In this trench, situated at 12,000 feet above sea level, are concentrated the population and economy of Tibet. The valley includes the chief cities of Tibet, including Lhasa, Shigatse, and Gyangtse, and most of the meager agriculture and animal husbandry.

The climate of the Tibetan highlands is conditioned by its great elevation and by the encircling mountains. The high altitudes and the rarefied air combine with intense insolation and strong radiation to produce sharp temperature contrasts between night and day and between the dry winters and moist summers. Conditions differ widely, depending on elevation and exposure. In the northern Tsinghai plateau, for example, the winter lasts six months and the summer is characterized by a wide diurnal temperature range with frosts mornings and evenings and afternoon readings of up to 85° F (29° C). In the Chang Tang plateau the average annual temperature is 23° F (—5° C), with summers virtually absent. Only in a few months does the average temperature rise about 32° F, and even during the warmest months, water freezes at night.

By contrast, southeastern Tibet has a relatively mild climate, resembling the conditions of western Yünnan. Lhasa monthly averages range from 32° F (0° C) in January to 63° F (17° C) in July. Lhasa is at an elevation of 12,200 feet, where intensive radiation and the long winter reduce the growing season to 140 days, from May to September. This is also the rainy season when the valleys of southeastern Tibet come under the influence of the monsoon from the Indian Ocean. Lhasa's average annual precipitation is 64 inches, most of it occurring in July and August. However, annual rainfall is highly irregular from year to year, ranging from 200 inches to 20 inches.

The high, nearly parallel ranges in southern Tibet operate as an effective rain barrier. Almost none of the moisture crosses the Trans-Himalayan ranges into the Chang Tang plateau and the Tsaidam basin. The average annual precipitation there is less than 4 inches.

Differences in climate, vegetation, and agricultural land-use are all conditioned by elevation. In the lowest valleys, below 5,000 feet, a very mild climate prevails, making possible the cultivation of corn and tea. From 5,000 to 10,000 feet, the cultivation of corn, potatoes, and grains is possible, with the first two crops dropping out above 10,000 feet. On rainy slopes, a slim forest growth is found below 11,500 feet, followed by highland steppe and meadows. The snow line is generally found at 16,000 feet in the Tibetan highlands.

Most of the population live along the eastern and southern margins of the Tibetan highlands, where lower elevations provide meager agricultural and grazing possibilities. Cultivators are settled in valleys and intermontane basins, while herdsmen migrate over the upland pastures.

The main agricultural districts are the Sining valley east of the lake Koko Nor and the Brahmaputra valley, especially in the neighborhood of Lhasa. Barley, buckwheat, rye, and peas are the leading crops. Barley, the staple grain of the Tibetans, is made into tsamba, a national food made of parched barley, butter, and tea. Barley grows at elevations up to 11,500 feet. It is sown in April and harvested in August.

Animal husbandry is the basic economic activity of the highlands. The main grazing lands are in the valleys of southern Tibet, the upper reaches of the Yellow and Yangtze rivers, and the Tsaidam basin. The stock is driven into the uplands after the melting of the snows. In the fall, it is returned to the valleys and foothills. Yak, sheep, camels, and horses make up the bulk of the herds. The yak is the typical Tibetan draft animal; its endurance and surefootedness make it well suited for highland travel.

Mineral exploitation includes the coal of the Tatung mines north of Sining and salt, borax, potash, and bromine from some of the saline lakes on the highlands. Starting in the mid-1950's, a major resource development effort was undertaken in the Tsaidam basin, involving mainly exploration for petroleum and natural gas. Some oil wells were put into operation, notably at Lenghu, and small refining facilities were constructed in the late 1950's. The economic recession that followed the failure of the Great Leap led to the abandonment of the Tsaidam development projects, but they were renewed in 1969.

Transportation continues to be dependent on highways, except for the Sining valley, linked to the Chinese railroad system in 1959. The principal motor roads focus on Sining and Lhasa. They are the Tsinghai-Tibet road, between those two cities, the Sining-Yüshu (Jyekundo) road, continuing on into the Chamdo area of eastern Tibet, and the Szechwan-Chamdo-Lhasa highway, all of which were in operation by the middle 1950's. Other roads link Tibet with Sinkiang, via the Aksai Chin area, and with Nepal, or reach into the Himalayas along the frontier with India.

Tibetans make up the largest ethnic group in the Tibetan highlands, although a Chinese influx since the middle 1950's has undoubtedly reduced the Tibetan component in the total population. Of the total 1953 population of 3 million, Tibetans made up 1.8 million, including 516,000 in Tsinghai and 1.27 million in Tibet. With the exception of Chinese-settled Sining basin in the extreme northeast, virtually all of Tsinghai Province is organized into Tibetan autonomous chou: Haisi (jointly with Mongols and Kazakhs), Haipei, Hainan, Hwangnan, Ngolog, and Yüshu. Smaller ethnic minorities, totaling 250,000, notably the Hui, Salar, Tu (Mongor), and Mongols, have been set up as autonomous hsien in the Sining area. Tibet, after a long period of provisional status, was formally inaugurated in 1965 as the Tibet Autonomous Region, one of five such province-level administrative units in China. The influx of ethnic Chinese into the Sining basin, but also into key support centers throughout the Tibetan highlands, may have raised the Chinese component of the population from 900,000 in 1953 to perhaps 1.5 million in the late 1960's.

TSINGHAI PROVINCE
Capital: Sining; area: 280,000 sq. mi.; population: 2.5 million

The population and economic activities of Tsinghai have been concentrated in the Sining area east of lake Koko Nor. The Sining area, situated west of Lanchow, the capital of Kansu Province, is the northeastern gateway to Tsinghai and the Tibetan highlands. Proceeding up the Sining River (also known as the Hwang Shui) from Lanchow, Chinese settlers have penetrated deeply here into Tibetan ethnic territory. Economic development of this northeast corner of Tsinghai was further stimulated in 1959, when Sining was reached by a railroad from Lanchow, and the intensive industrial development of Lanchow spilled over into the Sining area, less than 100 miles away.

Sining, the capital of Tsinghai, is situated on the south bank of the Sining River at an elevation of 7,500 feet. It evolved as a processing center for the surrounding agricultural district, which produces mainly such grains as spring wheat and barley, and as the transport hub for the Tibetan nomadic herding areas of the Tsinghai hinterland. In the late 1950's and through the 1960's, its traditional industries (flour-milling, wool, meat products) were supplemented by metal products and chemicals. Steel from a small local smelter is used in the manufacture of ball bearings, electrical equipment, pumps, and farm implements. Chemical minerals, such as salt, potash, and borax, from the Tsaidam basin to the west provide the basis

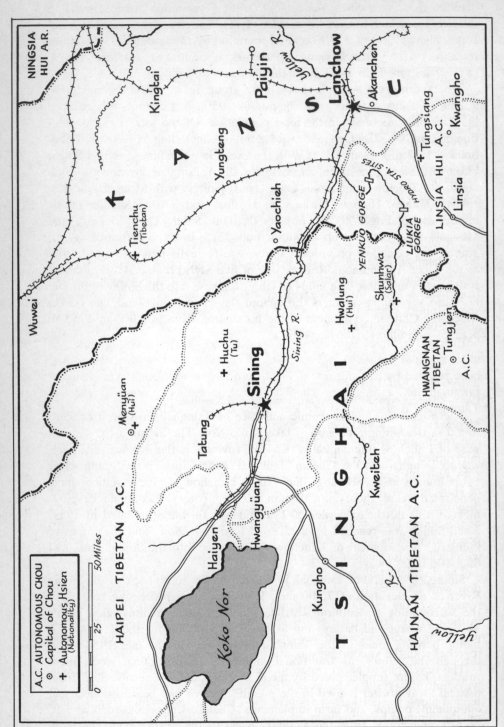

Map legend:

A.C. AUTONOMOUS CHOU
⊙ Capital of Chou
✝ Autonomous Hsien
(Nationality)

0 25 50 Miles

NINGSIA HUI A.R.

K A N S U

Kingtai ○
Paiyin
Yellow R.
Lanchow ★
Akanchen ○
Tungsiang ✝
LINSIA HUI A.C.
Kwangho ○
Linsia ○

Yungteng ○

Tienchu ✝
(Tibetan)

Yaochieh ○

HYDRO STA. SITES

YENKUO GORGE

LIUKIA GORGE

Shunhwa ✝
(Salar)

Hwalung ✝
(Hui)

Sining R.

Wuwei ○

Menyüan ⊙✝
(Hui)

Huchu ✝
(Tu)

Sining ★

HAIPEI TIBETAN A.C.

Tatung ○

Hwangyüan ○

Haiyen ○

Koko Nor

T S I N G H A I

HWANGNAN TIBETAN A.C.

Tungjen ⊙
A.C.

Kweiteh ○

Kungho ○

HAINAN TIBETAN A.C.

Yellow R.

TABLE 57
CITIES OF THE TIBETAN HIGHLANDS

City	City Level	Function	Population (*in thousands*) 1953	1957	1970 est.
TSINGHAI					
Sining	subprovincial	manuf., trade	94		300
Former Cities	*Period*				
Chiehku					
(Jyekundo)	1951–53				
Golmo	1960–65				
Lenghu	1959–64				
Tachaitan	1960–64				
TIBET					
Lhasa	subprovincial	trade, light manuf.			70

for a chemical industry. A polyvinyl chloride resin plant, opened in 1965, uses acetylene from limestone (via calcium carbide) and hydrogen chloride from salt. A small nitrogen fertilizer plant was inaugurated the following year. Sining's population, 94,000 in the 1953 census, subsequently rose to about 300,000 by 1970.

Energy for Sining's industries is provided by coal mines at Tatung, 25 miles north of Sining. A rail spur was extended to Tatung after Sining had been reached by the railroad in 1959. In addition to serving as a chemical raw material (as in the production of hydrogen for ammonia synthesis), Tatung coal is also burned in a local thermal-power station. Another source of power is a 24,000-kilowatt hydroelectric station near Sining. Though construction on the plant was begun in 1959, during the Great Leap, it was interrupted in the early 1960's and completed only in 1966.

A railroad spur also leads 60 miles westward from Sining to the town of Haiyen, near the eastern shore of the lake Koko Nor. The Chinese have disclosed no particular industrial activities necessitating the construction of the Sining-Haiyen line, which represents the initial segment of the proposed railroad to the Tsaidam basin. Some reports have associated Haiyen with facilities for nuclear-weapons production.

The Tsaidam railroad project was announced in the 1950's in conjunction with an intensive effort to develop the petroleum and other mineral resources of the Tsaidam basin. Construction beyond Haiyen was abandoned in the early 1960's as the entire Tsaidam development was inactivated. It was not immediately apparent whether rail construction was being resumed together with the announced renewal of Tsaidam projects in 1969.

The development effort began in the middle 1950's, after the first highways into the Tsaidam basin had been completed. An east-west road extended along the northern margin of the Tsaidam salt swamp from Chaka, on the Sining-Lhasa highway, to Mangyai, northwest of Kansen, in the west. Another east-west road was laid along the southern margins of the Tsaidam swamp from Golmo, on the Sining-Lhasa highway, to Mangyai. The two roads were linked by a north-south route running from the Ansi-Tunhwang area of northwest Kansu across the Nan Shan mountains south to Golmo. Food for the geological exploration parties was supplied by state farms at Golmo and at Telingha, on the northern east-west road.

The special status of the Tsaidam basin was reflected administratively in late 1956 by the establishment of a separate Tsaidam Administrative District, with its headquarters at Tachaitan (Great Chaitan, a Chinese phonetic rendering of Tsaidam). The new settlement of Tachaitan was situated on the northern edge of the salt swamp, at the junction of east-west and north-south roads. A saline lake next to the settlement yielded borax, potash, bromine, and other salts from its brines. As development of the Tsaidam basin proceeded, Tachaitan was raised in 1960 to the status of city.

In the meantime, an intensive oil-exploration program had uncovered significant petroleum fields in folded Miocene sandstones striking northwest-southeast. The most promising oil accumulations were discovered in 1958 at Lenghu, 125 miles northwest of Tachaitan, near the junction of the Sinkiang and Kansu borders. The reserves at Lenghu were estimated at 150 million tons, and an annual output of 3 million tons by 1962 was planned. Lenghu was promptly organized as a city in 1959, and, under the crash program techniques typical of the Great Leap, a small refinery with a designed capacity of 300,000 tons of crude oil was reported to have opened in August, 1959. Crude oil and refined products were transported by tanker-trucks eastward to Lanchow.

Development of another oil-producing district was begun northwest of Mangyai, a road junction in the western part of the Tsaidam basin. Industrial activity in the area was reflected by the establishment in 1958 of a Mangyai work council. (A work council, kung-tso wei-yüan-hui in Chinese, was a specific urban type of administrative unit established in the Tsaidam basin during its early development program.) Production wells were drilled at Yushashan ("oil sands mountain"), 50 miles west-northwest of Mangyai, near the lake Ghaz Kul, and at Yuchüantze ("oil spring"), 30 miles northwest of Mangyai. A 100,000-ton refinery was reported inaugurated at Yuchüantze in March, 1959, as another Great Leap crash project.

A work council, suggesting the initial phase of resource development, was also established in 1958 at Mahai, 40 miles west of Tachaitan, near a newly discovered gas field. Another work council, set up in 1958 at the road junction of Golmo, on the main highway to Tibet, was raised to the status of city in 1960. Finally, the development program also involved an exclave of the Tsaidam basin, in the southwest corner of Tsinghai, where the work council of Tanglha Shan (in the Chinese phonetic rendering, T'ang-ku-la Shan) was established in 1958 on the main highway in the Tanglha Range, near the northern border of Tibet. The character of the resource development in the Tanglha Range, requiring the establishment of a separate administrative exclave, was not disclosed.

The failure of the Great Leap policy was soon reflected in the inactivation of the development effort in 1962–63. Administratively, interruption of the Tsaidam program was indicated in early 1964 by the abolition of the special Tsaidam Administrative District and of the urban status of its resource-development centers: the cities of Lenghu and Tachaitan, and the work councils of Mangyai, Mahai, and Tanglha Shan. A year later, in early 1965, the city of Golmo was demoted to hsien status. The Tsaidam district was reincorporated into an ethnic autonomous territory, the Haisi Mongol-Tibetan-Kazakh Autonomous Chou, from which it had been separated in 1956, when the development effort began. It was not immediately apparent whether the announced renewal of the Tsaidam program in 1969 was associated with restoration of the former urban centers and other administrative changes.

The Haisi ("west of the lake") chou, named for its location west of lake Koko Nor, was established in 1954 with its headquarters at Tulan, a settlement on the Tsinghai-Tibet highway that also bears the Mongol name Tsagan Usu ("white water"), rendered in Chinese transcription as Ch'a-han Wu-su. The chou was formed through the amalgamation of three autonomous hsien established for the Mongol, Tibetan, and Kazakh communities. The Mongols, representing one of the southernmost Mongol outliers in Tibetan ethnic territory, had their headquarters in the Tulan area; the Tibetans at Tienchün, to the north; and the Kazakhs at Golmo, to the west. From 1959 through 1963, while the Tsaidam program was under way, the Haisi chou was administered from the Tsaidam city of Tachaitan. Following inactivation of the Tsaidam effort, the headquarters of the autonomous chou moved to Telingha, 110 miles east of Tachaitan. In the middle 1950's, before the influx of Chinese for the Tsaidam program, the population of the Haisi chou was given as 20,000, of whom half were Kazakhs.

North of the lake Koko Nor, in the uplands of the Nan Shan, is the Haipei ("north of the lake") Tibetan Autonomous Chou. It was established in late 1953 with a population of 70,000, including 24,000 Tibetans. The chou's administrative center, Menyüan (the former Weiyüan), is also the seat of a Hui Autonomous Hsien, situated in the Tatung valley north of the Sining agricultural area.

South of lake Koko Nor is the Hainan ("south of the lake") Tibetan Autonomous Chou, established about the same time (December, 1953) as its northern counterpart. A Chinese influx into the Kweiteh farming district, on the upper Yellow River, south of Sining, raised the population of the Hainan chou from 100,000, at the time of its founding, to about 200,-000 by 1963, converting the Tibetan component of about 60,000 from a majority to a minority. However, the administrative center of the Tibetan chou has remained in a Tibetan settlement known in Chinese as Kungho and in Tibetan as Chhagbugchhag (in Chinese phonetics, Ch'ia-pu-ch'ia).

East of the Hainan chou is the Hwangnan ("south of the Yellow") Tibetan Autonomous Chou, established in 1953 south of the Yellow River along the Kansu border. Its population was 72,000, including 64,000 Tibetans, and its administrative seat was established at Tungjen, site of the Lungwu lamasery. Northeast of Tungjen is the small town of Paoan, home of the Paoan ethnic minority, speaking a Mongolic language and professing Buddhism. The Paoan, including a related Moslem group across the border in Kansu Province, number 5,500.

South of the Hwangnan chou, on the right bank of the upper Yellow River, is another southern Mongol enclave in Tibetan ethnic territory. It is constituted as the Honan Mongol Autonomous Hsien, formed in 1952 with its headquarters in the settlement of Yu-kan-t'an. The total Mongol population of Tsinghai in the 1953 census was 26,000.

Three other autonomous hsien border on the Chinese-inhabited Sining agricultural basin. These hsien, all established in February, 1954, are based on the Tu, Hui, and Salar minorities.

The Huchu Tu Autonomous Hsien has its seat at Huchu, 20 miles north-northeast of Sining. The hsien population is 180,000, including 20,000 of the titular Tu minority. Tu is the name given by the Chinese to the so-called Mongor, a term that itself apparently reflects the Chinese pronunciation of "Mongol." The Tu, or Mongor, who number 53,000 in the Sining basin and adjoining parts of Kansu, are a Buddhist people speaking a Mongolic language. They engage in agriculture and stock-herding.

Southeast of Sining, in the upper Yellow River valley, are the Hui and Salar autonomous hsien. The Hui hsien has its seat at Hwalung, 45 miles southeast of Sining, and the Salar have their headquarters at Shunhwa, on the south bank of the Yellow River, 70 miles southeast of Sining. The Shunhwa Salar Autonomous Hsien at the time of its founding in 1954 had a population of 42,000, including 22,000 of the Salar nationality, a Turkic-language Moslem group. The total Salar population is 31,000.

The deeper hinterland of Tsinghai is occupied by two larger Tibetan autonomous chou: the Ngolog (in Chinese phonetics, Kuo-lo) Tibetan Autonomous Chou, in the upper reaches of the Yellow River, and the Yüshu Tibetan Autonomous Chou, in the upper reaches of the Yangtze River.

The Ngolog chou, named for a Tibetan tribe, was established in 1954, with its original headquarters at the Chalang lamasery, on the Yellow River. The administrative seat subsequently moved repeatedly but has remained since 1959 at Machin (formerly known as Tawu), on the northern slopes of the Amne Machin Mountains. The chou had a population of 110,000 at the time of its founding, 90,000 deriving a livelihood from stock-herding and 20,000 from the growing of crops.

The Yüshu chou was established in 1951, with its administrative center at Yüshu, a major subregional center in southern Tsinghai. Until 1953, the capital briefly enjoyed the status of city and was then officially called Chieh-ku, the Chinese phonetics for its Tibetan name Jyeku (another Tibetan form is Jyekundo). After the abolition of municipal status, it reverted to its Chinese name, Yüshu. The town is a highway hub, with roads leading northeast toward Sining and south into eastern Tibet and western Szechwan. The population of the chou is about 100,000, mainly Tibetan.

TIBET AUTONOMOUS REGION
Capital: Lhasa; area: 470,000 sq. mi.; population: 1.5 million

Before the Chinese Communists established their political and military authority in Tibet in 1950–51, this region had maintained virtual independence under the fourteenth Dalai Lama, who was installed in 1940 and assumed ruling powers in 1950 at the age of sixteen after a ten-year regency.

The control of the Dalai Lama extended to the eastern part of Tibet known as Kham, with its center at Chamdo (Chinese phonetics, Ch'ang-tu). Although the Tibetans were in effective control of the Chamdo area, bounded on the east by the upper Yangtze River, the Chinese claimed the area and showed it on their maps as part of Sikang Province. In apparent recognition of its special character, the area was organized as a separate administrative entity, the Chamdo Area (Chinese, ti-ch'ü), which in the 1953 census had a population of 300,000. At first part of Sikang Province, the Chamdo area was joined to Tibet after the abolition of Sikang Province in 1955.

Meanwhile, the Chinese Communists had signed in May, 1951, an agreement with the Dalai Lama government for the occupation of Tibet, and late in 1951, Chinese troops entered Lhasa, the Tibetan capital. The agreement pledged Peking not to alter the existing political system in Tibet or the powers of the Dalai Lama, but it also provided for Chinese control through the appointment of a military and administrative committee to implement the agreement.

Under the terms of the 1951 agreement, the Chinese-sponsored Panchen Lama was installed at the Tashilhunpo monastery near Shigatse, traditional seat of the Panchen Lama, a religious dignitary second only to the Dalai Lama. However, the Chinese enhanced the powers of the Panchen Lama as a counterweight to those of the Dalai Lama.

After a prolonged visit by the Dalai Lama and the Panchen Lama to Peking in the autumn of 1954, the Chinese Communists set up in 1955 a Preparatory Committee for the Tibet Autonomous Region, including the two Tibetan dignitaries and representatives of the Chamdo area and the Peking Government.

However, implementation of Communist reforms envisaged by the committee was delayed because of opposition from the Dalai Lama and the reported outbreak of a rebellion among the Khamba tribesmen of eastern Tibet. After a visit to India by the Dalai Lama and the Panchen Lama in

November, 1956, on the 2,500th anniversary of the death of Buddha, Mao Tse-tung announced that the reforms would be postponed at least until after completion of the second five-year plan (1958–62).

The Khamba uprising spread to central Tibet, and Chinese efforts to suppress the unrest led to a rebellion in Lhasa in March, 1959, during which the Dalai Lama fled to India. His departure eliminated the bulwark of resistance to Chinese influence. The Panchen Lama, who dissociated himself from the Lhasa rebellion, stayed on in Tibet, but declined to accept the chairmanship of the Preparatory Committee in place of the Dalai Lama. After a rift with the Chinese in the middle 1960's, he was reported to have been deposed.

The flight of the Dalai Lama, the consolidation of Chinese control in Tibet, and open friction over the disputed border led to the brief Chinese-Indian frontier war of October-November, 1962. Under a cease-fire declared unilaterally by Peking, the Chinese in the eastern (Assam) sector of the boundary withdrew to the McMahon Line, claimed by India as the international boundary. In the western (Kashmir) sector, the 1962 war left both sides along the Chinese claim line, leaving the Aksai Chin area under Chinese control.

The consolidation of Chinese control in Tibet, following the Dalai Lama's flight in 1959, may be said to have been completed in 1965, when the Preparatory Committee stage gave way to the formal inauguration of the Tibet Autonomous Region.

Economically, Chinese control manifested itself in the construction of a network of motor roads in Tibet. Two major highway-building periods may be distinguished. In the middle 1950's, the Chinese opened the 1,250-mile Tsinghai-Tibet highway and the 1,400-mile Szechwan-Tibet highway, placing Lhasa within two weeks' overland travel from the railheads of Sining in Tsinghai and Chengtu in Szechwan. A 380-mile truck road was also completed from Lhasa through Shigatse and Gyangtse to India's Sikkim border at Yatung in the Chumbi valley. In the west, Sinkiang was linked with Tibet by a motor road across the Aksai Chin area. In the second stage, roughly the 1960's, the trans-Tibetan highway and the Tibet-Nepal highway were completed. The trans-Tibetan highway connected Lhasa via Shigatse along the great valley of southern Tibet with the Aksai Chin road in the west. The Tibet-Nepal highway runs from Lhatse, on the trans-Tibetan highway, through Tingri and the border town of Nyalam into Nepal to Katmandu.

The construction of roads, in turn, facilitated the region's economic development, including the development of fuel and energy sources (local coal mines and small hydroelectric projects) and some manufacturing for local consumption.

Since the middle 1960's, Tibet has been divided administratively into five districts and the municipal area of Lhasa, which covers a vast territory in central Tibet of about 30,000 square miles. The districts are: Ngari

(in Chinese phonetics, A-li), in western Tibet, with its headquarters at
Shihchüanho, a new Chinese settlement adjoining Tashigong at the point
where the Aksai Chin road crosses the upper Indus River; Shigatse, in the
central valley west of Lhasa, with its capital at Shigatse; Shannan ("south
of the mountains"), situated south of the eastern section of the Trans-
Himalaya, with its headquarters at Tsetang, another Chinese stronghold, on
the upper Brahmaputra River just north of the Tibetan town of Nedong;
Nagchu (in Chinese phonetics, Na-ch'ü), north of Lhasa, with its center at
Nagchu, a highway hub (also known by the Chinese name Heiho); and
Chamdo, in eastern Tibet, with its seat at Chamdo, a town of 2,500 popu-
lation on the upper Mekong River.

Lhasa, the Tibetan capital, is situated at an elevation of 12,000 feet, on
a left tributary of the Brahmaputra. The city is dominated on the northwest
by the spectacular Potala, a palace-monastery that served as the residence
of the Dalai Lama. The fostering of small manufacturing and a Chinese
influx raised the city's population to about 70,000 in the 1960's.

Shigatse, Tibet's second urban center, is situated on the Nienchu River,
a right tributary of the Brahmaputra. Shigatse's development has been
fostered by the construction of the trans-Tibetan highway westward and the
motor road leading south via Gyangtse toward the Indian border. It is near
Shigatse that the Panchen Lama had his residence in the Tashilhunpo
monastery. Shigatse's population has probably risen above the 20,000 reported in the early 1950's.

17. Trends and Prospects

Glancing back at the detailed survey of economic development since the Communists assumed power in Peking in 1949, we find two basic tendencies of regional development. The first, corresponding to the period of heavy investment in industry at the expense of agriculture in the 1950's, was marked by a distinct westward orientation toward the underdeveloped interior regions of China. The second, associated with a period of more balanced development, has been focusing to a greater extent on the heavily populated eastern part of the country.

The initial westward push was motivated by a number of factors. One of the foremost was a desire to ensure a more uniform pattern of industrialization, which had been limited largely during the pre-Communist period to the eastern coastal areas and to Manchuria. Industry in eastern port cities, notably Tientsin, Tsingtao, and Shanghai, had been promoted by both Western and Chinese domestic investment. The location of these centers was influenced for the most part by access to imported raw materials, accumulated skills, and capital rather than by proximity to mines or internal markets. Manchuria was developed as an appendage of the Japanese economy, with the region's resource base furnishing the foundation for iron and steel, light metals, and other sectors of heavy industry. Relatively few industrial centers were situated in the interior. They included the Taiyüan complex in Shansi, Wuhan on the middle Yangtze River, and the Changsha area in Hunan. During World War II, Southwest China also received the first impetus, with the establishment of modern industry at Chungking and Kunming.

But it was not until the 1950's that a concerted effort was made to reduce the traditional preponderance of the eastern seaboard by expanding industry in the interior. The new inland industries were designed to make greater use of domestic resources for the benefit of the internal market. They were established both in agricultural areas and near newly developed mineral-resource sites. Examples of agricultural-processing industry can be found in the greatly expanded cotton textile capacity constructed in the cotton-growing areas of the North China plain, notably at Chengchow in Honan and at Shihkiachwang in Hopei. Mineral-resource development spurred the growth of such cities as Hantan in southern Hopei, where an iron and steel industry and other metal-processing arose in the late 1950's.

The westward trend of that early period was also related to the need for the domestic production of commodities in which China was heavily dependent on foreign sources. The prime example was petroleum, which was produced in negligible amounts in China in the early 1950's and had to be imported in large amounts, mainly from the Soviet Union. Early Chinese oil development was concentrated in outlying western regions, notably at Yümen in Kansu and at Karamai in Sinkiang. It was partly to provide access to these distant resource areas that the Chinese undertook the construction of the ambitious Sinkiang railroad project, which was to link Lanchow with the Sinkiang capital, Urumchi. The western oil-field development and the construction of the railroad, in turn, led to the establishment of a great industrial complex at Lanchow, with oil-refining, petrochemicals, and other industries.

Finally, the development program of the interior was also related to strategic factors and to the Soviet-Chinese alliance. Strategic considerations were evident in the construction of industrial centers in the Chinese heartland, far from exposed border areas, at a time when military thinking was still dominated by ideas of conventional land warfare. China's close relationship with the Soviet Union during the 1950's was evidently also a significant factor in the general westward expansion of the Chinese economy toward the Soviet borders in Central Asia. These ties were perhaps best reflected by the great transcontinental railroads that were to link the two countries. One was the Trans-Mongolian railroad, whose inauguration in late 1955 substantially shortened the overland route between the developed regions of the Soviet Union and China, compared with the earlier connection through Manchuria. The other transcontinental link was the Sinkiang railroad, originally envisaged as an additional through route between China and the Soviet Union, though not completed.

The Great Leap Forward marked the watershed between this early westward orientation of regional development and the new eastward look that was to follow. The collapse of that crash program of economic development, in which China overextended itself, and the associated withdrawal of Soviet aid led to a retrenchment of economic activity and a reappraisal of priorities. Instead of the emphasis on heavy industry that characterized the period of the 1950's, a new economic policy of balanced development gave more priority to agriculture and its support industries, such as chemical fertilizers and farm implements. The new policy inevitably focused renewed attention on the heavily populated agricultural regions of China, away from the resource-oriented projects in the underdeveloped western part of the country. In the absence of Soviet support, China's limited investment capabilities were thus reoriented from costly industrial and transport development in the west to more intensive economic growth in the historical population core of the east. The shift in regional emphasis was perhaps best illustrated by the inactivation of the Tsaidam Basin, a mineral-rich area of northwestern Tsinghai, where a major development effort was under way in the late 1950's. The failure of the Great Leap was followed by a halt in the construction of an access railroad, the gradual shutting down of economic activity, and, finally, the administrative elimination of urban areas associated with the resource-development program in the Tsaidam Basin. In 1969 the Tsaidam program was renewed, but the focus of economic activity continued to be on the population core of China proper.

Additional factors in the 1960's reinforced the new eastward orientation associated with a more balanced policy of economic development. The search for adequate domestic petroleum resources that had been a major driving force in the westward movement was crowned with success in quite another direction, the Taching oil field of northern Manchuria. Although the older western producing districts at Yümen and Karamai continued to provide a significant share of China's petroleum, the Taching field became the nation's leading supplier. It was situated far more favorably to the industrialized northeastern quadrant of China than the more remote western oil areas. Instead of investing in costly western access railroads, the Chinese used their limited capital construction funds for the building of a special rail outlet for the Taching oil field, to relieve the traffic load on the relatively dense but heavily used Manchurian rail net.

Changed strategic considerations and the Chinese-Soviet split also were in favor of the new eastward look. The advent of the nuclear era with intercontinental ballistic missiles in a sense eliminated the security afforded by interior location in the days of traditional land warfare. With any point equally vulnerable to nuclear-missile attack, it became in a sense immaterial whether strategic industries were located in distant western areas or in the more accessible east. The end of the alliance with the Soviet Union furthermore removed another stimulus for westward expansion. In fact, the gradual decline of Chinese-Soviet overland trade in the 1960's and the growing commercial dependence of China on Japan, Western Europe, and other overseas sources gave renewed importance to economic activity in eastern coastal regions.

Finally, despite official Chinese disclaimers that cost-effectiveness weighs heavily in economic decision-making, it may be assumed that Peking derives greater benefit from investing its limited capital resources in the developed eastern regions with ample labor supplies and nearby markets than in sparsely populated outlying western areas.

The regional-development policy emphasizing the populated east is operating at two levels. One represents modern industrial and resource development projects that are financed by the central government and are controlled through its provincial administrations. These projects, whether in mining or in manufacturing, generally involve significant production capacities, and their output is shipped over considerable distances to consuming areas. Production establishments of such magnitude are usually associated with the expansion of existing urban centers or the creation of new urban complexes. The other level of regional development consists of a multitude of small rural industrial projects designed to meet local needs. These rural activities had a precedent during the Great Leap Forward, but apparently overextended local capabilities, as in the famous backyard-iron-furnace campaign, and were largely abandoned in 1960. After the Chinese economy began to recover from the recession of the early 1960's, local small-scale industry was again encouraged on a more moderate basis. By 1970, it seemed to account for a significant portion of economic production, ranging from small coal mines and ironworks, through the manufacture of simple mineral fertilizers, to the making of farm tools and other engineering products.

The outlook for the 1970's is for continued emphasis in regional development on the main agricultural and industrial regions of the eastern half of China, in the form of both centrally financed modern projects of substantial capacity and the small-scale rural activities for local needs. Investment in transportation is likely to focus on connecting lines in the more populated regions rather than on new pioneering railroads in outlying areas. However, existing western transport routes—notably, the railroad from Lanchow to Sinkiang—may be expected to serve as axes of development in coming years by providing access to potential resource sites along the way,

Methodology and Bibliography

In the middle 1950's, when research for the first edition of *China's Changing Map* was under way, the flow of economic information and statistical releases was adequate to ensure directly an overview of regional development in Communist China. The imposition of statistical secrecy and a virtual blackout on other information about the population and economy since 1960 have required a more indirect approach in tracing regional developments in the 1960's for the second edition. This approach was based on the assumption that certain changes in the territorial-administrative structure reflect particular economic developments. For example, the creation of a city ("shih") in an area where no significant urban center had existed was interpreted to mean that a new industrial complex had arisen, usually based on mining or another resource-oriented activity. Conversely, the elimination of a city and its demotion to town ("chen") level was taken to reflect a decline in importance or the abandonment of the industrial project for which the city was initially established.

ADMINISTRATIVE UNITS

The starting point for this approach was therefore detailed analysis of changes in the territorial-administrative organization of Communist China during the 1950's and the early 1960's before publication of this type of information, too, was halted in early 1966, at the start of the Cultural Revolution. A number of basic sources were used to trace the administrative evolution:

Jen-min shou-tse (*People's Handbook*), an annual series of official reference books published in Peking through 1965. Each contains, under the section titled "T'u-ti, Jen-k'ou" ("Land and Population"), a listing of administrative units as of the time of publication.

Survey of China Mainland Press, prepared by the American Consulate General in Hong Kong, provided announcements of administrative changes that could be used as a cross-check against the annual published lists in *Jen-min shou-tse*. The last announcement of administrative changes, before the Cultural Revolution cut off this type of publication, covered the period from October, 1965, to February, 1966, and was published in No. 3666 of the *Survey of China Mainland Press.*

Mainland China: Administrative Divisions and Their Seats. Gazetteer No. 70.

337

Washington: U.S. Board of Geographic Names, January, 1963. A useful reference for pre-1949 Nationalist names and for Communist names as of 1960, based on *Chung-hua jen-min kung-ho-kuo hsing-cheng ch'ü-hua chien-ts'e (Digest of Administrative Divisions of the People's Republic of China)*. Peking: Ministry of Interior, 1960.

Administrative changes were also traced by comparison of successive editions of administrative maps published in Peking. The maps were particularly useful in showing changes in the location of hsien seats, since Chinese practice superimposes the hsien name on the local name when the administrative seat is moved from one place to another. The last available administrative map published in Peking before the Cultural Revolution interrupted the issuance of maps for public use is:

Chung-hua jen-min kung-ho-kuo ti-t'u (Map of the People's Republic of China). Peking: Map Publishers, March, 1966. This map, which is the fifth edition of an administrative map first published in June, 1957, shows the administrative-territorial organization of Communist China as of December, 1965.

Although the detailed record of administrative changes thus ceased with the start of the Cultural Revolution in 1966, subsequent developments could be inferred from scattered news items and radio broadcasts. The most significant changes during the Cultural Revolution, which did not appear to have upset the basic structure of the administrative system, were the restoration of Tientsin as a centrally administered city in 1967 and the dismemberment of the western and eastern extremities of the Inner Mongolian Autonomous Region in late 1969. Similarly, it became evident in the course of 1971 that the generic term for the intermediate type of civil division between province and hsien level was being changed from special district ("chuan-ch'ü"), which apparently suggested impermanence, to area ("ti-ch'ü").

CURRENT INFORMATION

Once the administrative pattern was known, the next step was to interpret these territorial changes in terms of economic construction projects and regional development. In the absence of comprehensive sources that described the location of economic activity during the 1960's, this information had to be assembled from official Chinese news items and radio broadcasts. The principal sources monitoring these transmissions are:

Survey of China Mainland Press, American Consulate General, Hong Kong.

Current Background, American Consulate General, Hong Kong.

Selections from China Mainland Magazines, American Consulate General, Hong Kong.

Daily Report: Chinese People's Republic (until July, 1971, entitled *Communist China*), Washington, D.C., Foreign Broadcast Information Service.

Additional information was culled from the reports on China published by the U.S. Joint Publications Research Service (JPRS), a translation agency of the United States Government. JPRS reports have appeared in a number of series since the service began in late 1957. The current series, which began in 1968, is titled *Translations on Communist China*. However, the reports of all JPRS series have also been given a consecutive JPRS numeration. Useful bibliographies are:

Contemporary China, a bibliography of reports on China published by the U.S. Joint Publications Research Service, edited by Richard Sorich. New York: Joint Committee on Contemporary China of the American Council of Learned Societies and the Social Science Research Council, 1961.

China Bibliography, JPRS 45174, April, 1968.

The foregoing digests of news items, radio broadcasts, and other current information, all of which are available from the National Technical Information Service, U.S. Department of Commerce, Springfield, Virginia 22151, constituted the basic sources of information used in preparation of the second edition of *China's Changing Map*. Additional sources of a more general nature that were consulted mainly for the period up to 1960 follow under subject headings:

POPULATION AND ETHNIC GROUPS

AIRD, JOHN S. *Estimates and Projections of the Population of Mainland China: 1953–1986*. Washington, D.C.: Bureau of the Census, Series P-91, No. 17, 1968.

————. "Population Growth and Distribution in Mainland China," in Joint Economic Committee of the U.S. Congress, *An Economic Profile of Mainland China* (hereafter referred to as *Economic Profile*), 1967, pp. 341–401.

————. *The Size, Composition and Growth of the Population of Mainland China*. Washington, D.C.: Bureau of the Census, Series P-90, No. 15, 1961.

Atlas Narodov Mira (Atlas of the Peoples of the World). Moscow: GUGK, 1964. The distribution of China's ethnic groups appears on Plates 42–49.

BRUK, S. I., editor. *Chislennost' i rasseleniye narodov mira (Numbers and Distribution of the Peoples of the World)*. Moscow: Academy of Sciences U.S.S.R., 1962. China's ethnic groups are discussed on pp. 144–46, 175–76.

————. *Naseleniye Kitaya, MNR i Korei (The Population of China, the Mongolian People's Republic and Korea)*; an explanatory text for an ethnographic map of these countries. Moscow: Academy of Sciences U.S.S.R., 1959. The discussion of China's ethnic groups, one of the most complete in the literature, appears on pp. 3–34 (translated as JPRS No. 3710, August 1960).

FIELD, ROBERT MICHAEL. "A Note on the Population of Communist China," *The China Quarterly*, No. 38, April-June, 1969, pp. 158–63. An analysis of provincial population figures.

————. "Chinese Provincial Population Data," *The China Quarterly*, No. 44, October-December, 1970, pp. 195–203. An amplification of the previous article, with provincial population figures reported in Chinese media from 1957 to 1970.

LATTIMORE, OWEN. *The Mongols of Manchuria*. New York: Howard Fertig, 1969 (reprint of original 1934 edition).

NI, ERNEST. *Distribution of the Urban and Rural Population of Mainland China: 1953 and 1958*. Washington, D.C.: Bureau of the Census, Series P-95, No. 56, 1960.

ORLEANS, LEO A. "China's Population Statistics: An Illusion?" *The China Quarterly*, No. 21, January-March, 1965, pp. 168–78.

————. "Propheteering: The Population of Communist China," *Current Scene* (Hong Kong: USIS), No. 24, 1969.

SHABAD, THEODORE. "The Population of China's Cities," *The Geographical Review*, 1959, No. 1, pp. 32–42.

TODAYEVA, BULYASH KH. *Mongol'skiye yaziki i dialekty Kitaya (Mongolic Languages and Dialects of China)*. Moscow: Oriental Literature Publishers, 1960.

TSAI PING-WEN. "Mainland China's Population Problem Analyzed," *Fei-ch'ing yen-chiu (Studies on Chinese Communism)*, Taipei, April 10, 1969, pp. 32–46 (translated as JPRS 48262, June, 1969).

ULLMAN, MORRIS B. *Cities of Mainland China: 1953 and 1958*. Washington, D.C. Bureau of the Census, Series P-95, No. 59, 1961.

BASIC STATISTICAL RELEASES OF THE 1950'S

First Five-Year Plan for Development of the National Economy of the People's Republic of China in 1953–1957. Peking: Foreign Languages Press, 1956, 232 pp.

Annual Plan Fulfillment Reports:

1952 and 1953: Supplement to *People's China,* November 16, 1954.

1954: *Current Background,* No. 360, September 29, 1955.

1955: Supplement to *People's China,* July 16, 1956.

1956: Supplement to *People's China,* September 1, 1957.

"Communiqué on Fulfillment and Overfulfillment of China's First Five-Year Plan," *Current Background,* No. 556, April 15, 1959.

"Proposals of the Eighth National Congress of the Communist Party of China for the Second Five-Year Plan for Development of the National Economy (1958–1962)," adopted by the congress on September 27, 1956. Supplement to *Hsinhua News Agency Release,* undated.

"Communiqué on China's Economic Growth in 1958," *Current Background,* No. 558, April 20, 1959.

"Communiqué on Fulfillment of 1959 Plan," *Peking Review,* January 26, 1960.

"Text of Deputy Premier Li Fu-chun's Report on Draft 1960 Economic Plan," *Current Background,* No. 615, April 5, 1960.

Osnovnyye pokazateli razvitiya narodnogo khozyaystva Kitayskoy Narodnoy Respubliki (Statistical Abstract of the National Economy of the Chinese People's Republic). Moscow: Gosstatizdat, 1958 (translated from *Kuo-min ching-chi t'ung-chi t'i-yao* [*Statistical Abstract of the National Economy*], appended to the pamphlet *Kuan-yü 1956 nien-tu kuo-min ching-chi chi-hua chih-hsing chieh-kuo ti kung-pao* [*Communiqué on Fulfillment of the 1956 Economic Plan*], Peking, 1957). This source gives basic annual statistics from 1952 through 1956.

Ten Great Years. Peking: Foreign Languages Press, 1960 (translated from *Wei-ta ti shih-nien,* Peking, 1959). This source gives basic annual statistics from 1949 through 1958.

ECONOMY IN GENERAL

CHEN, NAI-RUENN. *Chinese Economic Statistics: A Handbook for Mainland China.* Chicago: Aldine, 1966; Edinburgh: Edinburgh University Press, 1967.

ECKSTEIN, ALEXANDER. *Communist China's Economic Growth and Foreign Trade.* New York and Maidenhead: McGraw-Hill, 1966.

ECKSTEIN, ALEXANDER, editor. *China Trade Prospects and U.S. Policy.* New York: Praeger, 1971.

———, WALTER GALENSON, and TA-CHUNG LIU, editors. *Economic Trends in Communist China.* Chicago: Aldine, 1968; Edinburgh: Edinburgh University Press, 1969.

FIELD, ROBERT MICHAEL. "Chinese Communist Industrial Production," in *Economic Profile, op. cit.,* pp. 269–95.

———. "Industrial Production in Communist China: 1957–1968," *The China Quarterly,* No. 42, April-June, 1970, pp. 46–64.

GALENSON, WALTER. "The Current State of Chinese Economic Studies," in *Economic Profile, op. cit.,* pp. 1–13.

———, and NAI-RUENN CHEN. *The Chinese Economy Under Communism.* Chicago: Aldine, 1970.

Kitay segodnya (China Today). Moscow: Nauka, 1969, 336 pp. The Chinese economy of the 1960's is discussed on pp. 52–129.

Kitayskaya Narodnaya Respublika: Ekonomika, gosudarstvo i pravo, kul'tura (The Chinese People's Republic: Economy, State and Law, Culture). Moscow: Nauka, 1970, 226 pp. The economy of the 1960's is discussed on pp. 46–112.

KLATT, WERNER. "A Review of China's Economy in 1970," *The China Quarterly*, No. 43, July-September, 1970, pp. 100–120.

LI, CHOH-MING. *Economic Development of Communist China*. Berkeley: University of California Press, 1959.

MUROMTSEVA, ZOYA A. *Problemy industrializatsii Kitayskoy Narodnoy Respubliki (Problems of Industrialization in the Chinese People's Republic)*. Moscow: Nauka, 1971.

PERKINS, DWIGHT H. "Economic Growth in China and the Cultural Revolution (1960–April 1967)," *The China Quarterly*, No. 30, April-June, 1967, pp. 33–48 (see also comments by Werner Klatt and reply by author in *The China Quarterly*, No. 31, July-September, 1967, pp. 151–58).

RISKIN, CARL. "Small Industry and the Chinese Model of Development," *The China Quarterly*, No. 46, April-June, 1971, pp. 245–73.

SHABAD, THEODORE. "China's 'Leap Forward' Reconsidered," *Far Eastern Survey*, October, 1959.

———. "China's Year of the 'Great Leap Forward,'" *Far Eastern Survey*, Part I, June, 1959; Part II, July, 1959.

WU YUAN-LI. "Planning, Management and Economic Development in Communist China," in *Economic Profile, op. cit.*, pp. 97–119.

———. *The Economy of Communist China: An Introduction*. New York: Praeger, 1965; London: Pall Mall Press, 1966.

FUEL AND POWER

ASHTON, JOHN. "Development of Electric Energy Resources in Communist China," in *Economic Profile, op. cit.*, pp. 297–316.

BEREZINA, YU. I. *Toplivno-energeticheskaya baza Kitayskoy Narodnoy Respubliki (Fuel and Energy Base of the Chinese People's Republic)*. Moscow: Oriental Literature Publishers, 1959 (translated as JPRS 3784, August, 1960).

IVANOV, V. D., and YE. P. KAZAKEVICH. *Gidroenergeticheskiye resursy Kitayskoy Narodnoy Respubliki i ikh ispol'zovaniye (Hydroelectric Resources of the Chinese People's Republic and Their Utilization)*. Moscow: Gosenergoizodat, 1960 (translated as JPRS 9838, August, 1961).

MEYERHOFF, A. A. "[Petroleum] Developments in Mainland China, 1949–1968," *The American Association of Petroleum Geologists Bulletin*, August, 1970, pp. 1567–80.

WANG, K. P. "The Mineral Industry of Mainland China [in 1964]," in Bureau of Mines, *1964 Minerals Yearbook*, Vol. IV, pp. 1165–80.

———. "The Mineral Industry of Mainland China [in 1968]," in Bureau of Mines, *1968 Minerals Yearbook*, Vol. IV, pp. 189–200.

———. "The Mineral Resource Base of Communist China," in *Economic Profile, op. cit.*, pp. 167–95.

WU YUAN-LI. *Economic Development and the Use of Energy Resources in Communist China*. New York: Praeger, 1963.

VYSOTSKIY, I. V., editor. *Geologiya nefti (Geology of Petroleum)*, Vol. 2, Section II: "Oil Deposits of Foreign Countries." Moscow: Nedra, 804 pp. Oil deposits of China are discussed on pp. 321–51.

IRON AND STEEL

CHANG, KUEI-SHENG. "Nuclei-formation of Communist China's Iron and Steel Industry," *Annals of the Association of American Geographers,* June, 1970, pp. 257–85 (see also commentary by Theodore Shabad and author's reply in *Annals, op. cit.,* December, 1970, pp. 807–9.

HSIA, RONALD. "Communist China's Iron and Steel Bases," *China Mainland Review,* University of Hong Kong, September, 1966.

NIKOLAYEV, S. A., and L. I. MOLODTSOVA. "The Present State of the Chinese Iron and Steel Industry," *Soviet Geography, Review and Translation,* October, 1960, pp. 55–71 (translated from *Geografiya i khozyaystvo,* No. 6, 1960, pp. 34–44).

WU YUAN-LI. *The Steel Industry in Communist China.* New York: Praeger, 1965; London: Pall Mall Press, 1965.

OTHER INDUSTRIAL SECTORS

CHAO, KANG. *The Construction Industry in Communist China.* Chicago: Aldine, 1967; Edinburgh: Edinburgh University Press, 1968.

CHENG, CHU-YUAN. *The Machine Building Industry in Communist China.* Chicago: Aldine, 1971.

LIU, JUNG CHAO. *China's Fertilizer Economy.* Chicago: Aldine, 1970.

AGRICULTURE

BUCK, J. L., O. L. DAWSON, and YUAN-LI WU. *Food and Agriculture in Communist China.* New York and London: Praeger, 1966.

DAWSON, OWEN L. *Communist China's Agriculture.* New York: Praeger, 1970.

FIELD, ROBERT MICHAEL. "Chinese Grain Production," *The China Quarterly,* No. 46, April-June, 1971, pp. 350–53. Comments on SWAMI-BURKI article (below).

————. "How Much Grain Does Communist China Produce?," *The China Quarterly,* No. 33, January-March, 1968, pp. 98–107.

LIU SHIH-CH'I. *Geografiya sel'skogo khozyaystva Kitaya (Geography of Agriculture of China).* Moscow: Foreign Literature Publishers, 1957 (translated from *Chung-kuo nung-yeh ti-li,* Shanghai, 1956).

PERKINS, DWIGHT H. *Agricultural Development in China, 1368–1968.* Chicago: Aldine, 1969.

Provincial Agricultural Statistics for Communist China. Ithaca, N.Y.: Committee on the Economy of China, 1969.

SWAMY, SUBRAMANIAN, and S. J. BURKI. "Foodgrains Output in the People's Republic of China, 1958–65," *The China Quarterly,* No. 41, January-March, 1970, pp. 58–63. Presents an official Chinese grain production series.

Voprosy geografii sel-skogo khozyaystva Kitayskoy Narodnoy Respubliki (Problems in the Geography of Agriculture of the Chinese People's Republic). Moscow: Academy of Sciences U.S.S.R., 1959.

TRANSPORTATION

CHANG KUEI-SHENG, "The Changing Railroad Pattern in Mainland China," *Geographical Review,* Vol. 51, 1961, pp. 534–48.

IL'IN, A. I., and M. P. VORONICHEV. *Zheleznodorozhnyy transport Kitayskoy Narodnoy Respubliki* (*Railroad Transportation in the Chinese People's Republic*). Moscow: Transzheldorizdat, 1959, 162 pp.

LIPPIT, VICTOR D. "Development of Transportation in Communist China," *The China Quarterly*, No. 27, July-September, 1966, pp. 101–19 (reprinted in *Economic Profile, op. cit.*, pp. 661–76).

SHIRYAYEV, S. L. *Transport Kitayskoy Narodnoy Respubliki* (*Transportation in the Chinese People's Republic*). Moscow: Oriental Literature Publishers, 1962, 108 pp.

———. *Zheleznodorozhnyy transport Kitayskoy Narodnoy Respubliki* (*Railroad Transportation in the Chinese People's Republic*). Moscow: Nauka, 1969, 140 pp.

STEPANENKO, S. I. *Vodnyye puti Kitayskoy Narodnoy Respubliki* (*Waterways of the Chinese People's Republic*). Moscow: Rechnoy Transport, 1959, 82 pp.

WU YUAN-LI. *The Spatial Economy of Communist China: A Study of Industrial Location and Transportation*. New York: Praeger, 1967; London: Praeger, 1968.

ATLASES AND GEOGRAPHY BOOKS

AFANAS'YEVSKIY, YE. A. *Sychuan'* (*Szechwan*). Moscow: Oriental Literature Publishers, 1962, 267 pp.

Central Intelligence Agency. *China: Provisional Atlas of Communist Administrative Units*. Washington, D.C., 1959.

———. *Communist China Administrative Atlas*. Washington, D.C., 1969.

———. *Communist China Map Folio*. Washington, D.C., 1967.

CRESSEY, GEORGE B. *Land of the 500 Million*. New York: McGraw-Hill, 1955; Maidenhead: McGraw-Hill, 1955.

HERRMANN, ALBERT. *An Historical Atlas of China*. New edition edited by NORTON GINSBURG. Chicago: Aldine, 1966; Edinburgh: Edinburgh University Press, 1967.

HU, HSÜEH-WEI, et al. *Hua-tung ti-ch'ü ching-chi ti-li* (*Regional Economic Geography of East China*). Peking, 1959 (translated as *Vostochnyy Kitay*, Moscow, 1962).

Institute of Geography, U.S.S.R. Academy of Sciences. *The Physical Geography of China*. Published as JPRS 32,119, 1965, and New York and London: Praeger, 1969.

KALMYKOVA, V. G., and I. KH. OVDIYENKO. *Severo-zapadnyy Kitay* (*Northwest China*). Moscow: Geografizdat, 1957.

OVDIYENKO, I. KH. *Kitay* (*China*). Moscow: Uchpedgiz, 1959.

SUN P'AN-SHOU et al. *Hua-chung ti-ch'ü ching-chi ti-li* (*Regional Economic Geography of Central China*). Peking, 1958 (translated as *Tsentral'nyy Kitay*, Moscow, 1961).

TENG CHING-CHUNG et al. *Hua-pei ching-chi ti-li* (*Economic Geography of North China*). Peking, 1957 (translated as *Severnyy Kitay*, Moscow, 1958).

TREGEAR, T. R. *A Geography of China*. Chicago: Aldine, 1965; London: University of London Press, 1965.

———. *An Economic Geography of China*. New York: American Elsevier, 1970; London: Butterworth, 1970.

WATSON, FRANCIS. *The Frontiers of China*. New York: Praeger, 1966; London: Chatto & Windus, 1966.

WU CH'UAN-CHÜN et al. *Ekonomicheskaya geografiya Kitayskogo Priamur'ya* (*Economic Geography of China's Amur Valley*). Moscow, 1960.

—— et al. *Tung-pei ti-chi'ü ching-chi ti-li* (*Regional Economic Geography of Manchuria*). Peking, 1959 (translated as *Ekonomicheskaya geografiya Severo-Vostochnogo Kitaya*, Moscow, 1963).

GEOGRAPHICAL BIBLIOGRAPHY

A useful bibliography on the geography of China has been prepared by Theodore Herman of Colgate University:

The Geography of China: A selected and annotated bibliography, edited by Theodore Herman. University of the State of New York, Foreign Area Materials Center, Occasional Publication No. 7, 1967 (obtainable from Foreign Area Materials Center, 33 West 42d Street, New York, N.Y. 10036).

Index

THE AUTHOR: Theodore Shabad has been
with the *New York Times* since 1953, alter-
nating as Desk Editor for Soviet Affairs and
correspondent in Moscow. He returned to the
Times Moscow bureau in September, 1971. He
is the author of *Geography of the USSR*
(1951) and *Basic Industrial Resources of the
USSR* (1969)